MODERN BRITISH JEWRY

Modern British Jewry

GEOFFREY ALDERMAN

CLARENDON PRESS · OXFORD
1992

Oxford University Press, Walton Street, Oxford OX2 6DP
Oxford New York Toronto
Delhi Bombay Calcutta Madras Karachi
Petaling Jaya Singapore Hong Kong Tokyo
Nairobi Dar es Salaam Cape Town
Melbourne Auckland
and associated companies in
Berlin Ibadan

Oxford is a trade mark of Oxford University Press

Published in the United States
by Oxford University Press, New York

British Library Cataloguing in Publication Data
Data available

Library of Congress Cataloging in Publication Data
Alderman, Geoffrey.
Modern British Jewry / Geoffrey Alderman.
Includes index.
1. Jews—Great Britain—History. 2. Great Britain—Ethnic relations. I. Title.
DS135.E5A585 1992
941'.004924—dc20 92-899
ISBN 0-19-820145-1

Typeset by Hope Services (Abingdon) Ltd.
Printed and bound in
Great Britain by Bookcraft Ltd.,
Midsomer Norton, Bath

For
Marion Joan

Preface

I WAS not trained as an historian of Anglo-Jewry, and although I met and enjoyed the company and hospitality of the late Dr Cecil Roth when I studied at Oxford I was not at that time tempted to follow him in researching and writing about the Jewish communities of Britain. It was while preparing a book on the British electoral system that I pondered why no one had ever confronted the development of Anglo-Jewish voting habits. I determined to repair this omission, and in due course wrote *The Jewish Community in British Politics*, published by Oxford University Press in 1983. Shortly after the appearance of this book the then honorary officers of the Federation of Synagogues (of which I am a lifelong member) commissioned me to write the Federation's centenary history, published in 1987, while an approach from the European Science Foundation led, eventually, to a study of *London Jewry and London Politics 1889–1986*, which Messrs Routledge published in 1989.

It is fair to say that each of these works has attracted controversy. My view is that I am merely one participant in a movement, a reaction to the public-relations history that British Jewry had been accustomed to read hitherto, and of which (it must be said) Cecil Roth had been an accomplished exponent. Roth's *History of the Jews in England*, which Oxford University Press first published in 1941, virtually ended with Emancipation, in 1858. The period 1858–1905 was dismissed in four pages; the period after 1905 Roth did not regard as history at all. Albert Hyamson's history of *The Sephardim in England*, which appeared ten years later, devoted precisely thirteen pages to the twentieth century, and left much unsaid into the bargain. Hyamson's excuse was that 'the historian ought never to deal or attempt to deal with events of which he has a personal knowledge'. It was, I think, for the same reason that the *History of the Jews in Britain since 1858*, which was written by the late Dr Vivian Lipman (a pupil of Roth) and which was published posthumously in 1990, contained but fifteen pages on the development of Anglo-Jewry over the past fifty years; the sensitive issues were quickly passed over, or simply ignored in favour of bland description. Vivian (a good friend) was as aware as I was of the growing body of scholarly research, by a younger generation of British, American, and Israeli academics, whose findings have revolutionized our understanding of modern Anglo-Jewish history. We talked often of these themes. But he knew, and I knew, that the book he was writing would never expose the new reality. It would—at most—merely hint at what had been discovered: the existence of warts would not be denied, just heavily camouflaged.

In the work which follows I have deliberately set out to tell the story warts and all. My immeasurable debt to the work of others must be apparent from the notes and references, and I have, on another page, made some acknowledgement of the help received from a wide variety of organizations, libraries, and individuals. Even within the generous word-limit permitted to me by Oxford University Press a great deal of selection has been necessary—of facts, of issues, and of themes. The selection I have made is of course subjective, but informed; I hope no one will think it outrageous. Readers wishing to pursue topics in more depth can use my bibliographical references as the starting point, supplemented by entries in such invaluable works of reference as the *Encyclopaedia Judaica* and the *Blackwell Companion to Jewish Culture* edited by Dr Gloria Abramson. There are no maps in my work, for in truth nothing I could have offered would have equalled the maps in Martin Gilbert's *Jewish History Atlas* (London, 1969) or the more recent *Atlas of Modern Jewish History* compiled by Professor Evyatar Friesel (New York, 1990).

My work has been most magnificently funded by the Leverhulme Trust, through whose generosity my College was able to provide me with the services of a full-time research assistant for three years. Other grants in support of the research have come from the Nuffield Foundation, the Marc Fitch Fund, the Freshwater Group of Companies, and Leslie Mann (Kosher Butcher) Ltd. of Hendon; my research assistant and I were thereby able to consult a wide variety of library and archival collections in Britain, the United States, and Israel. In addition, in 1989 I had the great good fortune to be elected to a Loewenstein–Wiener Fellowship by American Jewish Archives, Cincinnati, Ohio, United States; I was thus enabled, both to sample the riches of this archival repository and, at the same time, to use the resources of the adjacent Klau Library, one of the world's great Judaica collections. I must also record here my thanks to Royal Holloway & Bedford New College, which as my employer has supported my research without question, and whose grant to me of a period of sabbatical leave proved invaluable during the later stages of the project.

Throughout this work the post of my research assistant has been held by Dr Sharman Kadish. The labours of a research assistant are particularly onerous, but pivotal to the success of any project. Dr Kadish's painstaking attention to the outcome of goals set by me has been exemplary, and her prodigious knowledge of Anglo-Jewish politics during and immediately after the First World War has been an additional source of inspiration.

It is customary for an author to thank his wife for having put up with and sustained him during his work—so customary, indeed, that I feel the acknowledgement is in danger of becoming otiose, or at least taken for granted. Those who are unfamiliar with these matters should therefore know that a book (like the one now presented) which is a labour of love is also all-consuming in the attention it demands; the author thinks of it and little else. This itself can destabilize a human relationship. But if one adds to this risk which many authors run the additional strain imposed by communal pressures, which can so easily seep from the professional level and infect family life, one begins to realize what a tower of strength Marion has been and must have been to me over the past four years. She has rescued me from despair as assuredly as my religious faith has sustained me at moments of sorrow and anger.

I should, in conclusion, point out that in the pages which follow the phrases 'Anglo-Jewry' and 'British Jewry', and their derivatives, are used interchangeably.

G. A.

Royal Holloway & Bedford New College,
University of London
27 Tammuz 5751
9 July 1991

Acknowledgements

I WISH to record here my gratitude to the following persons and organizations, who freely and most generously gave access to their archives and libraries, and whose advice and assistance proved invaluable both in the course of the research and in the task of writing the text:

American Jewish Archives, Cincinnati, United States (especially its Director, Dr A. Peck); Anglo-Jewish Archives, London; British Library, London; Board of Deputies of British Jews (especially its Executive Director, Mr D. Massel); Central Zionist Archives, Jerusalem; Office of the Chief Rabbi of the United Hebrew Congregations, London; the late Mr H. Diamond, JP; Federation of Synagogues, London; Dr W. Fishman; Greater London Record Office; the late Dr B. Homa; House of Lords Record Office; Institute of Historical Research, University of London; Jabotinsky Institute, Tel Aviv; Rabbi Dr I. Jacobs; Jewish Board of Guardians (now Jewish Care); Jews' College London; the Library of the Jewish Theological Seminary of America, New York; the Klau Library of Hebrew Union College, Cincinnati, United States (especially Dr Ida Cohen Selavan); Thomas P. Linehan; the late Dr V. D. Lipman; Councillor H. J. Lobenstein, MBE; London Board for Shechita; Public Record Office, London; the Library of Royal Holloway & Bedford New College, University of London; United Synagogue, London; University College London; the Library and Archives of the YIVO Institute for Jewish Research, New York.

Transcripts of Crown-copyright records in the Public Record Office, London, appear by permission of the Controller of Her Majesty's Stationery Office. A quotation from the Solomon Schechter Papers appears courtesy of the Library of the Jewish Theological Seminary of America, New York, United States.

Contents

List of Tables

List of Abbreviations

BD	Archives of the Board of Deputies of British Jews
BUF	British Union of Fascists
CBF	Central British Fund for German Jewry
CP	Communist Party
CZA	Central Zionist Archives, Jerusalem
EZF	English Zionist Federation
FJPC	Foreign Jews Protection Committee
GLC	Greater London Council
JC	*Jewish Chronicle*
JJS	*Jewish Journal of Sociology*
JPC	Jewish People's Council against Fascism and Anti-semitism
JRU	Jewish Religious Union for the Advancement of Liberal Judaism
JSS	*Jewish Social Studies*
JSSM	Jewish Secondary Schools Movement
LBJRE	London Board of Jewish Religious Education
LCC	London County Council
NAFTA	National Amalgamated Furnishing Trades Association
Parl. Deb.	*Parliamentary Debates*
PP	*Parliamentary Papers*
PPC	Palestine Protest Committee
PRO	Public Record Office
RSGB	Reform Synagogues of Great Britain
SDF	Social-Democratic Federation
TAC	Trades Advisory Council
TJHSE	*Transactions of the Jewish Historical Society of England*
ULPS	Union of Liberal and Progressive Synagogues
UOHC	Union of Orthodox Hebrew Congregations
WJC	World Jewish Congress

I

British Jewry on the Eve of Emancipation

THERE has never been a precise method of calculating the number of Jews in the United Kingdom. Religious affiliation has never formed the subject of a question in the British (as distinct from the Irish) census and, even if such information had been sought, problems of definition would abound. Orthodox Judaism defines a Jew as a person born of a Jewish mother or converted by a reputable *Beth Din*. This definition begs other questions. The Jewishness of the mother must itself be recognized and accepted. What is meant by a 'reputable' *Beth Din*? The British State has recognized as Jews persons upon whom no 'reputable' *Beth Din*, applying strict *Talmudic* maxims, would ever confer such a status. A person born a Jew, and recognized as such by Jewish orthodoxy, may drift far away from Jews and from Judaism, may transgress the precepts of orthodox Judaism, and may marry out of the faith. Such a person would still be accorded the status of a Jew by orthodox rabbis; only those who had embraced another faith, or whose repudiation of Judaism had been particularly stubborn or heinous, would run the risk of having this status withheld.

An uncircumcised Jewish male will still be a Jew. An unmarried Jewess who 'marries out' will none the less give birth to children who are fully Jewish. The Nazi Holocaust devoured many who claimed that they were not Jewish, and some, indeed, to whom this identification (based upon the most painstaking research into their ancestry) came as a dreadful shock.

In this work I define as Jewish any person who considered or considers him or herself to be such, or who was or is so regarded by his or her contemporaries. This definition thus carries with it no religious or communal overtones, but it does have the merit of combining self- with popular ascription, and so is inclusive rather than exclusive. It also happens to be particularly useful in relation to estimates of the Jewish population of Britain, more especially in the mid-nineteenth century.

These estimates come from Jewish and non-Jewish sources; their proximity is therefore all the more remarkable. In 1830 Sir Francis Henry Goldsmid (1808–78) used statistics of burials carried out under Jewish auspices in London, multiplied by the ratio of deaths to the general population of the capital, to compute a figure of around 18,000 as the total of London's Jewish population; he assumed that Jews in the provinces amounted to half this total, and so arrived at an estimate of 27,000 as the Jewish population of Great Britain.[1] J. E. Blunt, also writing in 1830, surmised that these estimates were too low, and put forward a figure of 37–38,000 (20,000 in London).[2] In 1845 Dr Nathan Marcus Adler (1803–90), on taking up his appointment as Chief Rabbi of the *Ashkenazi* Jews, had addressed a questionnaire to all the congregations of the British Empire acknowledging his authority.[3] Basing himself on the results of these inquiries, Henry Mayhew reported in 1851 that the total number of Jews in Great Britain was then 35,000.[4] Two years later Reverend John Mills, in his study of *The British Jews*, observed that 'it is generally calculated that they amount, in round numbers, to about 30,000—some 25,000 in London and its suburbs, and the remainder in other parts of the United Kingdom'. He added, however, that calculations based on mortality rates would suggest a somewhat lower figure for London—perhaps 20,000—giving a grand total of 25,000.[5]

A number of important qualitative judgements must be grafted on to these calculations. The first concerns the relatively large number of Jewish paupers, who had no synagogal affiliation. Mills

[1] F. H. Goldsmid, *Remarks on the Civil Disabilities of British Jews* (London, 1830), 69–71.

[2] J. E. Blunt, *A History of the Establishment and Residence of the Jews in England* (London, 1830), 75.

[3] Office of the Chief Rabbi of the United Hebrew Congregations, Chief Rabbinate Archives, MS 104: 'Statistical Accounts of all the Congregations in the British Empire 5606/1845' (now deposited in the Greater London Record Office, Acc 2712/VIII/107). The replies to this questionnaire have been transcribed by Rabbi Dr B. Susser and are printed in A. Newman (ed.), *Provincial Jewry in Victorian Britain* (London, 1975).

[4] H. Mayhew, *London Labour and the London Poor*, 4 vols. (London, 1861–2), ii. 117.

[5] J. Mills, *The British Jews* (London, 1853), 256.

gave it as his opinion that almost half the Jews of Britain were members of the 'lower class': 'Many are in daily want of the necessaries of life, and a still larger number [are] scarcely able to obtain sufficient to support existence.'[6] Secondly, even among the better-off, synagogue affiliation was by no means the universal rule; and, in any case, Chief Rabbi Adler's survey did not include full returns for worshippers at every synagogue.[7] So any overall population estimates based upon synagogal affiliation are minima only.

We are therefore probably on safe ground in asserting that the Jewish population—however defined—of the United Kingdom at the time (say) of the Great Exhibition of 1851 numbered around 30 to 35,000 souls. We are on even safer ground in adding that the vast majority of these—perhaps as many as 25,000 and certainly no fewer than 20,000—lived in London. The minimum of 20,000 is suggested in several ways. Mills, relying on the death rate figures issued by the London Committee (Board) of Deputies of British Jews, supported this figure, which was also that arrived at by Mr Liddle, a medical inspector of the General Board of Health, who based himself on information supplied by the secretaries of the major synagogues in the capital.[8] Dr V. D. Lipman used the statistics of children attending Jewish voluntary day schools in London to reach a similar conclusion, and demonstrated that calculations based upon the number of births, marriages, and deaths, as recorded by the Board of Deputies in 1852, support this computation.[9]

Dr Adler's survey reflected the overwhelming preponderance of London in the geographical distribution of British Jewry—a picture whose broad outlines were confirmed and sharpened in the returns of the 1851 Census of Worship.[10] Within London the Jews had concentrated themselves in three well-defined and relatively compact areas. The estimate given by Mayhew agrees with qualitative evidence, that very roughly two-thirds of the Jews of London still

[6] Ibid. 257–8.

[7] In particular, the returns for Southampton, Portsmouth, Norwich, and the Manchester Old Hebrew Congregation were incomplete.

[8] V. D. Lipman, *Social History of the Jews in England 1850–1950* (London, 1954), 9.

[9] Ibid. 10.

[10] V. D. Lipman, 'A Survey of Anglo-Jewry in 1851', *TJHSE* 17 (1951–2), 187–8.

resided in the City of London (more particularly in the wards of Aldgate and Portsoken) and the streets of Whitechapel, to the immediate east of the City (more precisely, the area of Rosemary Lane (Royal Mint Street) as far as Wellclose Square, at the eastern end of Cable Street; the area of Goodman's Fields, between Royal Mint Street and Whitechapel High Street; and the area to the north of Goodman's Fields, from Houndsditch eastwards as far as Commercial Street).[11] In these combined localities Jews constituted, in 1851, almost 10 per cent of the total population; in some more specific locations, in particular streets and squares, the proportion was certainly much higher.

To this area of settlement (in which certainly until the third decade of the nineteenth century almost the whole of London Jewry resided) I shall apply the term 'East End', though the employment of such an epithet in relation to any period before the 1850s is probably anachronistic. Mayhew referred to the 'East-end' in his survey of London published in 1861 and 'the east end of the City' was described as a specific area of concentrated Jewish settlement in Dickens's *Dictionary of London* first published in 1879.[12] By the 1880s the description was in common usage, and the geographical limits to which it was applied had expanded to include 'the Tower Hamlets' of Aldgate, Whitechapel, Spitalfields, Ratcliff, Shadwell, Wapping, Mile End, and Limehouse—the areas, in short, which were grouped within the Borough of Stepney created in 1899. These areas all became, to a greater or lesser extent, places of distinct Jewish settlement, as did the boroughs of Bethnal Green to the north and Poplar still further east; in time the 'East End' was redefined in the public mind, so that it embraced such places too.[13]

Certainly, within the East End defined as the eastern parts of the City and the western areas of Whitechapel were to be found, by the mid-nineteenth century, all the major constituents and institutions of Jewish communal life, some of them having a national as well as a local role and importance. Here, within reasonable walking distance of each other, were the synagogue of the Spanish & Portuguese Jews in Bevis Marks (erected 1701) and the three major

[11] Mayhew, *London Labour*, ii. 117; J. Weale (ed.), *London Exhibited in 1851* (London, 1851), 531–7.

[12] Mayhew, *London Labour*, ii. 118; *Dickens's Dictionary of London* (London, 1880), 145.

[13] See the discussion by R. Kalman, 'The Jewish East End—Where Was It?', in A. Newman (ed.), *The Jewish East End 1840–1939* (London, 1981), 3–15.

Ashkenazi houses of worship—the Great Synagogue (established 1690) in Duke's Place, the Hambro', in Fenchurch Street (1707), and the New Synagogue (1761), originally in Leadenhall Street but later moved to Great St Helens, east of Bishopsgate. Here, too, at 1 Smith's Buildings, Leadenhall Street, was to be found the *Beth Hamedrash*, the 'House of Study' which had originated in the eighteenth century and which incorporated the *Beth Din* of the *Ashkenazim.*[14] In 1860 the Jewish Board of Guardians in London moved into its own premises at 13 Devonshire Square, just east of Houndsditch and strategically located between the City offices of the magnates who ran the Board, and the Jewish poor to whom they ministered in Whitechapel and beyond.[15] The largest of the Jewish almshouses in London (Joel Emanuel's, founded 1849) was located in Wellclose Square, and the largest Jewish school, the Jews' Free School (opened in 1822) was situated in Bell Lane, Spitalfields.[16]

Why had the Jews settled in the City of London and its immediate eastern environs? Jews had been expelled from England in 1290, but during the sixteenth century small groups of Marranos (crypto-Jewish refugees from the Spanish Inquisition) were to be found enjoying a precarious existence in London and Bristol.[17] The Jews whom Oliver Cromwell and his Council of State had permitted to meet for private worship in 1656 were Marranos, originating mainly from the Canaries, Amsterdam, Brazil, and the West Indies, who appear to have established themselves in the City of London during the 1630s. The members of this, the Spanish & Portuguese Jews' Congregation, were collectively known as *Sephardim.* They followed a ritual and mode of Hebrew pronunciation that was and has remained distinct from that of the German- and Yiddish-speaking *Ashkenazim* of central and eastern Europe. The synagogue in which they originally worshipped was located in the City of London, in Creechurch Lane; later, in 1701, a magnificent new house of worship, modelled on the Portuguese synagogue in Amsterdam, was erected nearby, in Bevis Marks, where it still stands.

[14] P. Ornstein, *Historical Sketch of the Beth Hamedrash* (London, 1905), 1.

[15] V. D. Lipman, *A Century of Social Service 1859–1959* (London, 1959), 42.

[16] See generally S. S. Levin, 'The Origins of the Jews' Free School', *TJHSE*, 19 (1960), 97–114.

[17] V. D. Lipman, *A History of the Jews in Britain since 1858* (Leicester, 1990), 1–2.

The choice of the City as the place of the Resettlement is not difficult to understand. In most of Europe at that time, Jews were excluded from settlement in capital cities; to be able to live openly in London was therefore a novelty and a privilege. The original Marrano community of the Resettlement was composed of wealthy merchants, attracted to London in part because of its commercial importance, but mindful at the same time of the ability to be able to call upon the protection of the State should this have become necessary. London therefore offered a measure of security as well as of opportunity. The requirements of the orthodox Jewish Sabbath dictate that worshippers reside within walking distance of the synagogue, since riding on the Sabbath is forbidden; and around the synagogue are naturally established other communal services and agencies, such as schools, butcher shops (to sell *kosher* meat and poultry, slaughtered according to religious precepts), and *mikvaot* (ritual baths). To all these desiderata may be added the wish of Jews—even if their degree of religious observance is not of the strictest—to live in reasonably close proximity to each other on social grounds.

Sephardim continued to emigrate to Britain, and specifically to London, both from the West Indies, the Iberian peninsula, and Holland and from North Africa, Gibraltar, and Italy, throughout the eighteenth century.[18] But, partly on account of a high rate of assimilation into Gentile society, their numbers remained small; in 1800 the *Sephardim* of London did not total more than about 2,000.[19] The *Ashkenazim*, by contrast, were then at least ten times more numerous, their numbers swollen by influxes from Holland and Germany, and by the continuous westward migration of poor Jews seeking to escape persecution and deprivation in central Europe. For rich and poor Jews alike, settlement in London, in Britain, had one other outstanding advantage. The Resettlement had been permitted, but it had never been enacted. In general, therefore, the laws of England did not recognize or confer (either in a positive or in a negative sense) any special status upon 'Jews' as such, and discriminated against Jews only in so far as Jews, like

[18] V. D. Lipman, 'Sephardi and other Jewish Immigrants to England in the Eighteenth Century', in A. Newman (rapporteur), *Migration and Settlement* (London, 1971), 37–46.

[19] Lipman, *History of the Jews*, 4; T. M. Endelman, *Radical Assimilation in English Jewish History 1656–1945* (Bloomington, Ind., 1990), 10.

other Dissenting minorities, were not members of the Established Church. The Revolutionary and Napoleonic wars brought Jewish immigration to Britain to a virtual halt. As the balance between foreign-born and British-born Jews resident in Britain tilted in favour of the latter around the mid-nineteenth century, such legal discriminations as were suffered by the Jews became the objects of increasingly critical attention.[20]

By 1850 the City of London, overcrowded and archaically administered, was ceasing to be a residential area. Jews had for some considerable time been moving beyond its square mile, eastwards into the areas of Whitechapel already described. There were legal and economic as well as social reasons for this movement. To begin with, the law (on the initiative of the non-Jewish merchant classes of London in the late seventeenth and eighteenth centuries) imposed severe restrictions upon Jews wishing to do business within the boundaries of the City. A Jew who wished to practise as a stockbroker was obliged to purchase an expensive licence from the Court of Aldermen. The number of Jews who could operate on the Royal Exchange, buying and selling commodities, had in 1697 been limited to twelve out of a total of 124. On the death or resignation of one of these Jewish brokers, the Lord Mayor was accustomed to exact a huge fee for the transfer of the broker's medal.[21]

More irksome still were the restrictions upon Jews engaging in retail trade of any description within the City. The statutes of the City obliged all those wishing to operate as retailers to be admitted as freemen. This was a course of action not open to professing Jews, since it entailed the swearing of a Christian oath. The restriction had been compounded in 1785, when the Court of Aldermen had approved a standing order to the effect that not even baptized Jews could purchase the freedom.[22] The standing order was rescinded in

[20] In London, in 1841, 90% of the Jewish population was British born; in Manchester, in the third quarter of the 19th cent., nearly half the Jews were British born, and in Birmingham about three-quarters: V. D. Lipman, 'The Structure of London Jewry in the mid-19th century', in H. J. Zimmels, J. Rabbinowitz, and I. Finestein (eds.), *Essays Presented to Chief Rabbi Israel Brodie* (London, 1967), 253; B. Williams, *The Making of Manchester Jewry 1740–1875* (Manchester, 1976), 372; Birmingham Jewish History Research Group, *Birmingham Jewry 1749–1914* (Oldbury, 1980), 36.

[21] T. M. Endelman, *The Jews of Georgian England 1714–1830* (Philadelphia, 1979), 22.

[22] Ibid. 80.

1828; two years later Jews obtained entry to the freedom of the City by special oath. But by then it was too late to reverse the developing pattern of settlement which these restrictions had, in part, dictated. Economic factors had also impinged upon and affected this pattern. As Dr Lipman has observed, British Jewry in 1850 resembled a pyramid, but one whose base was much broader and flatter at the bottom relative to its midriff.[23] The *St. James's Medley* estimated in 1855 that about five-twelfths of London Jewry were of the 'lower classes', barely making a living.[24] This estimate agreed with that of John Mills, who reckoned that about half the Jews living in the capital in the early 1850s belonged to the 'lower class'.[25]

Until the 1880s we cannot talk of the existence within Anglo-Jewry of a significant proletariat in the Marxist sense of that term—a manual working class with a distinct socio-economic ethos and culture. The only substantially Jewish industrial employment to be found in London before 1880 were the cigar- and cigarette-making activities of a small community of Dutch, mainly *Sephardi* Jews; the records of the Bevis Marks synagogue show that between 1841 and 1880 over a fifth of the bridegrooms married there were makers of cigars.[26] Jewish-owned firms, such as Godfrey Philips and Salmon & Gluckstein, began to appear in the East End in the 1840s and 1850s.[27] Jews still formed but a small proportion of the total number of licensed tobacco manufacturers in Britain. None the less, by the late 1880s Booth could report of cigar-making that 'this trade, so far as the masters in East London are concerned, is almost entirely in the hands of the Jewish community'.[28]

The tobacco industry in general had been encouraged by the lowering of duties on imports of tobacco after the end of the Napoleonic Wars; it required little by way of initial capital outlay, and on the employment side was initially favoured by Jewish authorities concerned with schemes of apprenticeship for young lads, no doubt because it offered a settled employment untarnished by association with street trades and low living. But conditions were far from satisfactory. 'The manufacture of cigars sold at the

[23] Lipman, *Social History*, 27.

[24] *St. James's Medley* (Nov. 1855), 235–6.

[25] Mills, *British Jews*, 257.

[26] G. H. Whitehill (ed.), *Bevis Marks Records Part III* (London, 1973), 10, 13.

[27] H. Pollins, *Economic History of the Jews in England* (London, 1982), 97.

[28] C. Booth (ed.), *Life and Labour of the People of London*, 1st ser. iv (London, 1902), 221.

lowest rates [Mayhew observed] is now almost entirely in the hands of the Jews, and I am informed by a distinguished member of that ancient faith, that when I treat of the Hebrew children, employed in *making* cigars, there will be much detailed of which the public have little cognisance and little suspicion.'[29] This was indeed the case, as the reports of two Royal Commissions on Children's Employment (1843 and 1865) made clear.[30]

In 1858 the combination of low wages and wretched working conditions led to the first recorded strike of Jewish workers anywhere in the United Kingdom. An 'Oppressed Cigar Maker' wrote to the *Jewish Chronicle* in the following terms:

> The masters being unable to procure English workmen . . . to submit to the lowering of wages, resort to the practice of travelling to Holland and other parts of the continent, and, exaggerating the state of the cigar trade in England, fill the poor Dutchmen's minds with buoyant hopes of *high* wages. Arriving in a strange land with their wives and families they too soon discover that not only have they been duped but are as badly off as they were in their own country.[31]

Sweatshop conditions existed in the tobacco trades well before sweating achieved national prominence in relation to sectors of the clothing industry, and the need to address this problem motivated the Jewish authorities to press for legislation: firstly, in two enactments in 1867 permitting workshops which closed on the Jewish Sabbath (roughly sunset Friday to nightfall Saturday) to open late on Saturday evening; secondly, through legislation passed in 1871 allowing Jewish-owned workshops to operate on Sundays provided they had closed during the Sabbath.[32] In spite of these provisions, however, conditions in the industry remained at such a level that by the 1870s the Jewish Board of Guardians had determined to dissuade clients from entering it.[33]

By mid-century the image so popular in the eighteenth and early nineteenth centuries, of the Jew as a pedlar and hawker, was no longer grounded in fact. Again, the Spanish & Portuguese marriage registers provide some statistical back-up for this view; in the 1840s

[29] Mayhew, *London Labour*, i. 442.
[30] These are discussed in Pollins, *Economic History*, 123.
[31] *JC* (15 Jan. 1858), 38.
[32] Pollins, *Economic History*, 275 n. 45; J. Wigley, *The Rise and Fall of the Victorian Sunday* (Manchester, 1980), 123, 127.
[33] Pollins, *Economic History*, 32.

over 20 per cent of bridegrooms were hawkers and general dealers, but in the decade 1851–60 this proportion fell to 11 per cent, and by the 1870s was less than 9 per cent.[34] In 1796 the London magistrate Patrick Colquhoun had estimated the number of Jewish old-clothes men operating in the capital at 'upwards of two thousand'; Mayhew's view was that by 1849 the total had declined to between 500 and 600.[35] Jews were moving rapidly into craft skills such as cap and slipper making, watch, shoe, and umbrella manufacturing, glazing, and the renovation of clothes.[36]

The process by which this had come about had been complex. It is relevant to point to the desire of even the poorest Jews for self-improvement, but this is not by itself a sufficient explanation. Typically, Jewish boys would begin their street careers by selling oranges and nuts, and then progress to 'sponges, combs, pocket-knives, pencils, sealing-wax, paper, many-bladed pen-knives, razors, pocket-mirrors and shaving-boxes'.[37] But hawking was an arduous occupation, and a hazardous one. Jewish pedlars in London were subject to a great deal of abuse and even physical attack, so that the temptation to move from the selling of such articles on the streets to the retail trade, and even to the wholesale selling of these wares to other would-be hawkers, was very great.[38] We might also note that case-law dating from 1812 set down the rule that although hawkers (that is, itinerant salesmen) in London needed licences, stallholders (operating from fixed premises) did not; hence the Jewish preference for fixed markets.[39]

At the lowest levels there can be no doubt that the Jews were displaced by the Irish, whose share of the population of the capital rose from 4 to 7 per cent between 1801 and 1851, whilst that represented by the Jews declined from 1.7 to 1.0 per cent over the same period.[40] The Irish were prepared to accept lower standards

[34] Whitehill, *Bevis Marks Records*, 10; V. D. Lipman, 'Trends in Anglo-Jewish Occupations', *JJS*, 2 (1960), 202–5.

[35] P. Colquhoun, *A Treatise on the Police of the Metropolis* (3rd edn., London, 1796), 159; Mayhew, *London Labour*, ii. 121.

[36] M. A. Shepherd, 'Popular Attitudes to Jews in France and England, 1750–1840', D.Phil. thesis (Oxford, 1983), 241; J. H. Stallard, *London Pauperism amongst Jews and Christians* (London, 1867), 9, 100.

[37] Mayhew, *London Labour*, ii. 118.

[38] G. Alderman, 'Jews in the Economy of London (1850–1940)', in E. Aerts and F. M. L. Thompson (eds.), *Ethnic Minority Groups and Economic Development (1850–1940)* (Leuven, 1990), 58.

[39] Shepherd, 'Popular Attitudes', 244.

[40] Ibid. 247, 258.

of living than were the Jews, and their acquiescence in narrower profit margins had helped deprive the Jews of the dominance of the fruit trade by the end of the 1850s. The decline of the turnpikes also had an effect. Jewish pedlars relied much on the coaching trade generated by turnpikes, the tolls of which were leased by the City of London to Jews, such as Lewis Levy. In the 1820s William Cobbett had waged a campaign against Jewish control of London toll-gates; in the 1830s road improvers succeeded in freeing much of central and west London from all road tolls; by the late 1830s, in the face of railway competition, income from turnpike tolls had collapsed.[41] Jewish pedlars were, in this way, deprived of their best markets.

The leaders of the Jewish communities in London had their own special reasons for hastening the demise of the Jewish pedlar. The peddling and criminal fraternities interacted in a manner that was both embarrassing and dangerous. The involvement of Jews—and Jewesses—in the receiving and disposing of stolen property had probably been exaggerated by the popular press, and certainly by the 1850s the stereotype (however authentic it might once have been) no longer corresponded with reality. Yet the public opprobrium brought about by genuine cases of Jewish criminality—the dramatic escape from police custody in 1827 of Ikey Solomons (on whom Dickens is thought by some to have modelled Fagin in *Oliver Twist*), the trial of Sol Litsenberg (indicted at Marlborough Street Police Court in 1830 for running a gang of twenty juvenile thieves in the vicinity of Leicester Square), the scandals resulting from cases of Jewish-run houses of easy virtue (condemned by *Ashkenazi* Chief Rabbi Solomon Hirschell in 1836)—all these factors galvanized the communal leadership, and led it in the direction of operating and encouraging schemes of apprenticeship by means of which young co-religionists might have their energies channelled into honest and respectable pursuits.[42]

The records of the *Talmud Torah* from which the Jews' Free School developed show that schemes of apprenticeship, more particularly in the tailoring, pencil-making, watch-making, and glass-cutting trades, were being promoted throughout the period of

[41] Ibid. 246–7.

[42] On Solomons see J. J. Tobias, *Prince of Fences: The Life and Crimes of Ikey Solomons* (London, 1974); on Litsenberg, Shepherd, 'Popular Attitudes', 305; on Jewish-owned brothels, *Weekly Herald* (3 July 1836), 2; and see the Report from the Assistant Handloom Weavers Commissioners, *PP* 1840, xxiii (159), 112.

the Napoleonic Wars.[43] The records of a *Sephardi* charity for the period 1823–39 confirm that tailoring and shoe-making were the most favoured forms of apprenticeship, followed by the tobacco industry and the manufacture of pens and pencils.[44] In 1850 the residential Jews' Hospital at Mile End was apprenticing boys to tailoring, shoe-making, cabinet-making, and hat-making outlets; girls were taught housework, needlework, and cooking before being placed in service at the age of 15.[45]

As Dr Pollins has observed, many of these trades were undergoing technological changes that reduced the value of craftsmanship, and created instead a demand for cheap semi- and unskilled labour, the need for which was subject to seasonal fluctuation.[46] Jewish youngsters were, in short, being directed towards occupations that would become, by the 1870s if not earlier, infamous as repositories of the sweating system. In relation to the tobacco trades the threat was perceived (as we have noted) and action taken. But in general, during the first half of the nineteenth century, it either went unnoticed or was simply not regarded as a matter to which high priority need be given.

At all events, by 1850 Jews in London were largely engaged in the making, wholesale selling, and retailing of items which they had peddled at street level a couple of generations before. A classic example is presented in the career of Moses Moses, an old-clothes dealer who took leases on two shops in Covent Garden from which second-hands and misfits were sold. Later Moses & Co. produced cheap ready-mades, its methods of production (subcontracting to sweaters) causing it to be attacked by *Punch* in 1848.[47] Jewish predominance in the trade in second-hand clothes—centred on 'Rag Fair' (Rosemary Lane) and 'Petticoat Lane' (Middlesex Street, east of Houndsditch and north of Whitechapel High Street)—had a special origin. In the 1840s the rise of a workshop industry catering for a mass market in cheap clothing threatened the livelihoods of

43 Levin, 'Origins of the Jews' Free School', 108–9.

44 P. L. S. Quinn, 'The Jewish Schooling Systems of London, 1656–1956', Ph.D. thesis (London, 1958), 192*b*.

45 S. Stein, 'Some Ashkenazi Charities in London at the End of the Eighteenth and the Beginning of the Nineteenth Centuries', *TJHSE* 20 (1959–61), 77; *JC* (13 June 1851), 281.

46 Pollins, *Economic History*, 121–2.

47 *Punch*, 14 (1848), 127; and see 'Parson Lot' [Charles Kingsley], *Cheap Clothes and Nasty* (London, 1850). The enterprise, as Moss Brothers, later specialized in clothes hire.

clothes pedlars; these obtained their supplies from markets whose rapid decline was being assisted by the determination of the police to stamp out criminal activities.[48] Petticoat Lane was given a new lease of life through the foresight of a number of Jewish entrepreneurs, who set up covered clothes exchanges off Houndsditch.[49] These initiatives saved Petticoat Lane from extinction, and at the same time helped lift the trade from the bad reputation which the leaders of Anglo-Jewry found so worrying.

As the City of London declined as a residential area the wealthiest Jews, engaged in banking and stock- and commodity-broking, and an increasing number of the well-to-do Jewish bourgeoisie, moved away, more particularly to the 'West End'. But before examining Jewish settlement west of the City, it needs to be borne in mind that certainly until the 1870s most middle-class members of London Jewry continued to reside, if not in the City, then certainly in the East End, near their businesses. The orange and nut markets in Duke's Place, Aldgate, were said to have been the exclusive preserve of Jewish merchants, who lived in comfortably furnished houses in the square, in which were situated three public houses, all kept by Jewish licensed tobacco manufacturers.[50] 'Almost every shop [Mayhew recorded] has a [Hebrew] Scripture name over it.'[51] The area around Goodman's Fields (bounded by 'the four streets'—Mansell, Alie, Leman, and Prescott) housed the importers, manufacturers, and wholesalers of a range of goods, including cigars, pencils, and sealing-wax.[52] Wholesale dealers in foreign bric-à-brac, such as feathers and shells, lived to the immediate east of the Tower of London; it was here, in Upper East Smithfield, that Marcus Samuel (the first Viscount Bearsted and founder of the Shell Transport & Trading Company) was born in 1853.[53] Retail jewellers congregated in the vicinity of Whitechapel, Houndsditch, and Bevis Marks.

In these neighbourhoods Jews of all economic conditions lived practically side by side; hawkers and old-clothes dealers dwelt in

[48] Shepherd, 'Popular Attitudes', 269.

[49] Mayhew, *London Labour*, ii. 26–7; Proceedings of the Select Committee on Sunday Trading (Metropolis), *PP* 1847, ix (666), qq. 1120–5.

[50] Lipman, *Social History*, 32.

[51] Mayhew, *London Labour*, i. 86–91.

[52] Lipman, 'Structure of London Jewry', 261–4; V. D. Lipman, 'Jewish Settlement in the East End of London 1840–1940: The Topographical and Statistical Background', in Newman (ed.), *The Jewish East End*, 27.

[53] R. Henriques, *Marcus Samuel First Viscount Bearsted* (London, 1960), 14–15.

the same streets as families wealthy enough to employ more than one servant.[54] We should note too that the spread of Jews out from the original area of settlement in the City had led to a flourishing of minor *Ashkenazi* houses of worship, some of them branches of the City congregations. Chief among these was the Rosemary Lane Synagogue (*Machzike Torah*—'Upholders of the Law'), dating from 1748; a 'Polish Synagogue', a dependency of the Great, which evolved as a *minyan* in Cutler Street; and the Gun Square Synagogue, Spitalfields, a dependency of the New Synagogue and founded—also by Polish immigrants—in 1792.[55]

The continued if small-scale migration of Jews from Poland—and, to a lesser extent, from Germany—after 1815 led to the establishment of other congregations in London. These were often (as had been the case with the Cutler Street community) in the nature of *landsmannschaften*—that is, organizations of Jews from the same town or district of origin—sometimes evolving from study-groups or benefit or friendly societies, comprised, perhaps, of men in the same trade or calling. They could provide modest financial payments at times of need, including *shiva* benefit during the period of seven days confined mourning following the death of a parent or close relative, when orthodox practice enjoins that no work be performed. Mills noted that in the early 1850s in London there were 'twenty of these institutions, comprising about two thousand members'.[56] The first to become a true synagogal body, the *Chevrat Menahem Avelim Chesed Ve'Emeth* (Society for Comforting Mourners and Burying the Dead) was established as the Sandy's Row Synagogue in Spitalfields in 1851; many of the *chevrot* that sprang up over the following thirty years were also located in the Spitalfields area.[57]

The Jewish East End in 1851 did not extend much beyond a line through Commercial Street north of Whitechapel High Street, Leman Street south of it, and Wellclose Square, south of Cable Street. The Square housed the Joel Emanuel almshouses and the Hand-in-Hand Asylum for aged and 'decayed' tradesmen, dating

[54] Lipman, 'Structure of London Jewry', 264–8.

[55] C. Roth, 'The Lesser Synagogues of the Eighteenth Century', *Miscellanies of the Jewish Historical Society of England*, 3 (1937), 5–6.

[56] Mills, *British Jews*, 291.

[57] Lipman, 'Jewish Settlement in the East End', 29.

from 1840.[58] Further out, at Mile End (a mile or so further eastwards) were to be found the Spanish & Portuguese Hospital, the *Ashkenazi* Jews' Hospital (which, as we have seen, also undertook the training of boys and girls), a collection of almshouses in Devonshire Street, and the two major communal cemeteries, that of the Spanish & Portuguese Jews on the northern side of Mile End Road, and that of the *Ashkenazim*, close by in Alderney Road.

As we have observed, the majority of London's Jews lived at this time in the East End. Most of the remainder lived in the ever more fashionable West End—that is, London west of Temple Bar. As we might expect, the West End attracted in the main the wealthier elements in the community. A few of these had already equipped themselves with country seats, in Highgate and Hackney, Richmond and Roehampton, Teddington and Twickenham, Kew and Isleworth.[59] Most, however, preferred to remain in London. Until the end of the eighteenth century they had continued to live above their businesses in the City, or in the more desirable squares east of it. But around 1800 the wealthier families began to move out, more particularly in the direction of Kensington, Belgravia, and Mayfair, as well as to Kennington, Islington, and Bow. The trickle soon became a flood: Nathan Mayer Rothschild (1777–1836) from St Swithin's Lane to Piccadilly, Moses Montefiore (1784–1885; his next-door neighbour) to Park Lane, the Goldsmids to Regent's Park and Marble Arch. By the 1840s 'the great Anglo-Jewish families, interconnected by marriage, [had] settled in dynastic clusters in Mayfair or the West Central district'.[60]

As it happened, the nucleus of a Jewish community in the West End already existed, formed from the craftsmen whose jewellery, watch-making, and embroidery shops had been established there from the middle of the eighteenth century. We know that a *minyan* met at the Westminster home of Wolf Liepman around 1768; such was the origin of the Western Synagogue, originally located in Denmark Court (off the Strand) but later (1826) removed to St Alban's Place.[61] In 1810 dissident elements in the Western

[58] Lipman, *Social History*, 23.

[59] Endelman, *Jews of Georgian England*, 126–7; V. D. Lipman, 'The Age of Emancipation, 1815–1880', in id. (ed.), *Three Centuries of Anglo-Jewish History* (Cambridge, 1961), 70.

[60] Ibid. 71.

[61] A. Barnett, *The Western Synagogue through Two Centuries 1761–1961* (London, 1961), 22.

Synagogue had seceded to form a separate congregation originally located in Dean Street, Soho, later relocated in Brewer Street and later still (1826) reopened in Maiden Lane, Covent Garden.[62]

Estimates of the Jewish population of the West End are difficult to compute. The Western Synagogue claimed in its reply to Chief Rabbi Nathan Adler's questionnaire that it catered for the needs of some 1,000 souls; the Maiden Lane congregation probably served about half this number. In 1840, eighteen *Sephardim* and six *Ashkenazim* had resolved to establish a place of worship which would be neither *Ashkenazi* nor *Sephardi*, but 'British'; as a result, two years later, the first English 'Reform' Synagogue, the West London Synagogue of British Jews, opened its doors in Burton Street; in 1849 the congregation removed to Margaret Street, Cavendish Square. The reasons for this secession, and the circumstances in which it took place, will be explained in due course. Here we may note that the secessionists complained, *inter alia*, that there would otherwise have been no place for them to worship in the area of Westminster in which they lived.[63] Naturally, the Reform Synagogue did not feature in Adler's survey. But in the 1851 census it claimed an average Sabbath attendance of 140, so that the total number of persons in the congregation might have been as high as 500.[64]

But the combined totals for the three West End communities mentioned so far certainly do not reflect the total number of Jews living there, because we know that many residents of the West End continued to maintain their membership of City synagogues. In 1853 the Spanish & Portuguese had opened a branch synagogue in Wigmore Street, and two years later, under the auspices of the Great Synagogue, an *Ashkenazi* branch synagogue—the Central Synagogue—was consecrated in Great Portland Street.[65] In all, therefore, it is possible that in mid-century between 4,000 and 5,000 Jews lived in London's West End.

[62] Lipman, *Social History*, 14. The Maiden Lane synagogue rejoined the Western in 1907, and the Western itself merged with the Marble Arch constituent of the United Synagogue in 1991.

[63] M. Leigh, 'Reform Judaism in Britain (1840–1970)', in D. Marmur (ed.), *Reform Judaism* (London, 1973), 20.

[64] Lipman, 'A Survey of Anglo-Jewry in 1851', 177.

[65] A. Hyamson, *The Sephardim of England: A History of the Spanish and Portuguese Jewish Community, 1492–1951* (London, 1951), 313–14; M. Adler, *The History of the Central Synagogue 1855–1905* (London, 1905), 18.

Around 'the Borough', in Southwark, south London, a third distinct grouping of Jews may be identified. In 1851 two synagogues existed there: one dating from the mid-eighteenth century (perhaps to serve the needs of Jewish inmates of the debtors' prison) but now very much in decline, known as Nathan Henry's Synagogue, situated behind his house in Market Street; the other, the Borough Synagogue, founded by secessionists in 1823 and located in Prospect Place, St George's Road. On Nathan Henry's death in 1853 his synagogue closed. But the Prospect Place establishment grew, serving the needs of Jewish retailers in the area. The 1851 census returns suggest that between 300 and 400 Jews lived in Southwark at this time.[66]

Both in numbers and in economic status the Jews of London exercised the preponderating influence in ordering the affairs of British Jewry. Until the very end of the nineteenth century provincial Jewries were not only small in absolute numbers, but much less well endowed in terms of infrastructure and personnel. Yet it was, perhaps, for this very reason that they could sometimes be fiercely independent, resisting subordination to the capital by refusing to bestow support—and hence legitimacy—upon the institutions and initiatives which emanated from their London co-religionists. The origins of provincial Jewry combine elements of general economic development with those drawn from the specific historical demography of Jews in post-Resettlement Britain. Some provincial communities had originated in the needs of itinerant pedlars, who wished for a place of rest during the Sabbath—a *pied-à-terre* which might, in time, become a warehouse or even a retail shop:

> The foundation of Provincial Jewish Congregations in England [Lucien Wolf wrote] was almost exclusively the work of the . . . Germano-Polish section of the Hebrew people . . . [who] were for the most part exceedingly poor and were glad to settle anywhere as long as the locality afforded the chance of making a modest livelihood. In this way, towards the beginning of the eighteenth century, the leading British ports . . . received a sprinkling of Jewish settlers. The more prosperous among them set up stores for trading with the seafaring population. Those who were absolutely destitute became pedlars . . . As soon as a pedlar had saved a little money . . . he would set up shop on his own, preferentially in the centre of the district

[66] Lipman, 'A Survey of Anglo-Jewry in 1851', 177; see generally M. Rosenbaum, *History of the Borough Synagogue* (London, 1917).

which he had worked as a pedlar, and the peripatetic trinket-seller would blossom out into a jeweller and silver-smith . . . Each shop-keeper would become the controller of a fresh set of tied pedlars . . . Thus it came about that at the centre of nearly every provincial congregation was a jeweller and silversmith, and that in some of the larger towns those jewellers, who had originally been forced into the trade by the necessity of dealing in merchandise that was at once portable and profitable, became eventually bullion merchants and even bankers.[67]

Wolf's account was a romantic oversimplification: not untrue, but partial. Of the four categories of provincial Jewish communities that comprised Dr Lipman's typology—seaports, inland market centres, newer industrial centres, and pleasure resorts—Wolf's explanation holds true certainly for *some* of the seaports and *some* of the inland county towns.[68] Even in relation to the seaport communities, while the story of the pedlar appears authentic in the case of Falmouth (founded about 1740, one of the earliest provincial Jewries) and Portsmouth (1742) it does not suffice as a general explanation of the rise of Jewries in other naval towns: for example, Chatham (*c*.1750) and Sheerness (1790).[69]

Most of the provincial Jewries that existed in the mid-nineteenth century had been established in the period of fifty years that followed the accession of the first Hanoverian monarch, George I, in 1714; many owed their foundation to the efforts of German-Jewish immigrants, who came from rural townships and whose passage to England was encouraged by the free travel that was available on mail-packets until 1771. The expansion of England's population in the eighteenth century created a demand for the crafts and callings which they practised. These ranged from work in glass, jewellery, and precious metals to professional occupations such as optical work and dentistry. Very few were tailors, but the great expansion of the Royal Navy at the end of the century led to a growth in demand for the services of private contractors, who could supply ships with stores and clothing; in 1816 the Navy List recorded the names of no less than 140 Jewish navy agents, in ports as far apart as Portsmouth, Plymouth, Sheerness, Chatham,

[67] L. Wolf, 'The Origins of the Provincial Communities', in L. Wolf, *Essays in Jewish History*, ed. C. Roth (London, 1934), 137–8.

[68] Lipman, *Social History*, 18.

[69] See generally C. Roth, *The Rise of Provincial Jewry* (London, 1950).

Liverpool, Dover, Falmouth, Sunderland, North Shields, and Brighton.[70]

In 1850 most of these navy-port congregations were still flourishing; some, indeed, had not yet reached the limit of their growth. Falmouth, Penzance, Sheerness, and King's Lynn were in decline. But the Memorial Synagogue in Chatham, dedicated in 1870, served a community that had been in existence since about 1750.[71] Dover, where Jews had lived perhaps since the 1750s, did not obtain its first purpose-built synagogue until 1862.[72] The Southampton community was not formally established until 1833, and a permanent house of worship not constructed until 1864.[73] Portsmouth, the estimated Jewish population of which was about 300 at this time, could by 1874 support a school, two benevolent institutions, and a set of almshouses, built by the community in 1857; by 1901 (encouraged, no doubt, by the growth of the town as a holiday resort) the congregation also boasted no less than three *kosher* restaurants.[74]

The development of seaside resorts in the second half of the nineteenth century gave new leases of life to other Jewish communities. Great Yarmouth, where Moses and Judith Montefiore had spent their honeymoon in 1812, did not acquire a synagogue until 1847; the congregation appears to have been all but extinct by 1877, but was resurrected in 1899 and, on the strength of an unprecedented influx of Jewish visitors, engaged the services of the Revd S. Pearlstein, formerly of Exeter, who acted as minister, teacher, and *shochet*.[75] The Jewry of Ramsgate was built upon the fact that the Montefiores chose to reside there. Sir Moses built the synagogue (consecrated 1832) entirely at his own expense, and erected the Judith Lady Montefiore Theological College in 1866; by 1901, when its resident Jewish population was said to number about 130, the town had six *kosher* restaurants and boarding houses.[76]

[70] C. Roth, 'The Portsmouth Community and its Historical Background', *TJHSE*, 13 (1932–5), 186; see also G. L. Green, *The Royal Navy & Anglo-Jewry 1740–1820* (London, 1989), chs. 7, 8, 9.

[71] Roth, *Provincial Jewry*, 49.

[72] Ibid. 55.

[73] Ibid. 100.

[74] Newman (ed.), *Provincial Jewry*: entry for Portsmouth.

[75] *JC* (8 Sept. 1899), 17; (7 Sept. 1956), 18.

[76] Newman (ed.), *Provincial Jewry*: entry for Ramsgate.

Brighton had attracted Jews both as residents and as visitors since the end of the eighteenth century; when peace was made with France in 1815, Chief Rabbi Hirschell resided in the town, the Jewish population of which expanded rapidly after the construction of the synagogue in 1823. The Sabbath census of 1851 suggests a Jewish population in Brighton of about 150, which included teachers, shopkeepers, tradesmen, and pawnbrokers; in 1867 the synagogue had to be enlarged, and was replaced by a new building, in Middle Street, in 1874.[77] We might also note that the growth in popularity of inland spa resorts resulted in the establishment of small Jewish communities at Bath, where a synagogue was dedicated in 1842 to serve a community of about 50 souls, and at Cheltenham, where a community of about twice that size had opened a synagogue in 1839.[78]

The resident Jewish populations of the seaside towns were never very large in Victorian times; some, like Brighton, were virtual dormitories of London, their members often owing primary allegiance to one of the London congregations to which they belonged. Very different indeed were the Jewries that developed in the large industrial and commercial ports that expanded with the growth of Britain's overseas trade in the nineteenth century. Chief among these were Bristol, Hull, Liverpool, and Newcastle upon Tyne. Two of these (Hull and Liverpool) may be distinguished from the others on account of the fact that their relatively small resident Jewish communities had to cater for numbers of immigrants and transmigrants which, even in mid-century, could be substantial.

At Hull, where (following the healing of a communal schism) a synagogue had been erected in 1826, there were in 1837 about thirty-five resident Jewish families; the total Jewish population in 1851 has been estimated at 200, but the number of immigrants from Russia, Poland, and Germany landing at the port annually could reach twice that number. Next to London, Hull was the main port of entry into Britain from the Continent. Particularly in and after the European revolutions of 1848–9, the Jewish community there was obliged to spend considerable sums in providing relief for

[77] D. Spector, 'Brighton and Hove—1837–1901', in Newman (ed.), *Provincial Jewry*; Roth, *Provincial Jewry*, 34–9.

[78] See generally M. Brown and J. Samuel, 'The Jews of Bath', *Bath History*, 1 (1986), 150–72; M. A. Shepherd, 'Cheltenham Jews in the Nineteenth Century', *JJS* 21 (1979), 125–33; B. Torode, *The Hebrew Community of Cheltenham, Gloucester and Stroud* (Cheltenham, 1989).

impoverished co-religionists from central Europe, some of whom settled in the town. In 1852 the synagogue was much enlarged, while the Jewish school attached to it was educating forty boys and girls; in 1863 a separate girls' school was set up. By then the community had equipped itself with two benevolent institutions, a Philanthropic Society established in 1848 and the *Meshivas Nephesh* Benefit Society, which came into being the following year. Judge Finestein has calculated that in 1870 about 500 Jews lived in Hull. Four years later some foreign-born Jews, more traditional and meticulous in their approach to religious observance, established their own, separate house of worship, while the older and more Anglicized elements began to move to fashionable districts, residence in which was (no doubt) felt to accord with their more affluent and assimilated status. These trends were to become typical of Jewish life in many provincial towns during the second half of the century.[79]

Liverpool was in 1850 the largest provincial Jewish community, with an estimated population of 1,500.[80] Originating in the second half of the eighteenth century, by the mid-nineteenth Liverpool Jewry was possessed of two synagogues—the result of a schism in 1838—the Old Hebrew Congregation in Seel Street (erected 1807) and the New Hebrew Congregation in Hope Place (1842). The causes of the split had little to do with religiosity, but arose rather out of a revolt against the methods by which those who ruled in Seel Street maintained themselves in power. The details will be examined in due course. The revolt itself reflected fundamental alterations in the socio-economic structure of Liverpool Jewry and, as such, was symptomatic of the far-reaching effects which economic growth and the consequent rise of an Anglo-Jewish bourgeoisie were having, and were to have, upon many provincial communities. In some respects, too (though the analogy must not be pressed too far) the conflict in Liverpool mirrored that out of

[79] I. Finestein, 'Hull', in Newman (ed.), *Provincial Jewry*; Lipman, *Social History*, 22–3.

[80] On Liverpool Jewry see B. L. Benas, 'Records of the Jews in Liverpool', *Transactions of the Historical Society of Lancashire and Cheshire*, 51 (1899), 45–84; B. B. Benas, *Later Records of the Jews in Liverpool* (n.p., 1929); id., 'A Survey of the Jewish Institutional History of Liverpool', *TJHSE* 17 (1951–2), 23–38; P. Ettinger, *Hope Place in Liverpool Jewry* (Liverpool, 1930); D. Hudaly, *Liverpool Old Hebrew Congregation 1780–1974* (Liverpool, 1974); and the entry in Newman (ed.), *Provincial Jewry*. The most reliable estimate of the Jewish population of Liverpool is given by Williams, *Manchester Jewry*, 133.

which the West London Reform congregation had been born, and anticipated that which was to afflict the Manchester community some years later. Certainly, disenchantment with what were perceived as ultra-conservative ruling cliques, and alienation from forms of divine worship regarded as archaic and off-putting, were common to all three.

By mid-century Liverpool Jewry could boast a full complement of social and educational facilities: a Jewish day school, founded in 1842 and having 38 boys and 45 girls on its books; a Philanthropic Society, dating from 1811; a Ladies' Benevolent Institution, founded in 1849 for the relief of poor married women during confinement, sickness, and *shiva*; and a Hebrew Provident Society, dating from 1850, which provided a small number of pensioners with weekly doles. In part, these welfare societies had been set up to deal with the problems resulting from the large number of foreign Jews who, taking advantage of cheap rail and sea travel, made the cross-country journey from Hull and other east coast ports in order to obtain a passage to America. Here again, we must note the parallels between the experience of Liverpool and that of London, and the similarities in the expedients to which the Jews in both cities resorted to cope with the problems of the Jewish poor in the mid-century.

Liverpool also boasted one of the finest Anglo-Jewish preachers in the English language, David Meyer Isaacs (*c.*1810–79). The Western Synagogue in London had in 1817 begun to experiment with sermons in English (as opposed to German or Yiddish), delivered by Rabbi Tobias Goodman, who may have preached at Seel Street two years later.[81] At the prompting of Moses Montefiore, Bevis Marks substituted English sermons for Portuguese in 1829.[82] Isaacs set an altogether higher standard, an accomplishment all the more remarkable since 'though not an Englishman, his accent and fluent acquaintance with the English language would proclaim him of English birth'.[83] He was in fact born a Dutchman, and had come to England in 1818, when his father had opened a private school in Spitalfields; subsequently he acted as companion to the blind wife of Chief Rabbi Hirschell, and received instruction in *Talmud* from

[81] Barnett, *Western Synagogue*, 50–1.

[82] L. Wolf, *Essays in Jewish History* (London, 1934), 313.

[83] J. Picciotto, *Sketches of Anglo-Jewish History*, ed. I. Finestein (London, 1956), 333.

Dayan Israel Levy. In 1832 he was engaged as minister in Bristol and in 1835 was appointed to deliver English sermons at Seel Street and to act as 'Second Reader' to its secretary, David Woolf Marks (1811–1909). In all, Isaacs spent twenty-seven years in Liverpool, moving to the New Congregation in 1851 after a dispute over his salary and eventually leaving for the Great Synagogue, Manchester, in 1862.[84]

The remaining seaport Jewries in existence in the mid-nineteenth century were, by comparison with Liverpool, exceedingly small; unlike Hull, however, they experienced neither the expansion nor the problems associated with immigrants and refugees. Bristol, where the nucleus of a community can be detected in the 1750s, had a Jewish population of about 300 a century later; a new synagogue (a converted Quakers' meeting house) was consecrated in 1842.[85] Because it did not feature on any recognized transmigration route, the growth of Bristol's Jewish community was slow and faltering; one estimate put the size of the community in 1906 at just over 800, but another (1914) indicated virtually no growth in sixty years. In spite of having a few wealthy families within the congregation (pre-eminently the Alexander family, whose fortune was based upon wide shipping and marine insurance interests), the Bristol community was really not well-to-do. Partly as a result, it could not afford to retain the services of ministers of religion for more than a few years, after which (like David Isaacs) they moved on to more lucrative positions. Aaron Levy Green (1821–83), born in London, served at Bristol from 1838 to 1842 before returning to the capital, working first at the Great Synagogue and then (1855) at the Central; he became (the *Jewish Chronicle* observed) '*the* minister who established in England the Jewish pulpit and made it felt to be a necessary adjunct of the Synagogue'.[86]

The Jewry of Newcastle upon Tyne numbered no more than about 100 in 1851; its synagogue had been erected thirteen years earlier, perhaps as a response to the activities of Christian missionaries.[87] The honour of being the oldest Jewish community

[84] On Isaacs see Williams, *Manchester Jewry*, 91–2; *JC* (9 May 1879), 11.

[85] On Bristol Jewry see generally A. Schlesinger, 'Victorian Jewry in Bristol', in Newman (ed.), *Provincial Jewry*.

[86] *JC* (16 Mar. 1883), 11; Green was a regular contributor to the *Chronicle*, under the pseudonym 'Nemo'.

[87] This paragraph is based on entries in Newman (ed.), *Provincial Jewry*, and

in the north-east (and of being the first provincial Jewry to send a representative to the Board of Deputies) belonged in fact to Sunderland, where a synagogue had been established in 1781. By the 1850s the Sunderland community numbered about 250 souls, divided into a 'Polish' congregation (based apparently upon an eastern European group of *chassidic* Jews) and a community of Dutch and German origin. The two congregations were formally united in 1857, and a new synagogue was consecrated in 1862. An estimated 50 to 100 Jews were located at Tynemouth (North Shields), though a house of worship was not provided (rented) until 1873. The Jews of South Shields had no organized religious life until the erection of a synagogue in 1862; until then Jews who lived on the south side of the Tyne crossed the river by ferry to join their brethren in Tynemouth for divine worship, paying their fares in advance so as not to desecrate the Sabbath. The communities on both sides of the river seem in general to have occupied themselves as ships' chandlers, retail and credit drapers, tailors, cabinet makers, and pawnbrokers. A handful of Jews—small tradesmen and ships' chandlers—resided in the port of Hartlepool. Significant growth of Jewish communities in the neighbourhoods of the rivers Tyne, Wear, and Tees had to wait until the era of mass immigration at the end of the century.

By the 1850s eight 'county' towns can be identified as possessing Jewish communities.[88] Most of these dated from the mid-eighteenth century. Only Exeter had over 100 members.[89] The small congregation at Canterbury was in decline. Oxford had a Jewish population (mainly second-hand clothes dealers and cigar merchants) of about fifty. Services at Cambridge had been suspended, though Cambridge Jewry, like Oxford, was to grow again at the end of the century, after it had become possible (1871) for Jews to matriculate into and take higher degrees and accept fellowships at these ancient seats of learning.[90] At Bedford there was a synagogue catering for five

L. Olsover, *The Jewish Communities of North-East England 1755–1980* (Gateshead, 1980).

[88] Data in this paragraph are taken from Newman (ed.), *Provincial Jewry*, and Roth, *Provincial Jewry*.

[89] On the Jewries of south-west England see B. Susser, 'The Jews of Devon and Cornwall from the Middle Ages until the early 20th Century', Ph.D. thesis (Exeter, 1977).

[90] Acts of Parliament in 1854 and 1856 made it possible for professing Jews to take Bachelors degrees at Oxford and Cambridge respectively. Higher degrees, fellowships, and offices at these universities were not open to professing Jews until

members; an organized community at Gloucester had collapsed, the remaining members having attached themselves to that at Cheltenham.

The historian of East Anglian Jewry has observed that 'by the middle of the nineteenth century Ipswich Jewry had already disappeared'.[91] This judgement appears premature, since the town possessed a synagogue at which, on census Sabbath in 1851, ten congregants were observed; but the statement would certainly hold true for the 1890s. Norwich appeared to be in a flourishing condition, for in 1849 a new, purpose-built synagogue, costing £500 and serving a community of about seventy-five souls, had been opened amid a flurry of publicity; in truth, this renaissance was due to the exertions of a few monied enthusiasts, pre-eminently Joel Fox, a member of the Town Council and the local Board of Guardians. By the early 1870s the community was in dire financial straits, and had to use the correspondence columns of the *Jewish Chronicle* to appeal for funds.[92]

North of the Border, there were as yet no organized communities in Aberdeen or Dundee.[93] Glasgow had a synagogue in the city centre to serve a congregation—about twenty-six families—of merchants, furriers, and tradespeople, originating for the most part from Poland and Germany. The Edinburgh community dated formally from 1816; there were perhaps a hundred Jews in the

the passage of further legislation in 1871. The impetus which led to the abolition of these remaining restrictions was provided by the case of Numa Hartog (1846–71), who achieved the status of Senior Wrangler in the Cambridge Mathematical Tripos in 1869, but found himself unable to enter upon a college fellowship: see his entry in *Dictionary of National Biography*. In Scotland, religious tests were by the 19th cent. no longer required for university entrance, so that 'the Scottish Universities, alone, allowed Jews to graduate as doctors': K. Collins, *Go and Learn: The International Story of Jews and Medicine in Scotland* (Aberdeen, 1988), 11–12.

[91] H. Levine, 'The Jews of East Anglia', in Newman (ed.), *Provincial Jewry*.

[92] *JC* (31 May 1872), 133; and see generally H. Levine, *The Norwich Hebrew Congregation 1840–1960* (Norwich, 1961).

[93] On Scottish Jewry see A. Levy, 'The Origins of Scottish Jewry', *TJHSE* 19 (1955–9), 129–62, and the same author's *The Origins of Glasgow Jewry 1812–1895* (Glasgow, 1949). Also useful are S. Daiches, 'The Jew in Scotland', *Records of the Scottish Church History Society*, 3 (1929), 196–209, and M. Rodgers, 'Glasgow Jewry', in B. Kay (ed.), *Odyssey, the Second Collection* (Edinburgh, 1982), 113–23. There is a full bibliography compiled by H. L. Kaplan in K. E. Collins (ed.), *Aspects of Scottish Jewry* (Glasgow, 1987), 87–96. T. Benski, 'Glasgow', in Newman (ed.), *Provincial Jewry*, declares that the size of Glasgow Jewry in 1858 'must have been over 300'; this estimate appears to be based merely upon the seating capacity of the synagogue (260), and seems to me excessive.

Scottish capital at the time of Nathan Adler's survey. In Wales there was a small but thriving community (about fifty strong) in Swansea, that could trace its origins back to the 1740s. A synagogue existed in Cardiff, and one was erected in Merthyr Tydfil in 1848.[94] In Cardiff the Jews congregated in the old part of the city, around Bute Street, where they established a medley of shops, clothing, and pawnbroking businesses.[95] Jewish pedlars were certainly tramping the valleys of Glamorganshire and Monmouthshire, but of the valley Jewries associated with the growth of the South Wales coalfields there was as yet no trace.

Dublin boasted a community of perhaps 150 souls—for the most part gold and silversmiths, watchmakers, traders in snuff and tobacco merchants, clothiers and grocers, but including also itinerant salesmen and pedlars. There was a handful of Jews in Limerick and Cork. Jews certainly lived in Belfast, but the community there was not organized until 1864, on the initiative of Daniel Jaffe, a merchant from Hamburg who had first visited the city in 1845 to purchase linen for export to the Continent and America; other founders of the Belfast congregation were also from Germany, mainly merchants engaged in the export of cloth and jute.[96]

The picture of early Victorian provincial Jewry painted thus far is of a patchwork of communities mostly dating from the mid to late eighteenth century and mostly located in what were still semi-rural areas or in seaports. Jewries located in the large and growing inland industrial towns were still small: about fifty Jews in Nottingham, perhaps twice that number each in Coventry and Sheffield, Dudley, Wolverhampton, and Leeds, but only a handful in Leicester.[97] Apart from London, only three English cities had in 1851 Jewish communities of over 500 persons. Of these, Liverpool has already been cited; it remains to outline those located in Birmingham and Manchester.

Jews had certainly lived in Birmingham since the early eighteenth

[94] G. Alderman, 'Into the Vortex: South Wales Jewry before 1914', in Newman (ed.), *Provincial Jewry*.

[95] U. Henriques, 'The Jewish Community in Cardiff, 1830–1914', *Welsh History Review*, 14 (1988), 269–71.

[96] L. Hyman, *The Jews of Ireland* (London, 1972), 157–8, 203–5, 210, 218.

[97] Lipman, *Social History*, 24; on Sheffield see A. Krausz, *Sheffield Jewry* (London, 1980); on Leicester, A. Newman, *Leicester Hebrew Congregation 1874–1974* (Leicester, 1974).

century; it was in Birmingham that many of the cheap fancy goods sold by pedlars were made, and the town's geographical location made it a most convenient centre for hawkers and pedlars. The 1851 religious census suggests a Jewish population of between 750 and 1,000; research based upon names occurring in the general census has put the figure for the resident Jewish community at approximately 730; to this perhaps another fifty, representing the itinerant population and paupers, should be added.[98] Certainly, the Sabbath attendance recorded at the synagogue, in Severn Street—253—was the largest of any single provincial congregation. In 1856 a splendid new house of worship, built on Singer's Hill, was consecrated by Chief Rabbi Adler in the presence of local dignitaries and representatives from several of the London communities as well as from other provincial congregations.[99] Attached to the synagogue was a Hebrew School; grants to the needy were made by a Philanthropic Society established in 1828, and by a Benefit Society dating from 1853.

Birmingham Jewry was a trading community, whose members originated from Poland, Prussia, and other parts of Germany; less than half of those engaged in trade were British born. The poorest occupations (especially glazing and hawking) were the preserve of Polish immigrants. Crafts such as jewellery and tailoring were well represented in the community, but many of the shopkeepers combined more than one speciality: clothiers, for example, might also be pawnbrokers.[100] Although the overwhelming mass of the community lived in the city centre, even in 1851 the more affluent were beginning to escape to healthier parts north of the centre and to its west, in the village of Edgbaston.[101]

The Jewish community of Manchester was not as old as that of Birmingham, but by the mid-nineteenth century its size was greater, it had two synagogues (Haliwell Street and Ainsworth Court, Long Millgate), and the merest hint of a *Sephardi* presence. The origins of Manchester Jewry conformed strictly to Lucien Wolf's model: a number of pedlars, from Germany via Liverpool, settled permanently in Manchester in the 1780s, opened small shops in the rundown neighbourhood around Shudehill, Long Millgate and Miller

[98] *Birmingham Jewry 1749–1914*, 13, 36.

[99] Z. Josephs (ed.), *Birmingham Jewry, ii. More Aspects 1740–1930* (Oldbury, 1984), 14.

[100] *Birmingham Jewry 1749–1914*, 37–8.

[101] Ibid. 16.

Street in the 'Old Town', hired a room for public worship, and organized the provision of a burial-ground at Pendleton.[102] The arrival of wealthy textile merchants from Germany (including Nathan Mayer Rothschild from Frankfurt in 1799 and Solomon Levi Behrens from Hamburg in 1814) added status as well as wealth to the community, and as the economy of Manchester 'took off' after 1815, Jewish traders and shopkeepers were drawn to it, sometimes from declining communities in the seaports and the midlands and south of England.

Other Jewish traders came from Holland, Germany, and France; in the 1840s Manchester also, and inevitably, attracted poorer Jews from Poland. By the end of the 1850s the number of Jews in Manchester had overtaken that in Liverpool, and totalled about 1,800. Of these fully one-third came from eastern Europe; two, Abraham Nissim Levy and Samuel Hadida, hailed respectively from Constantinople and Gibraltar.[103] As with London, the social structure of Manchester Jewry resembled a pyramid: cotton traders, professionals, and solid retailers were located at the top, below them came modest shopkeepers, and at the bottom was a poor eastern European working class, mostly itinerant traders and semi-skilled manual workers. And, as in Birmingham, this class structure soon exhibited a geographical dimension. The poorest Jews inhabited the slums of Red Bank, north of Old Town. The wealthier elements had for some twenty years been moving into middle-class suburbs mainly to the north of the city, at Cheetham Hill, where the Great Synagogue was consecrated on 11 March 1858. Two weeks later 'The Manchester Congregation of British Jews'—in fact, a Reform Synagogue—was opened nearby, in Park Place. The Reformers were mainly of German origin, and their motives in raising the banner of revolt were as much social as doctrinal. They chose as their first minister the enigmatic Rabbi Dr Solomon Marcus Schiller-Szinessy (1820–90), a Hungarian scholar whose career was and continued to be a byword for controversy, and of whom we shall learn more in due course.[104]

This survey of provincial Jewry has been locational and congregational in form. In summary, we can say that British Jewry in the mid-nineteenth century was dominated by London; that

[102] Williams, *Manchester Jewry*, ch. 1.

[103] Ibid. 83.

[104] Ibid. ch. 10; R. Loewe, 'Solomon Marcus Schiller-Szinessy, 1820–1890', *TJHSE* 21 (1962–7), 148–89.

there were some forty-three small communities (generally no larger than 500 persons and often very much smaller) elsewhere in the British Isles, many of which were to disappear completely by the end of the century, but a few of which were to grow as industrial expansion proceeded; and that there were three cities—Birmingham, Liverpool, and Manchester—which supported Jewish communities of greater size, though they were still very small compared with London; roughly half of the Jews living in the provinces in the 1840s dwelt in these three cities. We can also make a number of generalizations about the structure and characteristics of the provincial Jewries; these characteristics had important consequences for the relationship of these congregations to London, and to the institutions which London Jewry alone was able to support.

The first point worthy of note is that, certainly until the 1840s, the vast majority of provincial communities were governed by constitutions which mirrored those of the major London synagogues. The outstanding feature of these schemes of governance was their highly oligarchic aspect. Synagogue membership was divided into three classes (of males), of which the most important—but often the least numerous—were (using the *Ashkenazi* terminology) the *Ba'ale batim* (literally, 'masters of the house', or 'householders'). These 'privileged' members alone had the power to vote at general meetings, and to be elected as honorary officers; refusal to serve as an honorary officer, or to undertake other prescribed duties, might entail a fine or other penalty. In some communities the privileged members alone had the right to permit others to enter into this category of membership (and might blackball aspiring entrants) and in others the right of entry devolved upon the sons or sons-in-law of those already 'privileged'. Many ceremonial honours of ritual, such as being called to the Reading of the Law from the *Torah* Scroll, had to be offered in the first instance to privileged members, and only with their approval could these honours be conferred upon other categories of member. Of these there were generally two, the *Toshavim* (literally 'Sojourners'), who rented seats in the synagogue, and the *Orahim* ('Strangers') who, while being permitted to worship in the synagogue, had no rights whatever pertaining to its administration or to the ceremonial honours connected with it.[105]

[105] V. D. Lipman, 'Synagogal Organization in Anglo-Jewry', *JJS* 1 (1959), 80–93; *JC* (11 Jan. 1901), 14–16.

But it needs to be stressed that ultimate power in a synagogue very often did not reside even with the privileged members, in spite of the fact that they were invariably obliged to pay a hefty entrance fee for being such. Only privileged members could become honorary officers, but honorary officers were elected by ex-honorary officers, or 'Elders', and it was with such relatively minute groups, numbering no more than twenty or thirty, that ultimate power lay. In the eighteenth century, constitutional arrangements such as these were justified, and justifiable, in terms of the manner in which organized communal life had been established and synagogues built. Typically, a select group of monied families was responsible for building the synagogue, paying for its upkeep, purchasing the cemetery, and, indeed, for providing the resources that continued to support the entire infrastructure of communal life. Examples of such leadership can be drawn from virtually every provincial community: George Alexander and Bethel Jacobs in Hull, for example, Alexander Jacob and Ephraim Franklin in Manchester, David Barnett and Jacob Phillips in Birmingham.[106]

In time, and certainly by the 1840s, the scions of these families had managed to integrate to a remarkable degree with the non-Jewish societies in which they dwelt, and had come to play a full part in local politics. At Bristol, for example, we find Joseph Frankel Alexander standing as a candidate in municipal elections as early as 1835.[107] At Birmingham David Barnett, the Russian-born merchant and factor, became in 1839 a founder-member of the Corporation. On taking the oath he objected, of course, to the words 'on the true faith of a Christian'; the Town Clerk having referred to precedents in London and Southampton, the Mayor then declared that 'Mr. Barnett must be allowed to take the declaration in his own way'—which he was.[108] The process of local political emancipation was made much simpler by the passage in 1845 of the Jewish Municipal Relief Act, which allowed professing Jews to hold any and every municipal office. But in some respects that Act merely gave formal recognition to a state of affairs that had already come about.

[106] On these, see Finestein, 'Hull', in Newman (ed.), *Provincial Jewry*; Williams, *Manchester Jewry*, 133; and Josephs, *Birmingham Jewry*, 13.

[107] Schlesinger, 'Victorian Jewry in Bristol', in Newman (ed.), *Provincial Jewry*.

[108] J. T. Bunce, *History of the Corporation of Birmingham*, 2 vols. (Birmingham, 1878, 1885), i. 163.

Just as the unreformed system of elections to the Westminster Parliament gave power to the landed classes, who alone (it was argued) had an economic stake, or interest, in the well-being of the nation, so the manner in which synagogal life was ordered bestowed authority on those whose stake in the establishment and running of communal institutions was felt to be greatest, and who might reasonably be regarded as fit and proper guardians of the communal image. Reform of the national electoral system came about as a direct consequence of shifts in the economic base of British society; first the industrial bourgeoisie (1832) and then (1867) working-class heads of households were admitted to the parliamentary franchise. The pace of reform in synagogal government was also forced as a consequence of economic and social change affecting the basic structure of Jewish communal existence.

Here again (and as with political emancipation) the process of democratization began in the provinces earlier than in London, partly because of the more immediate impact of industrialization and partly because it was in fact easier to initiate reforms in small communities than in large ones. At Liverpool a revolt against the arbitrary rule of an élite of privileged (or 'free') members broke out in 1838 under the leadership of a wealthy jeweller, Barnett Lyon Joseph, recently arrived from Bristol. The grievances of the disaffected were many, and included arbitrary taxes imposed by the ruling oligarchy (such as compulsory payments for circumcision), exhorbitant imposts on the sale of *kosher* meat, and the perpetuation of class distinctions even within the communal cemetery.[109] Central to the demands of the Liverpool rebels was their insistence that while the distinction between privileged members and mere seat-holders might remain, the latter must be given the right to participate in the formulation of the regulations governing synagogal life, including matters pertaining to the raising of communal revenues. The ruling oligarchy, led by the banker Elias Mozeley, refused to give way, and neither the intervention of Chief Rabbi Hirschell nor a clumsy attempt to involve the Board of Deputies could prevent the establishment of a secessionist congregation in 1842.[110]

[109] B. L. Joseph, *Address to the Seatholders of the Liverpool Congregation* (Liverpool, 1838), quoted in L. P. Gartner, 'Urban History and the Pattern of Provincial Jewish Settlement in Victorian England', *JJS* 23 (1981), 45.

[110] BD Minute Book, vol. 5, 12 Sept. 1842; Ettinger, *Hope Place*, 29.

At Manchester the indignities suffered by seat-holders were not as great, and the ratio of seat-holders to free members was much more favourable (almost two to one, whereas in Liverpool it had been of the order of thirty to one). But the irritation arising from taxation without representation went very deep. There was also a generational dimension to the controversy. Manchester Jewry was a rapidly growing community which had attracted many young traders from other provincial centres and from Germany. In August 1844, and following the refusal of the oligarchy to give ground, 'about twelve or fifteen members, mostly young unmarried men', broke away from the Haliwell Street synagogue and established themselves at Ainsworth Court.[111] Within a year the new community had obtained recognition for marriage purposes from Chief Rabbi Adler and the Board of Deputies.[112]

Subsequently, traditions arose that the Manchester rebels had religious reform as an ultimate objective, that they wished to instal an organ, and, perhaps, introduce liturgical changes.[113] There is no contemporary evidence that any such modifications to orthodox ritual were contemplated; indeed, in 1851 the rebels returned to Haliwell Street, and the secession was pronounced at an end. Yet events at Liverpool and Manchester, following so soon upon the establishment of the Reform congregation in London, most certainly acted as warnings to other communities, so that by the end of the 1840s many had begun to reform the old 'vestry' system (as it was known), at least to the extent of making entry into the class of privileged members easier and less costly, and permitting seat-holders a greater voice in the ordering of communal affairs.[114]

In 1842 the Western Synagogue in London abolished the system of privileged members, and declared every seat-holder eligible for election as an honorary officer.[115] But the trend towards greater democratization was resisted by the largest London synagogues, partly because so much communal income depended upon the existence of a class of privileged members required and prepared to

[111] *JC* (8 Dec. 1848), 80.

[112] BD Minute Book, vol. 5, 13 Aug. 1845; Williams, *Manchester Jewry*, 140.

[113] P. S. Goldberg, *The Manchester Congregation of British Jews, 1857–1957* (Manchester, 1957), 9; M. Margoliouth, *The History of the Jews in Great Britain*, 3 vols. (London, 1851), iii. 125; *Jewish World* (7 Sept. 1877), 6.

[114] V. D. Lipman, 'Origins of Provincial Anglo-Jewry', in Newman (ed.), *Provincial Jewry*.

[115] Barnett, *Western Synagogue*, 186.

pay handsomely for the privileges they enjoyed. In the Great Synagogue, the Hambro', and the New the vestry system appears to have been maintained in more or less full working order at the time of their amalgamation as the United Synagogue in 1870.[116] However, nowhere were the dangerous anachronisms of the system more in evidence, or the dire consequences of their survival and defence more dramatically illustrated, than within the community of the Spanish & Portuguese Jews of the capital.

At the time of the Resettlement the Spanish & Portuguese Jews were not compelled to live in a ghetto; but they chose—in effect—to do so (even though their ghetto had no physical dimensions) out of a deep sense of insecurity, which was reflected in the rules—*Ascamot*—which they framed for their own self-government in 1663.[117] These *Ascamot* were written in Portuguese; the edition of 1819 had an English translation, but it was not until 1850 that English became the language in which the *Ascamot* were themselves composed.[118] The constitution of 1663 put the control of the synagogue and of the community into the hands of two wardens (*Parnassim*) and a Treasurer (*Gabbay*). These three gentlemen, who together constituted the executive (*Mahammad*), were chosen from amongst the privileged members of the congregation (the *Yehidim*) and they, together with a number of *adjuntos* (ex-members of the *Mahammad*) chose their successors. The *Mahammad* was, in effect, the executive committee of the Elders (*Velhos*); its powers were almost unlimited:

> They appointed officials, issued ordinances, interfered with totalitarian absolutism in the private lives and extra-synagogal activities of members, acted as a court of arbitration to prevent quarrels between Jews from being aired publicly, suppressed commercial practices and speculations which created public prejudice, [and] imposed stringent monetary and social penalties on the recalcitrant.[119]

[116] Mills, *British Jews*, 125–6; A. Newman, *The United Synagogue 1870–1970* (London, 1977), 11, 32.

[117] The *Ascamot*, translated into English, will be found in L. D. Barnett (ed.), *El Libro de los Acuerdos* (Oxford, 1931).

[118] Hyamson, *Sephardim*, 336. The equivalent *Tekanot* of Duke's Place were published in Hebrew and Yiddish until 1810; the first edition in English (and Hebrew) appeared in 1827. The Minutes of the Board of Deputies, originally in Portuguese, were kept in English from 1778: E. Adler, *London* (Philadelphia, 1930), 199; C. H. L. Emanuel, *A Century and a Half of Jewish History* (London, 1910), 7–8.

[119] C. Roth, *A History of the Jews in England* (2nd edn., Oxford, 1949), 188.

The exercise of such authority was originally justified on the ground of communal well-being: the safety and standing of the congregation depended (it was argued) upon the preservation of a particular public image. But these objectives demanded, in turn, the formulation of others, designed to make it possible for the self-perpetuating oligarchy that ran the Spanish & Portuguese Jews' Congregation to exercise a wide degree of social control upon Jews both beyond as well as within the circle of Bevis Marks. For example, no member of the congregation could publish any work without the permission of the *Mahammad*, or make representations of a political nature to official and governmental bodies. In particular, under the provisions of the notorious *Ascama* No. 1, and under pain of the most severe ecclesiastical penalty (namely *herem*, or ban, under which no *kosher* meat would be supplied to the wrongdoer, neither would his son be circumcised, nor would he be buried in the communal cemetery), it was absolutely forbidden to establish another *Sephardi* congregation.[120] Originally this awesome prohibition was without limit; but in 1784 it was restricted to the area within a radius of four miles from Bevis Marks, and in 1809 to six.[121]

By 1830 the *Sephardi* community of London was past its prime, having suffered from a very high rate of intermarriage, migration to America, and the marriage of its womenfolk to members of the *Ashkenazi* communities, by which it was now overwhelmingly outnumbered.[122] Intermarriage was of course a reflection of a decline in religious observance, and this decline was evidenced in other ways, such as a marked lack of decorum during synagogue services. The *Mahammad*, far from responding positively and constructively to this state of affairs, retreated into pettiness and narrow constitutionalism. Its insistence that Isaac d'Israeli accept the office of *Parnass* (which he did not want and for which he was totally unfitted) and the fines which, in consequence, they attempted to impose upon him, led to a protracted and unseemly quarrel (1813–17) that resulted in the withdrawal of the d'Israelis from

[120] See generally I. Epstein, 'The Story of Ascama I of the Spanish and Portuguese Jewish Congregation of London with special reference to Responsa material', in M. Ben-Horin *et al.*, *Studies and Essays in Honour of Abraham A. Neuman* (Leiden, 1962), 170–204.

[121] Hyamson, *Sephardim*, 188, 241.

[122] Endelman, *Jews of Georgian England*, 172.

Bevis Marks and the baptism of their children—including the future Prime Minister Benjamin.[123]

During the following two decades complaints about synagogue decorum increased in number and intensity, and focused especially upon the length of services.[124] At the same time there were demands for a branch synagogue to be established in the West End, where an increasing number of the *Sephardi* aristocracy now lived. The debate was prolonged and acrimonious. The ruling elements among the *Yehidim* moved too slowly on the question of decorum, and were dubiously successful in defending *Ascama* No. 1.[125] On 15 April 1840 a meeting of twenty-four gentlemen at the Bedford Hotel, Southampton Row, resolved to establish a synagogue that would be neither *Ashkenazi* nor *Sephardi*, but 'British'; the West London Synagogue of British Jews was formally opened in Burton Street, Euston, on 27 February 1842.[126]

The dissidents of Burton Street had put forward demands that of themselves bore no particular relationship to the Reform movement that had originated in Germany at the beginning of the century. By far the most radical of their demands was for the abolition of the observance of the 'Second Days' of festivals, a rabbinical institution which applies only in the Diaspora; in urging this reform, they were actually out of step with the German reformers, who raised the issue in 1845 only to dismiss it as of no central significance.[127] We can also point to developments in the Great Synagogue, the Hambro', and the Western—for example, the limited reform of synagogue services so as to stamp out indecorum at the Hambro' in 1832—that sprang from the same purely practical concerns that motivated the West London reformers.[128]

[123] Hyamson, *Sephardim*, 242–6.

[124] *JC* (24 Mar. 1845), 122–3.

[125] Hyamson, *Sephardim*, 279.

[126] Leigh in Marmur, *Reform Judaism*, 24.

[127] R. Liberles, 'The Origins of the Jewish Reform Movement in England', *Association of Jewish Studies Review*, 1 (1976), 141. In Israel, and as ordained in the Hebrew Bible, only the first and last days of Passover and of Tabernacles are observed as holy days, when no work is performed, and only one day is so observed for Pentecost; in the Diaspora, two days—the 'Second Days'—are observed in each case, at the commencement and conclusion of Passover, at Pentecost, and at the commencement and conclusion of Tabernacles. At the Frankfurt conference of 1845 the German Reformers decided that the Second Days no longer had a religious significance, but that Second Day services might still be provided if there was a demand.

[128] C. Roth, *The Great Synagogue 1690–1940* (London, 1950), 252; Barnett, *Western Synagogue*, 182–6; D. Philipson, *The Reform Movement in Judaism* (2nd edn., New York, 1931), 93.

The seceders were united less in a conscious wish to establish a new species of Judaism, doctrinally different from that into which they had been born, than by a desire to have sole charge of a place of worship that would conduct itself, from a technical point of view, in a particular way. They obtained as first minister of their congregation the services of the Revd David Wolf Marks, whose theology, if anti-*Talmudic*, certainly did not amount to a rejection of the notion of divine revelation.[129] The *Forms of Prayer* which the congregation issued in August 1841, and in the drafting of which Marks, assisted by Hyman Hurwitz (1770–1844; the first Professor of Hebrew at University College London[130]) had played the major part, was a remarkably conservative document. Based upon the traditional *Sephardi* prayer-book, the practical changes of a liturgical nature which it introduced were minimal. References to the Temple sacrifices, to the idea of a return to Zion, and to belief in the coming of the Messiah, were all retained. We might also note that an organ was not introduced into the West London Synagogue until 1859, and that until 1918 the separation of men and women at divine services was strictly maintained.[131]

The founders of the Burton Street place of worship would certainly have denied that they were establishing a *movement*. But Chief Rabbi Hirschell, supported by his *Dayanim* and by the *Dayanim* of the *Sephardim*, thought otherwise, and (9 September 1841) set forth a solemn denunciation, or 'Caution', against the use of *Forms of Prayer*, on the grounds that its compilation amounted to a rejection of the authority of the Oral Law—that is, the *Talmud*. On 22 January 1842 the religious authorities of the *Ashkenazi* and *Sephardi* communities in London issued a 'Declaration' which was published throughout the British Empire, and sent to orthodox communities in Europe, North America, Turkey, and Palestine. Anyone using the heretical prayer-book was branded a sinner. The seceders themselves were denied 'any communion with us Israelites in any religious rite or sacred act'; a *herem* was thus

[129] M. J. Goulston, 'The Theology of Reform Judaism in Great Britain—A Survey', in Marmur, *Reform Judaism*, 56.

[130] On Hurwitz see S. Stein, *The Beginnings of Hebrew Studies at University College* (London, 1952), 10–22.

[131] Leigh in Marmur, *Reform Judaism*, 26; M. A. Meyer, *Response to Modernity: A History of the Reform Movement in Judaism* (New York, 1988), 175–6.

placed upon them.[132] This ban was in fact lifted in March 1849.[133] And, as we noted earlier, a branch of Bevis Marks was established in the West End four years later. The West London Synagogue remained for the rest of the century the preserve of a small number of wealthy and interrelated families—hardly the stuff of which true religious reformations are made.

The ultimate significance of what had taken place lay in a quite different direction. At the Bedford Hotel in 1840 a small band of *Sephardim* and *Ashkenazim* (the group included nine Mocattas and three each from the Montefiore, Henriques, and Goldsmid families) had rebelled against established religious authority. Worse than that, they had rejected the norms of communal discipline. And it was true, indeed, that as early as 1830 the banker Isaac Lyon Goldsmid (1778–1859), as Moses Montefiore noted in his diary, had warned the Board of Deputies that if it did not support his campaign for political emancipation, he would 'establish a new Synagogue with the assistance of the young men . . . [and] . . . would alter the present form of prayer to that in use in the [Reform] Synagogue at Hamburg'.[134]

There was, in short, a most definite connection between the establishment of the West London congregation and the wider ambitions of its founders, and this connection lay in their seeming determination to hijack the political—rather than the religious—leadership of British Jewry. The fact (as we shall see) that so many of the rebels of Burton Street were leading protagonists of political emancipation, and had found or were to find themselves at loggerheads with the Board of Deputies in this regard, was not a coincidence.[135] The refusal of the Western Synagogue, and of the authorities in Liverpool and Manchester, to publish Solomon Hirschell's Caution, not to mention the bad taste of the Plymouth congregation in burning it, served merely to underline how necessary, in the eyes of the religious and lay leaderships of British Jewry, was the containment and isolation of this revolt.[136] The

[132] Hyamson, *Sephardim*, 285. Epstein, 'The Story of Ascama I', 186, and Lipman, *History of the Jews*, 22, both deny that this Declaration amounted to a *herem*; but the plain meaning of the words quoted can have no other implication.

[133] Hyamson, *Sephardim*, 287, 293.

[134] L. Loewe (ed.), *Diaries of Sir Moses and Lady Montefiore*, 2 vols. (London, 1890), i. 83.

[135] Liberles, 'Origins of the Jewish Reform Movement', 127.

[136] Leigh in Marmur, *Reform Judaism*, 24.

birth pangs of Reform Judaism in Britain were bound, therefore, to have profound repercussions upon the organizational mechanisms through which these leaderships were accustomed to exercise communal influence and control, as well as upon the conduct of the leaders themselves.

The religious leadership of British Jewry was primarily expressed and exercised through the Chief Rabbinate. The office of 'Chief Rabbi' had evolved from that of the Rabbi of the Great Synagogue, Duke's Place. But the process of evolution was by no means inevitable. The position of British Jewry *vis-à-vis* the state differed fundamentally from that which regulated the legal status of Jewish communities in mainland Europe. There were in Britain no 'Court Jews' or *Landesrabbinat*, the members of which might, under the official auspices of the Government, pose as the sole authorized spokesmen of the community. Nor were there any *yeshivot*, *Talmudic* academies whose rabbinical heads might have emerged as natural communal leaders.[137] The Spanish & Portuguese Jews had established for themselves the office of *Haham* (literally 'Wise Man')—in effect a presiding communal rabbi, but his writ could hardly run beyond London since there was not, until the very end of the nineteenth century, any *Sephardi* community of significant size in any provincial centre. Nor was the office of *Haham* found to be indispensable even in London. Twenty-two years separated the death of *Haham* Moses d'Azevedo from the appointment of his successor, Raphael Meldola, in 1806. Meldola, an Italian scholar of great repute, but also of a temperamental and quarrelsome nature, died in 1828. The office of *Haham* was not filled again until Benjamin Artom (1835–79; also Italian) was appointed in 1866.[138]

In truth, the purely religious demands made upon any *Haham* by the relatively small congregation of Spanish & Portuguese Jews was not great; during the long gaps between successive holders of the office, essential tasks such as the authorization of marriages and divorces, and the supervision of meat supplies (co-ordinated from 1804 by a London Board for Shechita, run jointly with the *Ashkenazim*), could be carried out by lesser clerics. The provincial Jewries were almost exclusively *Ashkenazi* in composition. But they were, in the main, far too small to maintain and finance the

137 N. Cohen, 'Non-Religious Factors in the Emergence of the Chief Rabbinate', *TJHSE* 21 (1962–7), 304–9.

138 Hyamson, *Sephardim*, 226, 342.

apparatus of separate rabbinates; nor did they possess sufficient status to represent themselves, in the eyes of international Jewry, as autonomous *kehillot*—that is, totally self-governing congregations, as were commonplace in central and eastern Europe—even if they had wanted to. In the vast majority of provincial congregations, as Chief Rabbi Adler's survey of 1845 revealed, one man—usually the *shochet*—would act as synagogue minister and teacher, a general religious factotum, but not one expected to display or possess more than a modicum of learning.

For rabbinical scholarship and leadership the provincial communities naturally looked, therefore, to the *Ashkenazi* synagogues in London. During the eighteenth century there was no one undisputed *Ashkenazi* 'Chief Rabbi' in the capital. Aaron Hart, Rabbi of the Great Synagogue 1704–56, was recognized by the Portsmouth community as the authority to whom all questions of ritual, including the authorization of marriages and the licensing of *shochetim*, had to be submitted.[139] His successor, Hart Lyon, was recognized as their spiritual leader by both the Hambro' and the New. There was a moment, towards the end of the century, when the title of 'Rabbi of London and the Provinces' (by which Hart Lyon's successor, David Tevele Schiff, styled himself) was in serious dispute. Meshullam Zalman, who was then Rabbi of the New and the Hambro', contested it, and claimed the support of a majority of the Portsmouth community. But the challenge was never successfully pressed home, and in 1780 Zalman left London an embittered man.[140]

David Schiff was in practice 'Chief Rabbi', and the authority of his successor at Duke's Place, Solomon Hirschell (Hart Lyon's son), was never in doubt. Hirschell, Rabbi of the Great Synagogue from 1802 to his death in 1842, was known as 'Chief Rabbi of the German and Polish Jews in England'. His authority was supported by the Hambro' and the New, and was recognized in colonial outposts as distant as New Zealand, South Africa, and Australia.[141] But it received very considerable if indirect (and unintended) legal force at home after the passage of the Registration Act of 1836.

139 Roth, 'The Portsmouth Community', 169.

140 C. Roth, 'The Chief Rabbinate in England', in I. Epstein, E. Levine, and C. Roth (eds.), *Essays in Honour of the Very Rev. Dr. J. H. Hertz* (London, 1942), 374–6.

141 Ibid. 378–9.

That measure (section 30) recognized the President of the Board of Deputies as the sole authority competent to certify to the Registrar-General the names of marriage secretaries of synagogues 'of Persons professing the Jewish Religion'. Under the leadership of Moses Montefiore (whose presidency of the Board spanned, with gaps, the period 1835–74), it was established that such certification would not be given without authorization from one of the Board's two ecclesiastical authorities—either the *Haham* or other designated official of the *Sephardim*, or the 'Chief Rabbi'. This meant, in short, that Hirschell could exercise a very substantial measure of veto over the recognition (and, therefore, establishment) of all new *Ashkenazi* congregations in the British Empire.[142]

It was under the aegis of Hirschell's successor, Nathan Marcus Adler, that the office of Chief Rabbi took on substance as well as form. Born in Hanover (and therefore a subject of the Elector, who happened also to be King George III of the United Kingdom), Adler came from a distinguished rabbinical family; his father, Mordecai, 'was in fact the unofficial head of the Hanoverian Jews'.[143] Like his distinguished German contemporary, Samson Raphael Hirsch, who rescued German-Jewish orthodoxy from the twin assaults of Christianity and Reform by preaching and practising the transmission of orthodoxy alongside secular, general knowledge, Nathan Adler combined an intense rabbinical apprenticeship with an equally thorough general education.[144] He was no obscurantist. At the university cities of Göttingen, Würzburg, and Erlangen he had obtained a thorough secular as well as rabbinical education, and in 1829 was appointed *Landesrabbiner* (Chief Rabbi) of Oldenburg, from which, later the same year, he accepted a call to become the first official Chief Rabbi of Hanover. His election—by an overwhelming majority—as Chief Rabbi in London, came in 1845; he held the post until his death.

[142] A. Newman, 'The Chief Rabbinate and the Provinces, 1840–1914', in J. Sacks (ed.), *Tradition and Transition: Essays Presented to Chief Rabbi Sir Immanuel Jakobovits* (London, 1986), 218.

[143] H. D. Schmidt, 'Chief Rabbi Nathan Marcus Adler (1803–1890): Jewish Educator from Germany', *Leo Baeck Yearbook*, 7 (1962), 290.

[144] On Hirsch (1808–88) see J. Katz, 'Sources of Orthodox Trends', in J. Katz (ed.), *The Role of Religion in Modern Jewish History* (Cambridge, Mass., 1975), 29–34; and see generally R. Liberles, *Religious Conflict in Social Context: The Resurgence of Orthodox Judaism in Frankfurt Am Main, 1838–1877* (Westport, Conn., 1985).

Nathan Adler was, in contrast to his predecessors at Duke's Place, a rabbinical scholar of international repute, most famous for his work *Netinah laGer*, a study, published in 1875, of the Aramaic translation of the Hebrew Bible known as the *Targum Onkelos*. As Chief Rabbi in Britain he claimed an allegiance which his predecessors at the Great Synagogue could not, for his was the first election in which provincial communities (twenty-one in all) participated as well as the major London *Ashkenazi* congregations.[145] The survey of 1845, which he initiated shortly after his induction, revealed a series of Anglo-Jewish communities in which observance of orthodox practice was lax, synagogue attendance poor, and educational facilities woefully deficient.[146] This state of affairs seems to have reinforced his own personal inclination: that the orthodox structure in Britain was much too weak to permit the growth of self-governing communities, as existed on the Continent, and that what was needed was strong centralization of religious institutions, naturally under his control.[147]

In 1847 Adler published his *Laws and Regulations for all the Synagogues in the United Kingdom*. The powers to which he laid claim—to be able to superintend religious observances in the synagogues, and even to sanction the building of new synagogues and the formation of new congregations—appeared extravagant. But he was able, in very substantial measure, to enforce them through a wide variety of devices: his position in relation to the Board of Deputies, and the consequent recognition he was able to secure from the provincial communities, whose religious functionaries had in practice to be licensed by him; his ceaseless campaigning for more Jewish day schools, and for the funds with which to build them; and by dint of his own personal charisma.[148] At bottom, Nathan Marcus Adler was 'Chief Rabbi' because that was how he was treated by the non-Jewish world—by Government departments, by Parliament, and by the general press.

[145] For a full list of the participating communities see A. Newman, 'The Chief Rabbinate', in Newman (ed.), *Provincial Jewry*.

[146] The survey (see n. 3 above) revealed, *inter alia*, that the laws regulating sexual intercourse within marriage had largely fallen into abeyance; only half the congregations surveyed possessed a *mikvah*, the rest (in Rabbi Dr Susser's words) 'evading the issue by reference to public baths or the proximity of the sea'. There were very few Jewish day schools of quality, and even at these the number of children attending represented only a small proportion of the total.

[147] Williams, *Manchester Jewry*, 129, 193.

[148] Newman in Sacks, *Tradition and Transition*, 218–20.

During his tenure of the post Adler's authority was only seriously challenged once, by Dr Schiller-Szinessy in Manchester. In the late 1840s and 1850s a number of itinerant self-styled 'rabbis' passed through England; that any of them was in possession of an authentic *semicha* is extremely doubtful. Schiller-Szinessy was, and, what is more, he had acquired in Hungary and Germany a thorough secular education, holding a doctorate from the University of Jena. His arrival in England, a political refugee, caused something of a stir. He began preaching, first in London, then in Birmingham and Manchester, on the themes of liberty, equality, and fraternity, and on the task of the Jew to further these principles, and he wrote for the *Jewish Chronicle* on these subjects, as applied to the Habsburg Empire. We may conclude, too, that his preaching in this vein struck an Anglo-Jewish community increasingly preoccupied with its own political status as particularly relevant.[149] In October 1850 the Haliwell Street congregation in Manchester determined to obtain Chief Rabbi Adler's approval for the appointment of Schiller-Szinessy as their local rabbinical authority.[150]

Adler's wariness before agreeing to this arrangement was well founded. Schiller-Szinessy had a good track record as an opponent of Reform; he had denounced the conference of Reform rabbis held at Frankfurt in 1845.[151] His intellectual and rabbinical credentials were comparable with those of Adler himself. At the same time Adler was well aware of the separatist tendencies to be observed within the larger provincial communities; to have rejected Schiller-Szinessy would have provided ammunition for schismatics, some of whom were known to have played with Reform ideas. Adler therefore approved Schiller-Szinessy's appointment, but on the strict understanding that in carrying out his duties he would act under Adler's authority, and that when called to the Reading of the Law he could only be addressed as *Morenu* ('Our Teacher', the customary title by which rabbis are addressed) with Adler's approval.[152]

[149] *JC* (21 June 1850), 289–90; (28 June), 297–8; (13 Sept.), 389; (27 Sept.), 405. See also S. M. Schiller-Szinessy, *The Olden Religion in the New Year: A Sermon Preached in the Birmingham Synagogue*, trans. M. Nathan (London, 1850).

[150] Williams, *Manchester Jewry*, 186–7.

[151] Ibid. 186.

[152] Office of the Chief Rabbi of the United Hebrew Congregations, Copy Letter Book, vol. 2 (1851–4), 3 Mar. 1852 (now deposited in the Greater London Record Office, Acc 2712/VIII/1).

Schiller-Szinessy took up his duties on these understandings, and quickly effected a reunion of the two Manchester synagogues. Only then did the precise form of his ultimate ambition take shape. He began describing himself as 'Local Rabbi'; to win support among the apathetic and the uncommitted, he began preaching the need for 'reform' of the synagogue service; he acted as an independent rabbinical authority in the recognition of a convert; and in December 1851, having exploited local separatism for all it was worth, he was rewarded by being confirmed as 'Local Rabbi . . . subject to the jurisdiction of the Chief Rabbi'.[153]

A less patient man might have over-reacted at this point. Adler did not fall into this trap. He did nothing to impugn Schiller-Szinessy's orthodoxy. Indeed at a meeting in Manchester the following May the Chief Rabbi indicated that he might be prepared, should a suitable vacancy arise, to appoint him a *Dayan* on his *Beth Din*.[154] The great weakness in Schiller-Szinessy's plan to set himself up as an independent rabbi, on the European model, by exploiting local separatist prejudices, lay in the fact that he was forced to rely on the support of true Reformers, such as Professor Tobias Theodores (1808–86), who taught German at the newly established Owen's College.[155] Adler's reliance on the reluctance of the more traditionally minded to support such a *mésalliance* was a gamble, to be sure. But the odds shifted heavily in favour of the Chief Rabbi when the Reform party in Manchester (the majority of whom, like Theodores, were German immigrants) openly declared their programme of introducing 'necessary and salutary improvements into the public worship of the Synagogue' (23 May 1853), and once Adler had begun to impose the sanctions implicit in his predecessor's ban against the West London Synagogue—for example, by prohibiting marriages between orthodox and Reform partners.[156]

Schiller-Szinessy's ambition foundered on the rock of marriage. At the beginning of 1856 he attempted, first in Manchester and then in Hull, to determine upon his own authority whether marriages might or might not be performed, without reference to the Chief Rabbi in London.[157] Now the authorization and

[153] Williams, *Manchester Jewry*, 192, 209–10.

[154] Ibid. 215–16.

[155] On Theodores see *Manchester Guardian* (28 Apr. 1886), 5, and *JC* (30 Apr. 1886), 10.

[156] *JC* (3 June 1853), 275; Wolf, *Essays in Jewish History*, 326.

[157] Williams, *Manchester Jewry*, 241–4.

recognition of marriages lies at the very root of Jewish identity; a marriage that is not recognized by orthodox communities internationally can have the most severe repercussions, both for the partners involved, for their offspring, and for the congregation that permitted it to take place. Reformers were and are prepared to incur such opprobrium. Those in charge of Manchester Jewry at this time were not and, bolstered by the arrival of meticulously observant Polish immigrants at Red Bank, the conservatives made a stand: if local autonomy meant more freedom for Reformers to remodel the community, and thus to endanger its orthodox credentials, they wanted none of it. Schiller-Szinessy resigned—he was in effect sacked—and, because he had nowhere else to go, became Rabbi to the small Reform congregation established in Manchester soon afterwards. Its radicalism, culminating inevitably in the abolition of the observance of 'Second Days', was too much even for him. In 1860 he left Manchester, and in 1863 took up an academic post at Cambridge University, eventually becoming its Reader in Talmudic and Rabbinic Literature.

In this way, and at the price of permitting a second Reform congregation to come into being, Nathan Adler successfully defended the authority of his office. He had also, albeit incidentally, established the primacy of the *Ashkenazi* rabbinate over that of the *Sephardim*, who it will be recalled were without a *Haham* at this time. But we should not be in the least surprised that his staunchest ally in the struggle to contain the Reform movement should have been none other than the acknowledged lay leader of the Spanish & Portuguese Jews, the stockbroker and banker Moses Montefiore, President of the Board of Deputies. Both men were utterly determined to uphold, not merely the orthodox character of British Jewry, but the principle of centralized communal institutions, based upon the major London congregations. Both considered that the price they had to pay—the emergence of small, self-identified Reform congregations in Manchester and London—was exceedingly modest by comparison.

The London Committee (known from 1913 as the Board) of Deputies of British Jews traces its origins back to the first half of the eighteenth century, when the Spanish & Portuguese congregation appointed *Deputados* to deal, *ad hoc*, with political matters. The formal date of foundation of the Committee is generally taken to be 17 December 1760; it was on that day, following separate expressions of devotion to the new King George III, that the Elders of the Great Synagogue agreed to hold joint meetings of 'the Two Nations' to discuss any relevant 'publick affair'.[158] Such joint meetings were very infrequent. Between 1802 and 1812 it appears that no President was appointed who might have summoned the Deputies together. The Committee met in 1817 after a gap of five years, and in 1828 after a gap of eight years.

The meeting in 1828 was called to consider matters relating to political emancipation; and it was partly on account of mounting activity and concern over this issue that meetings became more frequent thereafter. Under the leadership of Moses Montefiore the institution assumed a definitive shape. Previously it had met at infrequent and irregular intervals, a semi-formal gathering of representatives of Bevis Marks, the Great, the Hambro', and the New. Now (May 1835) the requirements of structure and national representation were recognized:

> This meeting [it was resolved on 11 May] is convinced that it would be of essential advantage to the Interests of the Jews of Britain, that in all matters touching their political welfare they should be represented by one Body, & inasmuch as the general Body of Deputies have long been recognised as their representatives, it is highly desirable for the general good that all British Jews should so acknowledge them, having a sufficient number of Members from each Congregation to ensure the accordance of their proceedings with the general wishes of the Jews.[159]

Accordingly, the following year the Board acquired its first formal constitution, permitting the affiliation of other London congregations; provincial congregations were also invited to join. The Board remained—as it was bound to remain—a London-dominated body. The adhesion of the smaller communities was slow in coming about. The Western and Maiden Lane congregations in London agreed to send representatives, but of the provincial communities only Sunderland responded positively, and its representation soon lapsed on the grounds of poverty. None the less, in time the power conferred on the President of the Board under the 1836 Registration Act served as an encouragement to provincial

[158] G. Alderman, *The Jewish Community in British Politics* (Oxford, 1983), 8; A. Newman, *The Board of Deputies of British Jews 1760–1985: A Brief Survey* (London, 1987), 4–5.

[159] BD Minute Book No. 2: resolution of 11 May 1835.

congregations to agree to make nominations to it, even though the legislation did not actually require such affiliation, and even if those nominated had their permanent residence in London. When Montefiore became President, the Board comprised twenty-two Deputies: seven each from Bevis Marks and the Great, and four each from the Hambro' and the New; the Board's running expenses were shared in roughly equivalent proportions. By 1854 the total had risen to fifty-seven; of these less than half (25) represented London congregations, but of the provincial Deputies a further eleven actually lived in the capital.[160] The method of allocating the Board's expenses clearly acted as a continuing disincentive to affiliation by poorer provincial bodies; only in 1883 was the system overhauled, so that member congregations paid fees based, not upon a proportion of total expenditure, but simply upon their individual memberships.[161]

Montefiore's tenure of the Presidency was only a qualified success. As we shall see, his attitude to political emancipation was generally unhelpful. This meant that the Board did not play in this struggle the central role that might have been expected of the body that claimed to be the representative organ of British Jewry. Others made the running, while Montefiore busied himself with journeys to foreign parts in order to take up what he regarded as the far more pressing claims of oppressed Jewries abroad. These epic voyages—to the Middle East over the Damascus Blood Libel (1840), to Rome over the Mortara Affair (1859), to Russia (1846 and 1872), to Constantinople and Morocco (1863–4), and seven times to the Holy Land (1827, 1838, 1849, 1855, 1857, 1866, and 1875)—were productive of little concrete good (the release of Damascus Jews accused of ritual murder being the one exception worthy of mention), though they probably had an uplifting effect upon the morale of those co-religionists on whose behalf they were undertaken. To conclude (as the historian of the Board of Deputies does) that while serving to boost his own prestige and status they also 'emphasised the significance of the Board' seems excessively charitable.[162]

[160] N. Grizzard, 'The Provinces and the Board 1851–1901', in Newman (ed.), *Provincial Jewry*, 11.

[161] Board of Deputies, *Annual Report 1883*, 37.

[162] Newman, *Board of Deputies*, 14; for details of Montefiore's foreign excursions see S. Lipman and V. D. Lipman (eds.), *The Century of Moses Montefiore*

By nature an autocrat, Montefiore found it difficult to come to terms with the Board's enlargement and very limited democratization. He seems to have looked upon the conduct of Board business as almost a private, family affair, and could never adjust properly—or positively—to its necessary reform to meet changing circumstances. When the enlarged Board met for the first time on 12 August 1838, his friend and secretary Louis Loewe (1809–88) noted from Montefiore's diary that the President appeared 'to have apprehended some difficulty in managing' the new body.[163] He had little liking for attention to the details of administration, and delayed too long the appointment of a professional secretary (the solicitor Sampson Samuel, appointed 1838).[164] The collection of basic communal statistics, relating to synagogue membership, births, deaths, and marriages, was not commenced until 1849.[165] Although the Board resorted to *ad hoc* standing committees from time to time, it was not until 1854 that a standing general purposes committee was created.[166]

Above all, Montefiore allowed his personal prejudices to influence his duty to uphold the representative status of the Board. He resented the establishment of Reform congregations in Britain not merely on account of his own staunch orthodoxy, but because he saw their foundation—rightly—as a challenge to the centripetalism of which he was (also) such a stout defender. He supported the authority of Nathan Adler in refusing to grant recognition for marriage purposes to the Reformers, and in 1853, when four provincial congregations (Chatham, Norwich, Portsmouth, and Sunderland) elected adherents of Reform (three of whom were Londoners) as their Deputies, he used his casting vote to keep them out; he had done so (he later revealed) with pleasure, and on 'religious grounds'.[167]

In 1836, acting with the Board's approval, Montefiore informed the Government that the Board was 'the only official channel of

(Oxford, 1985), pt. II. The most authoritative study of Montefiore is the volume in Hebrew by M. Samet, *Moses Montefiore: Reality and Myth* (Jerusalem, 1989).

[163] Loewe, *Diaries*, i. 144.

[164] I. Finestein, 'Montefiore as Communal Leader', in Lipman and Lipman (eds.), *Century of Moses Montefiore*, 51.

[165] Grizzard, in Newman (ed.), *Provincial Jewry*, 2.

[166] Finestein in Lipman and Lipman (eds.), *Century of Moses Montefiore*, 54.

[167] I. Finestein, 'The Anglo-Jewish Revolt of 1853', *Jewish Quarterly* (Autumn/Winter 1978–9), 112; *JC* (9 Dec. 1853), 79.

communication for the secular and political interests' of British Jewry.[168] But this claim needed to be credible, and such credibility was difficult to sustain when an articulate, vocal, and distinguished—albeit small—section of British Jewry, embracing many of the leading emancipationists, was excluded from its deliberations. Of course the West London congregation did not accept this state of affairs in silence. Montefiore kept Reformers out of the Board; the ban on them was not lifted until 1874, and not until 1886 (the year following Montefiore's death) were terms mutually agreed by which Deputies from the West London Synagogue—Sir Julian Goldsmid and Sir Philip Magnus (1842–1933)—might take their seats.[169] Meanwhile, however, the West London Synagogue had sought and obtained, in the Marriage and Registration Act of 1856, 'practically all the powers in relation to registration of Jewish marriages' which the 1836 Act had given to the President of the Board of Deputies alone.[170] Moreover, the school which the Reformers had opened was recognized by the Government for the purpose of grant aid.[171]

How were the Jews at large, particularly those in the provinces and those who did not belong to the ruling circles of the larger congregations, informed about these momentous events? The earliest true Anglo-Jewish newspaper (as opposed to conversionist bulletin), *The Hebrew Intelligencer*, made a brief appearance (three issues) in 1823. *The Hebrew Review and Magazine of Rabbinical Literature*, edited by Solomon Hirschell's secretary, Rabbi Dr Morris Raphall (1798–1868), was published between 1834 and 1836.[172] The reduction of the Stamp Duty on newspapers to one penny seems to have acted as an inducement to the production of more ambitious ventures, aimed at a wider readership. In 1840 the statistician Jacob Franklin obtained the support of Sampson Samuel, Dr Raphall, David Aaron de Sola (Cantor at Bevis Marks), and a recent immigrant from Bohemia, the University of Vienna graduate Dr Abraham Benisch (1811–78) for the production of a

[168] I. Finestein, 'The Anglo-Jewish Revolt of 1853', *Jewish Quarterly* (Autumn/Winter 1978–9), 112; *JC* (9 Dec. 1853), 108.

[169] Ibid. 110; Leigh in Marmur, *Reform Judaism*, 33.

[170] H. S. Q. Henriques, *Jewish Marriages and the English Law* (Oxford, 1909), 38–9.

[171] Leigh in Marmur, *Reform Judaism*, 32.

[172] [C. Roth], *The Jewish Chronicle 1841–1941* (London, 1949), 3–8. On Raphall see Lipman, 'The Age of Emancipation', in Lipman, *Three Centuries of Anglo-Jewish History*, 101.

fortnightly journal, *The Voice of Jacob*, launched in September 1841 on the basis of a subscription fund to which the Montefiore, Rothschild, and other monied families contributed.[173]

The following month the *Jewish Chronicle* appeared. It was the brainchild of an enterprising printer and bookseller, Isaac Vallentine, one of the founders, in 1860, of the Jewish Association for the Diffusion of Religious Knowledge (later the Jewish Religious Education Board). To assist him in the launch of his newspaper Vallentine obtained the collaboration of David Meldola, son of the late *Haham* and then virtually spiritual head of Bevis Marks, and Moses Angel (1819–98), an alumnus of University College London who taught at the Jews' Free School (of which he was to become Headmaster).[174] Vallentine took the precaution of obtaining the approval of the Revenue authorities for his newspaper to be regarded as a 'class' paper, meant for a strictly limited readership; in consequence, it was not subject to the Newspaper Tax and could be despatched, post free, to any part of the country.

In 1842 the *Jewish Chronicle* and *The Voice of Jacob* merged, under the latter's title and under Angel's editorship. Two years later, Vallentine and Jacob Franklin having fallen out, the *Chronicle* was resurrected under the banner of *The Jewish Chronicle and Working Man's Friend*. In 1848 *The Voice of Jacob* ceased publication. Benisch began producing a journal of his own, *The Hebrew Observer*, in 1853, but it soon became clear that British Jewry could not support two rival periodicals, both of them weeklies. They coalesced as the *Jewish Chronicle and Hebrew Observer* and, under Benisch's editorship (1854–69), the paper became the authoritative journalistic voice of British Jews.[175]

Benisch was not, as it turned out, a good business man. But he was 'a good scholar and organiser and in many respects a born publicist'.[176] His reporting of events of concern to Jews the world over was professional and remarkably comprehensive. He had become editor of the *Chronicle* at a crucial turning-point in the affairs and status of British Jewry. In 1848 the paper had been refused permission to report the proceedings of the Board of

173 [Roth], *Jewish Chronicle*, 10.

174 *JC* (13 Nov. 1891), Jubilee Supplement, 14–15; (9 Sept. 1898), 8–10.

175 [Roth], *Jewish Chronicle*, chs. 4, 5.

176 Ibid. 81; and see J. M. Shaftesley, 'Abraham Benisch as a Newspaper Editor', *TJHSE* 21 (1962–7), 214–31.

Deputies. But five years later, at the height of the controversy over the admission of Reformers, the request was granted.[177] Benisch used this freedom to expose the Board to ever greater public scrutiny. In short, he observed the spirit of greater democracy and greater openness that was at work within the Jewish communities in Britain, and harnessed that spirit for the good of Jews as well as for the good of his newspaper. The *Jewish Chronicle* became first and foremost a newspaper rather than a magazine. In the struggle for the political emancipation of British Jewry this was to be of inestimable importance.

[177] [Roth], *Jewish Chronicle*, 47. Finestein, 'The Anglo-Jewish Revolt', 113.

2

Emancipation Politics and Party Politics

THE issue of political emancipation dominated the communal agenda of the Anglo-Jewish leadership during the middle years of the nineteenth century. There was, however, no unanimity of view as to the strategy by which it might be attained, partly because those who ordered the affairs of the community were by no means united as to the degree of priority which it should be accorded. Nor was the issue one which agitated all—or even the majority—of Jews in Britain.

The story of the struggle for political emancipation, however told, must necessarily preoccupy itself with the efforts of a small group of (in the main) London-based communal grandees. Although, as we shall see, Jewish voters were involved, the Jewish voting public was exceedingly small, as was inevitable given the existence, even after the passage of the Reform Acts of 1832, of a narrow property-based franchise. The campaign for political equality was never a 'mass' movement:

> I was told by a Hebrew gentleman (a professional man) that so little did the Jews themselves care for 'Jewish emancipation', that he questioned if one man in ten, activated solely by his own feelings, would trouble himself to walk the length of the street in which he lived to secure Baron Rothschild's admission into the House of Commons.[1]

So reported Henry Mayhew in the 1850s. At about the same time the London correspondent of an American Jewish newspaper had noted that the Jews of Britain were as a whole 'quite indifferent' to the issue of emancipation; only a handful of ambitious men (he

[1] H. Mayhew, *London Labour and the London Poor* 4 vols. (London, 1861–2), ii. 126–7.

explained) cared at all about whether or not Jews could sit in Parliament.[2]

This anecdotal evidence undoubtedly overstated the case. Particularly after 1847, there was unquestionably a great deal of mounting excitement in the community as the saga of Lionel de Rothschild's crusade unfolded (he was elected MP for the City of London five times between 1847 and 1857), punctuated by the drama of Sir David Salomons's illegal entry into the House of Commons (as MP for Greenwich) by *force majeure*, and of his unbecoming expulsion therefrom (1851). But was all this activity, bringing as it did the inevitable national publicity, really good for the Jews? And what tangible communal benefit would derive from the presence in Parliament of a few MPs who happened to be professing Jews? Indeed, given that only a very small number of wealthy Jews could possibly have then afforded a career in national political life, the argument seemed at times very plausible that 'emancipation', defined in its narrowest political sense, was not likely to be of much advantage to most British Jews in the immediate future.

To most Jews in Britain (unlike their Continental counterparts) political equality was, in short, an irrelevance; for it was not in any sense a necessary prerequisite of social and economic freedom. In Britain the campaign for Jewish emancipation—or, more correctly, for the removal of the remaining civil disabilities affecting British-born professing Jews (of which the bar to a parliamentary career was but the most obvious)—did not touch the perceived essential interests of communal existence. Indeed, in some respects the campaign appeared to threaten freedoms already won and enjoyed. To understand why this should have been so, we need to separate out a variety of ways in which 'emancipation' might be defined in relation to the status of Jews in Britain in the mid-nineteenth century.

The campaign for Jewish emancipation is commonly supposed to have been triggered by the granting of Catholic emancipation by the Tory Government of the Duke of Wellington in 1829. The previous year the Test and Corporation Acts had been repealed. These enactments had imposed Anglican religious tests upon all those who sought public and municipal office; their simple repeal

[2] I. Finestein, 'Anglo-Jewish Opinion during the Struggle for Emancipation (1828–1858)', *TJHSE* 20 (1959–61), 133.

would have benefited Jewish and Christian Dissenters alike, because hitherto these groups had had to rely on Indemnity Acts which Parliament was accustomed to pass annually. But an amendment to the repeal, introduced in the House of Lords by the Bishop of Llandaff, inserted the words 'on the true faith of a Christian' into the declaration henceforth required of those taking up public office.[3] Following the grant of political rights to the Catholics, Jews, Unitarians, and atheists were alone subject to political disabilities because of their religious faith.

In relation to local government, the position of the Jews was not regularized until the passage of Lord Lyndhurst's Jewish Municipal Relief Act in July 1845; this measure permitted professing Jews to hold all municipal offices.[4] Before 1828 there are plenty of instances of Jews holding such posts. The surviving records of the parish of St James, Duke's Place, show that Jewish worthies in this most Jewish neighbourhood habitually stood for and were elected to parochial offices, from as early as 1748. What is remarkable, however, is that (the Bishop of Llandaff's amendment notwithstanding) the legislation of 1828 appears to have made little if any difference to this state of affairs.[5]

Part of the answer may indeed lie in the fact that parochial office was 'a burden and not a privilege'.[6] Whatever the strict requirements of the law might have been, ways had to be found of permitting this burden to be placed equally on the shoulders of Jewish as well as of Christian ratepayers. Certainly, during the late 1830s and 1840s the election of Jews to municipal office became almost commonplace. In 1838 A. Abrahams was elected as a councillor at Southampton, and in 1841 E. Emanuel became a councillor at Portsmouth; in 1839 David Barnett became a founder-member of the Corporation at Birmingham where, from mid-century, Jews were well represented among the Poor Law Guardians.[7] As an inevitable corollary, if otherwise qualified Jewish ratepayers were to be burdened with municipal office, their natural right to participate in the elections to office could not be

[3] *Parl. Deb.*, NS, xviii. 1591 (21 Apr. 1828).

[4] G. Alderman, *London Jewry and London Politics, 1889–1986* (London, 1989), 3.

[5] A. Rubens, 'The Jews of the Parish of St. James, Duke's Place, in the City of London', in J. M. Shaftesley (ed.), *Remember the Days: Essays on Anglo-Jewish History presented to Cecil Roth* (London, 1966), 189.

[6] Ibid. 182.

[7] Alderman, *London Jewry*, 3.

denied. Here again, common sense triumphed over legality. The practical right of Jewish ratepayers to participate in parish elections was so widely recognized—certainly in London—that as early as 1818 we find one City vestry resolving to admit proxies in order to enable Jews to vote whenever parish elections fell on Jewish holy days.[8]

At the parliamentary level the situation appeared much less favourable. Until the law was amended in 1835, returning officers had the right to demand the swearing of a Christian oath before permitting otherwise qualified persons to exercise the franchise. But it is clear that this requirement was frequently overlooked.[9] In May 1830 Sir Robert Wilson told the House of Commons that Jews habitually voted in parliamentary elections in Southwark because—quite simply—no one bothered to insist that they take the Christian oath.[10]

In London the position of Jews determined to embark upon political careers was much improved as a result of the exertions of the banker and philanthropist Sir David Salomons (1797–1873). In 1830 the Common Council had permitted Jews to become Freemen of the City, and so members of the City Livery Companies. In 1835 Salomons was elected one of the two City Sheriffs, obliging Parliament to legislate to enable him to enter office without having to take a Christian form of oath (Sheriff's Declaration Act, 1835).[11] His ambition to be elected an Alderman took much longer to fulfil. An amendment that would have permitted professing Jews to enter upon this office was defeated in the Commons in 1837 by a mere sixteen votes. However, that same year Moses Montefiore attained the shrievalty of the City, and (as was customary) was knighted into the bargain. Two years later Salomons served as Sheriff of Kent and in 1838 he, Moses Montefiore, and J. M. Montefiore all served as Commissioners of the Peace in that same county. In 1847, following the passage of Lyndhurst's Act, Salomons was at last admitted as a City Alderman. In 1855 he became the first Jewish Lord Mayor of London; the second Jew to hold this office, Benjamin S. Phillips (Lord Mayor 1865–6) had already, in 1846,

[8] E. M. Tomlinson, *History of the Minories* (London, 1907), 310.

[9] G. Alderman, *The Jewish Community in British Politics* (Oxford, 1983), 11; T. M. Endelman, *The Jews of Georgian England 1714–1830* (Philadelphia, 1979), 113.

[10] *The Mirror of Parliament*, 1830, vol. 2, col. 1781 (17 May 1830).

[11] C. Roth, *A History of the Jews in England* (2nd edn., Oxford, 1949), 252.

become the first Jew to gain election to the City's Common Council.[12]

In 1833 Lord Chancellor Brougham had observed that 'his Majesty's subjects professing the Jewish religion were born to all the rights, immunities and privileges of his Majesty's other subjects, excepting so far as positive enactments of law deprived them of those rights, immunities and privileges'.[13] By 1850 such 'positive enactments' were very few indeed. For those who cared about such matters the position in relation to local government (which played a much greater role in the lives of ordinary people in the nineteenth century than in the twentieth) was by mid-century one of absolute equality. If we add such other developments as the statutory recognition of the Board of Deputies (in the 1836 Registration Act), the right to engage in retail trade within the City of London, the establishment of the secular University College London (1828), and the admission of Jews to the Bar (1833), we must conclude that by mid-century the legal equality of Jewish with non-Jewish citizens of the United Kingdom was substantially complete.[14] This legal equality was complemented by an economic no less than a social emancipation, the latter an undoubted consequence of the former and epitomized by the close relationship between the three royal dukes of Kent, Sussex, and Cambridge and the Anglo-Jewish leadership at the beginning of the century.[15]

Why, then, did the matter of election to Parliament stir up such fierce emotions on both sides? To begin with, its symbolic importance was of course beyond measure, embracing as it did the right of Jews to vote for taxes as well as to pay them, and the right of the electors of the City of London to choose whom they wished to represent them in Parliament. These were classic Liberal positions, and it is hardly surprising that Whigs, Radicals, and Liberals, such as Lords Macaulay and John Russell, were to be found in the forefront of the struggle. Once Nathan Mayer's eldest son Lionel de Rothschild (1806–79) had been elected for the City (1847), his right to take his seat as a professing Jew became nothing more nor less than a struggle to convince the Peers that they had no

[12] Alderman, *London Jewry*, 3–4.

[13] *Parl. Deb.*, 3rd ser. xx. 239 (1 Aug. 1833).

[14] On Jews as barristers, see P. S. Lachs, 'A Study of a Professional Élite: Anglo-Jewish Barristers in the Nineteenth Century', *JSS* 44 (1982), 125–34.

[15] A. Gilam, *The Emancipation of the Jews in England 1830–1860* (New York, 1982), 4, 27–9; the Duke of Sussex was a leading emancipationist.

business meddling in the affairs of the Lower House. 'The city of London', the pro-emancipationist Conservative leader in the Commons, Lord George Bentinck, told John Wilson Croker, 'has settled the Jew question.'[16]

So it had, because two other issues central to the politics of mid-century Britain now came into play: the need to subordinate the wishes of the unelected Upper House to those of the elected Lower, and the desire to bring about a major disengagement between Church and State through an alteration in the Christian character of Parliament. These, again, were classic Liberal positions.[17] But they were also areas of great national contention. So it was that the right of professing Jews to be elected to and to sit in Parliament became submerged within a much wider debate. This helps explain why, although the City 'settled the Jew question' in 1847, the matter was not finally disposed of until an act of 1860 gave the force of statute law to the resolution which the Commons had passed in 1858 allowing Rothschild to take his oath in an acceptable, modified form.

It is wrong to suppose that those—and they were by no means located exclusively on the Tory side—who defended the status quo were either necessarily Jew-haters or necessarily bigots. They drew comfort from the opinions and demeanour of leading British Jews upon this matter, and cited them with scarcely concealed relish. The individuals on the Jewish side who forced the pace of emancipation comprised a small, self-selected group, mainly bankers, financiers, and philanthropists: the brothers Lionel and Mayer de Rothschild; David Salomons; Isaac Lyon Goldsmid and his son Francis Henry—all of whom stood as Liberals in the 1847 general election.[18] The Goldsmids were stalwarts of the Reform Synagogue, which Isaac had helped establish, and, as we have already noted, Reform families, such as the Goldsmids and the Mocattas, were among the leading and most outspoken emancipationists.[19] This

[16] Bentinck to Croker, 29 Sept. 1847, in L. J. Jennings (ed.), *The Croker Papers*, 3 vols. (London, 1885), iii. 138.

[17] See generally M. C. N. Salbstein, *The Emancipation of the Jews in Britain: The Question of the Admission of the Jews to Parliament, 1828–1860* (London 1982); P. Pinsker, 'English Opinion and Jewish Emancipation (1830–1860)', *JSS* 14 (1952), 51–94; and I. Finestein, *Post-Emancipation Jewry: The Anglo-Jewish Experience* (Oxford, 1980), *passim*.

[18] Alderman, *Jewish Community*, 23.

[19] Gilam, *Emancipation of the Jews*, 42–3.

identification was not accidental. Isaac Goldsmid and his friends campaigned for emancipation less because they personally felt the weight of such anti-Jewish measures as remained on the statute-book than because of the shame which (they argued) the existence of these measures brought to the status of British Jewry: the matter was one of principle rather than of practicalities:

> We desire to be placed on an equality in point of Civil Privileges with other persons dissenting from the Established Church not so much on account of the hardship of being excluded from particular stations of trust or honour, as on account of the far greater hardship of having a degrading stigma fastened upon us by the Laws of our country.[20]

But the Reformers also believed that British Jewry needed to put its own house in order, in part by accommodating itself to prevailing non-Jewish modes of worship, and by abandoning its claim to a national destiny separate from the destiny of the Britons amongst whom it dwelt. When he led a deputation to the Prime Minister, Sir Robert Peel, in 1845, to argue the case for municipal emancipation, Goldsmid put the matter quite explicitly: by reforming their ritual, the Jews (i.e. the Reformers) had proved that they were worthy of emancipation, which ought to be granted as a reward (so to speak) for their reforming tendencies.[21]

This was of course precisely the argument advanced by German Reformers, and it was bound for that reason to cause suspicion and resentment within the orthodox leadership. In Britain the proposition was never seriously advanced that the Jews might be granted legal equality once and only once they had abandoned their own peculiar forms of worship. The major argument of the opponents of emancipation was that the United Kingdom was a Christian realm, in the ultimate governance of which non-Christians should play no part. The British Reformers never argued for mass conversion to Christianity. But they did argue that Reform Judaism would itself bring full emancipation nearer; this was enough to arouse the ire of more conservative elements in the community.

The diaries of Moses Montefiore reveal a preoccupation with the fear that involvement in political life would lead inexorably to

[20] Peel Papers, British Library Add. MSS 40612, fo. 164ᵛ: petition to Sir Robert Peel from I. L. Goldsmid and 30 others, Feb. 1845. See also [I. L. Goldsmid], *The British Jew to his Fellow Countrymen* (London, 1833), 6.

[21] Gilam, *Emancipation of the Jews*, 42.

clashes between the requirements of orthodox observance and the demands of public office.[22] In 1837 he confided to his diary his resolve 'not to give up the smallest particle of our religious forms and privileges to obtain civil rights';[23] 'let them call me a bigot if they like', he remarked, 'it is immaterial to me what others do or think in this respect'.[24] Montefiore did not oppose the ideal of full emancipation, but he did feel that its claims needed to be subordinated to other concerns, such as oppressed overseas Jewries and the maintenance of orthodoxy. He was certainly not prepared to launch the Board of Deputies into a flamboyant public agitation, as was demanded by the Reformers and by the orthodox radicals, led by Salomons and Lionel de Rothschild.

This reticence led, in 1838, to a break between the Board and Isaac Goldsmid and, in 1845, to Montefiore and Goldsmid leading rival deputations to Peel on the emancipation question.[25] In October 1838 Salomons had been elected as the first *Ashkenazi* President of the Board; but he had resigned the office less than a month later, apparently because he objected to the exclusion of Reform Jews, a policy which he found it impossible to defend and which he felt hampered his political work.[26] Thereafter he concentrated on his own, highly idiosyncratic emancipation strategy which culminated in the events of 1851: having been returned as MP in the Greenwich by-election he took the Oath of Abjuration in an illegal form, voted in three divisions during the debate which followed, was required to withdraw from the Commons, was subsequently fined severely and visited with other civil penalties, and had to be rescued by retrospective legislation specially passed by the minority Conservative Government of the Earl of Derby and Benjamin Disraeli the following year.

All these events (it was argued) threatened to bring and perhaps did bring the community into disrepute. The circumvention of the authority of the Board of Deputies was particularly serious. In addressing Peel, Goldsmid had claimed to speak in the name of British Jewry. As long as no professing Jew could gain admission to Parliament, perhaps to articulate there 'Jewish' opinions at variance

22 L. Loewe (ed.), *Diaries of Sir Moses and Lady Montefiore*, 2 vols. (London, 1890), i. 107–8.

23 Ibid. 111.

24 Ibid. 108.

25 Alderman, *Jewish Community*, 20; Gilam, *Emancipation of the Jews*, 42.

26 A. M. Hyamson, *David Salomons* (London, 1939), 36. Between 1838 and 1840 the Board had 2 Presidents, Salomons and I. Q. Henriques.

with those of the religious and lay leaderships, the authority of both could be maintained reasonably intact. Conversely, once the claim for civil equality had been met, the very fact of its having been granted could or would be used, within the community, to bring about drastic alterations in the structure of communal power and the exercise of communal authority. Moses Montefiore's lack of enthusiasm for the cause of Anglo-Jewish emancipation was thus well grounded, and his cautious attitude enjoyed widespread support, no more so than from the religious leadership.

Some members of the clergy did go public in their support of civil and political equality. Morris Raphall, who became minister in Birmingham in 1841, had argued some years earlier that the denial of equal rights to the Jews threatened to impair 'the harmony of the social system'.[27] In 1850 Aaron Levy Green published a repudiation of the arguments advanced by a leading anti-emancipationist, George Croly.[28] In general, however, the religious leadership was either indifferent to the question, or openly hostile. No one knew what the effect of full emancipation might be upon the religious identification of British Jewry. Fundamentalists, such as Rabbi Joseph Crooll, argued that although Jews could dwell among other nations, they were not permitted to sink their own identities within those of the nations amongst whom they dwelt: the Jew was not an Englishman and, if he tried to become one, his Jewish identity — and destiny—would be lost.[29]

The eighteenth century had witnessed a stream of converts from Judaism to Christianity in England. Four of these, Menassah Lopes, Ralph Franco, Ralph Bernal, and David Ricardo, had secured election to Parliament during the first two decades of the nineteenth century, at a time when anti-Jewish missionary efforts had received a new, evangelical impulse through the foundation in 1809 of the London Society for Promoting Christianity among the Jews.[30] In 1826 the Philo-Judaean Society had been established. Its purpose—to kill Judaism by kindness—was far more sinister, for it proposed to bring about the conversion of British Jewry by aiding and

[27] *The Hebrew Review and Magazine of Rabbinical Literature*, 3 (15 Jan. 1836), 1.

[28] Gilam, *Emancipation of the Jews*, 56.

[29] Salbstein, *Emancipation of the Jews*, 78–84.

[30] Alderman, *Jewish Community*, 12; L. P. Gartner, 'Emancipation, Social Change and Communal Reconstruction in Anglo-Jewry, 1789–1881', *Proceedings of the American Academy for Jewish Research*, 54 (1987), 83.

abetting their civil emancipation and their social integration.[31] Some of the leading early non-Jewish champions of Jewish emancipation, such as Sir Robert Grant and Thomas Babington Macaulay, were Philo-Judaeans.

Against this background the argument that the political emancipation of Anglo-Jewry would lead to assimilation and complete loss of religious identity seemed, on the face of it, to be highly plausible; and it was on these grounds that a number of religious authorities openly repudiated the quest for political equality, and did not shrink from identifying themselves with Christian opponents of emancipation in this regard.[32] Neither Solomon Hirschell nor Nathan Adler, it must be emphasized, was of this view. But neither of them evinced much if any enthusiasm for the struggle. Asked by Isaac Goldsmid to support the emancipation campaign, Chief Rabbi Hirschell declined (1836), arguing that though he would not oppose the movement, he was apprehensive lest those who entered public life were moved to 'transgress the commandments'.[33] Dr Adler took the trouble to write to *The Times* denying the charge that he was indifferent to the quest for emancipation; he did, indeed, append his signature to a number of emancipation petitions.[34] But it was well known that he viewed the quest for political equality as one that did not merit high priority, and in general he stood aloof from it.

In fact, in so far as it is possible to measure their achievements, the work of the missionaries appears to have had little effect.[35] Synagogue attendance (as evidenced in the 1851 census) remained low, there was continued indifference to Jewish education, and continued neglect of the dietary and other laws. But incidences of outright apostasy appear to have declined by mid-century. Jewish opponents of emancipation were naturally haunted by the spectre of mass conversions, as had taken place in Germany and elsewhere in Continental Europe. The reality was that the civil and political emancipation of British Jewry, because it was unconditional and because it had been *preceded* by social and economic emancipation,

[31] On the Philo-Judaeans see Endelman, *Jews of Georgian England*, 78–85.

[32] Finestein, 'Anglo-Jewish Opinion', 116–17; U. R. Q. Henriques, *Religious Toleration in England 1787–1833* (London, 1961), 182–3.

[33] Quoted in Gilam, *Emancipation of the Jews*, 50.

[34] *Hebrew Observer* (15 Apr. 1853), 117; Gilam, *Emancipation of the Jews*, 50.

[35] T. M. Endelman, *Radical Assimilation in English Jewish History 1656–1945* (Bloomington, Ind., 1990), ch. 5.

acted (if anything) as a powerful breakwater against the exceedingly modest conversionist tide. In 1887 Oswald John Simon (1855–1932) explained to a missionary how emancipation had removed the most practical argument formerly used in favour of baptism: 'the most pious, the most learned, the most cultivated, and the most enlightened [Jews] remain honourably by the Covenant'.[36]

Measured at least by the yardstick of observance of the rites of passage, British Jews, while lax in their day-to-day practice of the orthodoxy to which they subscribed, remained none the less, throughout the nineteenth century, remarkably loyal to traditional values in some basic respects: they married in synagogues, their sons went through a ceremonial *barmitzvah* at the age of 13, the laws of mourning were observed at least in part.[37] Strict adherence to orthodox practices (such as Sabbath observance and *shiva*) undoubtedly declined, and there remained a significant level of intermarriage. But the *ethnic* identity of British Jewry appears to have been affected little (if at all) by the fact of emancipation. Rabbi (later Sir) Hermann Gollancz (1852–1930), subsequently Professor of Hebrew at University College London, frequently berated his upper-middle-class congregation at the Bayswater Synagogue, where he ministered 1892–1922, for its apathy and indifference to Jewish communal affairs; but he did not deem it necessary to refer explicitly to apostasy until 1911.[38]

In another respect, too, the fears expressed by Jewish opponents of emancipation proved groundless. In spite of the close association between the emancipation campaign and the Liberal Party, British Jewry never became exclusively identified with Liberal politics. David Salomons lost his Greenwich seat at the general election of 1852, but Lionel de Rothschild was re-elected. Thereafter, the motor that drove the engine of emancipation was fuelled by the gathering force of public opinion, much of it generated from within

[36] *Correspondence between Mr. Oswald John Simon and the Dean of Lichfield, Rev. George Margoliouth, and Rev. A. E. Suffrin, on Parochial Missions to the Jews* (London, 1887), 16.

[37] S. Sharot, 'Secularization, Judaism and Anglo-Jewry', *A Sociological Yearbook of Religion in Britain*, 4 (1971), 121–30.

[38] T. M. Endelman, 'The Social and Political Context of Conversion in Germany and England, 1870–1914', in id. (ed.), *Jewish Apostasy in the Modern World* (New York, 1987), 87. On Hermann Gollancz, see R. Apple, 'United Synagogue, Religious Founders and Leaders', in S. S. Levin (ed.), *A Century of Anglo-Jewish Life 1870–1970* (London, n.d.), 20–1. Hermann's brother, Sir Israel (1863–1930), a Shakespearian scholar, was a founder and the first Secretary of the British Academy.

the non-Jewish business classes.[39] This public opinion had a political dimension, for it reflected the rising tide of Liberalism that was to dominate British politics for the next quarter-century; between 1846 and 1874 the Conservatives held office for a total of five and a half years, but only as minority Governments. The electorate regarded the party as reactionary, the last refuge of vested interests that had no place in an industrial society. The refusal of the party to sanction the right of professing Jews to sit in the Commons was perceived as an integral component of this backward-looking mentality. In 1847 Bentinck had been forced to resign the Tory leadership because he supported Jewish emancipation. The Earl of Derby, Conservative leader in the Lords, was a confirmed opponent. On the other hand, Benjamin Disraeli, who became Conservative leader in the Commons, was a supporter.

The extent to which Disraeli's support was either genuine or consistent is a matter of debate.[40] He never denied or belittled his Jewish origins; on the contrary, he was proud of them. Yet during his first ten years as an MP (1837–47) he remained silent on the matter of Jewish emancipation, and on two occasions thereafter (1850 and 1854) he voted negatively on the issue. As with so much else in Disraeli's life, the key to an understanding of his motives lies in his appreciation of the road to power—his own road to the Conservative leadership, and his party's road to political victory. Out of the ruins of the Peelite Conservative Party, split irrevocably on the issue of the repeal of the Corn Laws in 1846, Disraeli and his supporters wished to build a new party; they could not do so while the attention and energies of their colleagues were diverted by narrow, sectarian obsessions—such as opposition to Jewish emancipation—which were essentially irrelevant to the concerns of mid-Victorian society.

In his novel *Coningsby*, published in 1844, Disraeli had warned his party that the power of Jewish voters was something they could not afford to ignore.[41] Until his leadership of the party in the Commons was beyond dispute, he dared not make too much of the emancipation issue. But after Rothschild's 1847 victory and the advertised determination of the Board of Deputies to support

[39] Alderman, *Jewish Community*, 20.

[40] The relevant chapters in Gilam, *Emancipation of the Jews*, and Salbstein, *Emancipation of the Jews*, offer contrasting views on this matter.

[41] B. Disraeli, *Coningsby* (Everyman edn., London, 1959), 207.

the campaign once more (in January 1848)—to say nothing of the support given by Lord Palmerston, easily the most popular politician of the era—the settlement of the matter acquired a new urgency. The continued refusal of the Tory peers to sanction legislation enabling Rothschild to take his seat as a professing Jew was exploited with much greater force by the Liberal Party, and came to be regarded by an increasing number of Conservatives as a danger as well as an embarrassment.[42]

In 1858, during the second minority Conservative administration headed by Derby and Disraeli, matters came to a head. The Liberal majority in the Commons threatened to permit Rothschild to take his seat regardless of the wishes of the Lords. Disraeli pressurized Derby into accepting a compromise (suggested by the anti-emancipationist Earl of Lucan) whereby each House was deemed to be free to determine for itself the form of oath to be administered to a Jew.[43] The Bill which was introduced to give effect to this settlement passed the Lords by 33 votes to 12 and the Commons by 129 votes to 55. Four Conservative front-benchers (including Disraeli) voted in favour of the measure; many more abstained. At the same time an amended Oaths Bill was also given parliamentary approval. On 23 July 1858 both measures passed into law. Scarcely a decade later, at the general election of 1868, the first Jewish Conservative parliamentary candidate appeared, Baron Henry de Worms (1840–1903; later Lord Pirbright).[44] The first professing Jew to take his seat in the Commons on the Conservative side, the obscure Nottinghamshire coal-owner Saul Isaac (1823–1903), was elected in 1874, appropriately enough at the same general election which gave Disraeli his first (and only) parliamentary majority.[45]

Lionel de Rothschild's ceremonial entry into the House of Commons to take his seat (28 July 1858) was an occasion of great communal rejoicing, but it also brought into the open a worry that had exercised communal leaders throughout the previous thirty years. Jews were overrepresented in the social strata from which the political classes were drawn, and there were enough of them with sufficient private wealth to make their candidatures an attractive

[42] *JC* (21 Jan. 1848), 400; *Morning Advertiser* (4 Mar. 1851), 2.

[43] Alderman, *Jewish Community*, 28; Gilam, *Emancipation of the Jews*, 163.

[44] On de Worms, see C. Bermant, *The Cousinhood* (London, 1971), 100–1; de Worms entered the House of Commons in 1880.

[45] On Isaac, see M. Caplan, 'Tory's First Jewish MP', *JC* (1 Mar. 1974), 9.

proposition regardless of their religious backgrounds. So the Jewish presence in the legislature grew with embarrassing speed. Lionel's brother, Mayer, was returned for Hythe at a by-election in 1859. At the general election later that year they were joined by David Salomons and, in 1860, by Francis Goldsmid. After the general election of 1865 no less than six Jews sat in the Commons; a further two were returned at by-elections during the lifetime of the 1865–8 Parliament.

Compared with the proportion which Jews comprised of the total population of the United Kingdom, they were already 'overrepresented' in the Commons, a state of affairs that has persisted ever since. As early as September 1858 this had become a cause of some communal concern.[46] Whatever the constitutional position of an MP, and whatever might have been his overriding duty to those who had elected him, and to those (whether electors or not) whom he represented in a territorial sense, it seemed very likely that the Jewish MPs would be regarded as spokesmen for their co-religionists.[47] These fears were soon dispelled. When Parliament reassembled after the general election of 1859 the *Jewish Chronicle* had thundered 'We are interested in it as citizens, not as Jews'.[48] And in 1872 the English-born patent-agent and poet Michael Henry (who had succeeded to the editorship of the paper following its purchase by a trio of communal grandees in 1869) reassured his readers thus:

> The House [of Commons] may have its Roman Catholic party, its Presbyterian party, its Evangelical party; but if of the six hundred and fifty-six gentlemen who compose the House of Commons, one third were members of the Jewish community, there would be no such thing as a Jewish party.[49]

There had indeed never been any intention on the part of the major Jewish protagonists of emancipation to create a Jewish 'lobby' at Westminster, less still to use the fact of a Jewish presence

[46] *JC* (3 Sept. 1858), 302.

[47] Ibid. (8 Feb. 1861), 4.

[48] Ibid. (27 Jan. 1860), 5.

[49] Ibid. (9 Aug. 1872), 262; the trio who had purchased the paper were Lionel Louis Cohen, founder of the Jewish Board of Guardians and of the United Synagogue, his brother-in-law Samuel Montagu (the future Lord Swaythling and founder, in 1887, of the Federation of Synagogues), and their close friend Lionel Van Oven. On Michael Henry see [C. Roth], *The Jewish Chronicle 1841–1941* (London, 1949), 81–2.

in Parliament to further Jewish interests; the right of professing Jews to sit in the Commons was to be the end in itself, not a means to other ends.

Some of the early Jewish MPs, by reason of their past communal involvement, were none the less expected to maintain a watching brief over Jewish interests at Westminster, and were happy to do so. David Salomons secured legislation (1871) enabling Jews who closed their factories or workshops on Saturdays to open them on Sundays for members of their own faith.[50] Francis Goldsmid ('the member for Jewry') made some of his greatest parliamentary speeches in condemnation of the attacks on Jews in the Danubian provinces and in Russia and Poland between 1862 and 1872.[51] In 1868 he was joined in the Commons by a fellow Reform Jew, John Simon (1818–97; MP for Dewsbury 1868–88); when Goldsmid was killed in a railway accident in 1878 Simon assumed the role of senior Jewish MP. It was Simon who organized, in 1872, the Mansion House protest meeting against the treatment of Jews in Serbia and Romania, who was one of the moving spirits behind the much larger protest in 1882 against the Russian pogroms, and who in 1888 intervened in the anti-Jewish agitation in Cork, enlisting the support of the Irish nationalist leader, Parnell. During the debate on W. E. Forster's Elementary Education Bill (1870) Simon had defended the right of Jewish children to absent themselves from school on Jewish Sabbaths and festivals.[52]

All these initiatives were useful, important, even vital. But many of them were extra-parliamentary, and even those that required a parliamentary presence could probably have been launched with the help of friendly non-Jewish MPs. The community did not want those MPs who happened to be Jewish to be regarded as a Jewish phalanx, the parliamentary arm of British Jewry. But it did expect—rightly or wrongly—the sympathy and support of Jewish members of the legislature as occasion demanded. The experience of the first half-century was, in this respect, most disappointing, and led the then President of the Board of Deputies, the barrister

[50] Hyamson, *David Salomons*, 88–9; *JC* (25 Aug. 1871), 6. See also J. Wigley, *The Rise and Fall of the Victorian Sunday* (Manchester, 1980), 207.

[51] D. W. Marks and A. Löwy, *Memoirs of Sir Francis Henry Goldsmid* (2nd edn., London, 1882), *passim*.

[52] On Simon see *JC* (2 July 1897), 21–5; *Dewsbury Reporter* (3 July 1897), 5.

David Lindo Alexander (1842–1922; President 1903–17) to make the following observation in December 1905:

> I have for some time past felt . . . that this Board on many occasions does not receive that co-operation and assistance from some of the Jewish members of Parliament, which it has a right to expect . . . and, further, that its efforts to procure the adoption of provisions and amendments, safeguarding Jewish interests are not infrequently hampered . . . by the want of unanimity amongst the Jewish members of Parliament.[53]

In short, although the events of 1858 had constituted a magnificent victory at the time, with the passage of years they appeared to many to have been an anti-climax. Two developments reflected the disappointment felt in this regard. By far the ablest of the early Jewish MPs was George Jessel (1824–83), elected Liberal MP for Dover in 1868. Jessel became Solicitor-General under Gladstone three years later, on the strength of an accomplished speech on the Bankruptcy Bill; later still he was appointed Master of the Rolls. Jessel had from 1855 to 1863 served on the Council of Jews' College, and he became a Vice-President of the Anglo-Jewish Association. But, as a parliamentarian, his undoubted talents were never employed within the ambit of Jewish communal affairs.[54] As for Lionel de Rothschild, who had spent so much time, energy, and money in the campaign to take a parliamentary seat, the burden he had won for himself apparently proved too heavy to bear: for not once during his entire membership of the Commons (1858–74) did he speak on the floor of the House.[55]

So it was that the larger hopes of those Jews who supported emancipation, and the more extreme fears of those who had opposed it or who had remained silent, were equally frustrated. Still, the wider process of emancipation inevitably had profound effects upon the community, and upon its relationship with the British polity as well as with Gentile society. To begin with, although it was true that emancipation had been, in the technical

[53] *JC* (8 Dec. 1905), 11.

[54] On Jessel see A. L. Goodhart, *Five Jewish Lawyers of the Common Law* (Oxford, 1949), 16–23.

[55] Lionel did, however, use his influence to secure the right of orthodox Jews to have their votes marked by the returning officer, in the event of a Saturday poll, when the secret ballot was enacted in 1872; the right did not, however, extend to Jewish high holy days—such as *Yom Kippur* (the Day of Atonement)—not falling on a Saturday. See Alderman, *Jewish Community*, 180, and H. S. Q. Henriques, *The Jews and the English Law* (Oxford, 1908), 247.

and legal senses, unconditional, the State had, almost surreptitiously, exacted a price in return for full civil equality. Nathan Marcus Adler feared that emancipation would entail the erosion of religious freedoms in the name of equality before the law. And so it was. If Jews wanted equality, they could have it; but, in that case, the laws which applied to the Gentiles would apply also to the Jews. In relation to the religious autonomy of the community, and more particularly in the matter of personal and marital status, the results were rather serious.

The special position of Jewish marriages, performed under the exclusive authority of the rabbinate, had been recognized and preserved in Lord Hardwicke's Marriage Act of 1753. But Lord Lyndhurst's Marriage Act of 1835, by rendering null and void all marriages 'within the prohibited Degrees of Consanguinity' as defined by canon law, clearly delimited the autonomy the Jews in Britain had enjoyed hitherto, to be able to marry within degrees of kinship laid down by the rabbis—principally marriage with the deceased wife's sister, or between an uncle and niece.[56] After 1835 such marriages had to be solemnized abroad, and in 1855 Adler told the Board of Deputies that 'as these marriages have been allowed from time immemorial, the great majority of the Jewish community do regard the prohibition . . . as a grievance and desire it to be remedied'.[57] It was certainly true that Adler and Montefiore were agitated on this issue, and that their anxiety was much deeper in this regard than in relation to the right of Jews to sit in Parliament.[58] But the Board itself was not greatly impressed by the Chief Rabbi's concern. His wish—to have amending legislation passed that would restore the Jewish exemptions—was never pressed. Had it been, it would undoubtedly have encountered fierce resistance from orthodox radicals like Salomons, for whom equality before the law was the greatest good.

In 1857 Salomons and Lionel de Rothschild intervened in another matter pertaining to rabbinical authority, namely the status in English law of a rabbinically authorized divorce, consequent

[56] I. Finestein, 'An Aspect of the Jews and English Law during the Emancipation: The Prohibited Degrees', *JJS* 7 (1965), 3–10; 5 & 6 William IV, c. 54.

[57] BD Minute Book No. 7 (1851–5), 321–3: Nathan Adler to Moses Montefiore, 1 Feb. 1855.

[58] I. Finestein, 'The Uneasy Victorian; Montefiore as Communal Leader', in S. Lipman and V. D. Lipman (eds.), *The Century of Moses Montefiore* (Oxford, 1985), 47.

upon the passage that year of the Matrimonial Causes Act. This measure had created a civil Divorce Court, which, *inter alia*, could dissolve a Jewish marriage. Adler and the Board of Deputies had tried to persuade the Government to insist upon a clause exempting Jewish marriages from such dissolution; influenced by Rothschild and Salomons, the Government desisted.[59] The precise status, in English law, of a *get* (bill of divorcement) authorized by a rabbi, remained thereafter in some doubt. Legal opinion obtained by the Deputies argued that the autonomy of the Jewish ecclesiastical authorities was unaffected by the 1857 legislation. For a time this was also the view of the State. But in 1866 the Registrar-General announced that he would no longer register rabbinic divorces; the implication clearly was that the civil authorities had ceased to regard them as sufficient.[60]

Henceforth a *get* could only be authorized after a civil divorce had been obtained, a state of affairs that was given judicial force in a case decided before the English courts in 1908.[61] By then the attitude of the Jewish leadership had changed too. Chief Rabbi Hermann Adler (1839–1911), Nathan's son, wished to stamp out the authority and independence of 'foreign rabbis' whom the refugees from Tsarist persecution had brought with them in the 1880s and 1890s. Both he and Lindo Alexander denounced them before the Royal Commission on Divorce and Matrimonial Causes in 1910, accusing them of encouraging religious divorces while couples remained civilly married, and of thus fostering bigamy and bastardy as defined by the law of the land.[62] Only Rabbi Dr Moses Gaster (1856–1939), appointed *Haham* in 1887, stood out against the Chief Rabbinate and the Board of Deputies on this issue. Gaster urged that 'no rabbi should be declared guilty of doing wrong when in the first place they do that which is commanded by the law of

[59] I. Finestein, 'Anglo-Jewry and the Law of Divorce', *JC* (19 Apr. 1957), 11.

[60] *PP* 1912–13, xx [Cd. 6481]: Royal Commission on Divorce and Matrimonial Causes; Minutes of Evidence, qq. 41,482 and 41,514 (13 Dec. 1910).

[61] G. R. Bartholomew, 'Application of Jewish Law in England', *University of Malaya Law Review*, 3 (July 1961), 104.

[62] *PP* 1912–13, xx [Cd. 6481]: Royal Commission on Divorce and Matrimonial Causes: Minutes of Evidence, qq. 41,363–41,507. A Jew may marry more than one wife; so long as his wives are unmarried or properly (i.e. rabbinically) divorced prior to the union, the issue of such partnerships do not have the religious status of *mamzerim* (bastards).

God'.[63] Nathan Adler would have agreed with him; Hermann, however, seemed happy to repudiate the religious freedom his father had held so dear.

The price paid for equality before the law thus continued to be exacted long after the excitement generated by the granting of political emancipation had died down. The boundaries between the civil state and the realm of British Jewry were redrawn. Within the Jewish community the preferred position of the new lines of demarcation was itself a matter of great dispute. Salomons quarrelled with Montefiore on the matter of divorce, but stood four-square with him in the campaign launched by the Deputies for exemption from what became the Metropolitan Interment Act of 1850. This measure (a response to the cholera epidemic of 1848) envisaged the closure of all private cemeteries; burials would henceforth have to take place in state-run burial grounds, located in the suburbs, where interment practices would be superintended by Edwin Chadwick's General Board of Health. However lax or unconcerned nominally orthodox Jews may be about Jewish ritual in life, their burial according to the precise requirements of orthodoxy generally becomes a matter of the greatest concern. So it was in 1850. The threat which the Interment Act posed to the sanctity of rabbinic burial laws united the Deputies, who lobbied furiously first for total and then (more successfully) for partial exemption: Jews were to have local autonomy within the national scheme. There was little enthusiasm for this compromise, and much relief when the Derby–Disraeli Government repealed the measure in 1852.[64]

Emancipation and its achievement also had a prolonged and pervasive effect upon British Jewry's perception of its own public image. Concern with the public face of the community was not new. But in the mid-nineteenth century this concern became passionate, and virtually institutionalized. Jewish writers were expected to describe the community to the non-Jewish world in

[63] University College London, Gaster Papers, bound vol. 18: Gaster to C. H. L. Emanuel (Secretary to the Board of Deputies), 17 Jan. 1911.

[64] A. Gilam, 'The Burial Grounds Controversy between Anglo-Jewry and the Victorian Board of Health, 1850', *JJS* 45 (1983), 147–56; Salomons saw the exemption of rabbinically sanctioned divorces from the general enactment of 1857 as a perpetuation by statute of Jewish civil inequality, but regarded proposed statutory interference with Jewish burial rites as an unjustified infringement of religious liberty.

glowing, even angelic terms: the purpose of the novelist and short story writer was not to examine real issues and tensions, less still to pose awkward and sensitive questions, but rather to provide well-written propaganda, to show that the Jews were deserving of civil and social equality, and that their full emancipation could not be construed as a danger to Christian Britain.

In the work of the Marrano descendant Grace Aguilar (1816–47), most notably *The Vale of Cedars*, a tale of the Spanish Inquisition published posthumously in 1850, Judaism is never closely defined, Jewish ritual is over-simplified, and Jewish festivals are described in terms of roughly concurrent Christian holy days; the Jews living in England differ from English Victorians only in point of their religious beliefs and practices, and even in this respect (Aguilar claimed) the two religions have many points of similarity. It has been said that Aguilar's Judaism was indeed 'a Christianised version'.[65] Aguilar herself confessed as much. In 1847 she published, in Chambers Miscellany, a very brief *History of the Jews in England*—the first such history written by an Anglo-Jewish author. 'Jews', she declared, 'are still considered aliens and foreigners . . . little known and less understood. Yet they are, in fact, Jews only in their religion—Englishmen in everything else.' 'A Jewish murderer, adulterer, burglar, or even petty thief', she added coolly, 'is actually unknown.'[66]

Admittedly, not all writers of the period were as uncritical and as superficial as this in their portrayal of their co-religionists. Charlotte Montefiore (1818–54), a niece of Sir Moses, argued against conversion in *Caleb Asher* (1845); Christian missionaries were berated for their lack of real interest in the welfare of Jews, and Jews were praised for their lack of interest in proselytizing. Matthias Levy, writing under the pseudonym 'Nathan Meritor', also argued against conversion (*The Hasty Marriage*, 1857), but he was equally scathing of Reform Judaism, in part (he argued) because it was a stepping-stone to intermarriage and conversion. However, the works of these authors, as of the sisters Cecile and Marion Moss, all sought to portray Jews as solid English citizens,

[65] L. G. Zatlin, *The Nineteenth-Century Anglo-Jewish Novel* (Boston, Mass., 1981), 39. See also Beth-Zion Lask Abrahams, 'Grace Aguilar: A Centenary Tribute', *TJHSE* 16 (1945–51), 137–48.

[66] G. Aguilar, *History of the Jews in England*, Chambers Miscellany, vol. 18, no. 153 (Edinburgh, 1847), 16, 18.

worthy if not wealthy, and thoroughly middle class in outlook if not in social status.[67] In *Caleb Stukely*, serialized in *Blackwood's Magazine* in 1842, Samuel Phillips (1815–74) depicted a different sort of Jew, the immigrant money-lender; the stereotype was thoroughly anti-Jewish, but Phillips's major purpose appears to have been to express his impatience at the length of time taken to Anglicize foreign Jews.[68]

The apprehension betrayed here was intensified in the second half of the century. The immediate post-emancipation generations felt that they were on trial, that they had to prove and to continue to prove that they were worthy of the rights and freedoms extended to them, and that they must somehow conform to Gentile expectations of acceptable Jewish behaviour. As Judge Finestein has emphasized, post-emancipation Anglo-Jewry was 'dominated by considerations of public image'.[69] In the literary sphere this obsession had a stultifying and dehumanizing influence. Jewish writers were expected to produce material that would project images designed to counterbalance those drawn by anti-Semites.[70]

The prototype is to be found in the work of Emily Harris (1844–1900). Harris later explained that the purpose of her novel *Estelle* (1878) had been that of 'plainly and truthfully delineating the life led by many a talented, aspiring, yet tender, and devout Jewish girl; her struggles, the strength and stedfastness [*sic*] of her religion; the single-mindedness and simplicity of her home life, all passing within the domestic household of an orthodox, intellectual Jew, her father'.[71] The Jewish family portrayed in the novel lived in a small English cathedral town and was hardly typical, therefore, of British Jewry. This was deemed not to matter, so long as the message conveyed by the work gave the desired impression.

The genre was continued by Benjamin Farjeon (1833–1903) and Samuel Gordon (1871–1927). Farjeon's literary output (especially *The Pride of Race*, which appeared in 1900) extolled the virtues of

[67] B. H. Cheyette, 'An Overwhelming Question: Jewish Stereotyping in English Fiction and Society, 1875–1914', Ph.D. thesis (Sheffield, 1986), 181.

[68] Zatlin, *The Nineteenth-Century Anglo-Jewish Novel*, 107, asserts that Phillips's Jewish identity cannot be firmly established. However, he was included in Rabbi Edward N. Calisch's *The Jew in English Literature* (Richmond, Va., 1909), 164, and it seems safe to so regard him; see also Endelman, *Radical Assimilation*, 103.

[69] Finestein, *Post-Emancipation Jewry*, 6.

[70] *JC* (20 May 1892), 9.

[71] Ibid. (27 May 1892), 12.

the 'English Jewish gentleman' and idealized them. 'The spirit of the English-born Jew, whose parents are also English-born', Farjeon explained, should be contrasted with the outlook of the 'Anglicized foreign Jew who, of late years, has overflooded the East End Ghetto.'[72] Gordon was himself an immigrant, from Prussia. His best-known work, the semi-autobiographical *Sons of the Covenant* (also 1900) earned praise because its idealized portrait of recently arrived Jewish immigrants in London's East End, wishing for nothing better than to marry into the assimilated Jewish gentry of the West End, represented (in the words of the *Jewish Chronicle*) 'all that is best and most typical in Jewish life and thought'.[73]

A reaction against such blatantly false portraiture was bound to come. It was previewed in *Dr Phillips. A Maida Vale Idyll* (1887), the first novel of 'Frank Danby', the pen-name of Julia Frankau (1859–1916), an accomplished and prolific writer who described the unashamed wealth-seeking that seemed to her to characterize upper-middle-class life in the Jewish West End, and the craving for social status that was to be found therein. Frankau was repelled by the type of Judaism and Anglo-Jewish existence which she experienced; her children were not brought up as in any sense Jewish.[74] *Dr Phillips* aroused the inevitable storm of indignation, but this was as nothing compared with the sense of outrage, even treason, that greeted the appearance in 1888 of the conceptually and stylistically brilliant *Reuben Sachs*, which fell from the pen of Amy Levy (1861–89).

Reuben Sachs is the best and most realistic account we have of the undisguised nepotism and the deep, irreverent materialism of the Jewish middle classes in London in the third quarter of the nineteenth century. Its author, the daughter of native-born English Jews (her father, Lewis, had made a fortune out of stocks and shares), was the first Jewess to become a student at Newnham College, Cambridge—a true daughter of the emancipation.[75] She was, of course, a supporter of women's suffrage. Her circle of friends included Eleanor Marx and she became, in 1888, a

[72] *JC* (8 Feb. 1901), 8.

[73] Ibid. (25 Jan. 1901), 17.

[74] Cheyette, 'An Overwhelming Question', 196–203; Endelman, *Radical Assimilation*, 136–7.

[75] On Levy see Cheyette, 'An Overwhelming Question', 187–95' and Beth-Zion Lask Abrahams, 'Amy Levy: Poet and Writer', *AJA Quarterly*, 6 (Oct. 1960), 11–17, and 'Amy Levy', *TJHSE* 11 (1924–7), 168–89. Levy was also the first professing Jewess to be cremated!

contributor to *Woman's World*, edited by Oscar Wilde. Sickened by the accepted standards of the Jewish milieu in which she had grown to adulthood, she set out to expose this environment in all its ultra-opulent and self-satisfied glory. *Reuben Sachs* is a story of romantic love sacrificed on the altar of wealth. The world it describes, of a coterie of Jewish families in Maida Vale and Bayswater, is a world in which men are preoccupied with making money, and their womenfolk with displaying whatever it can buy; Jewish values have been corrupted in the process.

The novel caused a sensation. The book was condemned in and by the *Jewish Chronicle*, and gave offence even further afield. 'It is to be lamented,' Rabbi Edward Calisch observed from the safety of the United States of America, that in the novel Amy Levy had chosen 'to give some of the less pleasing phases of Jewish character'.[76] But even Calisch, writing after her death, did not say that the picture she had painted was false. Her example was a major influence on Israel Zangwill (1864–1926), whose *Children of the Ghetto*, the first realistic literary portrait of East End Jewish immigrant life, appeared in 1892. 'She was accused [Zangwill recalled in 1901], of course, of fouling her own nest; whereas what she had really done was to point out that the nest was fouled and must be cleaned out.'[77] *Reuben Sachs* was a literary success. Its authoress became a communal outcast. In 1889 she published a short story—'Cohen of Trinity'—about a best-selling novelist who took his own life in the midst of his triumph; shortly afterwards Amy Levy herself committed suicide.

The manner of her death served to confer a spurious justification upon the oblivion to which the community at once consigned her memory.[78] During her lifetime the major concerns of the communal leadership, both in London and the provinces, had been to project images of 'good' citizenship, not to expose individual or collective shortcomings. In no sphere had this been more apparent than in relation to social problems, more especially those pertaining to the condition of the Jewish poor. We noted in the previous chapter the communal anxiety to which the continued existence of a Jewish

[76] *JC* (2 Aug. 1889), 12; (13 Sept.), 6; (6 Dec.), 6; Calisch, *Jew in English Literature*, 159.

[77] *JC* (25 Jan. 1901), 19. The most recent—and best—study of Zangwill is by J. H. Udelson, *Dreamer of the Ghetto* (Tuscaloosa, Ala., 1990).

[78] Abrahams, 'Amy Levy', 168.

pauper class had given rise. This anxiety was made worse by the relative ease with which foreign Jews could gain entry into Britain. The French wars had triggered a wave of xenophobia in England, leading to assaults on Jews and attacks on Jewish property (including the Birmingham synagogue in 1813). As wartime restrictions upon the entry and movement of aliens were abandoned after 1815, and as social pressures and political unrest in central and eastern Europe (more especially, persecutions under Tsars Nicholas I and Alexander II) drove Jews to seek new opportunities in the West, the incidence of Jewish pauperism in England became, again, a matter of concern.

Because of the origins and nature of Jewish immigration to Britain in the second half of the nineteenth century, the problem became the almost exclusive concern of the *Ashkenazi* community. Between the mid-1850s and the end of the 1870s the Jewish population of Britain increased from about 35,000 to over 60,000. Most of this increase can be attributed to immigration, and most of the immigrants came from Russia and Poland, generally young men, either unmarried or with wives and families whom they hoped would join them later. Dr Lipman estimated that by 1881 at least a quarter of the Jews in Britain were of Russian and Polish origin; but the proportion may have been nearer a third.[79]

The problem of the Jewish poor thus reappeared. It was compounded by the passage, in 1834, of the Poor Law Amendment Act, which sought to replace a system of 'outdoor' relief by one in which the only lawful method of relieving the impoverished was to be in separate workhouses for the aged and sick, for children, and for able-bodied males and able-bodied females, each workhouse to serve a group, or Union, of parishes, and to be maintained by a generally applicable poor rate. Now the Jewish community had made it a point of honour never to permit its poor to become a charge on the State. In the late eighteenth and early nineteenth centuries, in London, the *Ashkenazim* had furnished themselves with a range of charitable institutions to this end.[80] Most of these institutions operated in typical Victorian fashion as voting charities.

[79] V. D. Lipman, *A History of the Jews in Britain since 1858* (Leicester, 1990), 13; A. R. Rollin, 'Russo-Jewish Immigrants in England before 1881', *TJHSE* 21 (1962–7), 211.

[80] V. D. Lipman, *A Century of Social Service 1859–1959* (London 1959), 17–20, and the same author's *Social History of the Jews in England 1850–1950* (London, 1954), 52–3.

Each subscription purchased allowed one vote when a ticket was being allocated or when a place fell vacant in a home or almshouse. Inasmuch as the poor themselves could subscribe, the system incorporated an element of self-help; the subscription to the Bread, Meat and Coal Charity was deliberately fixed as low as one penny a week.[81]

But since benefits were allocated by lottery, each subscription was, literally, a gamble. The Jewish friendly society movement, which was to play such a central part in the life of the poor at the end of the century, was still in its infancy. If the poor could not obtain what they needed from the subscription charities, they could apply to individual synagogues—the Great, the Hambro', and the New—each of which had, as a matter of Jewish religious law, to provide sustenance for the needy (usually in the form of monthly allowances) dispensed by an officer—the *Gabbai Tsedakah* ('Overseer of the Poor')—especially appointed for this purpose. Members of a synagogue who had fallen upon hard times were entitled, as of right, to relief from the many trusts and bequests that had accumulated over the decades. Others, misleadingly termed the 'casual' poor, though they had no such right, were none the less entitled to look to the synagogue for relief, perhaps because they, or their parents, had been married in it. 'The evils of this right by marriage are very great', the Great Synagogue's Sub-Committee on the Poor observed in 1860, because 'the synagogue attracts to itself a generation of paupers, as sharers in its funds, from whom, until the family are all extinct, it can never be free'.[82]

But above and beyond these two categories of poor whom the synagogues were bound, by their constitutions, to relieve, there was a growing class of 'strange' or foreign poor, mainly recent immigrants, whose needs were met by the City synagogues jointly, under a succession of 'treaties'. In 1834 a new treaty, agreed largely through the influence of Nathan Mayer Rothschild, provided for a Conjoint Board (composed of officers from the three houses of worship), under whose direction the three overseers took turns in dispensing relief. The Great Synagogue agreed to bear half the cost, the New and the Hambro' a quarter each; the expenses of burying the foreign poor were to be shared in the same ratio.[83]

[81] Ibid. 19.

[82] Quoted in Lipman, *Century of Social Service*, 14.

[83] Ibid. 15.

The system inaugurated in 1834 had many defects. The sums granted—typically not more than about five shillings a month in the case of a foreign pauper—were not enough to relieve genuine poverty. Partly for this reason, and partly because of the rights to relief acquired by place of marriage, the system could be said to have perpetuated a pauper class. It was slow in operation. And it failed to distinguish properly between the needy and the greedy.[84] It could have been dismantled, and the fate of the Jewish poor placed in the hands of the Poor Law Commission, established under the Act of 1834. The Board of Deputies had, indeed, as a matter of principle, endeavoured to obtain special dietary and other facilities for Jewish inmates of workhouses when the Poor Law Amendment Bill was under discussion, and some dietary dispensations were apparently obtained from the Commission in 1842.[85] A few Jews undoubtedly did obtain poor relief in this way, as residents of the grim Union workhouses. At the end of the 1870s, when the total number of Jews living in London had reached about 46,000, the communal statistician Joseph Jacobs (1854–1916) estimated that in the capital alone there were over 10,000 Jewish paupers; yet only a handful of these were workhouse inmates.[86]

There were two reasons why communal leaders were determined not to permit significant numbers of the Jewish poor to obtain relief 'on the rates'. The first arose from a mixture of religious observance and social need. For it was undeniable that entry into the workhouse, a bleak enough prospect for the Victorian poor in general, was likely to be bleaker still for the Jewish poor, because of the splitting-up of families and the near impossibility of observing the minutiae of the dietary laws, the Sabbath, and other holy days. The second—equally compelling—related to the interests of the Jewish community at large. Jewish ratepayers were, like all ratepayers, assessed by the Poor Law Guardians for the maintenance of workhouses and other forms of relief to which all paupers might have access. The Jewish community could therefore claim, as a right of citizenship, that its poor, too, should be maintained in this way. The work of the secular authorities might, indeed, have been

[84] L. Magnus, *The Jewish Board of Guardians* (London, 1909), 14.
[85] Lipman, *Century of Social Service*, 12–13.
[86] J. Jacobs, *Statistics of the Jewish Population in London, etc. 1873–1893* (London, 1894), 9.

supplemented and supported in Jewish areas. But such a claim was never made, and such a plan was never discussed.

The argument prevailed that the right of asylum in Britain for Jewish refugees might be jeopardized should they ever be permitted to become a burden on the State.[87] The cumbersome and inefficient machinery erected by the City synagogues in 1834 was not, therefore, abandoned in its entirety. Instead, a refashioned scheme of co-operation was brought into existence. During the 1840s various plans for rationalizing and amalgamating Jewish charitable endeavours in London had been put forward, but all had foundered, on account of their over-ambitious nature and of the opposition of the memberships of the New and the Hambro' to the financial burdens they might have to bear.[88] But as the amounts spent by the Jewish charities in London rose (to an estimated £30,000 p.a. by the mid-1850s, exclusive of private donations), the need to find a viable solution became more urgent.[89]

In a series of articles in the *Jewish Chronicle*, Abraham Benisch proposed that the three City synagogues form 'a Board of Guardians', modelled upon but not as ambitious in its range of activities as the Jewish Comité de Bienfaisance that operated in Paris.[90] Benisch's plan involved the creation of an agency to co-ordinate existing charitable efforts. Ephraim Alex (1800–83), a dentist who was Overseer of the Poor of the Great Synagogue, made a different and more modest proposal: that the existing Conjoint Board be expanded and given an independent staff, to deal merely with the foreign poor. The 'appalling distress among the Jewish poor' during the severe winter of 1858–9 prompted renewed and more concentrated discussion of this proposal. In particular, the reluctance hitherto shown by the New and the Hambro' to participating in Alex's scheme was at last overcome.[91]

The London Jewish Board of Guardians met for the first time on 16 March 1859. Alex was elected President and the banker and financier Lionel Louis Cohen (1832–87) became Honorary Secretary. Ten years later Cohen succeeded Alex as President, and he in turn was succeeded as President first by his brother Benjamin

[87] Lipman, *Century of Social Service*, 10. [88] Ibid. 21.

[89] *JC* (25 Sept. 1857), 1156; the estimate was that of Abraham Benisch, editor of the *JC*.

[90] Ibid. (2 Oct. 1857), 1164.

[91] Ibid. (1 July 1887), 7; on Alex see ibid. (16 Mar. 1883), 3.

(1844–1909; President 1887–1900) and then by his son Leonard (1858–1938; President 1900–20). Lionel Cohen's forebears had been stalwarts of the Great Synagogue and he, like them, assumed the burdens of communal responsibility with enthusiasm and energy.[92]

The constitution and mode of operation of the Board of Guardians in its early years were largely the work of Cohen and Alex, and put into practice certain principles which informed the Board's approach not only to the relief of the foreign poor but, within a short space of time, to all manner of charitable work among the Jews of the capital. The work of poor relief was systematized; records were kept and information exchanged with other interested parties. Urgent cases were dealt with at once. The Board did not regard poverty as necessarily a crime, or as self-evident proof of idleness. Accordingly, loans and apprenticeships were financed side by side with schemes of cash and medical relief. Cases on the books for more than six months were freshly investigated. Jews wishing to emigrate (generally to the United States or the colonies), or to return to their country of origin, were given assistance. It was a condition of relief by the Board that children attended school; certificates of attendance were accordingly required. Relief was not available at all during the first six months' residence. What were termed 'confirmed paupers' were despatched to the mercies of the Poor Law.[93]

The overriding aim, however, was to put the poor in a position where they might fend for themselves. The problem of the Jewish poor was regarded as finite. Poverty caused by seasonal unemployment, or simply by a depression of trade or industry, was to be met by a policy of diversification, of schemes of training for a wider variety of occupations. In time, however, the Board of Guardians came to concern itself with the wider issues of housing and sanitation with which the poor had to contend. In 1862 the Board took over from the City synagogues the responsibility for medical relief, and for some years (until 1879) retained the services of its own medical officers. In 1865, on the initiative of the architect and communal worker Nathan Solomon Joseph (1834–1909), the Board took steps to remedy the deficiencies of the generally

[92] Bermant, *Cousinhood*, 178; Leonard Cohen's cousin, Hannah, was President 1930–40, and his son, Lord Cohen of Walmer, held the office 1940–7.

[93] Lipman, *Century of Social Service*, 28, 53–4.

inefficient and not infrequently corrupt vestries and district boards legally responsible for sanitation and housing in the metropolis, by appointing its own sanitary officer to inspect houses and to press landlords and local authorities to discharge their obligations. During the cholera epidemic of 1866 the Board also took it upon itself to provide twenty-seven standpipes for the supply of pure water.[94]

The Jewish Board of Guardians in London provided a model which the largest provincial communities soon followed. In the cases of Manchester and Liverpool, concerns similar to those which motivated the London congregations were intensified by local considerations stemming from particular economic and social circumstances. The stark condition of the Jewish poor of Red Bank, Manchester, the incidence of 'close, dirty, ill-ventilated and ill-drained habitations', of high rates of infant mortality, and even of cellar-dwellings, were well recognized by the end of the 1860s.[95] The general situation of the Jewish poor was made much worse because of the seasonal nature of the occupations in which they were engaged, and by the impact here (as in Liverpool) of the Lancashire Cotton Famine of 1862–4, in the miseries of which the Jewish poor shared to the full.

The ceaseless flow of new immigrants, many of whom lacked 'mechanical knowledge', exacerbated a problem that was already acknowledged to be beyond the means of existing charities to solve.[96] Inter-congregational rivalries, and the Reform controversy, resulted in added difficulties in the way of city-wide co-operation by the better-off Jews of Manchester in confronting the needs of their poorer brethren.[97] The formation in 1860 of the Hebrew Sick & Burial Benefit Society—the first Jewish friendly society in Manchester—was nothing less than a desperate attempt by a few of the communal leaders to encourage self-help among the less fortunate. It flourished after a fashion, but made little impact on the Jewish poor of the city as a whole.[98]

94 Alderman, *London Jewry*, 8.

95 Manchester Jewish Board of Guardians, *Third Annual Report* (1869–70), 10; *Fourth Annual Report* (1870–1), 10–11: cited in Williams, *Manchester Jewry*, 273.

96 Manchester Jewish Board of Guardians, *Sixth Annual Report* (1872–3), 6, quoted in B. Williams, *The Making of Manchester Jewry 1740–1875* (Manchester, 1976), 276.

97 *JC* (12 Nov. 1858), 5.

98 Williams, *Manchester Jewry*, 278–9.

This policy of drift was brought to a close by the onset of the Cotton Famine, by its exploitation by conversionists for their own well-publicized ends, and by a growing feeling of unease at the impact of an expanding class of Jewish paupers upon the public standing in Manchester of the Jewish community as a whole. Philip Falk, a businessman and a Reformer, put the case for 'an efficient system of dispensing charity in a liberal, and at the same time judicious manner—protecting the public from fraud . . . and promoting that feeling of self-dependence and self-reliance among the poor which alone can elevate them in the social scale'.[99] Here, indeed, was a topic upon which Reformers and orthodox could unite. For both, a solution to the problem of Manchester's growing army of Jewish paupers was viewed in the context of the need (perceived with an urgency just as great) to overcome the cultural, social, and religious insularity of the newest immigrants.

In February 1863 the Revd Samuel Landeshut (who had come from Bristol to serve the Old Congregation in 1859) arranged a conference of both congregations to address the problem and, in particular, to agree to the establishment of a Board of Guardians.[100] Initially it seemed that the idea was bound to fall victim to religious differences, focused upon the refusal of the orthodox to sanction the use of the Reform prayer-book in the most unlikely event of a Reform pauper being buried in an orthodox burial ground. But Landeshut was a patient man. In November 1866 he was able to announce to the *Jewish Chronicle* that 'a permanent Board of Guardians will be established [in Manchester], taking as its prototype the kindred institution of our brethren in the metropolis'.[101] The Manchester Board of Guardians held its first official meeting at the Jews' School, Cheetham Hill Road, on 1 July 1867. Philip Falk became President, and Landeshut and a Reform merchant, Henry Samson, served as joint secretaries.

The constitution of the Manchester Board followed that of London 'almost in every respect'.[102] Responsibility for poor relief in Manchester was henceforth communal and no longer synagogal. The overriding objectives of the new organization were deemed to be the discouragement of pauper settlement in the city, the promotion of emigration from it, and the encouragement of

[99] *JC* (18 Nov. 1864), 2: letter signed 'P. F.'

[100] Williams, *Manchester Jewry*, 281.

[101] *JC* (23 Nov. 1866), 2.

[102] Ibid. (3 July 1868), 7.

economic independence—and cultural assimilation—on the part of those paupers who remained. Accordingly, applicants new to Manchester were entitled to a single payment of only two shillings and six pence during their first month's residence in the city; and children between the ages of 5 and 13 had, as a condition of relief, to be sent to the Jews' School where (it was hoped) they would be taught to become 'useful members of society'.[103]

The events which led to the establishment of the Manchester Jewish Board of Guardians were watched closely in Liverpool, where attempts to deal piecemeal with various categories of Jewish poor had resulted in the familiar patchwork of well-motivated but overlapping charitable bodies—the Philanthropic Society, the Hebrew Mendicity Society, a Ladies Benevolent Institution, a Provident Society for elderly 'deserving Jews', and several other charity funds, in addition to the Hebrew Education Institution which was serving the needs of about 300 Jewish children (boys and girls) by the early 1870s. The Cotton Famine intensified a thousandfold the problems which the Liverpool communities had to face. The Old and New congregations had, as a result, to provide for the needs of able-bodied men and their families: in December 1865 there was a total of forty-five applicants for coal and blankets, of which no less than forty were from families with young children.[104] As in Manchester, continued immigration of Polish Jews complicated the problem still further.

The two congregations in Liverpool inevitably quarrelled over the apportionment of the increasing costs associated with relief work. A Hebrew Joint Relief Fund did not prove successful, but in 1876, following an initiative of the Revd Morris Joseph (1848–1930), of the Old Hebrew Congregation, a Liverpool Jewish Board of Guardians was established.[105] Its philosophy followed that of London and Manchester: to discourage casual begging, identify deserving cases, and attempt to deal once and for all with the problem of Jewish poverty by a mixture of loans, grants, and apprenticeships that would enable the poor to establish an independent existence.

[103] Ibid. (16 May 1873), 110.

[104] N. Kokosalakis, *Ethnic Identity and Religion: Tradition and Change in Liverpool Jewry* (Washington, DC, 1982), 90.

[105] Ibid. 92–3.

The Board of Guardians model established in London and developed in south Lancashire was adopted in other localities, though on a necessarily more modest scale. At Birmingham a Board of Guardians was set up in 1870, awkwardly coexisting with the much older Hebrew Philanthropic Society.[106] At Glasgow the Board of Guardians itself emerged out of the earlier Philanthropic Society; the Board of Guardians at Leeds dated from 1878.[107] Whether all these efforts would have succeeded in eradicating Jewish poverty is problematic. The approach adopted by these organizations was, however, predicated upon a dangerous assumption, namely that what was being confronted was finite in size. By the late 1870s it was becoming clear that emigration of Jews from eastern Europe was accelerating and that, moreover, its fundamental characteristics were changing.

As late as 1861 the Board of Guardians in London could report that 'Holland continues to supply the largest number of foreign paupers'.[108] And, as Professor Gartner has noted, a high proportion of Jewish immigrants to Britain before the 1870s appear to have been single men, without family responsibilities.[109] But by 1875 this pattern had broken down. With the end of the American Civil War, settlement in the United States again became an alluring proposition. In the case of Jewish families, powerful triggers were provided by the famine in north-east Russia in 1869–70 (as a result of which Jews were expelled from the border regions), by the systematic persecution of Jews in Romania (which began about the same time), by the Odessa pogrom of 1871, and by the repercussions for Russo-Polish Jewry generally of the Russo-Turkish conflict of 1876–8 and of the spread of civil unrest throughout the Russian Empire. Jews destined ultimately for North America were likely to regard England as a convenient staging-post.[110] In 1872 the Board of Guardians in London expressed, privately, its concern at 'the large influx of Jews from Poland', and in 1880 the *Jewish Chronicle*

[106] Z. Josephs (ed.), *Birmingham Jewry, ii. More Aspects 1740–1930* (Oldbury, 1984), 93–9.

[107] K. E. Collins, 'Growth and Development of Scottish Jewry, 1880–1940', in K. E. Collins (ed.), *Aspects of Scottish Jewry* (Glasgow, 1987), 14; E. Krausz, *Leeds Jewry: Its History and Social Structure* (Cambridge, 1964), 10; R. O'Brien, 'The Establishment of the Jewish Minority in Leeds', Ph.D. thesis (Bristol, 1975), 111.

[108] Jewish Board of Guardians, *Annual Report* (1861), 10.

[109] L. P. Gartner, *The Jewish Immigrant in England, 1870–1914* (London, 1960), 38–9.

[110] Lipman, *History*, 13.

commented that 'the larger proportion of our poor are invariably immigrants from Russia or Poland'.[111]

The phenomenon of the *chevrot*—the fraternities of Jews from central and eastern Europe, meeting for collective worship in any room that could be deemed vaguely suitable for the purpose, less interested in synagogue architecture and fashionable dress than in study of the *Talmud* and participation in Yiddish-based culture—could thus be observed well before the 1880s. The historian of Manchester Jewry has traced more than twenty *chevrot* in that city by the late 1870s; in London the full number will probably never be known.[112] The larger intra-communal tensions to which the *chevrot* gave rise will be examined in due course. Here it is sufficient to note that the twin calculations—that poverty might be eradicated and a substantial measure of acculturation achieved—which underpinned the idealisms of those who established the Boards of Guardians in London, Manchester, and elsewhere, began to be undermined even before the assassination of Tsar Alexander II in 1881. The mass immigrations that began in the 1880s in any case 'rendered all these calculations abortive'.[113]

But in the two decades that followed the achievement of political emancipation these developments, and the formidable problems to which they gave rise were, if perceived at all, not given a high communal priority. The energies and attention of communal leaders were focused instead upon refashioning the institutional framework of British Jewry and upon reinforcing the centripetal tendencies seen at work in the establishment of the Board of Guardians in London. A prerequisite deemed by some to be essential to this task was a healing of the wounds opened through the Reform controversy. Within the small, interrelated but *Haham*-less and (in truth) latitudinarian *Sephardi* community (and in spite of Moses Montefiore) the difficulties in the way of establishing a *modus vivendi* did not prove insuperable. Two leading lay members of Bevis Marks, Hananel de Castro and Haim Guedalla, put themselves at the head of a movement within their community for the removal of the *herem* on the *Sephardi* members of the West

[111] Jewish Board of Guardians, Minutes, 27 Nov. 1872; *JC* (20 Aug. 1880), 9.

[112] B. Williams, '"East and West": Class and Community in Manchester Jewry, 1850–1914', in D. Cesarani (ed.), *The Making of Modern Anglo-Jewry* (Oxford, 1990), 17; some of the more prominent *chevrot* in London are listed by G. Alderman, *The Federation of Synagogues, 1887–1987* (London, 1987), 20.

[113] Lipman, *Century of Social Service*, 75.

London Synagogue. Their humanitarian and essentially pragmatic arguments were reinforced by pecuniary considerations which were bound to carry weight with a lay leadership beset with financial problems. A campaign of attrition against those in charge of ecclesiastical affairs at Bevis Marks resulted, in 1849, in the lifting of the *herem*; in 1863 it was decided that offerings and legacies made to the synagogue by the seceders could, after all, be accepted.[114]

The influence which Nathan Marcus Adler had over the *Sephardim* in this matter was limited and to some extent counter-productive. But his attitude towards Reform did not soften. If anything, it hardened with age, and as the gospel of Reform, transmitted by German-Jewish merchants, was spread more widely within England. A Reform congregation was founded precisely in this way in Bradford in 1873.[115] Adler's resolve to make no concession to the Reformers remained complete, and without qualification: there was to be no accommodation with them, and no compromise that might afford them even a modest status in the communal hierarchy. The hand of friendship which Reverend Landeshut had extended to the Manchester Reformers (whose form of service now approximated much more closely to that of the Reform 'Temples' in the United States), and the holding of joint services, filled Adler with horror; he used the authority of his office to prevent Gustav Gottheil, the Reform Minister at Park Place, from preaching at the Great Synagogue in Manchester in 1872.[116]

In the struggle to meet the challenges of emancipation and assimilation, Adler and his allies relied essentially upon three weapons: the cloak of legitimacy; the umbrella of institutional protection; and the power of education. The first, the benefits of recognition and the concomitant threat of delegitimation, were, as we have seen, used to good effect in Manchester, and were, after a fashion, implemented some years later in London, in an attempt to

[114] A. Hyamson, *The Sephardim of England: A History of the Spanish and Portuguese Jewish Community, 1492–1951* (London, 1951), 293.

[115] M. R. Heilbron, 'Bradford', in A. Newman (ed.), *Provincial Jewry in Victorian Britain* (London, 1975); M. Leigh, 'Reform Judaism in Britain (1840–1970)', in D. Marmur (ed.), *Reform Judaism* (London, 1973), 36. On the activities of German-Jewish textile merchants in West Yorkshire see A. R. Rollin, 'The Jewish Contribution to the British Textile Industry: "Builders of Bradford"', *TJHSE* 17 (1951–2), 45–51.

[116] Williams, *Manchester Jewry*, 296.

prevent a friendly society composed of Dutch Jews (and dating from 1853) from establishing a permanent place of worship in Artillery Lane, Bishopsgate. The story of the Sandy's Row Synagogue—as it became known—provides a perfect illustration of the manner in which friendly societies, employing a rabbi or preacher to officiate at funerals, evolved through the stage of prayer- and study-groups into fully-fledged congregations. The story also provided an early opportunity for the protagonists and opponents of the *chevrot* to set out their arguments before the Anglo-Jewish public.

The Dutch Jews launched a public appeal for £500 to enable them to extend the lease of their synagogue building and to enlarge it. Their supporters, led by N. S. Joseph and the financier Ellis Abraham Franklin (1822–1909) extolled the virtues of independence and self-help. Their opponents, led by Lionel Louis Cohen, argued that the worshippers of Sandy's Row should be encouraged to join existing City synagogues, perhaps at reduced prices. This offer was not taken up. The renovated synagogue was opened in 1870, but it was consecrated by *Haham* Artom, Chief Rabbi Adler having refused to officiate.[117]

The irritation shown by Adler and Lionel Cohen towards Sandy's Row was all the greater because, earlier that year, Parliament had approved a scheme of amalgamation and rationalization of *Ashkenazi* synagogues in the City of London that promised a degree of central control unprecedented in modern Anglo-Jewish history. Formally, the foundation of the United Synagogue was nothing more nor less than the amalgamation of the Great, the New, and the Hambro' congregations into one body. Increasing co-operation between the three City synagogues had been foreshadowed in the Treaty of 1834, which, though concerned primarily with arrangements for meeting the needs of the Jewish poor, had extended also to more general questions of membership and the sharing of communal expenses; the Treaty had dealt with such matters as preventing the poaching of members, the division of profits derived from the London Board for Shechita, and the maintenance of a *Beth Din*.[118] As better-off Jews moved away from

[117] The story of Sandy's Row may be followed in *JC* (2 Sept. 1870), 3; (17 Nov. 1876), 518.

[118] Lipman, *Social History*, 55–6; see also C. Roth, *The Great Synagogue 1690–1940* (London, 1950), 237–8.

the City of London, and as the less affluent established their own independent places of worship in and around Whitechapel, the possibility that the Great, the New, and the Hambro' might find themselves confronted by an embarrassing dearth of members became very real.

In the short term this challenge was met by establishing branch synagogues, at Great Portland Street (a branch of the Great) and Bayswater (a branch of the Great and the New). These arrangements were, however, far from ideal, and gave rise within a very few years to further, and complicated, membership difficulties. Meanwhile, the number of minor synagogues, or *chevrot*, grew rapidly. In 1853 there had been only three identifiable minor synagogues in East London; by 1870 there were at least two score of them, with a combined membership of over 2,500 seat-holders, representing perhaps as many as 10,000 souls.[119] We should also note that although the expansion of London Jewry northwards was a phenomenon of the 1870s, the first signs of such a move were to be observed as early as 1861, when a prayer-group began meeting in Islington; it evolved into the North London Synagogue, opened in 1868.[120]

These memberships were of course quite beyond the control of the established City congregations, but they affected their operation in a number of ways. The provision of adequate burial facilities was one such problem; in 1857, following (at the instance of the Home Office) the compulsory cessation of burials at the Brady Street cemetery of the Great, an agreement between the Great and the New established a Conjoint Burial Board to manage the New Synagogue's cemetery at West Ham, with appropriate arrangements as to the sharing of expenses.[121] Another problem, scarcely less serious, was that stemming from falling membership rolls. In the early 1860s the Hambro' found itself in severe financial difficulties, and proposed (1863) an amalgamation with the Great; a committee of the Great examined the financial implications, and rejected the offer.[122] This was not the first occasion on which amalgamation of the City synagogues had been discussed. In 1859 a proposal from the New, for a union with the Great and the Hambro' as a condition precedent to the building of a further branch synagogue,

[119] See the letter from N. S. Joseph in *JC* (23 Sept. 1870), 3–4.
[120] Lipman, *Social History*, 69.
[121] Roth, *Great Synagogue*, 283–4.
[122] Ibid. 284–5.

had resulted in the appointment of a working party of the three communities, whose conclusion it was that:

Considering the present social conditions of the Jewish community in London—and with a view to their future well-doing—and to afford to the respective members and their families residing at the West End of the Metropolis increased accommodation by the establishment of another synagogue, it is the opinion of this committee that . . . there should first be an amalgamation of the three City and such other Metropolitan synagogues as may desire to unite with them.[123]

This recommendation, too, came to nothing, but the fact that it was not acted upon—at the very moment when the City synagogues had shown, through the establishment of the Board of Guardians, that they were indeed capable of joint action given a sufficient sense of urgency and direction—had significant repercussions. For the Bayswater synagogue, when established, was not a 'branch' in the sense of Great Portland Street; it had some degree of financial autonomy, it elected its own honorary officers and, after some argument, it was permitted to have its own marriage secretary. When the North London congregation applied to the Great for a loan of £1,100 to enable it to erect a new building, it was specifically provided 'that the said proposed synagogue shall not be a Branch of the Great Synagogue'.[124]

There is a tradition that the initiative that resulted in the formal union of the City synagogues came from Chief Rabbi Adler, who is said to have urged such a union during the course of conversation with the wardens of the Great, whom he had invited to breakfast in his *succah* during the festival of Tabernacles, 24 September 1866.[125] It is clear, not only that such an idea had been in the air for some considerable time, but that it had acquired new momentum some months earlier, through a fresh dispute between the New and the Great, over alleged poaching of members. But it is equally clear that Adler was preoccupied with the possibility of fragmentation of the London Jewry over which he claimed to exercise supreme ecclesiastical authority, and that his breakfast meeting imparted a sense of urgency and of mission where little had existed before. We know that Lionel Louis Cohen was present at that breakfast and that he emerged as the leading proponent of the

123 Quoted in A. Newman, *The United Synagogue 1870–1970* (London, 1977), 4.
124 Ibid. 5.
125 Roth, *Great Synagogue*, 286.

union Adler desired. Cohen's chief ally in this task, apart from the Chief Rabbi, was Dr Asher Asher (1837–89), who had been appointed Medical Officer of the Board of Guardians in 1862, and Secretary of the Great Synagogue four years later. Cohen became chairman, and Asher secretary, of a committee of the City congregations that drew up a scheme of amalgamation for submission to the Charity Commissioners; the scheme was brought into effect as the schedule to the Jewish United Synagogues Bill, which received the Royal Assent on 14 July 1870.

Several features of the Act, and of the organization—the United Synagogue—which it brought into being, deserve comment. The governing body of the new entity was (and is) the Council; the term 'Vestry', though it occurs in the Act, was never in fact employed by the new body.[126] Members of the Council had to be 'privileged', but all members could take part in their election. The Council in turn elected a President and two Vice-Presidents (the term 'Warden' was also dropped) as well as other officers, including two Treasurers of an amalgamated Burial Society. The United Synagogue was quite clearly not a federation of otherwise sovereign bodies. Each constituent synagogue was indeed to have its own local board of management, but annual budgets required the approval of the United Synagogue; founding and future constituents were therefore deprived of ultimate financial autonomy. The scheme also stipulated that the *minhag*, or ritual, of each constituent, was to be that of the German or Polish Jews. This requirement in effect prevented the adhesion of any non-orthodox body, but also that of any *Sephardi* community, and thus brought to an end the hopes, entertained by some as late as 1858, that one 'Chief Rabbi' might be appointed to serve as spiritual leader for both the *Ashkenazi* and *Sephardi* communities in Britain.[127] Whether the Spanish & Portuguese congregation would ever have agreed to such a proposition is highly doubtful; the appointment of *Haham* Artom in 1866 brought such speculations to an end. The United Synagogue scheme, as originally drafted, had spoken of 'the Chief Rabbi', under whose authority and control all religious matters were to fall. Gladstone's Liberal Government objected to the legislative underpinning of ecclesiastical jurisdiction in this way: the clause had to

[126] The term 'Council' formally replaced 'Vestry' in 1880.
[127] Hyamson, *Sephardim of England*, 306–7.

be modified.[128] Nathan Adler did not therefore become, by the authority of statute law, 'the Chief Rabbi', a British equivalent, so to speak, of a Continental *landesrabbiner*. But he did become, under the scheme scheduled to the Act, 'a Chief Rabbi', and the Deed of Foundation and Trust, executed by the officers of the United Synagogue in January 1871, gave him wide powers of rabbinical authority. As far as the *Ashkenazim* of Britain—indeed of the Empire—were concerned, he was 'the Chief Rabbi', and the non-Jewish world treated him as such.[129] The United Synagogue, for its part, became at once the largest synagogal body in Britain. By the end of the 1870s it comprised ten constituents with a total of over 2,500 male seat-holders.[130] Its presidents were generally Rothschilds and its vice-presidents invariably included a representative of the Cohen family; all in all, its list of honorary officers and Council members embraced much of the lay leadership of British Jewry.

Communities which joined the United Synagogue lost their independence, but they gained much in terms of access to the terminals of communal power; and, like the overwhelming majority of provincial congregations that put themselves under the jurisdiction of the United Synagogue's Chief Rabbi, their orthodox credentials were beyond dispute—even if their memberships were not particularly orthodox in practice. In this respect the United Synagogue set a standard; as an institution it was orthodox, but it admitted to membership all who were Jewish according to orthodox criteria, irrespective of their own personal degree of religious commitment. This was the essence of 'mainstream' British Judaism, and its flavour was to be found in the majority of provincial communities that flourished in the mid-nineteenth century.[131] Of course, Nathan Adler was much concerned to raise levels of religious observance. His preoccupation with the standards of

[128] PRO HO 45/8418: Lionel Louis Cohen to Home Office, 22 May 1870; United Synagogue, Council Minute Book 1870–79: 'Final Report of the Delegates appointed . . . for bringing the Scheme for the Union of the Synagogues into operation'. See also *JC* (15 July 1870), 5.

[129] A United Synagogue report of 1871 listed 17 provincial congregations as contributing to the fund for the upkeep of the office of Chief Rabbi, and 2 colonial communities (Melbourne and Sydney); the report lamented that there were 'no fewer than 21 Provincial and 15 Colonial Congregations participating in the benefits of the Chief Rabbi's supervision, who have never contributed to the Fund': A. Newman, 'The Chief Rabbinate', in id. (ed.), *Provincial Jewry*.

[130] Newman, *United Synagogue*, 216.

[131] Lipman, *History*, 26.

religious education then to be found within British Jewry has already been noted. To remedy the situation he found on taking up office, Adler placed his faith in the development of a network of Jewish elementary schools. His survey of 1845 had revealed that only in Birmingham, Liverpool, Manchester, and London were there schools of any substance; elsewhere there were either no schools, or small, fee-paying private establishments. Outside of the major centres, standards of instruction were not particularly high, partly because the remuneration paid to teachers was inadequate.

By the time of the foundation of the United Synagogue the situation had improved, at least to the extent that, as a result of Adler's efforts, more day schools had been established, so that perhaps as many as half the child population of British Jewry attended such schools.[132] But this achievement was itself controversial. The patchwork of Jewish voluntary schools, catering in the main for pupils up to the age of 12 or thereabouts, suffered from its association with mediocrity, and in any case never proved attractive to the more affluent sections of the community, who employed private tutors or else despatched their children to the more select private Jewish academies such as that opened in Highgate by Hyman Hurwitz and later (1842) removed to Kew by Leopold Neumegen (1787–1875), the Edmonton boarding-school run by H. N. Solomon (1796–1881), and Lewis Loewe's establishment at Brighton.[133] But from the mid-1870s there was an observable tendency for Jewish parents of middle-class status to send their sons to non-Jewish fee-paying schools, such as (in the capital) University College and the City of London schools, and Manchester Grammar School.[134] Through the exertions of Lionel Cohen a Jewish 'house' was established at Clifton College, Bristol, in 1879, and similar houses were established at Harrow and Cheltenham later on.[135]

The argument that a system of Jewish schools would act as a negative force in the process of social integration was persistently

[132] H. D. Schmidt, 'Chief Rabbi Nathan Marcus Adler (1803–1890): Jewish Educator from Germany', *Leo Baeck Year Book*, 7 (1962), 302.

[133] Lipman, *History*, 30; V. D. Lipman, 'The Anglo-Jewish Community in Victorian Society', in D. Noy and I. Ben-Ami (eds.), *Studies in the Cultural Life of the Jews in England* (Jerusalem, 1975), 154. On Solomon see J. Baum and B. Baum, *A Light Unto My Path: The Story of H. N. Solomon of Edmonton* (Edmonton, 1981).

[134] S. Singer, 'Jewish Education in the Mid-Nineteenth Century: A Study of the Early Victorian London Community', *Jewish Quarterly Review*, 77 (1986–7), 166.

[135] Bermant, *Cousinhood*, 183.

deployed. Following the passage of the 1870 Education Act which established ratepayer-financed school boards to supervise a system of state elementary schools, the argument carried even greater conviction; thereafter 'it became established communal policy . . . to regard Jewish day-schools as appropriate only for the areas of the foreign poor'.[136] The fear that Jewish schools would impede the process of social emancipation had a particular effect upon Nathan Adler's larger ambition, to set up an institution for the training of ministers and teachers of religion that would at the same time produce an élite of educated lay leaders. Several paths led him to this undertaking. Obsessed with the need to preserve his own status, and by the fear that this status would be irreparably compromised were other rabbis permitted to function alongside him, he opposed the right of any orthodox congregation anywhere in the Empire to appoint its own rabbinical authority without his approbation. This fiat even extended to members of his own *Beth Din*, whom he would not permit to be called to the reading of the *Torah* scroll by their rabbinical titles, and to his insistence that anyone invited by any of the City synagogues to address it must have his approval.[137]

But of course Adler himself could not function as a rabbi—let alone a 'Chief Rabbi'—in the pastoral sense. Congregations needed spiritual leaders who were locally based, and in the absence of rabbis they turned to other synagogue functionaries, principally the *chazanim* (cantors), who came to act—in effect—as non-ordained ministers of religion.[138] But whether they possessed the necessary qualifications to fulfil this role was questionable. A particular difficulty arose from the desire to have preachers ('lecturers') blessed with a complete command of the English language, this being considered in some quarters an important prerequisite of emancipation: 'We are anxious to obtain full emancipation [the *Jewish Chronicle* observed in 1849]; and would it not be a disgrace if we were told by our Christian opponents, that the Jews of England are so ignorant that they cannot find a lecturer in their

[136] Finestein, *Post-Emancipation Jewry*, 15. [137] *JC* (26 Nov. 1852), 62.

[138] S. Singer, 'The Anglo-Jewish Ministry in Early Victorian London', *Modern Judaism*, 5 (1985), 283–4; D. Englander, 'Anglicized not Anglican: Jews and Judaism in Victorian Britain', in G. Parsons (ed.), *Religion in Victorian Britain*, 4 vols. (Manchester, 1988), i. 249–51. Both Herman Hoelzel and Samuel Gollancz, who served as cantors in the Hambro' Synagogue from (respectively) 1845 to 1852 and 1855 to 1900, were ordained rabbis.

community?'[139] Whilst, therefore, Adler would remain the rabbinical authority of the *Ashkenazim* in Britain, synagogues under his jurisdiction required ministers who were neither cantors nor rabbis, but who had acquired a comprehensive training in the elements of Judaism and who could preach in the vernacular. It was with the object of training such a body of preacher-ministers that Jews' College was established.[140]

Despite its very strong *Ashkenazi* identity, Moses Montefiore had played a major part in supporting the foundation of Jews' College, and *Sephardim* were from the outset associated with its management (as they still are); a distinct training seminary catering for the needs of the Spanish & Portuguese community did not emerge until 1866, when Montefiore established at Ramsgate the Judith Montefiore College.[141] Jews' College, as originally conceived and founded, did not train rabbis; instead, it produced a succession of 'Reverends', complete with clerical dog-collars, who could administer and preach within their congregations but who were in no sense authorities in *halacha* (orthodox Jewish law). It had, originally, another purpose, to act as a grammar school to educate, to university-entrance standard, an Anglo-Jewish middle-class (male) élite; the site of the College—Finsbury Square, north London—was chosen as a fashionable neighbourhood that would attract the parents of such pupils.[142] This part of the scheme drew adverse comment from the start. Traditionalists found fault with the intrusion of secular subjects into the curriculum, but it was from the emancipationist side that the criticism was greatest; David Salomons was opposed to the idea of separate education for Jewish youngsters and argued that such an institution would be bound to act as a barrier to social equality.[143]

Jews' College opened its doors in 1855, but the school that

[139] *JC* (12 Jan. 1849), 109.

[140] I. Harris, *Jews' College Jubilee Volume, 1855–1905* (London, 1906), pp. iv–xii; A. M. Hyamson, *Jews' College, London, 1855–1955* (London, 1955), 15–23.

[141] The Judith Montefiore College was (as might be expected) well endowed, and flourished for a time, but was closed in 1896 following a scandal involving the alleged behaviour of certain of its students; henceforth the *Sephardim* made annual payments to Jews' College, and were represented on its governing body: Hyamson, *Jews' College*, 27, 65–7; C. Bermant, *Troubled Eden* (London, 1969), 207–8.

[142] Schmidt, 'Chief Rabbi Nathan Marcus Adler', 303.

[143] Gartner, 'Emancipation, Social Change and Communal Reconstruction', 102; Salbstein, *Emancipation of the Jews*, 121.

formed part of it failed conspicuously to attract a clientele of sufficient size; it was separated from the College in 1860. The first 'headmaster' of the College, Moses Montefiore's friend Louis Loewe (1809–88), a noted orientalist, later became Principal of the Judith Montefiore College; he was succeeded at Jews' College by the brilliant young rabbinical scholar Barnett Abrahams, 'father' of the *Sephardi Beth Din*; on Abrahams's premature death, in 1863 at the age of 32, the position fell (1865) to Michael Friedlander (1833–1910) who was Principal of Jews' College until 1907. Loewe and Friedlander both held doctorates from German universities and had also been educated in Jewish studies on the Continent; Abrahams, the son of a Polish rabbi, was the first Anglo-Jewish minister of religion to have gained a degree at a British university (University College London).[144] Yet in spite of this talented and appropriate leadership, Jews' College failed to make the impact upon which Nathan Adler had pinned his hopes. In its early years the College itself was unable to attract more than a handful of candidates for the ministry. Most of these came from poor families; ministerial salaries in the mid-nineteenth century generally reflected a lower-middle-class status, and the comparatively high turnover in ministerial positions is probably to be explained, at least in part, by 'congregational stress' resulting from economic factors.[145]

The *Jewish Chronicle* observed in 1890:

> It is useless to ignore the fact that the ministry is not a popular profession with us Jews. Parents of the wealthy class never dream of selecting it as a career for their sons . . . lads who do study for the ministry are almost exclusively drawn from the lower social strata . . . a mere opportunity for bread-winning that is seized upon by poor lads in default of anything better.[146]

The mid-Victorian Anglo-Jewish ministry did produce some excellent preachers, and Jews' College fulfilled a purpose, certainly in relation to the United Synagogue; by 1910, with only two

[144] On Loewe see R. Loewe, 'Louis Loewe: Aide and Confidant' in Lipman and Lipman (eds.), *Century of Moses Montefiore*, 104–17; on Abrahams see *JC* (20 Nov. 1863), 5; and on Friedlander, *JC* (16 Dec. 1910), 14–15.

[145] M. Goulston, 'The Status of the Anglo-Jewish Rabbinate, 1840–1914', *JJS* 10 (1968), 63; Gartner, 'Emancipation, Social Change and Communal Reconstruction', 103.

[146] *JC* (7 Nov. 1890), 13.

exceptions, every senior minister and preacher at the sixteen constituents of the United Synagogue was Jews' College trained.[147] But those with a scholastic bent invariably went abroad to complete their studies, a step made all the more necessary if they wished to obtain *semicha* (the rabbinical diploma). Simeon Singer (1848–1906), of the fashionable New West End Synagogue and author of what became the standard Anglo-Jewish prayer-book, obtained his rabbinical diploma in Vienna in 1890, and seven years later Dr Hermann Gollancz, of the Bayswater Synagogue (also of the United family) was granted his in Galicia.[148] In making these foreign excursions Singer and Gollancz were of course passing judgement on the state of rabbinical scholarship in Britain. But they were in excellent company. The most damaging indictment of the level of religious training given at Jews' College in the nineteenth century was made by none other than Chief Rabbi Nathan Adler himself, who proclaimed his lack of confidence in the College by sending his son Hermann to a *yeshivah* in Prague; there, in 1862, Hermann became a rabbi, and returned to London to act as secretary to his father and to teach at the College he had not attended.[149] In 1879 the school that had formed part of Jews' College was closed, and in the same year Nathan Adler moved into virtual retirement at Brighton. In 1880 the Council of the United Synagogue appointed Hermann 'Delegate' Chief Rabbi; no one, in truth, was more fitted for the uniquely British institution that the Chief Rabbinate had become.

In retrospect the decade of the 1870s might be regarded as the Indian summer of emancipated Anglo-Jewry. By universal consent, conflicts over religious practice and dogma were played down. The affairs of the community were in the hands of a small circle of very wealthy, interrelated families, whom the geneticist Redcliffe Salaman (1874–1955) correctly termed 'a beneficent oligarchy'.[150] Members of this cousinhood were not practising orthodox, but they evinced—certainly in public—a deep respect for orthodoxy, and they were certainly more observant than their counterparts in

[147] *JC* (30 Sept. 1910), 16.

[148] Apple, 'United Synagogue, Religious Founders and Leaders', 20–1, 23.

[149] See A. Schischa, 'Hermann Adler, Yeshivah Bahur, Prague, 1860–1862', in J. M. Shaftesley (ed.), *Remember the Days: Essays in Honour of Cecil Roth* (London, 1966), 241–77.

[150] R. N. Salaman, *Whither Lucien Wolf's Anglo-Jewish Community?* (London, 1953), 19.

Europe and the United States.[151] Very few were attracted to the Reform movement; the political considerations that had led German Jews to embrace Reform never existed in England, with the result that it was possible for the unique form of 'genteel orthodoxy of the United Synagogue' to flourish and grow, whereas in other circumstances it would almost certainly have been crushed.[152]

The oligarchy that governed Anglo-Jewry had become largely *Ashkenazi* in character. Moses Montefiore was almost the last important communal lay leader of the nineteenth century to come from the ranks of the *Sephardim*; the very last, the philanthropist and bullion broker Frederic David Mocatta (1828–1905) managed to belong simultaneously to Bevis Marks and to the Reform synagogue.[153] Montefiore finally retired from the Presidency of the Board of Deputies in 1874, and was succeeded by a nephew Joseph Mayer Montefiore, who had acted for him twice in earlier years. In 1880 the Presidency fell to another of Sir Moses's nephews, the brilliant Queen's Counsel and Liberal MP for Southwark, Arthur Cohen (1829–1914), who held the office until 1895. Arthur was a member of the great extended family of Cohens that included Lionel Louis and Benjamin. He was himself not an observant Jew, but he spoke scathingly of Reform Judaism and he took his obligations to orthodoxy very seriously (he was a Vice-President of the Council of Jews' College for twenty-six years), a fact reflected in his decision to resign the Presidency of the Board of Deputies when one of his daughters married out.[154]

Towards the issue of Jewish supra-national identity the cousinhood was, at bottom, ambivalent. The denial of such an identity had been a cardinal feature of the campaign for emancipation. In 1878 Hermann Adler reaffirmed this view:

> ever since the conquest of Palestine by the Romans we have ceased to be a body politic: we are citizens of the country in which we dwell. We are simply Englishmen, or Frenchmen, or Germans, as the case may be . . . Judaism has no political bearing whatever.[155]

[151] T. M. Endelman, 'Communal Solidarity among the Jewish Élite of Victorian London', *Victorian Studies*, 28 (1984–5), 497.

[152] Ibid. 503.

[153] On Mocatta see A. Mocatta, 'Frederic David Mocatta, 1828–1905', *TJHSE* 23 (1971), 1–10.

[154] See generally I. Finestein, 'Arthur Cohen, Q. C. (1829–1914)', in Shaftesley, *Remember the Days*, 279–302, and Lucy Cohen, *Arthur Cohen: A Memoir* (London, 1919), *passim*.

[155] H. Adler, 'Jews and Judaism: A Rejoinder', *Nineteenth Century* (July 1878), 134.

This view had been put forward countless times during the emancipation controversy, but it had not gone unchallenged from within the community. In 1847 the Jewish Association for the Removal of Civil and Religious Disabilities had declared 'Far be it from us . . . to renounce our faith in prophecy or to resign our hope in the eventual restoration of Israel'.[156] The orthodox prayer-books were not modified to exclude references to the hope of a restoration of Zion, and the practice of donating money to support Jews living in Palestine was not discouraged. When a British branch of the *Chovevi Zion* (Lovers of Zion) movement was inaugurated, in July 1891, to support the establishment of Jewish colonies in the Holy Land, Hermann Adler became an early contributor.[157]

The cosmopolitanism inherent in Jewish identity at this time impinged upon British Jewry in a much larger sense, however, through the need to alleviate the sufferings of Jewish communities living in societies less enlightened than that of the United Kingdom. Not only was such intervention a religious duty; it had become—especially through the well-publicized activities of Moses Montefiore—a source of communal pride. It had also become institutionalized, initially through the subscriptions paid by individual British Jews to the Alliance Israélite Universelle, founded in 1860 as an international agency to protect Jewish interests worldwide. By the beginning of the 1870s the Alliance had a membership of 13,370, of whom 382 resided in England and the British colonies.[158] French Jews did not constitute a majority of the membership of the Alliance, but its headquarters were in Paris and the French, in practice, dominated its proceedings. In March 1871 the British announced that they had determined to set up their own associated but independent body, the Anglo-Jewish Association, with the economist Professor Jacob Waley (1821–73) as its first President and the Hebraist—and Reform minister—Albert Löwy (1816–98) as its secretary.[159] The inability of the Alliance to function properly

[156] M. Margoliouth, *The History of the Jews in Great Britain*, (3 vols., London, 1851), ii. 263–4.

[157] Archives of the *Chovevi Zion* Association in England, CZA, A2/138: Hermann Adler to E. d'Avigdor, 12 Sept. 1891.

[158] Z. Szajkowski, 'Conflicts in the Alliance Israélite Universelle and the founding of the Anglo-Jewish Association, the Vienna Allianz and the Hilfsverein', *JSS* 19 (1957), 30.

[159] Council Minute Book of the Anglo-Jewish Association, vol. 1 (1871–81), Anglo-Jewish Archives, London, AJ/95/ADD (now transferred to the Parkes Library, University of Southampton).

during the Franco-Prussian War (1870–1) was used as the pretext for this initiative, but it was almost certainly not the true reason: the Germans did not break away until after hostilities had been concluded.

In addition to the undoubted continuing irritation at French control of Alliance business, a number of other factors played a part. The first related to a feeling of unease that Anglo-Jewish endeavours in the diplomatic sphere were seen to be part of an international movement. The efforts made by British Jews on behalf of disadvantaged co-religionists overseas had to be repatriated, as it were, and brought fully under Anglo-Jewish control. At the same time the Board of Deputies—described by the founders of the Association as 'a mere local institution'—was not felt to be prestigious enough or wealthy enough to undertake work of an international dimension; it was also argued that its constitution militated against swift action to deal with foreign emergencies.[160] The Anglo-Jewish Association was formed (an American correspondent was told in 1873) from 'the conviction that we English Jews as a body did not sufficiently identify ourselves with the mass of our oppressed brethren in imperfectly civilised countries, that the feeling of oneness was not sufficiently intense among us and that we consequently lagged behind in the discharge of the sacred duties which brother owes to brother'.[161]

Beyond this concern, however, lay the deep desire of Reform Jews—still excluded by Montefiore's fiat from participation in the work of the Board of Deputies—to make their views felt and their voices heard as spokesmen for British Jewry. The Anglo-Jewish Association was 'open to all Jews who accept as their guiding principle loyalty to their faith and their country'.[162] Abraham Benisch, one of the prime movers in the foundation of the Association, made no secret of his desire to see in it an apparatus

[160] *JC* (31 Mar. 1871), 11; J. M. Shaftesley, 'Dr. Abraham Benisch as a newspaper editor', *TJHSE* 21 (1962–7), 220–2.

[161] Szajkowski, 'Conflicts', 31.

[162] Quoted in Bermant, *Troubled Eden*, 107. In 1943 David Mowshowitch (1887–1957), formerly Lucien Wolf's secretary and then with the Board of Deputies, compiled an unpublished study of 'The Board of Deputies and the Anglo-Jewish Association', in which he drew attention to the importance of non-orthodox elements in the Association at its foundation, and commented that 'in the Anglo-Jewish Association this wing of the community began concentrating rather than in the Board': Archives of the Yivo Institute for Jewish Research, New York, Mowshowitch Collection, folder 153.

for the reconciliation of orthodoxy with Reform in Britain.[163] Its seven Vice-Presidents included a number of leading Reformers, notably Sir Francis Goldsmid and Sir Julian Goldsmid (1838–96), Liberal MP for Rochester, who became its President in 1886.

The forty-two members of the Association's Council embraced some of the most notable Anglo-Jewish figures of the day—four MPs, the *Haham*, Revd A. L. Green, Nathan Joseph, Professor D. W. Marks, F. D. Mocatta, a Rothschild.[164] The Association might indeed have become a rival to the Board of Deputies, offering in terms of prestige and professionalism what it lacked in terms of the legitimacy that democratic representation bestows. At first the Board of Deputies held aloof from it. But after its very effective intervention during the Balkan crisis of the late 1870s—and perhaps in an effort to limit the scope of its work to the international scene—the Board came to terms with it, and agreed in 1878 to the formation of a Conjoint Foreign Committee, consisting of seven representatives from the Board and seven from the Association. This Committee, dominated by the Association, constituted an Anglo-Jewish ministry of foreign affairs; its deliberations were conducted in secret and its conclusions were reported to neither of its constituent bodies.[165]

The Balkan crisis thus marked a watershed in the institutional history of British Jewry. It also had a far-reaching political significance. Benjamin Disraeli was now Prime Minister. His policy of refusing to allow the fact that there had been Turkish atrocities against Bulgarian Christians to result in any considerable increase of Russian influence in the region enraged Gladstone, who emerged from his first retirement to lead a crusade against the Ottoman Empire in the Balkans, and against Disraeli's threatened military intervention to force the Russians to yield up advantages won by the Treaty of San Stefano (March 1878). It never occurred to Gladstone to consider the position of Balkan Jews, whom Turkish rule had allowed 'a degree of tolerance far beyond anything conceded by Orthodox Christianity'.[166] Partly for this reason, and partly because Jews had considerable investments in Turkey, and

[163] Shaftesley, 'Benisch', 221.

[164] Anglo-Jewish Association, *Centenary Review 1871–1971* (London, 1971), 4.

[165] E. C. Black, *The Social Politics of Anglo-Jewry 1880–1920* (Oxford, 1988), 45.

[166] R. T. Shannon, *Gladstone and the Bulgarian Agitation* (London, 1963), 198–9; see also *The Times* (23 Dec. 1879), 6.

were loath to see them sacrificed on the altar of Gladstone's conscience, most British Jews supported Disraeli's Eastern policy, and actively opposed Gladstone's Bulgarian Agitation.

This Agitation coincided with the Buckinghamshire by-election (held on 21 September 1876), caused by Disraeli's elevation to the peerage. Buckinghamshire was Rothschild country. The attempts of the Liberals to make the Agitation a major issue in the campaign so enraged the Rothschild family that they were 'practically in open revolt', and had, by the beginning of October, 'gone Tory altogether'.[167] The *Daily Telegraph* (owned by the Jewish Levy-Lawson family) swung its influence behind Disraeli's policy.[168] While the Anglo-Jewish Association (later in collaboration with the Board of Deputies) petitioned the British Government on the need to secure the civil and political rights of Jews in newly independent Balkan states, the aged Lionel de Rothschild mobilized the considerable resources of his extended European family, and those of his German-Jewish banking associate Gerson von Bleichröder (Bismarck's banker and adviser) to influence proceedings at the Congress of Berlin called to resolve the crisis, and of which Bismarck was President.[169] The result was that the western European delegates at Berlin refused to sign a final treaty until Jewish anxieties had been allayed. The Treaty of Berlin, when signed in July 1878, thus contained definite guarantees of civil and political rights for the Jews of Romania, Bulgaria, and the Danubian principalities.[170]

For British Jewry this represented a very considerable victory; it was little wonder that when Disraeli returned in triumph from Berlin, Moses Montefiore (despite his ninety-four years) was the first to greet him at Charing Cross railway station.[171] But for the relationship between British Jewry and Liberalism the affair had an altogether more sombre significance. To begin with, the Bulgarian Agitation had had unpleasant anti-Jewish overtones, in which Disraeli's own ethnic origins were exploited to the full, particularly

[167] Alderman, *Jewish Community*, 37.

[168] *JC* (20 Oct. 1876), 458.

[169] Ibid. (29 Dec. 1876), 619; J. Cang, 'Anglo-Jewry and the Berlin Congress', *JC* (22 Jan. 1954), 15; Count Corti, *The Reign of the House of Rothschild*, trans. B. Lunn and B. Lunn (London, 1928), 449; see also F. Stern, *Gold and Iron: Bismarck, Bleichröder, and the Building of the German Empire* (London, 1977), 377–8.

[170] Cang, 'Anglo-Jewry and the Berlin Congress', 15.

[171] P. Goodman, *Moses Montefiore* (Philadelphia, 1925), 221.

by Liberal members of the intelligentsia such as Gladstone's friend and future biographer, John Morley.[172] Worse still, Gladstone himself had unleashed the full fury of his oratorical powers against Jews and Jewish influence. 'I deeply deplore', he told Leopold Gluckstein, author of a pamphlet on *The Eastern Question and the Jews*, 'the manner in which, what I may call Judaic sympathies, beyond as well as within the circle of professed Judaism, are now acting on the question of the East.'[173]

By the time the Berlin Treaty had been signed, little was left of the close relationship of the previous generation between Anglo-Jewry and Liberalism. Francis Goldsmid refused to support his party on the Eastern question.[174] John Simon, who had initially been supportive of Gladstone, turned against him at the end of 1879, after Gladstone had declined to speak out in favour of better treatment for Jews living under Christian rule in Romania.[175] Gladstone's refusal, when Prime Minister in the early 1880s, to become moved by the plight of Russian Jewry, or to get up an 'agitation' on its behalf, confirmed the coldness of the new relationship. Meanwhile, the secession of the Rothschilds had turned a great many City Jews into Conservatives, and seems to have acted as a green light to provincial Jewries also to demonstrate their support for Conservatism. This happened at Liverpool in 1876 and three years later at Sheffield, where the Conservative candidate won the support of Jews specifically because of issues of foreign policy.[176]

Other factors, coincidentally, played their part in destroying the old Jewish–Liberal relationship. The intrusion of radical philosophies into the Liberal policy-making process in the 1880s affected Jewish along with non-Jewish middle-class susceptibilities, and the exodus of many of the propertied classes from the Liberal Party, via Liberal Unionism, to the Conservatives, was one in which Jews were naturally involved. In 1886 Sir Julian Goldsmid and Ferdinand de Rothschild became Liberal Unionists; after 1886 no Rothschild was elected to the House of Commons as a Liberal. Any doubt which might have remained concerning the propriety of Jews

[172] R. Blake, *Disraeli* (London, 1966), 604–7; Alderman, *Jewish Community*, 38–9.

[173] *JC* (13 Oct. 1876), 438.

[174] Marks and Löwy, *Francis Henry Goldsmid*, 136.

[175] *The Times* (22 Dec. 1879), 8.

[176] *JC* (27 Oct. 1876), 469; (19 Dec.), 6, 10; (19 Aug. 1881), 9.

becoming Conservative supporters had in any case been removed in 1885, when Lionel Louis Cohen fought and won the North Paddington seat in the Conservative interest.

Lionel Louis Cohen was not of course the first Jewish Conservative MP, but he was the first to have held high office in the Jewish community, and the first to have held high office in the Tory party, being a Vice-President of the National Union of Conservative Associations. He had, by his own admission, spent the best years of his life fighting 'the domination so long exercised by the so-called Liberal party over the Jews, and the monopoly of the Jewish vote which they have exercised and even yet claim to enjoy'.[177] His boldness in standing for Parliament was indeed symbolic of the confidence that the Jewish middle classes had found in and through the exercise of their political rights. The path that he had chosen was a logical outcome of emancipation, and it was a path that was followed even by members of the Jewish clergy. Professor D. W. Marks was a Conservative sympathizer, as was Chief Rabbi Hermann Adler, whose public support for Lord Salisbury's Government at the time of the Boer War went far beyond a mere concern for the safety of British troops.[178]

Quite naturally, Amy Levy's anti-hero, *Reuben Sachs*, the Jew of Lancaster Gate, became a Conservative MP. 'Are we [one writer asked the readers of the *Jewish Chronicle* in 1888], because there was once a Liberal party, to bow down and worship Gladstone—the great Minister who was too Christian in his charity, too Russian in his proclivities, to raise voice or finger' to protect Russian Jewry?[179] The answer, at least from the Jewish middle classes, was a definite negative. In 1880 the Jewish contingent in the House of Commons was overwhelmingly Liberal (four Liberals as against one Tory); by 1900 it had become substantially Conservative (three Liberals but seven Unionists). The umbilical cord that had seemed to tie British Jewry to Liberalism had been cut at last, and with that act of severance a central characteristic of the drama of emancipation had been relegated from the present to the past.

177 Ibid. (1 July 1887), 7; the quotation is from a letter written on 8 Feb. 1874.
178 Alderman, *Jewish Community*, 42–4.
179 *JC* (7 Dec. 1888), 7.

3

Immigration and Social Control

THE world of emancipated British Jewry was turned upside down by the waves of immigration of Jews from Russia and eastern Europe that beat upon the shores of Britain in the quarter-century following the assassination of Tsar Alexander II. There was no facet of Anglo-Jewish life which was not affected by this immigration, just as there was no communal institution which could avoid responding, positively or negatively, to its imperatives. Ultimately the State itself was compelled to take notice. The Jewish immigrants changed the shape of the British polity as surely as they changed the structure of British Jewry: the Jewish experience and the British experience merged and affected each other in a manner far more central than that offered by emancipation itself.

As we have seen, England continued to attract Jewish migrants in the 1860s and 1870s; their motives in coming appear to have been mainly economic, though political unrest in central Europe, especially in Poland in the 1860s, added a momentum of its own; in his estimate, originally published in the *Jewish Chronicle* in 1883, Joseph Jacobs claimed that in the period 1865–81 about 12,000 Russian and Polish Jews, and about 7,000 from Germany and The Netherlands, had settled in England.[1] An estimate of 1871, prepared by the Statistical Committee of the Board of Guardians, had put the Jewish population of London at around 35,000.[2] In 1876 the *Jewish Chronicle* used the frequency of Jewish interments to arrive at a London population of just under 40,000, and a total Jewish population in Britain of 51,250.[3] Jacobs's estimate of 1882 was of a London Jewry of about 46,000; the figure for the country

[1] J. Jacobs, *Studies in Jewish Statistics* (London, 1891), 20.

[2] V. D. Lipman, *Social History of the Jews in England 1850–1950* (London, 1954), 65.

[3] *JC* (2 June 1876), 138.

as a whole was probably then around 60,000.[4] Dr Lipman has demonstrated that, on the assumption that the Jewish birth rate in mainland Britain, 1851–81, was identical with the non-Jewish, the total of British Jewry in 1880 would have been nearer 50,000 than 60,000.[5] His suggestion, that the difference is to be explained by immigration, is consistent with the picture painted by Joseph Jacobs of the dynamic of Jewish immigration to Britain over the previous two decades.

Jacobs's researches also provide the best guide we have to the social composition of London Jewry on the eve of the great immigrations. Using a variety of statistical indicators, Jacobs produced the rough socio-economic and topographical analysis of London Jewry in 1882 shown in Table 3.1. For the purpose of class analysis, Jacobs offered the typology shown in Table 3.2.

Many assumptions were built into this analysis, but the broad trends reflected therein have never been disputed. Almost a quarter of the Jews of London were paupers, and another fifth (each family unit of which earned about £100 a year) were numbered among the poorer working-class families of the capital, with an annual income that fell within the upper and lower limits outlined by Charles Booth as defining 'higher class' labourers.[6] But over two-fifths were in the middle-income bracket; over half London Jewry, in fact, were either prosperous or exceedingly well-to-do. There had thus been a significant alteration in the social composition of London Jewry (and almost certainly of British Jewry as a whole) since the mid-century: the poorer sections had contracted as a proportion of the whole (from over to under a half) and the middle-income groups had expanded (from a third to about a half). It was for this expanding middle class that the United Synagogue catered, erecting in north, west, and north-west London imposing ecclesiastical edifices in which the alumni of Jews' College could ply a uniquely English brand of Judaism, within a liturgical and organizational framework that had come to resemble the class distinctions then to be found in the Anglican Church.

In these synagogues seats were priced according to their proximity to the Ark (containing the *Torah* Scrolls) and the *Bimah*, the platform from which the service was conducted and on which

4 C. Roth, *A History of the Jews in England* (2nd edn., Oxford, 1949), 267.

5 Lipman, *Social History*, 65.

6 Ibid. 78; Booth's upper limit for this class was £130 p.a., and his lower, £91.

TABLE 3.1. *London Jewry in 1882*

	Families	Individuals
West London		
Professional and retired professional	300	1,200
'Rich merchants'	1,200	5,400
North, South, and East London		
Merchants	800	3,600
Professional and retired	200	800
London overall		
Shopkeepers	3,000	15,000
Petty traders (applying for casual relief)	2,000	8,000
Servants and assistants	—	1,000
Board of Guardians' cases		
Casuals	1,884	7,911
Chronic	234	
Other paupers	—	2,242
Russian refugees (recently arrived)	—	947
TOTAL		46,100

Source: J. Jacobs, *Studies in Jewish Statistics* (London, 1891), 13.

TABLE 3.2. *London Jewry by Class and Income, 1882*

Class	Numbers	Percentage %	Average Income £ p.a.
Upper	6,600	14.6	367
Middle	19,400	42.2	54
Lower	9,000	19.6	26
Pauper	11,000	23.6	12

Note: Upper: professional people and rich merchants; Middle: merchants with private houses; shopkeepers; Lower: petty traders and servants.

Source: *JC* (2 Feb. 1883), 10–11.

the Scroll or Scrolls were read. It was the opinion of the *Jewish Chronicle*, shortly after the establishment of the United Synagogue, that seat rentals in synagogues were more expensive than in English churches; the remedy proposed, however, was not to bring about a drastic lowering of rentals, but merely to lower them sufficiently to cater for 'the interests of the respectable middle classes'.[7] In the founding City synagogues, and the East London (admitted to the United Synagogue 1877) there was some lowering of rentals; in 1880 the average rental, including burial contributions, in the East London stood at £3. 7*s*. 3*d*. for the year; in the North London Synagogue the figure was £7. 1*s*. 8*d*., while in the Central, Bayswater, and the New West End the sums were over £11, £12, and £13 respectively.[8]

Rentals of this magnitude meant that only in the East London could working-class Jews afford to become seat-holders, and that even in that synagogue only the most highly paid members of the manual working classes could have joined: high seat rentals, one 'working man' told the *Chronicle*, were quite beyond the means of the 'genuine, honest and independent working class'.[9] Worshippers from these classes could of course *attend* any synagogue they pleased; generally (but not necessarily at the most crowded times of the religious calendar) they would be permitted to occupy such seats as happened to be vacant. This status was both unedifying and precarious, as a 'poor Jew' described in 1874:

> I am a regular attendant at one of our large synagogues. That is, I am what is styled by some of the petty officials a 'squatter'. I occupy, nearly all the year round, the seat of a gentleman who seldom has occasion to pray . . . I pray for him—my first prayer on entering the synagogue being that he might not come there that day . . . At the time of *Rosh Hashannah* [New Year] and *Yom Kippur* [Day of Atonement], of course I cannot occupy a seat . . . I am too poor to rent a seat . . . Why, then, should I be shut out entirely from publicly joining in the worship of God at the most solemn time of the year merely because I have the double misfortune to be poor and religious?[10]

Why, indeed? Class distinctions in constituents of the United Synagogue, however, went further than mere pecuniary considerations

[7] *JC* (28 Oct. 1870), 8.

[8] S. Sharot, 'Religious Change in Native Orthodoxy in London, 1870–1914: The Synagogue Service', *JJS* 15 (1973), 61–3.

[9] *JC* (17 Feb. 1888), 7.

[10] Ibid. (4 Sept. 1874), 367.

might have permitted. Poor women might find themselves refused admittance to the Ladies' Gallery, while men who wished to be called to the Reading of the Law on the *Bimah* had to wear a 'high hat'—the outward sign of upper- and middle-class respectability.[11]

For most members of the United Synagogue, the act of synagogue attendance itself was felt to be much more of a social than a religious obligation. Belonging to a synagogue was in any case more important than attending it. When the *British Weekly* carried out its census of religious worship in October 1886, it reported that only between 10 and 15 per cent of the total Jewish populations of west and north-west London attended synagogue on a Sabbath morning; the percentage attending on a weekday was very low throughout London.[12]

The services which were attended were of course orthodox in form, but their content—and length—were the subjects of constant criticism, particularly from those whose refined sensibilities were jarred on discovering the meanings of some of the prayers they were being asked to recite. An Association for Effecting a Modification in the Liturgy of the German Jews, formed in 1875, had as its object the modification and omission of certain parts of the prayers on account of 'the objectionable nature of their contents, unintelligibility of language, repetitions, [and] mode of recitation'.[13] Although the Association made little headway by itself, its aims were taken up elsewhere, and culminated in 1879, in a conference of United synagogues, the object of which was to present a list of suggested liturgical reforms for the sanction of Chief Rabbi Nathan Adler. Particular objection was taken to the *piyuttim*, medieval compositions which expressed, *inter alia*, desire for the blood of Jewish martyrs to be avenged.[14] This conference, chaired by Lionel Louis Cohen, reported in March 1880. In presenting its proposals it was disarmingly frank:

A few centuries ago, in nearly every country of Europe, Jewish worship was barely tolerated . . . It is consequently not surprising, if prayers first composed under the influence of feelings of resentment engendered by

[11] *JC* (22 Sept. 1882), 5; (20 Aug. 1886), 4.

[12] *British Weekly* (5 Nov. 1886), 3; (12 Nov.), 2–3; (26 Nov.), 16–17. See also S. Sharot, 'Secularization, Judaism and Anglo-Jewry', *A Sociological Yearbook of Religion in Britain*, 4 (London, 1971), 133–5.

[13] *JC* (2 Apr. 1875), 852; (30 Apr.), 71.

[14] Ibid. (27 June 1879), 9–10.

persecution, reflect traces of those bitter feelings . . . The present juncture appears opportune for the consideration of a moderate, judicious and temperate movement, in the direction of simpler services.[15]

Accordingly, the delegates asked for the removal of most *piyuttim* from the daily prayers, with the exception of some recited on the New Year and the Day of Atonement. They took exception also to the inclusion in penitential prayers of appeals for the intercession of angels, and then turned their attention to the presence, in the prayer-books, of passages from the *Talmud*, the sixty-three volumes of Oral Law upon which much of the daily life of the orthodox Jew is based. The *Jewish Chronicle* explained matters to the Chief Rabbi thus:

To-day the Jewish man of business . . . has no taste . . . for those Talmudic studies . . . The average Jew of to-day does not understand the language of those Talmudic extracts . . . The time has gone by . . . for the study of Talmudic literature in the synagogue. The synagogue, as everyone knows, was once literally the *Schul'*, the House of Study. It is now simply and solely the House of Prayer. Passages from the Talmud which were formerly in their place in the prayer book are, consequently, out of place in it now.[16]

Nathan Adler did not like any of these proposals, and refused to sanction some of them, such as the omission of *Talmudic* passages. Reluctantly, however, he gave way to the demands for the removal of *piyuttim* and other passages; his agreement to these modifications was said to have been partly responsible for his virtual retirement from the Chief Rabbinate that same year, 1880.[17] His son, Hermann, proved more accommodating. In 1889 a committee formed to oversee the building of a United synagogue in Hampstead asked for further modifications of ritual; other synagogues (the New West End, Central, and Borough) lent their support to this approach. On some matters Hermann stood firm, but on others—notably the shortening of services, the omission of the ceremonial recitation of the Priestly Blessings on festivals, and the introduction of verbal consents by the bride and bridegroom in the marriage service—he gave way.[18]

[15] Ibid. (5 Mar. 1880), 11.

[16] Ibid. (19 Mar. 1880), 10.

[17] Sharot, 'The Synagogue Service', 65; V. D. Lipman, 'The Age of Emancipation, 1815–1880', in id. (ed.), *Three Centuries of Anglo-Jewish History* (Cambridge, 1961), 85.

[18] *JC* (1 July 1892), 17–20; R. Apple, *The Hampstead Synagogue 1892–1967* (London, 1967), 42.

These modifications, and others which neither of the Adlers sanctioned but in which they appear to have acquiesced (such as the holding of 'confirmation' ceremonies for boys and girls, and of choral weddings, and the increased use of English for certain prayers and psalms) could just about be reconciled with orthodoxy in its loosest sense, though they would have had no place in the synagogues of Russia and Poland: the rabbis of old had not approved of them, but neither had they specifically prohibited them. Nor were they adopted uniformly by all United Synagogue constituents.[19] But on the issue of mixed choirs a watershed was reached. Strictly speaking, orthodox Judaism forbids men to hear the voices of women singing in synagogue, this being considered a form of lewdness.[20] At the ceremony which accompanied the laying of the foundation-stone at Hampstead (13 March 1892), Hermann Adler had refused to permit the use of a mixed choir; but the founding committee knew that he would not prohibit such an innovation once the synagogue had been established; this was indeed the case.[21] Four years later a mixed choir was introduced at the East London Synagogue; protesters seceded to form a quite distinct Stepney Orthodox Synagogue.[22] A mixed choir had already been introduced at the New West End Synagogue in 1895, and the practice was also adopted at the Brondesbury Synagogue, admitted to the United Synagogue in 1905.[23]

The United Synagogue was, as it remained for many years, a broad church. 'The content of the services', Dr Sharot has observed, 'remained predominantly traditional . . . however, the form . . . displayed a high degree of religious acculturation.'[24] Some United Synagogue constituents, particularly in the City, rejected the reforms of which others, in the suburbs, took full advantage. In

[19] Sharot, 'The Synagogue Service', 67–8.

[20] Babylonian Talmud, Tractate *Berachoth*, 24*a*.

[21] Apple, *Hampstead Synagogue*, 105–6.

[22] *JC* (19 June 1908), 16; Sharot, 'The Synagogue Service', 68. The Stepney Orthodox Synagogue became affiliated to the Federation of Synagogues in Mar. 1902.

[23] *JC* (24 May 1895), 16; (5 May 1911), 26.

[24] Sharot, 'The Synagogue Service', 69; for a contemporary critique of United Synagogue orthodoxy, written *c.*1886–7 by a disciple of Samson Raphael Hirsch, Solomon Herz, see J. Carlebach, 'The Impact of German Jews on Anglo-Jewry—Orthodoxy, 1850–1950', in W. E. Mosse *et al.* (eds.), *Second Chance: Two Centuries of German-Speaking Jews in the United Kingdom* (Tübingen, 1990), 410–13.

these latter communities, the middle classes who formed the core of United Synagogue membership demanded shorter, simpler ritual, characterized less by devotion than by decorum. If choir boys could not be obtained locally, then let them be paid to ride to the synagogue on the Sabbath (thus desecrating it, of course), because (the warden of the St John's Wood Synagogue explained in 1900) 'the choir was the chief attraction of the Synagogue'; the Board of Management at Brondesbury warned in 1906 that 'the management of the Synagogue . . . in our opinion *must* be a failure without a Choir'.[25]

Given this diversity, Hermann Adler attempted to steer a middle course, and his tolerance of practices which he must have known would be condemned by the standards of East European orthodoxy did at least hold together a Jewry which might otherwise have succumbed to the lure of Reformism on the German or American models. This was perhaps his greatest success. Simeon Singer's *Authorised Daily Prayer Book of the United Hebrew Congregations of the British Empire*, issued, with an elegant English translation, under the authority of Nathan Marcus Adler in 1890, defined parameters for the orthodox synagogue service that rapidly became accepted throughout the English-speaking world. Beyond them, and the doctrine and dogma which they reflected, Hermann Adler would not go. His veto of the appointment of the Revd Morris Joseph as the first Minister at Hampstead became a *cause célèbre*. Joseph (1848–1930), who described his Judaism as 'liberal conservative', was wanted by the scions of Hampstead, but his outspoken views on certain aspects of orthodoxy, and especially his condemnation of the 'mere thought' of the sacrificial rite as practised in Temple times ('the sooner such outworn, misused elements are eliminated from religion, the better') had damned him even in the eyes of Hermann Adler.[26] Joseph agreed, if appointed at Hampstead, to accept the ecclesiastical jurisdiction of the Chief Rabbi, but demanded complete freedom in the pulpit; Adler interviewed him, questioned him as to his views, and declared

[25] *JC* (18 May 1900), 24; Archives of the United Synagogue, Council Minute Book, vol. 3 (1903–8), 136–7: Brondesbury Synagogue to P. Ornstein, 4 Mar. 1906.

[26] M. Joseph, *The Ideal in Judaism and other Sermons preached during 1890–91–92* (London, 1893), 43, 48.

them, and him, to be unacceptable because contrary to the norms of 'traditional Judaism'.[27]

The letter Joseph subsequently wrote to the *Jewish Chronicle*, in which (having referred *en passant* to his approval of the use of the organ at Sabbath services) he stated his opinion that 'progress . . . is impossible within the confines of the Synagogue as by Rabbinical law established' must have amply comforted Adler in his decision. Morris Joseph obtained appointment as successor to Professor Marks at the West London Reform Synagogue (1893), where prayers for the restoration of sacrifices were no longer said. Hampstead appointed Aaron Asher Green (1860–1933, nephew of A. L. Green of the Central Synagogue), who, if he could not boast a particularly scholarly let alone original mind, possessed qualities as a preacher, pastoral worker, and eccentric Englishman that evidently endeared him to his flock.[28]

When Hermann Adler became Delegate Chief Rabbi on his father's retirement the centre of gravity of British Jewry still lay very much, therefore, with those middle-class Jews for whom the many varieties of United Synagogue Judaism were the religious models and the West End, Maida Vale, and Hampstead (or their provincial equivalents) the geographical goals. This delicate and finely balanced edifice was thrust into violent tremor by 'the demographic revolution of the Jewish people'.[29]

Between 1881 and 1914 about 2.5 million Jews from eastern Europe moved west. Most—about two millions—settled in the United States of America (dubbed in Yiddish the *Goldene Medina*, the Golden Land), the magnet which attracted so many of Europe's underprivileged and oppressed. Only about 150,000 settled in the British Isles, and it seems a safe assumption that many of these did not originally intend their stay to be permanent.[30] Britain—specifically England—was merely a stopping place on the way to America: a point of arrival at Grimsby or Tilbury or Newcastle or Hull, a cross-country train journey, and then a point of departure at Liverpool. The fact that it was often cheaper to travel to America via England than directly from Hamburg was well known; the

[27] H. Adler to F. Lyon, 19 May 1892, quoted in Apple, *Hampstead Synagogue*, 25.

[28] See generally Apple, *Hampstead Synagogue*, ch. 4.

[29] L. P. Gartner, 'Jewish Migrants en Route from Europe to North America: Traditions and Realities', *Jewish History*, 1/2 (Autumn 1986), 49.

[30] L. Kochan, 'Jews on the Move', *Listener* (27 May 1971), 677.

periods of frantic price-cutting in which shipping companies indulged on the North Atlantic run, from English ports, added its own compelling reason for breaking the journey in this way.[31]

But not all emigrants had the money to pay for their trans-Atlantic journey in one go; in that case, or if their cash simply ran out, they would seek whatever opportunities were available in England to earn a livelihood.

> Their goal is America [it was explained in 1886], and they stop en route in London. Sometimes they spend all they have in coming to London, and have no means to travel farther. Hence they remain here a short while until they learn a trade and save enough money to journey to the land of their choice.[32]

Inevitably, however, and without any advanced planning, a sojourn that was intended to be temporary could easily evolve into a permanent settlement. In this context it is important to remember that most emigrants from eastern Europe were not, in the narrow sense, political refugees or, in the narrow sense, the victims of persecution. Most came from Lithuania and White Russia, where there was comparatively little anti-Jewish violence. Of course, the Russian pogroms that followed the assassination of Alexander II, and which were renewed and intensified between 1882 and 1889, and again between 1902 and 1906, turned the trickle of Jewish refugees from Russia that had been observed before 1880 into a flood; restrictions imposed by the Russian authorities on Jewish residence, the forcing of Jews off the land while they were prohibited from living in cities, the expulsion of Jews from Moscow in 1891, all made it virtually impossible for most Russian Jews to participate in normal economic life.

In the west, pogroms and persecutions were regarded as the basic causes of Jewish emigration. In truth the picture was much more complex. The overriding reason for Jewish emigration from eastern

[31] Report of the Royal Commission on Alien Immigration, *PP* 1903, ix [Cd. 1742], minutes 16285–6; G. Halpern, *Die Jüdischen Arbeiter in London* (Berlin, 1903), 15; L. P. Gartner, *The Jewish Immigrant in England, 1870–1914* (London, 1960), 36. During the 'Atlantic Rate War', 1902–4, the price of a ticket from England to America fell from £6. 10*s*. 0*d*. to just £2.

[32] *HaYom* (24 Aug. 1886), quoted in Gartner, 'Jewish Migrants', 53. See also T. B. Eyges, 'Zikhroines fun die Yiddishe Arbeter Bavegung in London, England' (Yiddish; 'Memoirs of the Jewish Labour Movement in London, England') (MS in the Archives of the Yivo Institute, New York).

Europe to England was economic.[33] During the nineteenth century the Jewish population of the Russian Empire increased from one to over six millions.[34] Given the ever more onerous restrictions on Jewish life, this burgeoning population sought better prospects elsewhere. But the towns to which they were drawn could not support them; the flow was driven further west, and, eventually, overseas. Nor did this flow originate only in Russia or Russian Poland. The Jews of Galicia (then part of the Habsburg Empire) were politically emancipated in 1867 and were relatively persecution-free thereafter; but Jews emigrated from Galicia in greater proportion than they did from Russia.[35] From Romania, in 1899–1900, came a stream of *fusgayers* (walkers), a spontaneous march across Europe by young Jews searching to escape from persecution, famine, and hopelessness.[36]

The period of mass immigration of Jews from eastern Europe to Britain is conveniently dated from 1881; but given that there had been immigration before, the notion of a 'flood' was not appreciated at first. The famine in north-east Russia in 1869–70 had brought some migrants to Britain; young Jewish men, seeking to escape service in the Russian army during the war with Turkey in 1875–6, also made their way to England, where they found employment in the clothing industry in London and as waterproofers in Manchester.[37] The 1870s also brought to London some Russo-Jewish intellectuals, socialists such as Aaron Liebermann (1875) and Morris Winchevsky (the pen-name of L. Benzion Novochovitch, 1879) as well as some notable Russo-Jewish clerics, including Zvi Hirsch Dainow, a popular *maggid* (preacher) who was persuaded to use his oratorical powers against the socialists, and Rabbi Ya'acov Reinowitz (1818–93), who came to England in 1875 to visit his son-in-law Rabbi Susman Cohen, in Manchester, and whom Nathan Marcus Adler had the good sense to appoint as a *Dayan* to his *Beth Din*.[38]

[33] N. W Geldshteyn, *Di Idishe Wirtschaft in London* (Yiddish; *The Jewish Economy in London*) (Vilna, 1907), 1; and see V. D. Lipman, *A History of the Jews in Britain since 1858* (Leicester, 1990), 44.

[34] Gartner, 'Jewish Migrants', 50.

[35] Ibid. 54.

[36] Z. Szajkowski, 'Jewish Emigration Policy in the Period of the Rumanian "Exodus"', *Jewish Social Studies* 13/1 (Jan. 1951), 47–70.

[37] Gartner, *Jewish Immigrant*, 40.

[38] On Dainow see ibid. 105; on Reinowitz, the model for 'Reb Shmuel' in Israel Zangwill's *Dreamers of the Ghetto* (London, 1898) see *JC* (19 May 1893), 8.

The number of cases on the books of the Board of Guardians in London fluctuated between 2,000 or so at the beginning of the 1870s to over 2,500 by the end of the decade; in 1882 it reached almost 3,000 and in 1886, for the first time, it exceeded 4,000.[39] But these figures did not reflect the true extent to which the influx of Jewish refugees had thrown new burdens upon the Anglo-Jewish community. At the beginning of 1882, to deal with what was regarded as a grave but short-term emergency, a miscellany of the conventionally good and the indisputably great, including the Archbishop of Canterbury, Cardinal Manning, and Matthew Arnold, were persuaded by Baron Henry de Worms to support a great public meeting at the Mansion House, presided over by the Lord Mayor of London, to protest against anti-Jewish atrocities in Russia; a Mansion House Relief Fund was established, and the sum of £108,759 was collected to assist Jewish refugees both in England and on the Continent.[40] The Mansion House Fund was in practice administered by a 'Conjoint Committee' made up of administrators of the Fund and representatives of the Board of Guardians; from March 1882 it was this Conjoint Committee which shouldered the major (though not exclusive) responsibility for relieving immediate distress among the Russian refugees. In 1882 the Conjoint Committee dealt with 1,591 cases; thereafter the number of cases fell very sharply (to 93 in 1884), and did not again exceed 1,500 until 1892.[41]

In 1882 the Board of Guardians suspended its six months' residence rule as a charitable gesture of strictly limited duration, but only in the context of an avowed and advertised campaign to persuade immigrants to continue their journeys to America or the colonies, or to return whence they had come.[42] The Russo-Jewish Committee (formed in 1891 to make a new appeal for funds), because its purpose was to aid refugees fleeing religious persecution, repatriated relatively few of its clients. But the Board of Guardians was not so squeamish; between 1880 and 1914 the Board repatriated 17,500 'cases'—perhaps as many as 50,000 individuals.[43] Wherever possible, emigrants from eastern Europe who could not

[39] V. D. Lipman, *A Century of Social Service 1859–1959* (London, 1959), 276–8.

[40] *JC* (3 Feb. 1882), supplement; (27 Oct.), 6; *Daily Telegraph* (23 Jan. 1882), 4.

[41] Lipman, *Century of Social Service*, 290–1.

[42] *JC* (17 Feb. 1882), 14.

[43] Lipman, *Century of Social Service*, 94–5.

be persuaded to return, and who had no immediate plans to continue their journeys, were none the less offered financial assistance to settle elsewhere—mainly in the United States but also in Canada, Australia, South Africa, and Argentina. Steps were also taken to stop the emigration at its source: in 1884 and subsequently, advertisements were placed in the Jewish press in Russia and Romania warning intending immigrants to England of the many hardships they would face, informing them that during the first six months' residence the Board would do nothing to alleviate these difficulties, and calling upon those in authority within the Jewish communities there to do what they could to stem the flow at its source.[44] Chief Rabbi Nathan Adler added his own imprimatur to these pronouncements. At the close of 1888 he despatched to his colleagues in eastern Europe an impassioned plea, asking them to preach in their synagogues on the evils that awaited those orthodox Jews who set foot in Britain:

> Many of them are lost without livelihoods . . . at times they contravene the will of their Maker on account of poverty and overwork, and violate the Sabbath and Festivals . . . There are many who believe that all the cobblestones of London are precious stones, and that it is a place of gold. Woe and alas, it is not so.[45]

As late as 1880 the *Jewish Chronicle*, noticing that an ever greater proportion of the Jewish poor in London 'have been subjects of the Czar', looked to political reform in Russia as the best means of stemming the immigrant flow.[46] By 1882 this hope had of course been abandoned. Lionel Louis Cohen, then President of the Board of Guardians, warned that 'a movement is in progress which may assume vast proportions, and of which this country may not improbably become the centre'.[47] This movement could neither be stopped nor turned back upon itself; nor (it turned out) could it be hurried on, *en bloc*, to another country. At an international Jewish conference on migration, held in Berlin in the summer of 1891, it turned out that no Jewish community in the western world was

[44] G. Alderman, *The Jewish Community in British Politics* (Oxford, 1983), 52.
[45] *HaMaggid* (3 Jan. 1889), quoted in Gartner, *Jewish Immigrant*, 24.
[46] *JC* (20 Aug. 1880), 9.
[47] Jewish Board of Guardians, Minutes, 27 Feb. 1882, quoted in Gartner, *Jewish Immigrant*, 42.

willing to receive large numbers of immigrants.[48] The Russo-Jewish Committee made a grant of £25,000 to enable the Jewish community of Berlin to ship Jewish refugees direct to America, on the understanding that none would be sent to England without the prior consent of the Anglo-Jewish authorities.[49] But the Government of the United States had already begun to tighten its own immigration regulations; by the 1890s it was difficult for immigrants without money or relatives or friends already settled in the United States to gain entry there. The Hebrew Immigrant Aid Society in New York took steps of its own, as it had done in the early 1880s, to limit the flow of migrants, some of whom were repatriated.[50]

Some East European emigrants were bound to remain in England, either because they refused to be repatriated, or because they could not or would not be settled elsewhere. Some wanted to remain in England.[51] The fact that there was in England an established, well-to-do Jewish community, which had clearly been able to make its way in a non-Jewish environment, was an added attraction. Partly for this reason, and also because it was known that those contemplating immigration to or through England were influenced by reports of the welcome they might receive on arrival, private initiatives to assist them once they had disembarked were vigorously discouraged.

The most celebrated incident of this kind took place in London in 1885, when the attention of the Board of Guardians was drawn to the existence of a 'shelter' or 'home for the outcast poor' established by one Simon Cohen, a pious refugee from Poland, who had come to England in 1870 and had established himself as a prosperous baker in Aldgate. 'Simcha Becker' (as he was affectionately known) interested himself in the plight of his fellow Jews who arrived at the docks with little if any money, and very often without the slightest idea where they might find lodgings, let alone any means of employment. It was feared that in this condition they might become an easy prey to Christian missionaries, who waited at the dockside and offered food and shelter to those who would go

[48] M. Wischnitzer, *To Dwell in Safety* (Philadelphia, 1948), 70–2; *JC* (5 June 1891), 18; (12 June), 6, 9, 15; (19 June), 8–9; *The Times* (3 June 1891), 5; (6 June), 9.

[49] Gartner, *Jewish Immigrant*, 45.

[50] Z. Szajkowski, 'The Attitude of American Jews to East European Jewish Immigration (1881–1893)', *Publications of the American Jewish Historical Society*, 40/3 (Mar. 1951), 221–71.

[51] *JC* (3 Mar. 1882), 15.

with them, and also free medical aid, none of which was to be had from the Board of Guardians. In 1879 the baker of black bread and bagels in Aldgate arranged for premises at 19 Church Lane (which lay between the Commercial and Whitechapel Roads) to be used as a hostel for Jewish immigrants, where they were assured of shelter, clothes, *kosher* food, and even facilities for prayer and religious studies.[52]

The Anglo-Jewish authorities determined to put a stop to this charitable endeavour. In April 1885 the philanthropist F. D. Mocatta, active in the Board of Guardians (and a Vice-President from 1887), together with Lionel Alexander, the Board's Honorary Secretary, visited Cohen's shelter and pronounced it 'unhealthy'; they further reported that 'such a harbour of refuge must tend to invite helpless Foreigners to this country, and therefore it was not a desirable institution to exist'.[53] The authorities in Whitechapel were prevailed upon to have the shelter closed.

This precipitate action inevitably backfired. There was a protest meeting held at the Jewish Working Men's Club & Institute, Whitechapel.[54] Reports in the Jewish press warned of the dangers of alienating the newer immigrant Jewish community from the established leadership.[55] A section of that leadership had reached the same conclusion. Hermann Landau (1844–1921), a wealthy stockbroker who had emigrated from Poland to Britain in 1864, Samuel Montagu (1832–1911), the bullion broker and orthodox Jew from Liverpool who sat as Liberal MP for Whitechapel from 1885 to 1900, and Ellis Abraham Franklin, Montagu's business partner and brother-in-law, became sponsors of a new and more formalized establishment, which opened its doors at 12 Great Garden Street, Whitechapel, in November 1885, and which was known as the Poor Jews' Temporary Shelter; Franklin was its President (to be succeeded, later, by Landau) and Montagu its Treasurer. This Shelter served two meals a day, gave no financial assistance, and did not allow anyone to remain under its roof for

[52] The story is told in G. Alderman, *The Federation of Synagogues 1887–1987* (London, 1987), 7–8.

[53] Jewish Board of Guardians, Minutes, 13 Apr. 1885, quoted in Alderman, *Federation*, 8. On Mocatta, a leading figure in the Charity Organization Society, see E. C. Black, *The Social Politics of Anglo-Jewry 1880–1920* (Oxford, 1988), 20–2.

[54] *Die Tsukunft* (1 May 1885), quoted in Gartner, *Jewish Immigrant*, 52.

[55] Alderman, *Federation*, 8.

longer than two weeks. Even so, the Board of Guardians refused for fifteen years to become reconciled to it, demanding (*inter alia*) that it should admit only adult males and that those who did not find work after leaving the Shelter should be referred to the Guardians for repatriation. To these conditions those who managed the Shelter resolutely refused to adhere.

In time shelters, operating in a more modest fashion, sprang up in provincial centres. It was also in 1885 that Constance, Lady Battersea, daughter of Sir Anthony de Rothschild, took steps to establish a 'Jewish Ladies Society for Preventive and Rescue Work' (later, the Jewish Association for the Protection of Girls, Women, and Children), to rescue and if possible rehabilitate Jewish prostitutes, care for Jewish unmarried mothers, and protect Jewish girls travelling unaccompanied from incoming ships.[56] It is true that much money intended to assist transmigration was channelled through the Poor Jews' Temporary Shelter, and that increasingly after 1900 the Shelter and the Board of Guardians operated along parallel lines, helping immigrants and transmigrants alike.[57] None the less, it is difficult not to agree with Professor Gartner's conclusion that 'the Shelter and the Guardians originally embodied opposing outlooks on immigration policy', the one offering a helping hand of sorts, the other offering only repatriation, re-emigration, or, if these failed to attract, a stern charity dispensed in a manner designed deliberately to demean and even humiliate.[58]

Why did Jew treat Jew in this way? The historian cannot begin to answer this question without first drawing attention to the sheer physical impact upon Anglo-Jewry of the great immigration that took place between 1881 and the First World War. The sentiments and policies of the established Jewish community towards the immigrants can only be properly understood in the context of the magnitude—physical, cultural, social, religious, and political—of the phenomenon with which they were faced. On the eve of the Russian pogroms the number of Jews living in London was, as we have seen, about 46,000, and in the country as a whole around 60,000. By 1914 these totals had been dwarfed by the arrival of

[56] Constance, Lady Battersea, *Reminiscences* (London, 1922), 418–23. See also Lipman, *Century of Social Service*, 247–55; E. J. Bristow, *Prostitution and Prejudice: The Jewish Fight Against White Slavery 1870–1939* (Oxford, 1982), 236–7; and L. G. Kuzmack, *Woman's Cause: The Jewish Woman's Movement in England and the United States, 1881–1933* (Columbus, Ohio, 1990), 53–62.

[57] Black, *Social Politics*, 252–5.

[58] Gartner, *Jewish Immigrant*, 54.

about 150,000 immigrants; most found their way to London. Merely from a demographic viewpoint this amounted to a revolution. Between 1851 and 1881 London's Jewish population had grown at an annual rate of about 4 per cent.[59] But between 1881 and 1900 London Jewry expanded to approximately 135,000—an annual rate of growth of 10 per cent; of these, it was estimated in 1899 that roughly 120,000 were living in the East End.[60]

It was in East London, of course, that the settlement of Jewish immigrants was most marked and most visible; indeed, there is much truth in the assertion that it was the high concentration of foreign Jews in the Borough of Stepney (established as one of the new London boroughs created in 1899) that provided the ammunition for those who argued that there really was a Jewish 'problem' to be addressed by the nation at large. Stepney included the areas of Whitechapel, St George's-in-the-East, and Mile End, in which Jews had traditionally lived adjacent to the City of London, and into which the immigrants now poured just as their more prosperous English-born or Anglicized co-religionists were migrating northwards. According to the census of 1881, over three-quarters of the Russians and Poles (most of whom can be assumed to have been Jews, of course) who lived in London were located in these areas; by 1901 the proportion was just under 80 per cent.[61] By 1901 the alien population of Whitechapel had reached almost 32 per cent; in Mile End Old Town it was nearly 29 per cent. George Arkell's famous map of 'Jewish East London', prepared in 1899 for inclusion in the study of *The Jew in London* published under the auspices of Toynbee Hall, showed that some streets north and south of the Commercial and Whitechapel Roads were almost entirely Jewish by residence, and that Jews were spreading up to and (as it turned out) well beyond the borders of what was then regarded as East London:

[59] V. D. Lipman, 'The Structure of London Jewry in the Mid-Nineteenth Century', in H. J. Zimmels, J. Rabbinowitz, and I. Finestein (eds.), *Essays Presented to Chief Rabbi Israel Brodie* (London, 1967), 255.

[60] S. Fyne, 'London's Jewish Population', *JC* (14 Oct. 1955), 34; see also S. Waterman and B. Kosmin, *British Jewry in the Eighties* (London, 1986), 6. Joseph Jacobs put the Jewish population of London in 1902 at 150,000 (*Jewish Encyclopaedia* (New York, 1904), viii. 174), while in 1903 the statistician S. Rosenbaum [Rowson] gave an estimate of 144,000: 'A Contribution to the Study of the Vital and other Statistics of the Jews in the United Kingdom', *Journal of the Royal Statistical Society*, 68 (1905), 554.

[61] Lipman, *Social History*, 94.

The area covered by the Jewish quarter is extending its limits every year. Overflowing the boundaries of Whitechapel, they are spreading northward and eastward into Bethnal Green and Mile End, and southward into St. George's-in-the-East; while further away in Hackney and Shoreditch to the north, and Stepney, Limehouse and Bow to the east, a rather more prosperous and less foreign element has established itself. . . . Dirt, overcrowding, industry and sobriety may be set down as the most conspicuous features of these foreign settlements. In many cases they have completely transformed the character of the neighbourhood.[62]

In what became the borough of Stepney as a whole the alien population increased from 15,898 to 54,310 in the period 1881–1901; during the same period the number of habitable dwellings in the area fell from 35,300 to 31,500.[63] Here, through no fault of the Jews, was a social problem—and hence a political issue—in the making.

But it was for the established Jewish community itself that the immigrant influx posed the most immediate difficulties. By 1914 it is possible that London Jewry had reached 180,000.[64] The existing London Jewish community was, in short, swamped by the newcomers. In the provinces the impact of the immigration was less dramatic in terms of absolute numbers, but more startling in its relative effect. Between 1881 and 1911 the size of provincial Jewry more than quadrupled, from 20,000 to nearly 100,000.[65] Existing provincial communities were revitalized by the immigrants; others were virtually immigrant creations. Towns such as Birmingham (the Jewish population of which numbered 5,500 by 1911), Liverpool and Glasgow (7,000 each), Leeds (25,000), and pre-eminently Manchester (30,000) became major centres of Anglo-Jewry, with their own independent communal structures. By 1911 Jews constituted 2 per cent of the population of London but 5.8 per cent of the population of Leeds and 5.5 per cent in Manchester. Provincial Jewry as a whole possessed, for the first time, an existence of its own; it was no longer a mere adjunct of London.[66]

The true impact of the immigrations upon the size of British Jewry will almost certainly never be capable of definitive calculation. Substantial inaccuracies and omissions in surviving data relating to the number of aliens, and specifically of Jewish aliens,

[62] C. Russell in id. and H. S. Lewis, *The Jew in London* (London, 1900), 12–13.
[63] Lipman, *Social History*, 104. [64] Ibid. 100. [65] Ibid. 103.
[66] These figures are taken from the *Jewish Year Book* for 1911.

coming into the country at this time; the difficulties in distinguishing Jewish from non-Jewish aliens; the failure of the census (except in Ireland) to identify the religion as well as the nationality of aliens; all these factors make it impossible to derive authoritative totals for British Jewry or its geographical parts during this period. It is none the less probable that on the eve of the First World War there were as many as 250,000 Jews in Britain; the figure of 300,000 may be only a mild exaggeration.[67]

This great influx dismayed and at times terrified the Anglo-Jewish leadership; their reaction to it tested to the limit the meaning which they attached to the emancipation they or their fathers had fought for. Jews already settled in Britain objected to foreign-born Jews coming to Britain because these foreign Jews drew attention to themselves, and brought political controversy in their wake, so that the public mind became focused upon Jews as foreigners and a cause for concern at the very time at which the established Jewry was trying its hardest to blend itself, chameleon-like, into its non-Jewish environment. 'Up till the eighties', the *Jewish Chronicle* complained in 1903, the community 'was working out its own salvation undisturbed and at peace. The cruel action of the Russian Government has, however, unsettled and introduced a grave feature into the whole course of Anglo-Jewish development.'[68] The immigrants reminded British Jews of their lowly and foreign origins; worse still, they reminded the Gentiles. British Jewry wished to be thought of as modern; the immigrants gave, it was argued, the impression of primitivism, or at least of medievalism. The established community wished to stress its qualities as British citizens who happened to profess Judaism; the manners, customs, mores, and even politics of the immigrants all skewed the overall character of British Jewry in a quite opposite direction. As a result, the safety and standing of the community already here was felt to be in jeopardy. The *St. James's Gazette* argued in 1887 that the Jews were 'a people apart. Long as they may live among us they will never become merged in the mass of the English population.'[69] If that was really the case, emancipation itself was under threat.

Jews became news. Articles about them were written in local newspapers, in the quality press and in specialist journals, and they formed the objects of attention from social investigators and

[67] Lipman, *Social History*, 103. [68] *JC* (21 Aug. 1903), 17.
[69] *St. James's Gazette* (4 Apr. 1887), 5.

industrial reformers.[70] The evident concentration of Jewish immigrants in a few trades and occupations, in discrete areas of a limited number of large towns, only served to heighten public curiosity and concern. Many employments in Britain were, through prejudice and discrimination, simply not open to Jews. One can find examples of Jewish gas-fitters, Jewish house-painters, and even of Jewish blacksmiths and Jewish labourers in steel works. In 1901 the *Jewish Chronicle* recorded the existence of a Jewish branch of the Amalgamated Tinplate Workers' Union.[71] These were exotic exceptions to the rule. The Jewish immigrants needed to find employment in skills that they already knew or that could be readily acquired, and which, on account both of language and of religious requirements, kept them if at all possible within a Jewish milieu.[72]

For all these reasons they gravitated towards a small number of occupations that could be pursued at home, or in makeshift back-room workshops: in 1901 42 per cent of all Russian and Polish males in East London, and 54 per cent of females, were engaged in the tailoring trades; a further 13 per cent of the men were employed in boot, shoe and slipper manufacturing. The pattern in London was being repeated nationwide. By 1911 about half of all the Russians, Poles, and Romanians in England and Wales were engaged in some branch or other of the clothing trades, including footwear and headwear. In the three major cities of immigrant settlement, London, Leeds, and Manchester, the clothing industries were by far the most frequent avenue of employment. Another occupation for which immigrant Jews had a marked preference, and for the same reasons, was cabinet-making, in which 11 per cent of Russian and Polish males were employed in East London in 1901.[73]

It was the misfortune of the immigrants to have come to Britain at a time of economic recession and growing unemployment, which

[70] There is a useful list of the major articles, in so far as they related to the issue of sweating, in Gartner, *Jewish Immigrant*, 67.

[71] R. O'Brien, 'The Establishment of the Jewish Minority in Leeds', Ph.D. thesis (Bristol, 1975), 41; H. Pollins, *Economic History of the Jews in England* (London, 1982), 143–4; *JC* (8 Mar. 1901), 17. For Jewish blacksmiths in Glasgow *c.*1930 see K. E. Collins (ed.), *Aspects of Scottish Jewry* (Glasgow, 1987), facing p. 24.

[72] Pollins, *Economic History*, 145.

[73] D. M. Feldman, 'Immigrants and Workers, Englishmen and Jews: Jewish Immigration to the East End of London, 1880–1906', Ph.D. thesis (Cambridge, 1985), 57.

triggered a number of inquiries into social problems in the inner cities, turned the attention of the labour movement and the political community to discovering the causes of these ills, and led politicians to exploit the resulting public concern either for frankly political and opportunist ends, or as ammunition in the crusade against Free Trade, or because they genuinely believed that the alien influx menaced British values and the political and social norms of British society.[74] The origin of this public concern can be pinpointed with some accuracy. On 3 May 1884 the *Lancet* carried a short article reporting the findings of its 'Special Sanitary Commission' on a 'Polish Colony of Jew Tailors' that the Commission had discovered in Whitechapel.[75] The report focused upon sweating—the gross overwork and gross underpayment, in cramped, ill-lit and generally unhealthy conditions (which invariably included poor or even non-existent toilet and washing facilities) of workers in industries in respect of which employment was usually intermittent and for which there was an abundant supply to be had of cheap labour. As a matter of fact sweating in the London clothing trades pre-dated the great Jewish immigrations; indeed sweating was to be found in trades where no Jews had ever dared—or would ever dare—to set foot.[76] In Leeds and Manchester sweaters were keen to replace immigrant Jewish males with native-born English females, because these girls would work for lower wages and generally give less trouble.[77]

The *Lancet* article itself had not said that Jewish refugees were the only cause of sweating in the Whitechapel locality. Yet the prestigious nature of the journal in which the article appeared was seized upon by publicists and propagandists as evidence of an 'indissoluble connection' between immigration and sweating.[78] Within a short time the issue of sweating was subsumed within that of the alien presence, with the implication that the alleged unwholesome—and certainly un-English—life-style of the immigrants made them natural sweaters and natural victims of the

[74] See generally B. Gainer, *The Alien Invasion* (London, 1972), ch. 5.

[75] 'Report of the Special Sanitary Commission on the Polish Colony of Jew Tailors', *Lancet* (3 May 1884), 817–18.

[76] Pollins, *Economic History*, 147. On sweating in the London clothing trades see generally J. A. Schmiechen, *Sweated Industries and Sweated Labour: The London Clothing Trades 1860–1914* (Beckenham, 1984).

[77] Gainer, *Alien Invasion*, 44.

[78] Ibid. 80.

same.[79] In Leeds the chairman of the Sanitary Committee, Alderman Ward, had no doubt that Jewish tailors were 'very filthy', and that this was because they came 'from parts of Russia which are almost beyond the pale of civilization'.[80] In London John Burnett, a most respected moderate trade-union leader who had become the first Labour Correspondent to the Board of Trade, added an official imprimatur to these views. In his celebrated report on the sweating system in East London, published in 1887, Burnett declared that the causal relationship between sweating and alien immigration was beyond dispute:

These aliens have been chiefly German and Russian Jews, and there can be no doubt that the result has been to flood the labour market of the East End of London with cheap labour to such an extent as to reduce thousands of native workers to the verge of destitution.[81]

Arnold White, a writer and philanthropist of right-wing views who had begun in 1884 to interest himself in poverty in south and east London, added a new dimension to the debate. In his book *The Problems of a Great City* (1886) White addressed the issue of 'pauper foreigners', to whose presence in the capital he linked the distressed labour-market, the incidence of insanitary dwellings and—significantly—the spread of socialism.[82] By the beginning of 1888 White was talking openly about Jews rather than about aliens or foreigners.[83] In 1890 he made the first of several visits to Russia, and as a result adopted a tone towards Jews that was more racial in character. By the turn of the century he had convinced himself (and others) that the immigrant Jewish presence was a question 'not . . . of numbers, nor of habits, nor . . . of occupations . . . but the fact that, good, or bad or indifferent the orthodox immigrants belong to a race and cling to a community that prefers to remain aloof from the mainstream of our national life, by shunning intermarriage with Anglo-Saxons'.[84]

[79] *Yorkshireman* (16 May 1885), 314.

[80] *Leeds Daily News* (11 June 1888), 3. See also J. Connell, 'The Jewish Ghetto in Nineteenth Century Leeds: A Case of Urban Involution', *Urban Anthropology*, 10 (1981), 1–26.

[81] 'Report to the Board of Trade on the Sweating System at the East End of London by the Labour Correspondent to the Board', *PP* 1887, lxxxix (331), 4.

[82] See also A. White, 'The Invasion of Pauper Foreigners', *Nineteenth Century* (Mar. 1888), 414–22.

[83] C. Holmes, *Anti-Semitism in British Society 1876–1939* (London, 1979), 25.

[84] Royal Commission on Alien Immigration, Minutes of Evidence, *PP* 1903, ix [Cd. 1742], 16.

White's ability to make political capital out of these prejudices was limited by his own failure as a politician.[85] But the themes on which he wrote and spoke were taken up in political circles. In 1886 he and his disciple, the Tory Earl of Dunraven, a leading member of the Fair Trade movement, founded a Society for the Suppression of Immigration of the Destitute Aliens. In February 1888 Dunraven successfully moved in the House of Lords for a Select Committee to inquire into the sweating system.[86] In the Commons Lord Salisbury's Government bowed to pressure from East End MPs and agreed to establish a Select Committee on Alien Immigration. Arnold White serviced both committees, more particularly by searching out witnesses for their examination.[87]

In the short term neither of these parliamentary inquiries led to far-reaching results. The Lords' Committee concluded (as it was bound to, given the hard evidence placed before it) that 'undue stress has been laid on the injurious effect on wages caused by foreign immigration, inasmuch as we find that the evils complained of obtain in trades, which do not appear to be affected by foreign immigration'.[88] The Select Committee of the House of Commons felt that the immigrants were 'generally very dirty and uncleanly in their habits', but none the less showed themselves to be 'quick at learning, moral, frugal, and thrifty, and inoffensive as citizens'.[89] The only practical result of all these parliamentary labours was that the Board of Trade instituted annual returns of immigrants.

Thus far the Jewish community might be said to have emerged relatively unscathed: a great deal of information and misinformation had been spread about; some myths had been exploded; the right of entry into Britain had been preserved. In fact, however, the community had been thrown into a state of crisis as a result of which (as will be seen) the most extraordinary measures had been adopted by the ruling minority to take control of the immigrant majority. More immediately, the community was split on the issue of immigration control. Most responsible sections of communal opinion set their face against restriction, on broad grounds of

[85] On White see *Who Was Who 1916–1928*; he tried several times to gain election to Parliament, all without success.

[86] *The Times* (29 Feb. 1888), 6.

[87] Gainer, *Alien Invasion*, 81–4.

[88] Report of the Select Committee of the House of Lords on the Sweating System, *PP* 1890, xvii (169), xliii, para. 182 (28 Apr. 1890).

[89] Report of the Select Committee on Emigration and Immigration (Foreigners), *PP* 1889, x (311), xi (8 Aug. 1889).

principle and charity.[90] As long as the nation adhered to the policy of Free Trade this attitude could be characterized also as frankly patriotic: goods and persons were to enter Britain with equal freedom. But already in the 1880s there were dissentient voices. In 1886 the Board of Guardians in London had hinted that state control of Jewish immigration might have to be contemplated.[91] Jewish immigrants of modest means, who felt their slow climb upon the ladder of economic advancement threatened by new arrivals, added their weight to this argument. One of the most remarkable (and pathetic) aspects of the House of Commons' inquiry into immigration had been the evidence, in favour of restriction, afforded on behalf of an older generation of Dutch Jewish artisan immigrants.[92]

During the 1890s Jewish supporters of restriction grew bolder, and for a number of reasons. To begin with, although measures were taken, nationally and by the Jewish community, to attack the problem of sweating, the agitation linking sweating to the Jewish presence would not go away. The Factory Act of 1891 gave local authorities new powers to deal with unsuitable workshops, and with the passage of the Public Health (London) Act the same year the newly established London County Council was authorized to deal with insanitary conditions and overcrowding in the workshops of the capital. It was to David Schloss, the Honorary Secretary of the Board of Guardians' Sanitary Committee, that the LCC's Public Health and Housing Committee looked to provide information on the basis of which action could be taken.[93] In 1893 Schloss was able to report that 'a good deal' was being done 'to avoid the gross over-crowding of the workers, formerly so prevalent', and that, 'in some instances', steps had been taken 'to provide less inefficient ventilation'.[94] But a major difficulty in enforcing legislation was that sweatshop masters found it easy to evade the regulations. This, in turn, was facilitated by the dearth of inspectors and, more

[90] See e.g. the editorial in *JC* (26 Feb. 1886), 9.

[91] Ibid.; see also Russell and Lewis, *The Jew in London*, 167.

[92] Select Committee on Emigration and Immigration (Foreigners), Minutes of Evidence, *PP* 1888, xi (305), qq. 962–1315 (evidence of Henry Dejonge, cigar-maker). See also *JC* (28 Sept. 1894), 6–7: letter from I. Pou, 'Cigar Maker'.

[93] Greater London Record Office, LCC/MIN/7256: Minutes of the Public Health and Housing Committee, General Sub-Committee meeting, 4 Nov. 1892; Jewish Board of Guardians, *Annual Report 1892*, 83. See also Schmiechen, *Sweated Industries*, 139.

[94] Jewish Board of Guardians, *Annual Report 1893*, 81; *JC* (19 Jan. 1894), 6.

generally, by the economic system which made sweating such a viable proposition. The low pay which was such a central feature of the system was not tackled until the passage of the Trade Boards Act of 1909.

As with sweating, so with housing. We have already noted, in relation to Stepney, that Jewish immigrants moved into an area in which the housing stock was diminishing as the alien population was rising. In 1888 the average population density throughout London was 54 persons per acre; but in parts of Spitalfields it was found to be 286 (Christchurch) and 600 (Bell Lane).[95] Overcrowding was more or less endemic; the slums were notorious. Schemes of slum clearance, and the erection of warehouses and factories—and schools—made the housing shortage still worse. At the end of 1901 one East London newspaper reported that between 1875 and 1899 1,167 *fewer* persons had been provided with homes, in the districts of Whitechapel, Stepney, and Limehouse, as a result of clearances and rebuilding.[96] Inevitably, the housing shortage resulted in the raising of rents; in London as a whole rents rose between 10 and 12 per cent in the period 1880–1900, but in the East London boroughs the rise was of the order of 25 per cent.[97] Prospective tenants might also find themselves asked to pay 'key money' (often dubbed 'blood money') to the landlord or the outgoing tenant, merely for the privilege of moving in.[98]

The housing issue became, for obvious reasons, the most sensitive and explosive subject of controversy relating to the Jewish influx, both in London and in provincial centres. In Leeds the activities of 'Jewish capitalists' were blamed for the increase in rents in the Leylands, the area in which the Jewish immigrants had settled; both in Leeds and Manchester, as well as in London, the shortage of housing and the rise in rents were attributed to the Jewish immigrant presence.[99] Jews had more money to spend on rents; they had fewer qualms about multiple occupancy; where new 'model' dwellings were erected, Jews (it was said) were favoured

[95] H. E. Boulton, 'The Housing of the Poor', *Fortnightly Review*, NS 43 (1 Feb. 1888), 280.

[96] *Eastern Post* (2 Nov. 1901), 6.

[97] Feldman, 'Immigrants and Workers'. 62.

[98] Gainer, *Alien Invasion*, 41.

[99] Ibid. 42. On the rise of the Leylands as an area of Jewish settlement in Leeds see E. Krausz, *Leeds Jewry: Its History and Social Structure* (Cambridge, 1964), 21–2.

above non-Jews as tenants.[100] Jewish landlords favoured Jews, while towards their non-Jewish tenants they adopted rapacious and rack-renting practices. At Tredegar the activities of just one Jewish landlord were said to have sparked the anti-Jewish riots that spread through the mining communities of the valleys of South Wales in the summer of 1911.[101]

There are no simple answers to the questions raised here about the precise responsibility of Jewish immigrants for the ills of certain inner-city housing markets. The immigrants had, perforce, to live in slum properties, and could not fairly be blamed for their manifest inadequacies. Even in as well governed a city as Leeds, the immigrant quarter could be very deficient in basic amenities.[102] In London, where until 1899 responsibility for such matters lay with local Boards of Works not known for their efficiency or conscientiousness, the Jewish authorities themselves acted as sanitary inspectors. It was largely through the efforts of the Jewish Board of Guardians that a sustained campaign was launched in the late 1880s to provoke the Whitechapel District Board of Works into enforcing minimum sanitary requirements and providing adequate refuse collection.[103] The Guardians also lobbied the London County Council persistently on the need to address the problem of the Bell Lane rookeries, the clearance of which was announced during a county council by-election in Whitechapel in 1897.[104]

A specifically Jewish input was also made in the field of urban renewal, largely through the work of the East End Dwellings and the Four Per Cent Industrial Dwellings companies, both of which originated in an inquiry undertaken by the United Synagogue in 1884 into 'spiritual destitution' in the East End.[105] It was through the efforts of the Four Per Cent (whose directors included Nathan Mayer de Rothschild, Lionel Cohen, and Samuel Montagu) that the famous Charlotte de Rothschild Dwellings were constructed

[100] In spite of Lord Rothschild's assertion to the contrary, the tenantry of Rothschild Buildings, Whitechapel, was 'almost entirely Jewish': J. White, *Rothschild Buildings* (London, 1980), 72.

[101] G. Alderman, 'The Anti-Jewish Riots of August 1911 in South Wales', *Welsh History Review*, 6/2 (1972), 195; C. Holmes, 'The Tredegar Riots of 1911: Anti-Jewish Disturbances in South Wales', *Welsh History Review*, 11/2 (1982), 218–19.

[102] 'Report of the Lancet Special Sanitary Commission on the Sweating System in Leeds', *Lancet* (16 June 1888), 1209.

[103] Jewish Board of Guardians, *Annual Report 1889*, 22; *1890*, 75.

[104] *East London Observer* (27 Feb. 1897), 7.

[105] *JC* (27 Feb. 1885), 8.

around Flower and Dean Street, Whitechapel. Rothschild Buildings were the largest of a series of 'model' tenement blocks in the area (another was Nathaniel Dwellings, completed by the Four Per Cent Company in 1892) which had, by the mid-1890s, transformed the locality of the Ripper murders into one of poor but respectable Jewish inhabitants.[106]

The Jewish authorities were able to dispel, or to have dispelled, some of the wilder and quite unsubstantiated notions that gained currency about Jewish East London. It was true that the tenantry of Rothschild Buildings was overwhelmingly Jewish, but the statement made in the House of Commons by the Conservative MP for Bethnal Green South-West, Samuel Forde-Ridley, that the LCC's Boundary Street estate was 'now [1903] already nearly half full of aliens, who live under conditions we would not like to see our working classes subjected to' was shown (on the authority of the LCC's Housing Department) to be quite false: of 1,044 tenements on the estate, only 27 per cent were occupied by Jews and aliens, and there was found to be only one case of infringement of the Council's housing regulations.[107]

Jews did not constitute a health hazard. This accusation was frequently made, and in its most vicious form was expressed by the anti-Semite Joseph Banister in his book *England under the Jews*, which first appeared in 1901.[108] But the charge could not be made to stick. In 1889 a committee of the LCC appointed to investigate Bell Lane reported that it had not found 'that any considerable amount of squalor or disease prevailed. For this, the peculiar conditions under which the Jews, who form the majority of the inhabitants, live, as well as the numerous charitable dwellings, are doubtless responsible.'[109] In 1901 Dr S. Murphy, the LCC's Medical Officer of Health, pointed out that in the neighbourhood of Buckchurch Lane (St George's-in-the-East), 'the low death rate from all causes is interesting, because the population is almost a

[106] White, *Rothschild Buildings*, 20–30.

[107] Greater London Record Office, LCC/MIN/7381: Presented Papers of the Public Health and Housing Committee 1903–4 (Bundle 1): Memo. from the Housing Department of the London County Council to the Chairman of the Committee, 23 Feb. 1903; *Parl. Deb.*, 4th ser., vol. 118, col. 197 (18 Feb. 1903).

[108] Holmes, *Anti-Semitism in British Society*, 39–40.

[109] Greater London Record Office, LCC Minutes, 2 Aug. 1889: Report of the Housing of the Working Classes Committee.

wholly Jewish population'.[110] In Manchester that same year the death rate was 21.78 per 1,000, but among Jewish immigrants only 16.99 per 1,000; in the poorer areas of the city the general death rate was twice the Jewish figure; among children under 5 years of age the general death rate was 72.50 per 1,000, yet among immigrants' children it was only 55.88 per 1,000.[111]

None of this bore out Banister's claim that the country was being saturated by a 'stream of Semitic sewage'.[112] Only in relation to the incidence of tuberculosis can Jewish immigrants be said to have been disproportionate carriers of disease; that this was so was due entirely to the environmental conditions under which they worked, and of which they were the first victims.[113] By 1908 a leading campaigner for immigration restriction, John Foster Fraser, was honest enough to admit that 'the Jews are a healthy people. Excepting consumption they have a peculiar immunity from disease.'[114]

Intellectually, the Jews and their friends won the argument over sweating, and that over the threat allegedly posed by Jews to the nation's health. On the issue of housing and rents the outcome of the debate was less unequivocal. The Jewish influx into an area like Whitechapel in the 1890s, when the housing stock was diminishing, must have contributed its own burden to the East End's housing crisis. Of course Jews did not deliberately plan matters that way; but the effect was there for all to see. That Jewish landlords were more likely than native landlords to raise rents was a fact of life; that the rents they raised were usually those of their brethren from eastern Europe was merely a plea in mitigation.[115] The Jewish influx caused rents to rise; had it not been for the Jews, rents would either not have risen or would not have risen so much. It is also true that the clearance of slums, and their replacement by model dwellings, ensured housing for Jews at the expense of non-Jews. Perhaps for this reason Samuel Montagu insisted, in making a gift of £10,000 to the LCC in 1902, that the special housing complex

[110] Greater London Record Office, LCC/MIN/7381: Presented Papers of the Public Health and Housing Committee 1901–2 (Bundle 65): Memo. from Dr Murphy, 27 Mar. 1901.

[111] Gartner, *Jewish Immigrant*, 159.

[112] J. Banister, *England under the Jews* (London, 1901), 34–5.

[113] Gartner, *Jewish Immigrant*, 160–2.

[114] *Sunday Chronicle* (5 Jan. 1908), 3.

[115] H. S. Lewis in Russell and id., *The Jew in London*, 173–4.

for Whitechapel residents which the money was used to build on the Council's White Hart Lane estate, Tottenham, should be available 'without distinction of race or creed'.[116]

The effect of Jewish immigration upon the labour market was infinitely more complex. It was a common charge that Jewish workers displaced native workers, and that this happened because Jews accepted lower wages and were prepared to labour in inferior workplace conditions. Complaints of this sort were to be heard from the tailoring unions, both in London and the provinces, from the bespoke and ready-made ends of the clothing market, from the boot and shoe operatives, and even from the dockers: the dockers' leader Tom Mann, asserted (1891) that tailors and shoemakers, driven out of work by the aliens, hurried into dockland and added to the large pool of casual labour that was to be found there.[117]

Mann never substantiated this claim. It may well have been true. But if it was, it pointed to a still greater truth. There was always a pool of casual labour at the dockside, and its existence had nothing whatever to do with Jews. Similarly, Jewish immigrant workers were not the cause of low wage rates in the clothing and footwear industries. These occupations had attracted and were attracting female labour and agricultural labourers thrown off the land; what is more, they were trades notoriously susceptible to seasonal fluctuations in work, and they were beginning to feel the impact of the factory system. They were, in short, trades where high rates of unemployment were a fact of life.[118]

In the boot and shoe trades Jews accounted—at most—for about 4 per cent of the entire workforce; these trades were in the process of transformation from home and workshop production to the factory.[119] English boot and shoe operatives were loudest in their complaints about the aliens, and appear to have been the prime movers behind anti-alien resolutions passed by the Trades Union

[116] Greater London Record Office, LCC Minutes, 28 July 1903; *JC* (27 Nov. 1903), 12. See generally R. Thorne, 'The White Hart Lane Estate: An LCC Venture in Suburban Development', *London Journal*, 12 (Summer 1986), 80–8.

[117] *Evening News* (26 May 1891), 1. See also the evidence of Ben Tillett (Mann's collaborator in the organization of workers in the London docks), given to the House of Lords Select Committee on the Sweating System, *PP* 1888, xxi (448), qq. 12,662–6 (20 Nov. 1888).

[118] J. A. Garrard, *The English and Immigration: A Comparative Study of the Jewish Influx 1880–1910* (London, 1971), 164.

[119] Gartner, *Jewish Immigrant*, 75–6.

Congress in 1892, 1894, and 1895.[120] But their complaints lacked all substance. That of the tailors did not. The Jewish immigrant tailors gravitated towards the cheap, ready-made, and mass-produced end of the market; in a sense it was a market which they themselves created. A gentleman's suit that had cost £2. 10*s.* in 1880 could be bought for £1. 10*s.* in 1911; this was due to immigrant production methods.[121] Jews did not displace labour directly. But they did change tastes, adopting in the process new production methods, involving the subdivision of labour, that the English tailors, used to the principle of 'one man, one garment', found uncongenial and even immoral.

In Leeds the Jewish tailoring trade (supplying the large clothing factories) was dominated by about a hundred workshops, employing in 1891 about 1,800 workers; in London there were in 1893 no less than 758 shops that employed less than ten workers each.[122] Bigger, however, did not mean better, for sweating in the 'bedroom workshops' of Leeds was easily comparable with that to be found in the capital.[123] Sweating also flourished in the Jewish tailoring workshops that grew up in the Strangeways district of Manchester, and in Liverpool, Birmingham, Newcastle, and elsewhere, all with a result similar to that observed in London: the English workers were overtaken by a new type of production, and had either to concentrate on the lowest ends of the market ('slops') or the highest class of bespoke work.[124]

In the Jewish tailoring sweatshops that flourished in Britain at this time, workers and masters (whose status might easily descend to that of workers in bad times) earned their livelihoods in unpleasant conditions and under great mental strain.[125] A large number of Jews in London's East End lived at or below Charles

[120] Garrard, *English and Immigration*, 164; Alderman, *Jewish Community*, 67.

[121] Feldman, 'Immigrants and Workers', 84.

[122] Gartner, *Jewish Immigrant*, 88–9.

[123] J. Buckman, *Immigrants and the Class Struggle: The Jewish Immigrant in Leeds, 1880–1914* (Manchester, 1983), ch. 2. In view of Dr Buckman's researches, the conclusion of Professor Gartner (*Jewish Immigrant*, 89) that 'sweating in Leeds did not attain the notoriety which enveloped it in London' is clearly no longer tenable.

[124] Gartner, *Jewish Immigrant*, 91–3. See also R. H. Tawney, *The Establishment of Minimum Rates in the Tailoring Industry under the Trade Boards Act of 1909* (London, 1915), 5–9.

[125] Report of the Chief Inspector of Factories and Workshops, *PP* 1881, xxiii [C–2825], 16–21.

Booth's breadline (21*s.* per week); the average Jewish tailor in London or Leeds in the 1880s and 1890s might earn 7*s.* or 8*s.* a day, but would only work, on average, a three-day week.[126] But, perhaps because of a better communal and self-help infrastructure than was available to the non-Jewish poor, impressionistic evidence suggests that the degree of poverty within Jewish East London was not as great as that to be found in the area as a whole.[127]

In the final analysis, however, empirical evidence supporting one side or the other of the argument about specific features of the impact of Jewish immigration upon British society at the end of the nineteenth century and the beginning of the twentieth did not matter. By 1903 the housing crisis in Stepney had passed its peak, yet anti-Jewish (and not just anti-alien) feeling there ran higher than ever.[128] The influx of Jewish refugees and immigrants had changed the character of the neighbourhood. English posters were replaced with Hebrew ones; English theatres with Yiddish. Chapels became synagogues. At some of the schools operated by the London School Board (for example, Old Castle Street) Jewish children were in the overwhelming majority, and the Jewish Sabbath and holy days were observed; when Hermann Adler's daughter, Nettie, stood for election to the LCC at Central Hackney in 1910, one local newspaper complained that Sigdon Road School was 'entirely controlled by the Jewish calendar'.[129] Sundays took on the air of Saturdays, and Saturdays of Sundays;[130] English shops were displaced by Jewish (*kosher*) shops, and Jewish aromas were to be smelled instead of English fragrances. The English moved (or were forced) out as the Jews moved in: 'There is no end of them [a witness told the Royal Commission on Alien Immigration] in Whitechapel and Mile End. It is Jerusalem.'[131] 'Their habits are so

[126] Beatrice Potter, in C. Booth (ed.), *Life and Labour of the People of London*, 1st ser. iv (London, 1902), 50–4.

[127] Feldman, 'Immigrants and Workers', 114–15.

[128] M. J. Landa, *The Alien Problem and its Remedy* (London, 1911), 65. On the transition from anti-alien to anti-Jewish prejudice see Holmes, *Anti-Semitism*, 91–7.

[129] *JC* (14 July 1882), 13; H. B. Philpott, *London at School: The Story of the School Board 1870–1904* (London, 1904), 113; *Hackney Gazette* (7 Mar. 1910), 5.

[130] The Sunday Work of Jews Act of 1871, the provisions of which were incorporated into the Factory and Workshop Act of 1878, permitted Jews to work on Sundays if they refrained from work on Saturdays. Allegations that Jewish masters evaded the provisions of this legislation (for instance, by employing non-Jews to work on Saturdays) were widespread: *JC* (14 June 1895), 17; (21 June), 11; BD Minutes, vol. 13, 19 Jan., 7 Feb., and 15 Mar. 1896.

[131] Royal Commission on Alien Immigration, *PP* 1903, ix [Cd. 1742], q. 8,976.

different from ours', A. T. Williams, a member of the LCC for Stepney, told the Royal Commission, and they 'will not conform to our ideas'.[132] On the question of numbers, Williams had this to say at a public meeting at the People's Palace, Mile End, in January 1902:

I don't care for statistics. God has given me a pair of eyes in my head—(prolonged cheering)—and as I walk—(renewed cheering)—through Mile End or Cable-Street, as I walk about your streets, I see names have changed; I see good old names of tradesmen have gone, and in their places are foreign names—the names of those who have ousted Englishmen into the cold (Loud cries of 'Shame' and 'Wipe them out').[133]

It was left to A. J. Balfour, the Conservative Prime Minister, to sum up the feelings widely held beyond as well as within the areas of Jewish immigrant settlement. Speaking during the committee stage of the Aliens Bill in 1905, Balfour declared that:

A state of things could easily be imagined in which it would not be to the advantage of the civilisation of the country that there should be an immense body of persons who, however patriotic, able and industrious, however much they threw themselves into the national life, remained a people apart, and not merely held a religion differing from the vast majority of their fellow-countrymen, but only intermarried among themselves.[134]

During the 1890s the issue of this 'people apart' became highly politicized. The Association for Preventing the Immigration of Destitute Aliens could claim support from both Liberal and Conservative MPs, and from labour leaders such as Ben Tillett and J. Havelock Wilson.[135] In May 1892 the Conservative Government announced that an Aliens Bill was being prepared. The Liberals, in office between 1892 and 1895, refused to legislate on the matter, but this was partly because they did not wish to stab Free Trade in the back.[136] In July 1894 Lord Salisbury himself, in his private capacity, introduced an Aliens Bill which passed all its stages in the Upper House but was then dropped. Meanwhile, a group of Conservative back-bench MPs had determined to exploit the issue for party political purposes. The original movers in this stratagem

132 Ibid., qq. 1723–4.

133 *East London Observer* (18 Jan. 1902), 2.

134 *Parl. Deb.*, 4th ser. cxlix. 155 (10 July 1905).

135 *JC* (31 July 1892), 11; and see Gainer, *Alien Invasion*, 61–2.

136 Alderman, *Jewish Community*, 67.

were the members for Sheffield Central (Howard Vincent) and Thanet (James Lowther), but the initiative was soon grasped by a group of East London Tories including Thomas Dewar (St George's), H. Forde-Ridley (Bethnal Green South West), Claude Hay (Hoxton), and the Jew Harry Samuel (Limehouse).

At the October 1900 general election, a new and imposing populist Conservative emerged, Major William Evans-Gordon, who, having won the Stepney parliamentary seat back from the Liberals on a frankly anti-alien campaign, proceeded to organize a highly vocal pressure group, the British Brothers' League, to press for restrictive legislation.[137] The League was formally inaugurated in May 1901. The following August a 'Parliamentary Alien Immigration Committee' came into existence, consisting of fifty-two MPs who at once wrote to Lord Salisbury, the Prime Minister, demanding legislation.[138] All this agitation took place against a background of mounting, country-wide anti-Jewish prejudice, fostered by the right-wing jingoism and left-wing anti-capitalism which accompanied the Boer War, and from which even the Liberal Party was not immune.[139] Indeed it is worth noting that though the British Brothers' League was a Conservative-led and a Conservative-dominated body, it could boast all-party support; what is more, Jews, like Harry Samuel and Henry Norman (Liberal, Wolverhampton South), spoke on its behalf.[140]

It had become clear during the 1890s that there was a small but most influential Jewish lobby also in favour of legislation that would result in a stemming of the flow of Jewish immigrants to Britain. In 1892 Nathan Solomon Joseph (1834–1909), brother-in-law to Hermann Adler, architect of the Four Per Cent Company and of several United synagogues, and Chairman of the Sanitary Committee of the Board of Guardians, in justifying his call for parliamentary action to prevent the entry into Britain of 'helpless' Jewish paupers, explained that 'This class constitutes a grave danger to the community. Its members were always paupers and useless parasites . . . Many of these were never persecuted, but came with the persecuted . . . To admit an unlimited number of helpless

[137] For an account of the League see Gainer, *Alien Invasion*, 67–73.

[138] *JC* (30 Aug. 1901), 18.

[139] Garrard, *English and Immigration*, 191–2; C. Hirshfield, 'The British Left and the "Jewish Conspiracy": A Case Study of Modern Antisemitism', *JSS* 42/2 (Spring 1981), 95–112.

[140] *East London Observer* (18 Jan. 1902), 2.

souls, who are mere dead-weight, would not be mercy, but homicide.'[141]

What Joseph meant was that, through the politicized prejudice that they had aroused, the immigrants threatened the survival of the existing Jewish community in Britain. In March 1894 several members of the Jewish Board of Guardians assured the restrictionists of their support for 'such regulations as would discourage the immigration of undesirable persons, provided that precautions were taken to preserve inviolate the right of asylum'.[142] It was common knowledge that a number of Jewish MPs—most notably Benjamin Cohen (by then Conservative MP for East Islington and President of the Board of Guardians)—were of a like mind.[143] When the Royal Commission on Alien Immigration was established by Balfour's Government in 1902, Jewish artisans came before it to urge the case for restriction.[144] The argument that a distinction needed to be drawn between genuine refugees and those who might contribute to the economic well-being of the country, and not be a burden on it, on the one hand, and the diseased, those who might be regarded as criminals, paupers, and the generally 'undesirable', on the other, was obviously attractive and easily put. The Jewish Liberal parliamentary candidate Bertram Straus did so during the Mile End by-election of January 1905, which the Conservatives held by 78 votes in a contest in which aliens' legislation was a major issue.[145]

Who exactly might be categorized as an 'undesirable' was not defined by Straus, but other Jewish politicians wanted there to be no doubt that it included those who were physically fit and able to earn a livelihood, but whose mere presence contributed to social and economic problems. When A. T. Williams campaigned for a seat on the LCC at Stepney in 1901, he and his 'Moderate' (i.e. Conservative) running-mate issued to the Stepney electors a joint address which included a pledge to support legislative restriction on the immigration of alien paupers, because 'these unfortunate immigrants help to increase the poor rate, to lower wages, increase

[141] *JC* (17 June 1892), 9.
[142] *The Times* (21 Mar. 1894), 5.
[143] In addition to those Jewish MPs already mentioned we must add Louis Sinclair (Conservative, Romford): *JC* (13 Nov. 1903), 27.
[144] See the evidence of W. Silverstone, Z. Solomons, S. V. Amstell, and Isaac Lyons: Royal Commission on Alien Immigration, *PP* 1903, ix [Cd. 1742], qq. 12,249–55.
[145] *East London Observer* (14 Jan. 1905), 5.

the difficulty of Old Age Pensions, to crowd our already congested streets, and thus make the Housing Question the more difficult'.[146] The running-mate (not elected) was Edward Micholls, a wealthy Manchester cotton-spinner, and a Jew.

In their memoranda dissenting from the majority report of the Royal Commission, issued in August 1903, Sir Kenelm Digby (Permanent Under-Secretary at the Home Office) and Lord Rothschild (the only Jew on the Commission) objected to the repatriation of 'undesirable aliens' because, in Lord Rothschild's words, even if such measures 'were directly aimed at the so-called "undesirables" they would certainly affect deserving and hard-working men, whose impecunious position on their arrival would be no criterion of their incapacity to attain independence'. These were distinguished sentiments of principle, and the force with which they were put undoubtedly helped underpin the arguments of those who opposed the Bill which the Government introduced in 1904. But it has to be remembered that Rothschild himself played a double game: at the general election of 1900 he had supported Evans-Gordon at Stepney and another notorious anti-alienist, David Hope Kyd, who stood against Samuel Montagu's nephew, Stuart Samuel, at Whitechapel.[147]

The Bill of 1904, following the recommendations of the majority report, sought to exclude the entry into Britain of certain classes of aliens, the descriptions of which were widely drawn so as to include 'persons of notoriously bad character', 'persons without visible means of support', and 'persons likely to become a public charge'; pauper aliens could also be expelled, and the Local Government Board was to be empowered to control the settlement of those aliens allowed to stay by prohibiting settlement in certain areas. These provisions were hastily drawn and probably unworkable. What sealed their fate was a vigorous parliamentary assault by the Liberals, and in particular by Winston Churchill, who had just left the Conservative for the Liberal benches, and who had been adopted as Liberal candidate for Manchester North-West, in which there was a large Jewish electorate.[148]

[146] The election address is to be found in *London County Council Election 1901 Addresses in Alphabetical Order of Constituencies sold by W. Durrant of three Saint Andrews St Holborn Circus London E.C.*, in the British Library.

[147] Alderman, *Jewish Community*, 68.

[148] Ibid. 71.

The Bill was withdrawn. When a much modified measure (which included a right of appeal to an immigration board, and from which the reference to prohibited areas was entirely absent) was presented the following year, the Liberal Party experienced a change of heart. Sensing the popularity of the measure, the Liberals put up no more than a token resistance, while the Board of Deputies confined itself to admittedly important matters of amendment: in particular, to safeguard the rights of those who were genuine victims of religious persecution, and to provide for a right of appeal to the King's Bench against an expulsion order.

Outright opposition to the measure, which became law on 10 August, was left to a group of radical Liberals led by Charles Dilke and C. P. Trevelyan, and to the immigrants themselves. The Act gave a right of entry to immigrants seeking to avoid 'prosecution or punishment' on religious or political grounds, but not 'persecution'; the exclusion of transmigrants from the provisions of the legislation was due largely to the lobbying activities of the shipping companies.[149] It was not at the Board of Deputies that the principle of the legislation was condemned, but at the Jewish Working Men's Club, Great Alie Street, Aldgate, and by the Jewish socialist–Zionist party, *Poale Zion*, at Whitechapel.[150] Benjamin Cohen of course (together with three other Jewish Conservative and Unionist MPs) supported the Act.[151] Chief Rabbi Adler was reluctant to condemn it; 'we must frankly agree', he later wrote to the English Zionist Herbert Bentwich (1856–1932), 'that we do not desire to admit criminals, and that there is force in the argument against the admission of those [Jews] mentally or physically afflicted.'[152] At the general election of January 1906, in at least one constituency (Leeds Central, unsuccessfully defended by A. J. Balfour's brother, Gerald) Adler's influence was discreetly employed in the Conservative interest.[153] Politics, it seemed, was thicker than blood.

149 Garrard, *English and Immigration*, 46.

150 *JC* (19 May 1905), 7; (26 May), 16–17.

151 Ibid. (5 May 1905), 25; of the 12 Jewish MPs then in the Commons, 4 (3 Unionists and 1 Liberal) abstained and 4 (1 Unionist and 3 Liberals) voted against the Bill.

152 Herbert Bentwich Papers, CZA: A100, file 7a: Adler to Bentwich, 1 Apr. 1906.

153 Moses Gaster Papers, University College London: Gaster to Winston Churchill, 26 Feb. 1906. Hermann Adler had sent his nephew, Herbert, to Leeds to preach the virtues of Conservatism.

No one, in truth, had suffered more from the immigrant presence than Hermann Adler himself. For if it was true that the immigrants posed a challenge to the English way of life, it was even truer that, by their very presence, they constituted an affront to the Adlerian way of Judaism, and an assault upon the acculturative tendencies promoted so vigorously by those who felt themselves privileged to lead the community in the post-emancipation era.

If poor Jews [the *Jewish Chronicle* enquired in 1888] will persist in appropriating to themselves whole streets, in the same districts, if they will conscientiously persevere in the seemingly harmless practice of congregating in a body at prominent points in a great public thoroughfare like the Whitechapel or Commercial Road, drawing to their peculiarities of dress, of language and of manner, the attention which they might otherwise escape, can there be any wonder that the vulgar prejudices of which they are the objects should be kept alive and strengthened?[154]

For inasmuch as these 'peculiarities' of dress, language, and manner did give rise to prejudice, those migrants who remained in Britain had to be coaxed out of them. At the same time, the awesome consequences of a migrant take-over, by sheer weight of numbers, of the institutional basis of British Jewry had to be prevented. 'In ten or fifteen years', Nathan Joseph warned in 1893, 'the children of the refugees of to-day will be men and women, constituting in point of numbers the great bulk of the Jews of England. They will drag down, submerge and disgrace our community if we leave them in their present state of neglect.'[155] For these reasons, and side by side with the policy of repatriation, re-emigration, and restriction, there was implemented a programme of Anglicization and social control.

Communal leaders had no doubt that the long-term solution lay in education.[156] Jewish day schools were frowned upon by the Anglo-Jewish middle classes, but they received a new lease of life once the immigrant flow began to accelerate. By 1870 the Jews' Free School had no less than 1,600 boys on its roll, and 1,000 girls, taught by a staff of seventy (including pupil teachers); presiding over them all was the redoubtable Moses Angel (1819–98), headmaster for fifty-one years, who, even before the great immigration, had made no secret of his belief that the school's

[154] *JC* (28 Sept. 1888) 9.

[155] Ibid. (3 Feb. 1893), 16.

[156] Ibid. (20 Apr. 1888), 9.

overriding purpose must be to Anglicize the children entrusted to its care. 'Their parents', Angel told the newly established London School Board in 1871 'were the refuse population of the worst parts of Europe'; 'until they [the children] had been Anglicized or humanized it was difficult to tell what was their moral condition . . . [they] knew neither English nor any intelligible language.'[157] Angel's reference to 'refuse population' evoked communal disapprobation. But his condemnation of Yiddish as an unintelligible tongue had many supporters, and it was repeated, almost exactly twenty-four years later, by his successor, Louis B. Abrahams, who advised parents and pupils at the school prize-giving in 1905 to discard Yiddish, 'that miserable jargon which was not a language at all'.[158]

Once in the Jews' Free School, immigrant youngsters and the children of immigrant parents were weaned away from Yiddish as quickly as possible; their Yiddish-based cultural background and life-style were equally derided. Louis Abrahams urged parents to 'strengthen the efforts of teachers to wipe away all evidence of foreign birth and foreign proclivities'. The success of these efforts had already been recognized by the Government. Pupils 'enter the school Russians and Poles', a Board of Trade Report noted with evident satisfaction in 1894, 'and emerge from it almost indistinguishable from English children'.[159]

There were also in the capital by 1880 two Jews' Infants Schools (1,240 pupils), the Spanish & Portuguese School in Heneage Lane (350), the Stepney Jewish School (392; founded by the Adler family in 1863), the Westminster Jews' Free School (358), and a number of smaller establishments, such as the Bayswater Jewish Schools (founded 1867). Between them all these schools catered for about 5,600 children.[160] In the provinces there were by 1880 three Jewish schools in receipt of Treasury grants: Manchester (1,276), Liverpool (512), and Birmingham (389).[161] This provision was totally

[157] Quoted in Gartner, *Jewish Immigrant*, 223.

[158] *JC* (7 July 1905), 21.

[159] Quoted in Lipman, *Social History*, 147.

[160] Gartner, *Jewish Immigrant*, 224. Of these schools, the Bayswater, the 2 Jews' Infants, the Borough, the Westminster, and the Jews' Free School were in receipt of Treasury grants, which had been made available to Jewish schools since 1853; see C. Hershon, 'The Evolution of Jewish Elementary Education in England with Special Reference to Liverpool', Ph.D. thesis (Sheffield, 1973), 50.

[161] *JC* (1 Oct. 1880), 5.

inadequate to meet the demands of the great immigration. The gap was made good by the 'state' schools set up under the authority of local school boards following the passage of the Education Act of 1870; by 1901 the proportion of Jewish children in the capital attending Board schools was over 60 per cent.[162] At these schools children received instruction in Judaism from teachers employed first by the Jewish Association for the Diffusion of Religious Knowledge (established 1860) and later (from 1894) by the Jewish Religious Education Board.[163]

There was a certain irony in the very heavy dependence of the community on Board schools; less than a half-century before the community had boasted, in relation to the poor, that it would look after its own, and not rely on state aid. This dependence became heavier still following the passage of the Voluntary Schools Act in 1897, which freed voluntary schools from the obligation to pay rates, and increased the money available from the Treasury to support such schools; the Jewish schools of the metropolis at once formed themselves into the Jewish Voluntary Schools Association in order to be able to take advantage of this largesse.[164] By the beginning of the twentieth century the Jewish schools, both in London and the provinces, were utterly dependent upon state aid; this circumstance, and the fact that the Conservative Party was known to favour state support for denominational schools, to which the radical and Nonconformist wings of the Liberal Party were deeply opposed, acted as another force propelling the established Jewish community and the Conservative Party into an ever-deeper identity of interests.[165]

The Jewish voluntary-aided schools and the Board schools acted as a powerful mechanism by which immigrant children, and the children of immigrant parents, could be instructed in the ways of English and Anglo-Jewish society. Nor was the point lost that this function also reached out to the parents themselves. In a paper delivered to the Conference of Anglo-Jewish Ministers in 1911 (by which date over three-quarters of Jewish children in London were being educated at LCC elementary schools), the Revd S. Levy, observing that 'the national system of compulsory and free

[162] Gartner, *Jewish Immigrant*, 227–8.
[163] Lipman, *Social History*, 152.
[164] Hershon, 'Jewish Elementary Education', 114–15.
[165] Alderman, *London Jewry*, 24.

education' was enabling thousands of Jewish children 'to acquire English habits of thought and character', added that this process 'has inevitably a retroactive effect upon the parents in the home'.[166]

These roles were reinforced by a veritable battery of other devices, all brought into play with the object of Anglicizing the newcomers as quickly as possible. These ranged from the provision of free English language classes for adults (which the Russo-Jewish Committee began in 1894) to the establishment and fostering of a network of clubs and societies catering for both adults and young people. In these not only was the learning of English encouraged, but the new arrivals were introduced to the panoply of English cultural and leisure pursuits, such as swimming, football, and cricket. Typical of these organizations were the Jewish Working Men's Club (founded by Samuel Montagu in 1872), the Jewish Girls' Club (established by Lady Magnus in 1886), the West Central Jewish Girls' Club (established by Montagu's daughter, Lily, in 1893), and the Brady Boys' Club (founded in Whitechapel, under Lady Rothschild's patronage, in 1896).[167] The Jewish Lads' Brigade, founded in 1895 by Colonel A. E. W. Goldsmid, was 'substantially modelled' on the Church Lads' Brigade, in whose quasi-militaristic and religiously patriotic spirit it unashamedly followed; its aim, according to Commandant Goldsmid, was 'to instil into the rising generation all that is best in the English character, manly independence, honour, truth, cleanliness, love of active health-giving pursuits, &c.'—as if these admirable traits were not to be derived from a purely Jewish-Yiddish environment.[168]

As vehicles for the transmission of British values, and as purveyors of the benefits of social and cultural assimilation, clubs were of course invaluable. They were investments in the future, which is presumably why the wealthy Anglo-Jewish upper middle classes subscribed so generously to them. But neither clubs nor schools could address the religious separatism of the immigrants *en masse*; this separatism posed the greatest challenge to the social and organizational structure of British Jewry at the end of the

[166] Quoted in Lipman, *Social History*, 144.

[167] See generally H. Pollins, *A History of the Jewish Working Men's Club and Institute 1874–1912* (Oxford, 1981); L. Montagu, *My Club and I: The Story of the West Central Girls' Club* (2nd edn., London, 1954); and Black, *Social Politics*, ch. 5, 'Club Life'.

[168] C. Bermant, *Troubled Eden* (London, 1969), 88–9; *JC* (23 Aug. 1901), 6. On Goldsmid see C. Bermant, *The Cousinhood* (London, 1971), 242–3.

nineteenth century, and it demanded the most sophisticated response.

We have already noted how Nathan Marcus Adler sought to construct a religious superstructure for British Jewry that was radically different from that to be found in the Jewries of eastern Europe; he could do this because he had the support of the lay leadership, but also because the numbers of Jewish immigrants settling in Britain before the 1880s were small enough for them to be absorbed, without much difficulty, into the existing system. Leaving aside the small Reform congregations (none of which posed any threat to the status or authority of the Chief Rabbinate), the independent *chevrot* of very orthodox Jews to be found in London and Manchester could be accommodated within Nathan Adler's system, because in practice they acknowledged his authority, even though they had taken no part in his election.

It was true that these congregations lacked the decorum to be found in the United Synagogue (they would have said that their services possessed the noisy spontaneity for the absence of which the United Synagogue had unfortunately become famous). It was also true that the typical *chevra* met for worship in any back- or upstairs-room, attic, or hut that could be found for the purpose—partly because its members could not afford anything better (any more, as we have seen, than they could have afforded United Synagogue membership fees). The member of a *chevra* placed more importance upon what one did when one met for prayer, than upon the comparative luxury of the surroundings in which one prayed. The United Synagogue prayed in private. Members of *chevrot* were not ashamed to parade their boisterous Judaism for the whole world to see. In 1873 the *Jewish Chronicle* voiced its disgust at 'the undignified and highly objectionable accompaniment of a public procession of Jewish (?) ceremonial through London streets on the Sabbath of millions of our fellow-countrymen'.[169]

Adherents of the *chevrot*, in short, practised multiculturalism a century or more before the term was coined in relation to the impact of other ethnic minorities upon British society. For some this obstinacy which the orthodox Jewish immigrant displayed, in 'retaining habits and customs wholly unsuited to his surroundings

[169] *JC* (19 Sept. 1873), 413; the question mark occurs in the original text, and is itself a comment upon the Englishness of United Synagogue Judaism at that time.

and his new home', was fraught with danger.[170] But so long as the *chevrot* remained small in number they could be left alone, to pursue an exotic Judaism which might occasionally give rise to public comment, but which was generally felt to constitute an important safety-valve. The most widely held opinion about the *chevrot* that existed in England before the 1880s was, indeed, that they probably performed a useful role in Anglicizing groups of Jews who could not be reached in other ways. 'These members of the *Hebras*', the *Jewish Chronicle* explained in 1876, 'would feel strange in our synagogue. They must pass through a period of transformation. They must serve their apprenticeship to English feelings and English institutions. This service the *Hebras* perform for us.'[171]

There is a fundamental symmetry about the religious organization of the immigrants that came to Britain at the end of the nineteenth century, and a set of fundamental characteristics that were held in common, even if they were much more pronounced, and visible, in London than in the provinces. Wherever immigrants settled they established their own religious infrastructure. This might be centred around a fraternity—*chevra*, based, perhaps, upon the common origins of groups of immigrants—*landsmannschaften*—or upon a friendly society or trade union, or upon some religious precept. Or the religious life of the immigrants would be based upon a 'house of study', the *Beth Hamedrash*, by which was of course meant a house of religious study, which would double as a house of worship when the need arose. In Leeds, for example, immigrants kept away from the *Englische Shool*, the Great Synagogue erected in Belgrave Street, and founded instead, in the early 1870s, the *Beth Hamedrash Hagadol* (Great House of Study), the Central Synagogue and *Beth Hamedrash* in Templar Street (1885), the *Mariempoler Chevra* in Hope Street (1885), and the *Polnische Shool* (Polish Synagogue) in Byron Street (1893).[172] In Liverpool about twenty *chevrot* had been established by the end of the nineteenth century, some of them in converted churches or chapels.[173] In Glasgow a series of *minyanim* (prayer-groups) sprang up amongst immigrants settled in

[170] *JC* (28 July 1876), 259: letter from 'M.D.'

[171] Ibid. (24 Nov. 1876), 531.

[172] A. S. Diamond, 'A Sketch of Leeds Jewry in the 19th Century', in A. Newman (ed.), *Provincial Jewry in Victorian Britain* (London, 1975).

[173] N. Kokosalakis, *Ethnic Identity and Religion: Tradition and Change in Liverpool Jewry* (Washington, DC, 1982), 130.

the Gorbals in the 1880s, some of them *landsmannschaften* (Minkser Minyan, Odessa Minyan), others based upon the common occupations of their participants; the first synagogue proper was not built in Glasgow's South Side until 1901.[174] Even in a Jewry as small as Swansea (about 300 souls by 1900) the immigrants did not join the Goat Street synagogue opened in 1859, but established instead their own *Beth Hamedrash* in Prince of Wales Road (opened 1906).[175]

One other feature of immigrant settlement at this time deserves mention here: rabbis were amongst the immigrants, and whilst most *chevrot* were too poor to employ a rabbi, or indeed any religious official, some were not. Because of the migrations from eastern Europe, British Jewry experienced the novel sensation of having in its midst rabbinical scholars of high repute, trained in the *yeshivot* of Russia, Lithuania, and Poland, who were fully competent, in the eyes of orthodox Jewry, to authorize marriages and divorces, and to license *shochetim*.[176] Thus in Leeds the *Beth Hamedrash Hagadol* obtained, in 1901, the services of a distinguished Russian rabbinical scholar, Israel Chaim Daiches (1850–1937).[177] The immigrant Rabbi Shmuel Ya'acov Rabbinowitz (1857–1921) served in Liverpool from 1905.[178] Rabbi Avraham Shyne, formerly of Helsinki, ministered to the Gorbals community from 1885 to 1907.[179] The following year Rabbi Shmuel Yitzhak Hillman, of Bresen, in Russia, was appointed Communal Rabbi in Glasgow, where he served until 1914 and in which he succeeded in establishing a local *Beth Din*.[180]

In East London scores of *chevrot* sprang up after 1881, some with names which advertised the geographical origins of their members (the Grodno Synagogue, 44 Spital Street; the Kovno

[174] T. Benski, 'Glasgow', in Newman (ed.), *Provincial Jewry*; K. E. Collins, *Second City Jewry: The Jews of Glasgow in the Age of Expansion, 1790–1919* (Glasgow, 1990), 48–9.

[175] G. Alderman, 'Into the Vortex: South Wales Jewry before 1914', in Newman (ed.), *Provincial Jewry*.

[176] There is a useful list in B. Homa, *Orthodoxy in Anglo-Jewry 1880–1940* (London, 1969), 14.

[177] On Daiches see *JC* (23 June 1937), 15; (2 July), 12; *Jewish World* (14 Sept. 1906), 403; and Gartner, *Jewish Immigrant*, 247–8. The only periodical devoted to rabbinic scholarship to be published in England at this time, *Bet Va'ad la Hahamim* (*Assembly House of the Wise*) (1902–4), was Daiches's brainchild.

[178] Gartner, *Jewish Immigrant*, 193, 249; *JC* (17 June 1921), 13–14.

[179] Collins, *Second City Jewry*, 53.

[180] Ibid. 138–9.

Synagogue, Catherine Wheel Alley; the Warsaw Synagogue, Gun Street; the United Brethren of Konin Synagogue, 84 Hanbury Street; the Brothers of Petrikoff Synagogue, Sly Street). The names of others reflected the particular purpose of their founders (the Sons of the Covenant Friendly Society, Hope Street; the Holy Calling Benefit Society, 16 New Court; the *Chevra Kehol Chassidim* (Society of the Community of the Pious), 35 Fieldgate Street). Others, again, simply expressed an ethical principle or contained a biblical reference (the Glory of Jacob Synagogue, 18 Fieldgate Street; the Love and Kindness Synagogue, Prescot Street). Most of these *chevrot* existed in makeshift accommodation of which the premises of the *Chevra Kehol Chassidim* were not untypical:

> This Chevra numbering 52 members . . . partakes of the character of a Beis Hamedrash being open all day for study. The members contribute 5d a week, the income aggregating to about £100 per annum. There is a mutual benefit fund; loans being advanced to members free of interest . . . The synagogue is approached through a somewhat dingy passage, and is built in the same way as many workshops in that locality, on what was originally the open space at the back of the house. There are between 80 and 90 seats for males, and no provision for females.[181]

Most of the London *chevrot* could not afford full-time rabbis. But enough of them could, so that a veritable academy of rabbis from eastern Europe became concentrated in the capital: David Rabinowitz and Moshe Avigdor Chaikin at the Peace & Truth Synagogue, Old Castle Street; Eliyahu Shalom Regensberg and Ya'akov Dimovitch at the *Ain Ya'akov* (Well of Jacob) *chevra*, Artillery Lane; Shmuel Kalman Melnick of Princelet Street, and, above all, Avraham Aba Werner (1837–1912), formerly a *Dayan* in Tels, Lithuania, and subsequently Rabbi in Helsinki, who in 1891 arrived in London to take up the post of Rabbi to the *Chevra Machzike Hadath* (Society of the Upholders of the Religion), an alliance of two rigidly orthodox communities, one of German and Austro-Hungarian immigrants in Stoke Newington, North London, the other of Russian and Polish immigrants located in Booth Street, Spitalfields.[182]

[181] Federation of Synagogues Building Committee Report, 19 Jan. 1897, quoted in Alderman, *Federation*, 12–13.

[182] B. Homa, *A Fortress in Anglo-Jewry* (London, 1953), 7–8; Gartner, *Jewish Immigrant*, 209; Homa, *Orthodoxy*, 22.

Avraham Werner accepted the invitation to become the spiritual head of this body in the late summer of 1891, shortly after Hermann Adler had been confirmed as Chief Rabbi. The two events were most certainly not coincidental. As Delegate Chief Rabbi in the 1880s Hermann had become an object of ridicule and contempt among the immigrants. This was not simply on account of his relative leniency in the matter of reform of the synagogue service, or his Anglican clerical garb (complete with gaiters), nor merely because, as we shall see, his right-wing and anti-trade-union stance was not one with which most immigrants felt they could identify. Their hostility to him was specifically directed at the religious role he arrogated to himself, and became focused initially upon his superintendence of the requirements as to *kosher* meat and poultry, and later upon his extreme reluctance to recognize the religious status of the many eminent rabbis who ministered to immigrant congregations.

These two issues were deeply intertwined. Grave misgivings about Adler's leniency in permitting (in his capacity as the more senior ecclesiastical authority of the London Board for Shechita) the sale of kidney suet and of unporged hindquarter meat, and in turning a blind eye to other infringements of orthodox practice regarding the preparation and sale of *kosher* meat and poultry, led the *Machzike Hadath* to appoint Werner as their rabbi, and then led him to authorize the establishment of an entirely separate *shechita* operation.[183] This move threatened the financial viability of the Shechita Board (whose fees for the killing of poultry were higher than those of the *Machzike Hadath*), but of far greater concern to Adler, and to the lay leadership of Anglo-Jewry, was the challenge that had been thrown down to Adler's competence as a rabbi and to his claim to be 'Chief Rabbi' and to be entitled to exercise the authority which it was assumed went with that office.[184] Each side declared the *shechita* of the other to be *trefah*—i.e. not *kosher*—and appealed to eminent Continental rabbis for support. The *Machzike Hadath* evolved into a distinct and independent *kehilla* (community), on the eastern European model, authorizing its own marriages and divorces, making its own arrangements for the supply of *kosher* food, and establishing

[183] Homa, *Fortress*, 29–31.

[184] A. M. Hyamson, *The London Board for Shechita 1804–1954* (London, 1954), 45–8.

its own *Talmud Torah* (religion school) which gave religious instruction in Yiddish.[185]

In 1898 the *Talmud Torah* and community moved into a converted chapel at the corner of Brick Lane and Fournier Street.[186] The Spitalfields Great Synagogue (as it was known) became the acknowledged centre of immigrant opposition to Adlerian and United Synagogue Judaism. Its fame spread. In 1902, under its influence, a separate *shechita* was established in Liverpool, supervised by Rabbi Gershon Ravinson.[187] The denunciation of this *shechita* as *trefah* by the Liverpool Shechita Board (which operated under Adler's authority) led to a much publicized libel action; Adler's competence was upheld, but the Liverpool Board (which had alleged bribery) had damages awarded against it.[188] The remaining years of Adler's life were dogged by *shechita* disputes of a similar kind, which reached the civil courts again in Manchester in 1907 and in London in 1911. In each case what was at issue was the right of immigrant groups to establish, and have recognized as *kosher*, slaughtering arrangements not sanctioned by the Chief Rabbi. The Manchester result followed that of Liverpool in recognizing the Chief Rabbi's authority. But in London the jury could not agree, with the result that the *exclusive* jurisdiction claimed by Adler was put in doubt; the London Board for Shechita refrained henceforth from referring to meat and poultry authorized by other rabbis as *trefah*.[189]

Adler's insistence on being recognized as a unique rabbinical authority contributed much to the erosion of his status and standing. A wiser man, knowing his own intellectual limitations, would have acted with circumspection and diplomacy. Adler acted with neither. In eastern Europe every Jewish community had its own rabbi. Hermann Adler regarded the whole of the British Empire as one community, presided over by one rabbi—namely himself. In eastern Europe matters of dispute within a community would be submitted to the local *Beth Din*, upon which would sit three *Dayanim*, appointed on the basis of their sagacity and religious reputation, and who would reach a binding decision by a majority vote. This was not at all the view of Hermann Adler, who made it clear, in accepting the position of Chief Rabbi in his own

[185] Homa, *Fortress*, 50–1. [186] Ibid. 54–5. [187] Ibid. 62.

[188] *JC* (26 Feb. 1904), 7; (4 Mar.), 8–11.

[189] Ibid. (12 July 1907), 34–5; (19 July), 30–1; (10 Feb. 1911), 8, 15–16; (17 Feb.), 19–21, 25–7; (28 July), 8. Hyamson, *London Board for Shechita*, 62–3.

right, following his father's death, that he would not consider himself bound by the authority of the *Beth Din*, or even feel obliged to consult it.[190] Noting that the Deed of Foundation and Trust gave exclusive responsibility for the religious administration of the United Synagogue to 'the Chief Rabbi', the United Synagogue's Executive Committee explained to the Council that the *Dayanim* 'are called upon to act in a consultative capacity only'.[191]

Even within this distinctly unorthodox framework, the London *Beth Din*, as operated by the United Synagogue, was not a tribunal in which immigrant Jews placed a great deal of faith. In 1870 its members consisted of Nathan Marcus Adler, the Revd A. L. Barnett, and the Revd Aaron Levy (1795–1875). The vacancy created by Barnett's death was not filled; Levy retired in 1872. In 1875 the *Beth Din* was formally taken under the wing of the United Synagogue, and the following year the Revd Bernard Spiers (1827–1901) was appointed *Dayan*. Spiers did not enjoy the confidence of the immigrants.[192] The appointment as *Dayan* of Ya'acov Reinowitz was more sympathetically received, and *Sha'alot* (questions pertaining to religious matters) were invariably referred to him for detailed scrutiny; but Reinowitz, though he eventually received a gratuity from the United Synagogue, was never employed by it, receiving instead a wage of £2 per week out of Hermann Adler's own pocket.[193] On his death, in 1893, his place was taken by his son-in-law, Susman Cohen, who retired in 1906.

Bernard Spiers died at the end of 1901. By that time, realizing that his refusal to award *Semichot* (rabbinical diplomas) himself, or to recognize those awarded by others, was causing friction within as well as beyond the orbit of the United Synagogue, Hermann Adler had been prevailed upon (1899) to confer *Semicha* upon two Russian-born but London (and Jews' College) educated Reverends,

[190] H. Adler to Secretary of the United Synagogue, 23 Nov. 1890, cited in A. Newman, *The United Synagogue 1870–1970* (London, 1977), 93. Adler added that 'The visitation of Provincial Synagogues and Schools is exclusively the function and duty of the Chief Rabbi, as is the visitation of a diocese by its Bishop.'

[191] Archives of the United Synagogue, Council Minute Book, 1880–91, vol. 1, part 2: Report of the Executive Committee, 3 Feb. 1891, as adopted by the Council, 17 Feb.

[192] Ibid.; Homa, *Fortress*, 15; R. Apple, 'United Synagogue: Religious Founders and Leaders', in S. S. Levin (ed.), *A Century of Anglo-Jewish Life 1870–1970* (London [1971]), 18. On Spiers see *JC* (3 Jan. 1902), 9–10.

[193] Homa, *Fortress*, 16.

Asher Feldman (1873–1948) and Moses Hyamson (1863–1948).[194] Early in 1902 these two newly-appointed rabbis were elevated to the *Beth Din*. There was a spontaneous revolt in the East End, where (1 March) a well-attended meeting at the Aldgate Baths protested against 'the action of the United Synagogue in attempting to elect as *Dayanim*, men in whom the East End has, and can have, no confidence whatever'.[195] This crisis had about it the making of a schism greater still than that caused by the *Machzike Hadath* revolt over *shechita*. The policy of appointing only 'English' *Dayanim* emanated from within the ruling circles of the United Synagogue, who saw in such appointments a way of Anglicizing the immigrants; Lord Rothschild, in particular, 'refused to consider an East European rabbi as a regular Dayan'.[196] Hermann Adler, either because he sympathized with the complaints or out of fear that his authority was about to be further eroded, persisted with the appointments of Hyamson and Feldman, but consulted also with Samuel Montagu, the President of the Federation of Synagogues, the umbrella body to which many of the East End *chevrot* belonged; as a result, the Federation's 'Minister', Moshe Avigdor Chaikin (1852–1928), was invited to participate in the work of Hermann Adler's *Beth Din* without, however, being assured of a permanent place on it and, indeed, without the title of *Dayan*.[197]

Some years later Montagu again intervened to bolster Adler's authority, by negotiating the admission into the Federation of the *Machzike Hadath*, as part of a settlement of the long-running *shechita* dispute. The resolution of this conflict had become more urgent following the publicity surrounding the Liverpool libel case and (later the same year) the publication of an official report (by a Committee of the Board of Admiralty) highly critical of the Jewish

[194] M. Goulston, 'The Status of the Anglo-Jewish Rabbinate, 1840–1914'. *JJS* 10 (1968), 73–6. The diplomas awarded to Hyamson and Feldman contained the extraordinary stipulation that, though rabbis, they could exercise their rabbinical functions only under the Chief Rabbi's supervision. In 1901 Adler was prevailed upon to approve changes in the curriculum of Jews' College permitting its students to take the rabbinical diploma: I. Harris, *Jews' College Jubilee Volume, 1855–1905* (London, 1906), pp. cxlii–cxliv; A. M. Hyamson, *Jews' College, London, 1855–1955* (London, 1955), 75–6.

[195] J. Jung, *Champions of Orthodoxy* (London, 1974), 80; Gartner, *Jewish Immigrant*, 208; *JC* (7 Mar. 1902), 13.

[196] Gartner, *Jewish Immigrant*, 208.

[197] Alderman, *Federation*, 39.

method of slaughter.[198] Financial pressures upon the *Machzike Hadath* had also become very acute. The institutions of the *Machzike Hadath* community remained in being, but under the terms of the settlement (16 February 1905) the overall authority of the Chief Rabbi was recognized 'provided that he acts in accordance with the *Shulchan Oruch* [Code of Jewish Law]'. In particular, Werner renounced his right to authorize marriages and divorces, and though the separate *shechita* remained in being, its administration passed henceforth into the hands of the London Board for Shechita.[199]

In more ways than one, therefore, the events of 1905 marked a watershed in the development of the relationship between the established community of Jews in Britain and the newer immigrants. The passage of the Aliens Act promised a drastic curtailment of the volume of Jewish immigration to Britain. Whether this hope was fulfilled quite in the way expected is a matter of dispute. Immigration from Russia and Poland fell, from over 12,000, in 1906, to under 4,000, in 1911.[200] But by 1906 immigration from Russia and Poland had probably passed its peak; the Act applied only to the 'undesirable' alien—defined largely in terms of destitution and criminal record—and the bulk of the new arrivals were admitted without inspection. Evans-Gordon and his associates were soon complaining bitterly about the negative impact of the measure. Yet, although the Act did not concern itself with transmigrants, its psychological effect was undeniable: news of its passage spread through the Pale of Settlement, and almost certainly acted as a deterrent.[201] The Liberal Government elected to office in January 1906 adopted a lenient approach, giving immigrants the benefit of any doubt as to their genuine status as victims of political or religious persecution.[202] But the Liberals did not repeal what they knew to be a popular measure.[203]

[198] Report of the Committee Appointed by the Admiralty to consider the Humane Slaughtering of Animals, *PP* 1904, xxiv [Cd. 2150], 10–11: *shechita* was recommended to be outlawed until 'some method of pre-stunning is devised'.

[199] *JC* (24 Feb. 1905), 18; Homa, *Fortress*, 65–7; Alderman, *Federation*, 26.

[200] Lipman, *Social History*, 143.

[201] Alderman, *Jewish Community*, 77–8; C. Holmes, *John Bull's Island: Immigration & British Society 1871–1971* (London, 1988), 72.

[202] Garrard, *English and Immigration*, 105; see also J. Pellew, 'The Home Office and the Aliens Act, 1905', *Historical Journal*, 32 (1989), 361–85.

[203] Nor did they accede to the Jewish request to abolish the £5 naturalization fee: *JC* (24 Apr. 1908), 7.

The tide of Jewish immigration to Britain thus receded. It left a Jewry—or, more accurately now, a series of Jewries—quite different from that which had existed but a quarter-century before. These differences were not merely religious and social; they were also cultural, political, and idealistic. In London, moreover, an entirely new synagogal body had been called into existence, which gave expression to these differences, and articulated them both internally and to the wider world. In response, as it were, the already established community erected defence mechanisms of its own to preserve an identity and an outlook suddenly under attack.

4
Strange Doctrines

THE dislocation which the great immigration from eastern Europe caused to the established structures of British Jewry went beyond mere numbers and extended into areas far removed from those of religious observance and ecclesiastical jurisdiction. The immigrants, whether orthodox or not in the Judaism they practised (and there were many who were non- or anti-orthodox)[1] were practically without representation in the institutional framework of British Jewry. Their *chevrot* were unwelcome as participants in the governance of the Boards of Guardians in London and the provinces. In London there was no immigrant participation in the management of the Guardians until March 1888, when the umbrella Federation of Synagogues was permitted one representative, thanks largely to the influence of the Federation's patron, Samuel Montagu. No Federation synagogue was represented on the Board of Deputies until 1889, when the Spital Square Poltava Synagogue (founded 1858) paid for and returned one Deputy.[2]

The participation of immigrant congregations in the supervision of *shechita* arrangements was a matter contentious on several grounds, touching as it did upon the authority of the Chief Rabbi, the presumed autonomy of local rabbinates, and the distribution of financial resources; for the fees customarily imposed by Jewish communities in respect of the slaughter of meat and poultry and the supervision of butchers' shops constituted a major form of communal taxation, the profits derived therefrom being distributed among the participating congregations. The exclusion of immigrant congregations from existing *shechita* arrangements carried with it, as we have seen, the threats of unwelcome publicity and schism. Yet

[1] L. P. Gartner, *The Jewish Immigrant in England, 1870–1914* (London, 1960), 192, suggests that only about half the 'eligible' Jews in East London belonged to *chevrot*.

[2] G. Alderman, *The Federation of Synagogues 1887–1987* (London, 1987), 22.

existing leaderships were slow to come to terms with the new reality.

In Manchester there was no communal Shechita Board until 1892. Prior to that date the affairs of *shechita* in Manchester had been administered by the Great Synagogue. In 1891 a conference of all the orthodox Jewish communities in the city resolved to establish a Manchester Shechita Board, 'controlled by . . . representatives from every synagogue', which was formally established early the following year.[3] Even so, the determination of some independent congregations to maintain separate *shechita* facilities continued to give rise to problems (and occasional court cases). By January 1894 the New Synagogue and Beth Hamedrash (established 1889) had gone further, by setting up its own Shechita Board and its own *Beth Din*. Partly in response, the Manchester Shechita Board felt it necessary to provide the services of *Dayanim* (Reverend Supervisors) to hear disputes relating to both private and religious matters; in 1902 the shape of a city-wide communal *Beth Din*, operating under the aegis of the United Synagogue's *Beth Din* in London, took on a definite form.[4]

The Liverpool Shechita Board dated from 1897; here, too, the established community had, perforce, to reach an accommodation with the immigrants; here, too, recourse was had to the secular courts, and here, too, the sheer size of the Jewry in which the immigration had resulted made it essential to appoint a rabbi (S. Y. Rabbinowitz) first to supervise *shechita* but also to act as a local ecclesiastical authority.[5] In London the right of the immigrants to take part in the supervision of *shechita* was not conceded until February 1901. In November 1888 Samuel Montagu, in his capacity as President of the London Shechita Board, believed that he had reached an agreement with the United Synagogue and the Spanish & Portuguese Jews' Congregation which would permit the Federation of Synagogues to have three representatives upon the Board, and a one-fifth share of the profits.[6] In fact, the Executive Committee of the United Synagogue was not then

[3] I. W. Slotki, *History of the Manchester Shechita Board . . . 1892–1952* (Manchester, 1954), 13.

[4] Ibid. 34, 52.

[5] N. Kokosalakis, *Ethnic Identity and Religion: Tradition and Change in Liverpool Jewry* (Washington, DC, 1982), 136.

[6] J. E. Blank, *The Minutes of the Federation of Synagogues* (London, 1912), 24–5; Alderman, *Federation*, 22.

prepared to tolerate such an arrangement, arguing that the Federation was a divisive body whose members omitted to take their proper share of London Jewry's financial burdens.[7] It was not until January 1899 that the United Synagogue relented, and not until another two years had passed that the Federation received its first remittance from the Board, a cheque for £76.

The *Chevrot B'nai Yisrael* (Federation of Synagogues) had been established on 16 October 1887, at a meeting of what were termed 'minor' synagogues, held on the premises of the Spital Square congregation, within the parliamentary constituency of Whitechapel, which had elected Samuel Montagu as its Liberal MP in 1885. By the time of Montagu's death, in 1911, the Federation embraced fifty-one London congregations, representing over 6,000 male members.[8] As the United Synagogue then had about 5,200 male seat-holders in membership, the Federation could justly claim to be the largest synagogal body in the United Kingdom.

That the *chevrot* of London's East End should have wished to federate themselves in order to provide services none of them could have provided individually, and which were not provided by the United Synagogue in a manner of which the immigrants approved, is perfectly understandable. To the general alienation which religious immigrants felt from Adlerian Judaism, and to the contempt in which they held his claim to be a reputable rabbinical authority, considerations of a severely practical nature came to be added. Even the lowest class of membership fees offered by the United Synagogue were beyond the means of most immigrants. But the question of burial facilities provided a much more poignant ground of complaint. The immigrants could carry out their religious observances without purpose-built synagogues, making do with a room or a hall hired for the purpose. But the provision of or access to a properly consecrated burial ground was essential. The United Synagogue had several, and was prepared to allow the burial of non-members, but at fees which most immigrants could not afford. In those cases where fees were not paid, burials were still carried out (as is required by Jewish Law), but in unmarked

[7] J. E. Blank, *The Minutes of the Federation of Synagogues* (London, 1912), 24–5; Alderman, *Federation*, 22; A. M. Hyamson, *The London Board for Shechita 1804–1954* (London, 1954), 42–4.

[8] Blank, *Minutes of the Federation of Synagogues*, 26.

graves, upon which no tombstones might be erected until all outstanding charges had been settled.[9]

The early minutes of the Federation reflect the anguish of the *chevrot* memberships at this distressing state of affairs. In July 1888 the United Synagogue agreed to reduce the charge for a 'second class' funeral to £3, but declined to alter the charge it made for children's funerals.[10] The impact of this decision can only be assessed in the light of the high rate of infant mortality then prevalent. The records of the Federation's own Burial Society, established on 15 April 1890, show that during the first two years and eight months of its existence it carried out 199 interments, of which no less than 117 (including 43 stillbirths) were of children under 1 year old.[11]

The leadership of the United Synagogue refused to address this issue until events had practically overtaken it. The solution favoured by the United Synagogue to the 'problem' of the East London *chevrot* was over ambitious and totally lacking in reality. In 1885 the United Synagogue's President, Nathan Mayer Rothschild (1840–1915; Lionel's eldest son and the first professing Jew to be raised to the peerage) persuaded the Synagogue Council to appoint a committee to address the subject of East End Jewry; 'unless the powerful leverage of the Council of the United Synagogue can be brought to bear [he argued], it is to be feared that the immigrants will remain "foreigners" in our midst.'[12] It was not until 1890, however, that a series of definite proposals emerged; the centre-piece of these was a plan to build one 'colossal' synagogue in Whitechapel, capable of seating 1,200 men and 200 women, membership (and associated burial rights) of which would be available for very modest sums.[13]

The United Synagogues's East End Scheme also incorporated plans for a variety of other institutions and facilities, such as a Savings Bank, court interpreters, reading rooms, and the provision, for the immigrants, of the services of a range of ecclesiastical

[9] Alderman, *Federation*, 13.

[10] Federation of Synagogues, Minute Book No. 1, 18 July 1888.

[11] Alderman, *Federation*, 13.

[12] *JC* (9 Jan. 1885), 9.

[13] V. D. Lipman, *Social History of the Jews in England 1850–1950* (London, 1954), 128–9. Given the true purpose of the 'colossal' synagogue scheme, it is difficult to agree with Professor Newman that 'it exemplified the basic feeling in the United Synagogue that something ought to be done to help the masses of London Jewry': A. Newman, *The United Synagogue 1870–1970* (London, 1977), 73.

officials, including a *Dayan*. Over the following eight years the Scheme underwent a number of changes; but only in its final (1898) form was the idea of a 'colossal' synagogue abandoned.[14] Such a synagogue could never have been self-supporting.[15] However large, it could never have accommodated more than a fraction of the totality of East End Jews. The expectation that immigrant Jews would want to attend it was ludicrous, and patently so in view of the fact that immigrants living in the vicinity of the Central and New West End synagogues had boycotted these places of worship, establishing their own *chevrot* instead.[16] The stipulation that members of the 'colossal' synagogue were not to enjoy to the full the rights of local autonomy and of representation at meetings of the United Synagogue Council open to members of other constituent synagogues merely added political injury to social insult.[17] A few peripheral features of the East End Scheme did eventually see the light of day. In 1905 the Jewish Institute was opened in Whitechapel; here was housed the *Beth Hamedrash*, the Court of the *Beth Din*, a reading-room and library, and here too the immigrants were offered lectures both religious and secular in content.[18]

In essence the East End Scheme was devised as an mechanism by which the immigrants might be Anglicized and controlled at the same time. 'Our motives are not wholly philanthropic', one United Synagogue leader admitted in 1891; 'our own personal interests are involved.'[19] The paternalism was too transparent, the mechanism itself was too unwieldy. In any case, by the time the Scheme was seriously discussed, the Federation of Synagogues was already in operation, achieving at least some of the objects of the ill-fated Scheme, but doing so in a manner far more gracious and infinitely more subtle.

No consideration of the origins and early history of the Federation is worth while that does not take into account the

[14] S. Sharot, 'Native Jewry and the Religious Anglicization of Immigrants in London: 1870–1905', *JJS* 16 (1974), 50–1, discusses the transformations which the scheme underwent in the 1890s.

[15] As Samuel Montagu pointed out: Lipman, *Social History*, 129.

[16] Sharot, 'Native Jewry and the Religious Anglicization of Immigrants', 50.

[17] Because the proposed synagogue would, in effect, have been subsidized by other constituents of the United Synagogue, its representation at the Synagogue Council was to be limited to 8, and its first wardens, board of management and representatives on the Council were to be chosen for it.

[18] *JC* (22 Mar. 1912), 28–9; P. Ornstein, *Historical Sketch of the Beth Hamedrash* (London, 1905), 12–13.

[19] *JC* (8 May 1891), 8.

complex motives and outlook of Samuel Montagu, its founder and the source of its early financial resource.[20] By the 1880s Montagu, a banker of vast wealth which he enjoyed using for philanthropic purposes, had become a leading member of the élite that ruled British Jewry; he was connected with every important initiative of that circle, including the London Shechita Board, the Jewish Board of Guardians, and the United Synagogue. But in a very fundamental sense he did not identify himself with the Anglo-Jewish gentry, nor did they identify with him. He was a self-made man, the son of a small tradesman in Liverpool, educated at the Liverpool Mechanics' Institute. His marriage to a sister of Lionel Louis Cohen brought him within the 'cousinhood'; but the place he occupied within it, though secure, was never comfortably enjoyed. In politics he was, and remained, a Liberal. In religious terms his orthodoxy was of the strictest.[21]

Montagu shared with other members of the cousinhood the fear that the visible presence of large numbers of Jewish immigrants in East London constituted a danger to the entire community. But he shared with the immigrants the view that United Synagogue Judaism represented a dilution of orthodoxy, and he understood better than any other member of the United Synagogue the reasons which drove the immigrants to seek an Anglo-Jewish future beyond the embrace of that institution. The absurdity of the East End Scheme struck him at once. In opposing the 'proposed Colossal Synagogue', to be subsidized by non-residents at the rate of £1,000 per annum, Montagu pointed to the facts (obvious to anyone who had taken the trouble to understand immigrant attitudes) that 'The Jews of Whitechapel desire to control their own Synagogues', and that, in consequence, they would not desert their 'small and numerous' places of worship for the proposed 'Colossal Synagogue'.[22]

The view prevalent among would-be opinion-formers in Anglo-Jewry was that the *chevrot* could and should be stamped out:

> It is because Jews have lived within themselves in other countries on the 'Hebra' principle that they have made the existence of Jews in those countries intolerable . . . the sooner the Hebra movement is crushed out of

[20] This paragraph is based on Alderman, *Federation*, 6–7, and C. Bermant, *The Cousinhood* (London, 1971), 197–207.
[21] Lily Montagu, *Samuel Montagu, First Baron Swaythling* (London, 1913), 18.
[22] *JC* (17 Jan. 1890), 6.

existence the sooner we will remove from our midst the only draw-back to the advancement of Jews in this country.[23]

Montagu, however, saw in the noisy spirituality of the *chevrot* something of great value—to which he was instantly drawn—and he determined, in any case, to make a virtue of necessity. As the local MP, Jewish to the core, and Yiddish-speaking into the bargain, he and he alone was in a position to confront the immigrants but at the same time to command their respect and their affection. He won the Whitechapel seat in 1885 after a vigorous and blatantly 'Jewish' campaign, during the course of which he attacked his brother-in-law mercilessly.[24] In 1886 he publicly expressed the hope that not a single Jew would vote Conservative.[25] In 1892 he retained the seat even though his Conservative opponent claimed to have a letter of support from Lord Rothschild, and in 1895 he retained it yet again (by thirty-two votes) in spite of the fact that his opponent undoubtedly did possess such a letter.[26] Whitechapel was one of only two Tower Hamlets parliamentary constituencies that never went Conservative between 1885 and 1900 (the other was Poplar). 'It is only natural', one newspaper observed, 'that a constituency which contains 50 per cent if not more, of Jewish people should return a Hebrew representative.'[27]

Montagu sought to devise a method by which the pious immigrants could continue to enjoy a form of religious self-government, but only within the existing framework of communal authority. More than any other leading member of the United Synagogue he recognized the dangers of schism. But he himself was no schismatic. Nor was he an opponent of Anglicization. The business of the Federation was conducted in English. No *chevra* was forced to affiliate to the Federation; *chevrot* which applied for affiliation might have their applications turned down (or accepted

23 *JC* (5 Dec. 1884), 7; see also ibid. (6 Feb. 1880), 9; (25 Feb. 1881), 10.

24 Ibid. (13 Nov. 1885), 10; his brother-in-law, Lionel Louis Cohen, had shocked the Anglo-Jewish world by standing, at that general election, as a Conservative candidate in North Paddington.

25 *JC* (2 July 1886), 9.

26 *Eastern Post* (9 July 1892), 5; *East London Observer* (20 July 1895), 6.

27 Ibid. It needs to be borne in mind that the overwhelming proportion of the Jewish inhabitants of Whitechapel at this time, because they had not been naturalized, did not have the vote (but see n. 155 below). In 1900 Whitechapel's registered electorate (5,004) formed only 6.4% of its total inhabitants: H. Pelling, *Social Geography of British Elections 1885–1910* (London, 1967), 42, 44.

on condition that improvements were carried out) if their premises were considered dangerous from the point of view of health and safety. But affiliation brought immediate benefits. There were no Federation membership fees. However, members of affiliated congregations could subscribe to the Federation's Burial Society, formed in 1890 to administer the burial ground at Edmonton, Middlesex, which Montagu had purchased (at a cost of nearly £1,000) and presented to the Federation the previous year.[28]

Montagu also associated himself with the general condemnation of the *chedorim* (literally 'rooms', usually in a teacher's house) in which the children of the immigrants were customarily given religious instruction. Here the *melammed* (teacher), usually a religious official such as a *shochet* or beadle, and almost invariably without formal training as a teacher, would supplement his other income by endeavouring to inculcate, through the medium of Yiddish and in surroundings totally unfitted for the purpose, an elementary education in Hebrew and Judaism into children whom he taught before school in the mornings and then again in the late afternoon and evenings.

Within the circle of the United Synagogue the *chedorim* were branded as obstacles to integration.[29] Montagu's approach was to bring about reform from within the world of the *chevrot*. The report (7 April 1891) of a committee appointed by the Federation to inquire into the state of religious education in the East End remains a masterly summary of the situation, all the more forceful because of the uncompromising critique it offered of the *chedorim* system:

> There are considerably more than 200 Chedorim in the East End, where at least 2000 boys from 5 to 14 years of age are trying to learn Hebrew . . . in the large majority of cases a bed room or kitchen is used . . . sometimes with a sick wife or child in the bed room, with cooking or washing being done in the kitchen. In nearly every instance the surroundings are of the most insanitary description, and the teachers in the most abject poverty.[30]

[28] Alderman, *Federation*, 13, 23–4. On the Federation's control of synagogue building policy in the East End see J. Glasman, 'London Synagogues in the late Nineteenth Century', *London Journal*, 13 (1988), 143–55.

[29] See *JC* (1 July 1898), special supplement, pp. v–vi: speech of Mrs N. S. Joseph at a 'Conference on Jewish Elementary Education' held at the Central Synagogue, London.

[30] Quoted in Alderman, *Federation*, 31.

Ideally the committee would have preferred to have seen the *chedorim* phased out, and replaced by more systematic instruction in London Board schools. However, realizing that, on grounds of cost alone, such a reform could not be realized, the committee made a more practical suggestion, that the *chedorim* be amalgamated and transferred, under the aegis of Federation synagogues, into more suitable accommodation. The *melamdim* were persuaded to undertake instruction in English, and to agree to have their pupils properly examined.[31] The Federation was a founding partner (1894) in the Jewish Religious Education Board, which endeavoured to provide more systematic and professional tuition for Jewish children attending schools in the public sector. The *chedorim* themselves were gradually superseded by *Talmud Torahs*, organized classes in religious instruction which were regularly inspected. In 1905 Montagu donated the sum of £1,000 to launch the *Talmud Torah* Trust, whose task it was to make sums available to such classes, conducted in connection with and often on premises provided by Federation synagogues.[32]

Montagu's munificence to the Federation and to Federation affiliates was prodigious. From time to time he made over to the Federation blocks of Treasury stock; he also gave very considerable sums towards the building or rebuilding of synagogues. In 1890 he funded the appointment of a Federation Minister, Dr Mayer Lerner (1857–1930; then Rabbi of Wurzheim, in Alsace), and in 1894 he provided the money to enable the Federation to acquire the services of the renowned *Maggid* of Kamenitsk, Chaim Zundel Maccoby (1858–1916), who had fled from Russia following the prohibition of his lecturing activities on behalf of the *Chovevi Zion* movement in the Pale of Settlement.[33] Maccoby continued to serve as Federation *Maggid* until his death. Lerner, disenchanted with Hermann Adler's acquiescence in liturgical reform, left England in 1894 to become *Oberrabbiner* of Altona and Schleswig-Holstein. In 1901 Montagu announced a gift of £1,000 to fund the salary, as Lerner's successor, of Avigdor Chaikin.[34] In his will he bequeathed the sum of £2,000 for the continued payment of salaries to Chaikin

[31] Quoted in Alderman, *Federation*, 31.

[32] Ibid. 36.

[33] There are sketches of Lerner and Maccoby in J. Jung, *Champions of Orthodoxy* (London, 1974), 1–67.

[34] Alderman, *Federation*, 35.

and Maccoby and left to the Federation all moneys owing to him in respect of loans made to various affiliated congregations.[35]

A variety of reasons have been offered, at the time and subsequently, to explain the Federation's establishment. Of Montagu himself it has sometimes been said that he desired to supplant Lord Rothschild as the undisputed lay leader of Anglo-Jewry, and that the launching of the Federation was designed to achieve this end. Such was the view put about by the gossip-mongers.[36] There is not a shred of evidence (even circumstantial) to support it. At its foundation Rothschild was offered, and accepted, the Presidency of the Federation, and actually presided at the second meeting of its Board of Delegates (16 January 1888). Montagu was the Vice-President; he became 'Acting' President, and then full President, only after a confrontation with Rothschild, at a meeting of the United Synagogue Council (4 December 1888) at which the opposition of the United Synagogue to the admission of the Federation to the London Shechita Board was discussed. 'I will withdraw from the meeting', Montagu declared, 'and will never again co-operate with your Lordship on any Committee.'[37] Even so, the Federation accorded Rothschild the courtesy title of Honorary President.

Montagu insisted that Rabbi Lerner exercise his religious authority 'under the jurisdiction of Dr [Nathan] Adler', and although the Federation entered a vigorous protest against its derisory allotment of two votes in the election of Hermann (as compared with the United Synagogue's 218), Montagu never failed to uphold Hermann Adler's authority and status, most notably in the matter of Hermann's dispute with the *Machzike Hadath*, as we have seen.[38] Indeed, in November and December 1891, when there were moves to forge an alliance between the Federation and the *Machzike Hadath*, Montagu used his authority to postpone indefinitely a plan to appoint a Federation committee 'to inquire into the prevalent rumours as to the condition of Kosher Meat as supplied in the East End of London'.[39] The Federation's Board of Delegates insisted that the examination of pupils in the *chedorim* take place 'under the sanction of the Chief Rabbi'.[40] Avigdor Chaikin's appointment was made with Hermann's approval;

[35] Ibid. 40–1. [36] *JC* (7 Dec. 1888), 5. [37] Ibid. 9.
[38] Federation of Synagogues, Minute Book No. 1, 7 April 1891.
[39] Ibid., Board meetings of 10 Nov. and 8 Dec. 1891.
[40] Ibid. 114: J. Blank to M. Harris, 7 Jan. 1892.

indeed the Chief Rabbi attended his installation ceremony (15 December 1901) at the New Synagogue, Great St Helen's, of which Mark Moses, a Treasurer of the Federation, was an Honorary Officer.[41]

In spite of the personal rift between Montagu and Rothschild (a rift which had not, however, prevented Rothschild from agreeing to perform the opening ceremony of the Federation's first, purpose-built, 'model' synagogue in New Road, near the London Hospital, in May 1892),[42] the Federation under Samuel Montagu's leadership remained very firmly within the jurisdiction of the Chief Rabbinate. For that reason alone, it could not be considered totally independent of the United Synagogue; nor, in view of its utter dependence upon Montagu's largesse, was it able to pursue a life of its own, driven by the larger aspirations of its members. This subservience to Samuel Montagu's personal wishes was to store up trouble for the future, after his death. So long as he lived, however, there was no risk of the Federation seceding (so to speak) from the Anglo-Jewish polity, as the *Machzike Hadath* had tried to do.

Towards the end of Montagu's life there is no doubt that he became exasperated with the unwillingness of his United Synagogue colleagues to recognize the Federation's numerical strength and communal status. The refusal of the United Synagogue to accord Avigdor Chaikin the status of a full *Dayan* was undoubtedly a turning-point. In July 1906 Montagu announced that Chaikin was 'to once more devote his entire time to the services of the Federation', and a year later, on his elevation to the peerage (as Lord Swaythling) he made known his decision to celebrate that honour by financing the appointment of a 'Chief Minister of the Federation', who would possess 'a great reputation for Orthodoxy, must be a Doctor of Theology & a good Orator, also a gentleman of refined manners . . . & able to take a prominent position among Jewish clerics'.[43]

'The Chief Minister of the Federation', Montagu told the Board of Delegates on 28 July 1907, 'would co-operate with the existing authorities, with the Chief Rabbi and with the Spanish & Portuguese Synagogue.'[44] The intention was clear: the man appointed would exercise his jurisdiction as an independent

[41] Alderman, *Federation*, 31; Jung, *Champions of Orthodoxy*, 77.
[42] *JC* (27 May 1892), 8.
[43] Alderman, *Federation*, 39–40.
[44] Ibid. 40.

rabbinical authority. The implication was also unmistakeable: the Federation of Synagogues would become thereby a *kehilla* in its own right, totally independent of any other. It seems that Montagu had in mind someone to whom he would offer the post. But he never did so, perhaps because he could not bring himself to take so drastic a step.

In June 1910 the Honorary Officers of the Federation, together with the Federation's Secretary, Joseph Blank, met their counterparts of the United Synagogue at New Court, the Rothschild headquarters, to discuss whether it might be possible (in Montagu's words) 'to prevent friction in the election of an eventual Chief Rabbi, when our respected Chief, who is over 70, is not able to work any longer at his post'.[45] Montagu offered a formal merger with the United Synagogue, but on terms which Rothschild rejected because Federation representatives on an enlarged United Synagogue Council would form a majority. Montagu also offered the United Synagogue a say in the appointment of the Federation's Chief Minister, who would be 'Delegate Chief Rabbi' and, eventually, Hermann Adler's successor. This offer, too, was refused.

Samuel Montagu died on 12 January 1911, just a few months before Hermann Adler, whose faltering authority he had in truth done so much to bolster. The United Synagogue set in motion the machinery to elect Adler's successor. Joseph Blank at once made it clear to his opposite number at the United Synagogue, Philip Ornstein, that the drama of 1890 was not to be replayed:

> If the Federation of Synagogues is to be properly represented on the body dealing with the election of the [new] Chief Rabbi, it must not be in proportion to its contribution to the Chief Rabbi's Fund . . . but to the immense interest it represents in the religious life of the community. It necessarily follows then, that the elective influence must be in proper ratio to the membership, which numbers 6,500 [males] in the 51 Synagogues represented.[46]

The response of the United Synagogue was to offer the Federation 28 votes; the Honorary Officers of the United Synagogue were to have no less than 75 at their disposal, not counting those votes cast by constituents of the United Synagogue, which would thereby command about 340 votes in all. There was no chance of the Federation accepting this arrangement.

[45] Newman, *United Synagogue*, 95–6.
[46] Blank to Ornstein, 23 Nov. 1911, quoted in Alderman, *Federation*, 45.

During the closing months of Hermann Adler's life there had been ominous indications that the principled separatism of the *Machzike Hadath* had struck chords elsewhere in British Jewry. At a Conference of Anglo-Jewish Ministers, in 1911, Rabbi Samuel Daiches (1878–1949) of Sunderland declared publicly that the Chief Rabbinate had 'crippled the community . . . [and] destroyed the sense of responsibility in congregation and Minister alike'.[47] During the interregnum that followed Adler's death the *Jewish Review*, endorsing Daiches's critique, observed in 1912 that Anglo-Jewry had been able to function without a Chief Rabbi; 'the need for a Chief Rabbi [it added] is not urgent.'[48] And at the Chief Rabbinate Conference in 1912 a deputation of immigrant rabbis demanded that the Chief Rabbi 'should not be allowed to interfere with the provincial Rabbi in questions appertaining to *Shulchan Aruch* [Code of Jewish Law] especially with regard to affairs of *Shechita*'.[49]

In December 1911, as a gesture of pacification aimed at the East End masses, the Council of the United Synagogue, on the motion of a Vice-President, Albert H. Jessel, agreed to ask the Federation whether it would permit Avigdor Chaikin to rejoin the *Beth Din* as a full *Dayan*, at a salary of £100 per annum.[50] To this the Board of the Federation enthusiastically agreed. This did nothing to alter the attitude of Federation members towards the larger question of participation in the election of Hermann Adler's successor. Hermann Landau, Mark Moses, and Joseph Blank travelled to the Continent to meet and interview between twenty and thirty applicants for the post of Chief Minister of the Federation. The choice, made by Louis Montagu, the second Lord Swaythling, under the terms of his father's trust deed, and confirmed by the Board of Delegates on 6 March 1912, fell upon Dr Meir Tsevi Jung (1858–1921), then Rabbi of Ungarisch Brod in Moravia. Eleven months later Dr Joseph Herman Hertz (1872–1946), like Jung a native of Hungary and at that time a rabbi in New York, was appointed Chief Rabbi of the British Empire. The Federation of Synagogues had taken no part in his election and declared, shortly afterwards, that it would refuse any longer to contribute to the Chief Rabbi's Fund.[51]

47 *JC* (23 June 1911), 15.
48 *Jewish Review* (May 1912), 6.
49 Quoted in Newman, *United Synagogue*, 98.
50 Alderman, *Federation*, 46.
51 Ibid. 45.

The Federation of Synagogues had clearly entered upon its majority, having outgrown the paternalism in which Samuel Montagu had clothed it at its birth. Had it, over the first quarter-century of its existence, achieved the objectives he and his associates had in mind, and in the furtherance of which he had invested so much time and money? In a letter published in the *Jewish Chronicle* some eighteen months after its foundation, Hermann Landau explained that:

> in the latter part of 1887 great dissatisfaction was expressed in the East End with existing ecclesiastical arrangements and meetings were actually held to organise a new Shechita Board, &c. The Federation was called into existence to prevent any development of this movement, and has, therefore, been the means of *preventing* communal disunion.[52]

Giving evidence to the Royal Commission on Alien Immigration in 1903 Montagu recalled (in somewhat exaggerated terms):

> I found there were different isolated [*sic*] minor synagogues in the East End of London which were disposed to quarrel among themselves and I formed the idea of amalgamating them together—quite a voluntary association—for their general benefit. The chief object was to get rid of the insanitary places of worship and to amalgamate two or three small ones together and have a suitable building. We have succeeded very well in that respect.[53]

Both these explanations were true. But they did not amount to the truth in its entirety. The Federation was called into existence as a means of preventing schism in Anglo-Jewry; as a means of bringing the mass of immigrant Jews in London in the 1880s within the discipline of the existing communal structures; and as a means of addressing some of the presumed causes of anti-Jewish prejudice. The Federation was, in fact, the largest single instrument of Anglicization, as well as of social control, that Anglo-Jewry possessed.

In this connection it is noteworthy that Samuel Montagu used the Federation to further an object dear to the hearts of the Anglo-Jewish leadership, namely to effect a dispersal of immigrants from the self-designated East London ghetto. Efforts to persuade immigrants to leave or simply not settle in the capital were

[52] *JC* (24 May 1889), 6.

[53] Royal Commission on Alien Immigration, Minutes of Evidence, *PP* 1903, ix [Cd. 1742], q. 16,772.

(inevitably) never a conspicuous success, the community established in Reading, Berkshire, in 1886, being the exception that proved the rule.[54] A new synagogue was opened in Reading in 1900, and the following year the congregation affiliated to the Federation.[55] In May 1902 the Federation hosted the first ever conference of Jewish communities of the British Isles, ninety-three delegates attending representing forty-three different congregations. Attention was drawn to 'the disadvantages caused by the overcrowding of Jews in our large towns', and to the desirability of 'a distribution from those centres to other places'.[56] It was on the basis of a resolution to this effect that Montagu set up the Jewish Dispersion Committee the following year, to offer employment and financial help to immigrants willing to move out of London; in this way Jewish families were sent to Reading, Leicester, Blackburn, Dover, and Stroud.[57] The policy of persuading Jews to move to the London suburbs, from which cheap transport was now available into the city-centre workplaces, was more successful. The Federation was instrumental, in the period 1903–7, in encouraging the establishment of communities in Walthamstow, Tottenham, Enfield, and Canning Town; in 1904 it gave notice that it would no longer assist 'in the establishment of new synagogues in the congested area in East London'.[58]

In all these respects, therefore, Montagu could argue, against his many detractors within the United Synagogue, that the formation of a Federation of the *chevrot* had been amply justified. But at the time of its foundation he had not, in fact, sought to explain its purposes in these terms at all. In his speech at the foundation meeting of the Federation Montagu had urged its formation in order to demonstrate a political point, that 'although there might be one or two Socialists' among the Jewish immigrants in East London, 'these were quite the exception to the rule'.[59] In 1889 he revealed this purpose in much more explicit terms:

> One of the principal objects of the Federation was to endeavour to raise the social condition of the Jews in East London and to prevent anything like anarchy and socialism . . . The blessings of the Patriarchs that they would

[54] Royal Commission on Alien Immigration, Minutes of Evidence, *PP* 1903, ix [Cd. 1742], 740–1: evidence of the Mayor of Reading.

[55] Alderman, *Federation*, 37.

[56] Blank, *Minutes of the Federation of Synagogues*, 37.

[57] Alderman, *Federation*, 37.

[58] Ibid. 38.

[59] *JC* (21 Oct. 1887), 7.

increase their cattle and amass wealth, and the prophecy that the poor would never cease out of the land, were in themselves evidence that Judaism did not recognise anything like social equality amongst all classes of people.[60]

Montagu's overriding object in funding Rabbi Lerner's appointment as Minister of the Federation was to enable the Federation 'to take the lead in combating this most serious evil', namely 'the influence of a few Atheists [i.e. socialists] over Jewish Working Men'.[61] Both Lerner and Maccoby were expected to preach against atheism and socialism, and both did so.[62] The Federation, in short, was a child of its times—the economic depression of the 1880s, the Marxist-inspired campaigns against unemployment which had resulted in riots at Hyde Park in February 1886 and at Trafalgar Square in November 1887, the growth of socialist-led and avowedly militant trade unions, the establishment of socialist political organizations.

Impoverished Jews working in the sweatshops of Leeds and London were bound to be influenced by these developments. The fact that they had brought with them from Russia and Poland a vibrant socialist tradition made this influence all the more inevitable. The immigrant presence—whatever its form—marked Jews out as foreigners. But in a very particular sense it also threatened to characterize them as purveyors of strange and revolutionary doctrines. W. H. Wilkins, Secretary of the Association for Preventing the Immigration of Destitute Aliens, warned in 1892 that Yiddish pamphlets circulating in the East End were spreading 'the vilest political sentiments'.[63] 'An undue proportion of the dangerous anarchists in this country', Arnold White later informed Lord Salisbury, 'are foreign Jews.'[64] S. H. Jeyes, a contributor to

[60] Ibid. (22 Mar. 1889), 12.

[61] Montagu to Blank, 6 Nov. 1889, quoted in Alderman, *Federation*, 28.

[62] Ibid. 30; E. C. Black, *The Social Politics of Anglo-Jewry 1880–1920* (Oxford, 1988), 212.

[63] W. H. Wilkins, *The Alien Invasion* (London, 1892), 48.

[64] White to Salisbury, 5 July 1894, quoted in B. Gainer, *The Alien Invasion* (London, 1972), 104. It was but a short step from the accusation of spreading anarchism to that of indulging in purely criminal activity. The charge that Jews were disproportionately represented among the criminal classes was resurrected at this time; it had no basis in fact, save, perhaps, in relation to prostitution; see C. Holmes, *Anti-Semitism in British Society 1876–1939* (London, 1979), 43–4; U. Henriques, 'The Jews and Crime in South Wales before World War I', *Morgannwg*, 29 (1985), 59–63; Gartner, *Jewish Immigrant*, 183–6; E. J. Bristow, *Prostitution and*

White's volume *The Destitute Alien*, gave his view that the alien influx, by reducing wages, strengthened 'that spirit of discontent and disorder on which the agitators live and batten, and which in time may pollute the ancient constitutional liberalism of England with the visionary violence of Continental Socialism'.[65] By 1901 a leading newspaper could claim that East End anarchists were 'almost invariably' Jewish immigrants.[66]

As with so many other accusations launched in the general direction of the Jewish immigrants, the truth of those relating to their alleged political sympathies is less important than the fact that such allegations gained a wide credence. In the popular mind Jewish refugees from Tsarist Russia had brought with them foreign philosophies of class war and social revolution; there was, therefore, a problem relating to image which the leaders of Anglo-Jewry had to address. To the extent that Jewish socialists and anarchists had in truth put down roots in England, and were in truth questioning the legitimacy of the existing (and in their view class-based) communal hierarchy, the problem required a solution all the more urgently.

There was no significant socialist presence within British Jewry prior to the great immigration. There were of course socialists of Jewish origin, mainly German *émigrés*, the most celebrated of whom was Karl Marx. But these individuals neither considered themselves members of British Jewry, nor were so considered by the community; the fact that they had Jewish backgrounds might have been convenient as a peg for anti-Jewish propaganda, but is of purely coincidental interest as a feature of Anglo-Jewish development. The home-grown early British socialist movements, such as the Owenites and the Chartists, contained no Jewish elements; Chartist newspapers had protested indignantly against persecution of Jews, but at the same time had had no compunction in bracketing Jews, along with 'jobbers, oppressors and murderers', as wealthy, parasitical enemies of the working classes.[67]

Prejudice: The Jewish Fight Against White Slavery, 1870–1939 (London, 1982), *passim*.

[65] S. H. Jeyes, 'Foreign Pauper Immigration', in A. White (ed.), *The Destitute Alien in Great Britain* (London, 1892), 189.

[66] *Eastern Post* (21 Sept. 1901), 6, quoting an article in the *Morning Standard*; the article is discussed in Gainer, *Alien Invasion*, 105.

[67] *Northern Star* (13 Nov. 1847), 8, quoted in E. Silberner, 'British Socialism and the Jews', *Historica Judaica*, 14 (1952), 34. See also A. Plummer, 'The Place of

But if the anti-Jewish discourse of early Victorian socialism acted as a deterrent to any Jewish–socialist alliance, the absence of anything approximating to a genuine, factory-based manual working class amongst the Jews was equally bound to distance British Jewry from a desire to identify with radical and trade-union movements. We have noted that the only substantially Jewish industrial employment to be found in London before 1880 was the cigar- and cigarette-making activities of the small community of Dutch Jews, and that the first recorded strike of Jewish workers in Britain involved this community, in 1858.[68] But poverty alone has never driven the poor into socialism; the many poor Jews in mid-Victorian England were as far from wanting to engage in class struggle (assuming, that is, that they understood the concept) as they were from wishing to supplant the cousinhood from its command of Anglo-Jewish institutions.

During the 1870s, and as a result of pressures in mainland Europe, a number of Jews with experience of trade-union and socialist organization made their way to London. For a brief moment in the early 1870s (the date is variously given as 1872 and 1874) a union of Lithuanian tailors existed in Whitechapel, founded by Lewis Smith, a Polish Jew who had come to England via the Polish uprising of 1863 and the Paris Commune of 1871.[69] It appears that a grand total of seventy-two members were recruited. The union lasted no more than a few weeks and then disappeared, its founder (setting a fashion which other frustrated organizers of Jewish workers in England were to follow) leaving for New York, where he became a successful labour leader.

In 1876 a somewhat more substantial socialist organization was established. A small group of intellectuals and semi-intellectuals discovered a leader in the person of Aaron Liebermann (?1849–80), a drop-out from both orthodox Judaism and the Technological

Bronterre o'Brien in the Working-Class Movement', *Economic History Review*, 2 (1929–30), 72, and M. Beer, *Fifty Years of International Socialism* (London, 1935), 104.

[68] H. Pollins, 'Anglo-Jewish Trade Unions, 1870–1914', Paper delivered to the Jewish Historical Society of England (16 Mar. 1977).

[69] W. Fishman, *East End Jewish Radicals 1875–1914* (London, 1975), 97, gives the date as 1872, the year of Smith's arrival in London; E. Tcherikower (ed.), *The Early Jewish Labour Movement in the United States*, trans. A. Antonovsky (New York, 1961), 181–2, gives 1874. See also A. R. Rollin, 'Russo-Jewish Immigrants in England before 1881',. *TJHSE* 21 (1962–7), 202–13.

Institute in St Petersburg, who had fled to Germany from the Tsarist police in 1875, and who had come thence to London to work on *Vperyod*, the Russian underground newspaper founded by the exiled Peter Lavrov.[70] On 9 May 1876 Liebermann and nine other politicized Russian-Jewish immigrants met at No. 40 Gun Street, Spitalfields, to found the *Agudas HaSozialistim HoIvrim BeLondon*—the Hebrew Socialist Union in London.[71]

Liebermann, who became the Union's secretary, proclaimed himself to be an international socialist; his views were thoroughly anti-bourgeois and anticlerical. In him, and in the Union he established, there was an inherent and unresolved contradiction: ideally, he wished to lead the Jews of Whitechapel out of Judaism and into socialism; but this was to be achieved through a specifically Jewish medium—his Union—the very existence of which was a recognition of the distinctive character of the Jewish working classes. Liebermann himself was not averse to restraining the anti-religious idealism of some of his comrades: a meeting planned for the night of Saturday, 29 July, was postponed because that night coincided with the commencement of the Fast of the Ninth of *Ab*, when orthodox Jews mourn the destruction of Jerusalem.[72]

The Union exhibited in its philosophy other fundamental confusions. It never managed to reconcile its proletarian aims with the fact that many of those whom it hoped to recruit (especially tailors) were in fact self-employed. It evinced a desire to unite Jewish and Irish immigrants in East London, forgetting that the Irish could be very anti-Jewish. Its anticlericalism was its undoing. Membership of the Hebrew Socialist Union never exceeded forty. Even so, within the area of Spitalfields in which it began to hold meetings in the summer of 1876 its fame, or notoriety, quickly spread. On 26 August 1876 a meeting held under its auspices at the Zetland Hall, Goodman's Fields, attracted several hundred workers.

[70] Fishman, *East End Jewish Radicals*, 101.

[71] The 'Hebrew Socialist Union' was the English name used by the group, although the correct translation of the Hebrew would be 'Union of Hebrew [i.e. Jewish] Socialists'. On the Union generally see the work in Yiddish by E. Tcherikower, *Der Onhayb Fun Der Yiddisher Sotsialistisher Bavegung (Liebermans Tekufeh) (The Beginning of the Jewish Socialist Movement (Liebermann's Period)*) (Warsaw, 1929), where, in cols. 533–94, the minute book of the Union is printed in full. Other source materials are listed in Gartner, *The Jewish Immigrant*, 104 n. 3.

[72] Fishman, *East End Jewish Radicals*, 108.

The demand for a maximum working day of ten hours was well received, but when Liebermann criticized the United Synagogue for imposing a high marriage fee of £3, and attacked local Jewish leaders, mentioning the Chief Rabbi by name, there was uproar: the meeting broke up in confusion.[73]

Jewish communal leaders had already taken steps to counter Liebermann's propaganda. Economic pressure was brought to bear upon Hebrew Socialist Union members by their employers. The oratorical powers of Zvi Hirsch Dainow (the *Maggid* of Slutsk) were employed against Liebermann and his comrades. A tailors' union was formed, but it was certainly not socialist, and collapsed after three months when its treasurer made off with its funds. Liebermann quarrelled with his associates, who accused him of being more Jewish than socialist. Suddenly, in December 1876, he left England. The Hebrew Socialist Union collapsed. When, after a period of revolutionary activity (and imprisonment) in Germany and Austria, he briefly returned to London in 1879, he was a spent force. He made the customary pilgrimage to America and there, in Syracuse, New York, he shot himself (November 1880).[74]

Exceedingly short lived though the Hebrew Socialist Union was, the general agreement among historians as to its significance is not mistaken. It was, as Professor Gartner has observed, the first Jewish socialist society in England; it organized the first Jewish labour meetings, and published the first Jewish socialist journal, *HaEmes* (*The Truth*).[75] The tailors' union it sponsored attracted 300 members. The attention paid to it by its Jewish detractors amounted to a compliment; the *Jewish Chronicle* was convinced that it had to be a front for missionary activity, a 'Conversionist Trick'.[76] Its brief existence threw into sharp relief the problem that was to face all succeeding Jewish socialist organs and all subsequent Jewish trade unions: whether their task was simply to act as a channel through which Jewish workers would enter the English working-class movements—the Anglicization of the Anglo-Jewish proletariat—or whether there was a specifically Jewish (and Anglo-Jewish) form of labour organization and of socialist philosophy that demanded a separate and autonomous articulation. As to the

[73] Ibid. 114–17; P. Elman, 'The Beginnings of the Jewish Trade Union Movement in England', *TJHSE* 17 (1951–2), 58–9.

[74] Alderman, *Jewish Community*, 49.

[75] Gartner, *Jewish Immigrant*, 106.

[76] *JC* (8 Sept. 1876), 364.

reason for its failure there can be no doubt. Liebermann's tragedy was to have launched the Hebrew Socialist Union at the very moment—1876—when, through the Bulgarian Agitation, Disraelian Conservatism was becoming ever more popular among all classes of British Jews. 'We socialists', one of its leaders candidly admitted, 'are widely hated in the city.'[77] Had Liebermann arrived a decade later, his impact would have been very different.

The great immigration to Britain neither consisted of nor did it result in the creation of a monolithic Jewish proletariat. The vision of a mass influx comprised exclusively of poverty-stricken but socialistically inclined Jews haunted the establishment and was naturally exploited by anti-Semites. This vision was, and has become, part of the mythology of the Jewish presence in Britain. Its basis in reality must be qualified. There is much anecdotal evidence pointing to the immigration of Jews whose social status might be reliably described as lower middle class. In the 1890s the Guardians in London noted that a new type of immigrant had begun to arrive, 'of a more capable and self-reliant nature than those who seek refuge here in times of acute persecution'.[78] These immigrants had money; their decision to come to England was based on rational choice, nurtured, perhaps, by information received from friends or relatives already settled here. They were neither frightened by the newspaper advertisements placed by the Anglo-Jewish authorities, nor were they intimidated or overawed by those who then controlled the affairs of British Jewry.

The Jewish authorities, in declaring immigrants of this type to be a phenomenon of the 1890s, were choosing to be highly selective in their presentation of evidence. The historian of Manchester Jewry has drawn attention to the way in which, between 1875 and 1914, 'the nascent Eastern European middle class [in Manchester] received a continuous flow of new recruits, a few arriving with capital and business or professional skills, most achieving modest economic success by enterprise'.[79] Ephraim Sieff and Michael Marks, if not exactly typical of this flow, were, however, dramatic

[77] Quoted in Tcherikower, *The Early Jewish Labour Movement*, 185.

[78] Jewish Board of Guardians, *Annual Report* (1897), 16.

[79] B. Williams, '"East and West": Class and Community in Manchester Jewry, 1850–1914', in D. Cesarani (ed.), *The Making of Modern Anglo-Jewry* (Oxford, 1990), 20–1.

examples of its potential.[80] In Manchester a class of immigrant *nouveaux riches* interposed itself between the Anglicized élite and the immigrant poor, taking the lead in the foundation and running of immigrant synagogues (such as Higher Broughton, founded in 1907), in the organization of alternative sources of charitable support (particularly through the establishment of friendly societies), and—ultimately—in promoting Zionism.[81]

In London the ability of immigrant parvenus to play such roles was restricted by the much stronger influence exerted by the established leadership and, of course, by the existence of the major communal institutions in the capital. None the less, the part played by Hermann Landau, who migrated from Poland in 1864, in attempting to influence the pace and direction of immigrant activities set a precedent which others were to follow. Morris Davis (1894–1985), who rose to become President of the Federation of Synagogues, 1928–44, and Labour Leader of Stepney Borough Council, 1935–44, was the son of well-to-do immigrants; his father, Joseph, born in Minsk in 1868, had settled in London at the end of the 1880s and made a very comfortable living from the liquor trade.[82] Circumstantial evidence also suggests that migration to London conferred the status of proletarian upon many Jews who had come from somewhat less humble backgrounds in eastern Europe: those who had been master artisans in Russia and Poland were obliged to become sweated employees in London, a transformation which they refused to regard as irreversible.[83] In this circumstance we may well detect an origin of their intense ambition for economic and social advancement, both for themselves and their children.[84]

Of these factors the English labour movement was well aware. English trade unionists were generally scornful of the ability of immigrant Jewish workers to organize for the purposes of collective action, pointing to the impermanence of Jewish trade unions, their

[80] I. Sieff, *Memoirs* (London, 1970), 6–13. See generally G. Rees, *St Michael: A History of Marks and Spencer* (London, 1969), chs. 1, 2.

[81] Williams, '"East and West"', 23–7.

[82] G. Alderman, 'M. H. Davis: The Rise and Fall of a Communal Upstart', *TJHSE* 31 (1988–90), 249–68.

[83] D. M. Feldman, 'Immigrants and Workers, Englishmen and Jews: Jewish Immigration to the East End of London, 1880–1906', Ph.D. thesis (Cambridge, 1985), 56.

[84] C. Russell in id. and H. S. Lewis, *The Jew in London* (London, 1900), 59.

lack of discipline, their apparent unwillingness to make common cause with English unions, and their seeming inability to produce capable leaders, as evidence in support of the contention that Jews had not 'the faintest idea of the principles of unionism'.[85] These alleged deficiencies were ascribed to a variety of causes, some of them frankly racist in implication, others springing from ignorance of the Jewish condition in the lands whence they had come. 'It must be remembered', C. Russell explained in 1900, 'that trade unionism is a new thing to the Polish Jew.'[86] Nothing could have been further from the truth.

The immigrant Jews came from societies which were rich in political and industrial organization. In the Pale of Settlement 'the Jewish strike movement . . . struck terror in the hearts of the employers'; Jewish factory-owners preferred hiring non-Jews because (in the words of one factory-owner) 'the Jews are good workers, but they are capable of organizing revolts . . . against the employer, the regime and the Tsar himself'. Jewish trade unions flourished for a time, and achieved considerable short-term successes.[87] Many of these unions owed their inception and organization to the inspiration of socialists. But Jewish socialism in the Pale of Settlement was split, initially between those who saw in revolutionary socialism the path which Jews had to take—but only in the company of other social-democratic groups—to free themselves from Tsarist oppression, and those who sought a solution to the Jewish condition through a unique form of socialist nationalism.

Adherents of the former view eventually established, at Vilna in October 1897, the anti-Zionist General Jewish Labour Movement in Russia, Poland and Lithuania—the Bund.[88] Those who espoused the socialist–nationalist philosophy (which was premissed upon the belief that the lack of a national homeland rendered impossible the normal development of a Jewish proletariat) were themselves divided—like the Zionist movement at large at this time. The territorialists, for whom any suitable territory was acceptable in

[85] *People's Press* (21 June 1890), 11. See generally the discussion in J. A. Garrard, *The English and Immigration* (London, 1971), 166–73.

[86] Russell and Lewis, *The Jew in London*, 81.

[87] E. Mendelsohn, *Class Struggle in the Pale: The Formative Years of the Jewish Workers' Movement in Tsarist Russia* (Cambridge, 1970), 22, 110–11.

[88] A. L. Patkin, *The Origins of the Russo-Jewish Labour Movement* (Melbourne, 1947), 138; O. I. Janowsky, *The Jews and Minority Rights (1898–1919)* (New York, 1933), 37– 40.

which Jewish national aspirations might be pursued within a broadly socialist framework, in time seceded from the Russian Zionist Organization to form the Zionist Socialist Labour Party (February 1905). A year later the Jewish Social Democratic Labour Party—*Poale Zion*—was formally constituted at Poltava, proclaiming Palestine as the only legitimate territory in which Jewish national self-determination might be pursued.[89]

Echoes of the quarrels between the territorialist, Zionist, and non- and anti-Zionist socialist tendencies in eastern Europe were to be heard in due course within Jewish immigrant circles in Britain. The *Poale Zion* activist Kalman Marmor (1879–1956), during a brief sojourn in England before settling in the United States, played a leading part in the establishment of the *Ma'aravi* (Western) society (1902–3), the forerunner of a number of *Poale Zion* groups which by 1905 had sprung up in London, Manchester, Leeds, and Liverpool. In 1905 Marmor edited *Die Yudische Freiheit* (*Jewish Freedom*), three issues of which appeared, and which attempted a synthesis of socialism and Zionism in an English setting. Yet as late as 1906 there is evidence of a species of *Poale Zion* thinking in London that was avowedly territorialist in its philosophy.[90]

Until the First World War support for *Poale Zion* amongst Jews in Britain remained very weak, its influence hardly comparable with that enjoyed by more mainstream socialists and, for a brief period immediately before the war, by the anarchists. But this must not be taken as evidence that the immigrants were for the most part anti-Zionist; rather, Zionism did not then occupy more than a peripheral place in their framework of reference, for the simple reason that its realization—settlement in Palestine—was not then a practical possibility. The concept of a Return to the Promised Land was of course deeply rooted within religious orthodoxy; socialist Zionism, for that reason alone, could not be automatically condemned as atheism. But even without a Zionist component, the notion that socialism was somehow incompatible with orthodoxy was something which most working-class immigrants refused to accept.

[89] Janowsky, *Jews and Minority Rights*, 42–6; N. Levin, *Jewish Socialist Movements, 1871–1917* (London, 1978), 411.

[90] G. Shimoni, 'Poale Zion: A Zionist Transplant in Britain (1905–1945)', in P.Y. Medding (ed.), *Studies in Contemporary Jewry*, ii. (Jerusalem, 1986), 228–30.

The teachings of the *Torah* could be said to embrace socialist principles, or at least to result in ends of which socialists could approve—such as the duty of the rich to distribute their wealth.[91] 'The Law of Moses', a deputation of the Jewish unemployed told Hermann Adler in November 1892, 'itself was Socialistic.'[92] Many of the Jewish trade unions in the Pale of Settlement managed to combine industrial militancy with fervent religious devotion.[93] It is true that a small number of publicity-seeking Jewish socialists in London organized free meals on fast days and ham sandwich picnics on *Yom Kippur*.[94] Of far greater significance was the mass of working-class Jews for whom there was not merely no conflict but a positive and deeply felt relationship between praying in a synagogue and then sitting in the same room to discuss socialist principles and organize industrial stoppages. On strictly religious grounds these immigrants rejected United Synagogue orthodoxy and its chief proponent, Hermann Adler; on class grounds they were minded to condemn the United Synagogue and the Board of Guardians as institutions fashioned by Jewish capitalists and exploiters, for whom Adler appeared to act as chief spokesman and apologist.

The opportunities for spreading the message of socialism within British Jewry, certainly in the major areas of immigrant settlement, were thus far greater in the 1880s than they had been in the 1870s. Though characterized by class subdivisions, a Jewish proletariat was in the process of formation in cities such as London and Leeds; moreover, its alienation, *ab initio*, from the existing communal leadership was assured, while at the same time its radicalization, through both the conditions of its own existence and its contact with indigenous radical movements, was likely to be much facilitated.

It was into this milieu that a disciple of Aaron Liebermann, L. Benzion Novochovitch, better known by his pseudonym Morris Winchevsky (1856–1930), had come in 1879.[95] Winchevsky appeared to have all the qualifications needed to make himself a superb socialist propagandist in London's East End. A Yiddish

[91] Alderman, *Jewish Community*, 54.
[92] *JC* (18 Nov. 1892), 10: speech of Lewis Lyons.
[93] Mendelsohn, *Class Struggle*, 109.
[94] See e.g. *JC* (23 Sept. 1904), 10.
[95] On Winchevsky, see Gartner, *Jewish Immigrant*, 106–10, and Fishman, *East End Jewish Radicals*, 138–51. Winchevsky's 2 volumes of memoirs were published, in Yiddish, in New York in 1927.

writer and socialist philosopher of great eloquence, he had attended the famous Vilna *Yeshivah*, and was thus able in his writings to summon up a rich variety of religious images. On 25 July 1884 he and a friend, Elijah Wolf Rabbinowitz (1853–1932) founded in London the first socialist newspaper in Yiddish, *Der Polisher Yidl* (*The Little Polish Jew*).[96] Through its columns Winchevsky hoped to popularize a brand of socialism which was undeniably Jewish in its focus without pandering to Zionism or religious orthodoxy, and which sought to confront and outface the wealthy Anglo-Jewish leadership.

Rabbinowitz had a more moderate—and pragmatic—outlook. He accepted religious advertisements for the paper, and, later, an election advertisement from Samuel Montagu. Winchevsky found these acknowledgements of bourgeois values beyond forgiveness. He left the paper and, with a group of like-minded friends, some of them social democrats and some of them anarchists, began publication of the *Arbeter Fraint* (*Worker's Friend*), the first issue of which appeared on 15 July 1885, from an editorial address in Spitalfields.[97] Its declared aim was 'to spread true socialism among Jewish workers'; it remained the major Yiddish socialist newspaper in Britain for the next decade.[98] The paper began as a monthly publication, becoming weekly only from December 1886. Its first editor, Philip Krantz (1858–1922), reflected in its columns the lofty idealism to which Winchevsky aspired, and which embraced the view that radicals, social-democrats, collectivists, communists, and anarchists could all find the strength to unite in an effort to sweep away the existing order, including, of course, all forms of religion.

Within the British labour movement as a whole at this time there was broad agreement that whatever changes were necessary to society could and would be implemented through the use of collective bargaining, and also by peaceful and parliamentary means. In following the line of argument that trade unionism was nothing but a harmful diversion of the energy of the workers from

[96] Its contents are examined in Fishman, *East End Jewish Radicals*, 140–51; and see W. J. Fishman, *Morris Winchevsky's London Yiddish Newspaper* (Oxford, 1985).

[97] A. Frumkin, *In Friling Fun Yidischen Sozialism* (Yiddish; *In the Springtime of Jewish Socialism*) (New York, 1940), 35–75, deals with the history of the *Arbeter Fraint*, of which Frumkin became editor in 1896.

[98] *Arbeter Fraint* (15 July 1885), 1; Tcherikower, *Early Jewish Labour Movement*, 188.

the struggle to attain revolutionary socialism, the *Arbeter Fraint* could hardly have endeared itself to the Jewish proletariat of East London; nor was the relentless anti-religious propaganda with which its revolutionary exhortations were accompanied calculated to make its message any more appealing. There was, in truth, not the slightest possibility of fomenting a Jewish socialist uprising in London. The realization of this awful fact drove Winchevsky to consider the possibility of parliamentary action. There were loud protests from the anarchists when the third issue of the paper urged socialists to participate in the 1885 general election.[99] Thereafter, socialists and anarchists struggled for mastery of the paper; by the spring of 1891 it was in anarchist hands. Winchevsky started a rival journal, *Freie Welt* (*Free World*, 1891–2), dedicated to 'violent social revolution'; it was—of course—a magnificent flop.[100] Krantz had departed for America in 1890, to be joined the following year by the *Arbeter Fraint*'s assistant editor, Benjamin Feigenbaum (1860–1932).[101] In 1894 Winchevsky followed them.

The doctrinal arguments between socialists and anarchists did not concern the bulk of immigrant Anglo-Jewry, and the columns of the *Arbeter Fraint* would be of interest only to students of radical philosophy were it not for two facts. The first was that the newspaper spawned a movement; the second was that the movement thoroughly unnerved the Anglo-Jewish leadership. In 1884 a Society of Jewish Socialists had been established in London; from this grew the International Workers' Educational Club, with premises at 40 Berner Street, off the Commercial Road. In June 1886 the Berner Street Club (as it was popularly known) assumed publication of the *Arbeter Fraint*, and from then until the anarchist take-over in April 1891 it served as the meeting-place for every sort of radically orientated Jewish immigrant in the capital. Similar clubs were established in Manchester, Leeds, Liverpool, Hull, and Glasgow.

The motives of those who were drawn to these clubs were mixed. Jewish radicals themselves admitted that some were attracted to them purely for social reasons.[102] No matter. It was at these clubs, and through the educational programmes and lectures which they arranged, that Jewish manual workers made their first

99 *Arbeter Fraint* (15 Sept. 1885), 17–18.

100 Gartner, *Jewish Immigrant*, 132–3; Levin, *Jewish Socialist Movements*, 132.

101 Gartner, *Jewish Immigrant*, 110.

102 Ibid. 112.

acquaintance with British socialists, such as William Morris and H. M. Hyndman, the founder of the Social-Democratic Federation (SDF). By the mid-1880s an East End, Jewish branch of the SDF had been organized, and other groups sprang up in the provinces in due course; in September 1905 a League of Jewish Social-Democratic groups was formed, affiliated to the SDF, which meanwhile (1900) had become a parent body of the Labour Representation Committee, the forerunner of the Labour Party.[103] The socialist clubs which drew their inspiration from Berner Street therefore acted as a conduit through which Jewish immigrant workers found their way into the mainstream British labour movement. More immediately, they acted as a stimulus to the organization of trade unions among these workers, taking as their cue the issue of sweating, to which, as we have noted, public attention began to be drawn at this time.

We are now in a position to understand why the activities of 'one or two Socialists' (to use Samuel Montagu's phrase) in the Jewish East End in the mid-1880s should have caused the Anglicized leadership of London Jewry so much consternation, and why the spectre of a socialist-led Jewish trade-union movement should have driven that leadership to desperate measures. The socialist presence lent credence to the accusation that Jewish immigrants were the means by which foreign, revolutionary doctrines had entered the British body politic. The socialists also threatened to use immigrant discontents—both in London's East End and in other cities—to challenge the existing power structure of British Jewry. It was true that the rather childish anti-religious sentiments paraded in the *Arbeter Fraint* failed to make much impression, and that the annual banquets which it sponsored on *Yom Kippur* in and after 1888 gave deep offence.[104] But the organization and co-ordination of protests and strikes against low wages and bad working conditions, almost invariably imposed by Jewish employers upon Jewish employees, gained widespread if transient support, and was bound to react unfavourably upon the communal image.

[103] Tcherikower, *Early Jewish Labour Movement*, 188; *JC* (13 Oct. 1905), 28. These early links between British and Jewish socialists had beneficial results. Both Hyndman and James Keir Hardie, founder of the Independent Labour Party and of the Labour Representation Committee, condemned the Kishineff pogrom (1903); the following year Hyndman denounced the Aliens Immigration Bill: Silberner, 'British Socialism and the Jews', 40–1.

[104] *Arbeter Fraint* (24 Aug. 1888), 2; (31 Aug.), 3; (21 Sept.), 2.

The formation of a Jewish Tailors' Union in London in the summer of 1883, and the establishment, under the leadership of Mark Moses (a prominent Jewish clothing contractor) of a Mutual Tailors' Association—a combination of masters—in Whitechapel the following year, were clear signals that an intra-communal class war was in the making in the Jewish East End, fuelled by the revelations in the *Lancet* and by public comments, made in March 1884 by an East End factory inspector, concerning the evasion of the provisions of the Factory Acts by Jewish master tailors.[105] The *Jewish Chronicle* urged the Board of Guardians to take pre-emptive action, by promoting the formation of non-socialist trade unions, whose major task it would be to ensure that existing factory legislation was enforced.[106] What seems to have been envisaged was a series of glorified friendly societies, exhibiting precisely the sort of ethos from which English unions were busy escaping. The Jewish friendly society movement did indeed experience a breathtaking renaissance in the 1880s and 1890s. By 1901 there were no less than 176 such societies in London alone, with over 26,000 members (mostly male) on their books; in Britain as a whole Jewish friendly societies numbered 270.[107]

But friendly societies catered for those in regular work, and could never act as weapons of industrial bargaining. Nor could the Board of Guardians expect to be taken seriously in the promotion of a moderate trade union, for it was in truth too closely identified with the Anglo-Jewish ruling élites. The task of organizing such a body thus fell to Samuel Montagu, the immigrants' friend. In 1886 he founded and supported the Jewish Tailors' Machinists Society, whose (unsuccessful) aim was to achieve a twelve-hour day without recourse to a strike.[108] In the succeeding years Montagu was to meddle further in the Jewish trade-union movement, much to the annoyance of the socialists. The exploitation by them, for frankly

[105] Fishman, *East End Jewish Radicals*, 136–7; *JC* (21 Mar. 1884), 5; (16 May), 10. On Mark Moses see *East London Observer* (28 May 1921), 4.

[106] Gartner, *Jewish Immigrant*, 117.

[107] See Lipman, *Social History*, 119–20; Black, *Social Politics*, 195–200; *JC* (11 Oct. 1901), 18–19; (8 Nov. 1901), 29. In considering published membership figures of Jewish friendly societies the incidence of multiple membership needs to be borne in mind. The *Jewish Chronicle* reckoned that at least 10% of male enrolments in London were double enrolments, 5% triple, 2.5% quadruple, and that 1% belonged to 5 and 1% to 6 different societies; this would reduce the number of adult males who belonged to at least one friendly society to about 15,000.

[108] Gartner, *Jewish Immigrant*, 118.

propaganda purposes, of the funeral in February 1887 of 'our comrade Simon Sweed, boot-finisher, 26 years of age, who fell victim to the present system of production' was an immediate trigger of the sequence of events that led to the foundation of the Federation of Synagogues in October.[109] Another trigger was certainly a heavy-handed and bungled attempt which Montagu and F. D. Mocatta made in the summer of 1887 to suppress the *Arbeter Fraint* by bribing the compositor and printer to sabotage its production; within three months the paper had acquired its own printing press, and was back in production.[110] The supreme duty which Montagu laid upon Rabbi Dr Lerner, the Federation's first Minister, of combating the influence which 'a few Atheists' had acquired over Jewish working men, has already been noted.

In spite of these efforts, by stages an authentic Yiddish-speaking Jewish trade-union movement came into existence, covering various branches of the clothing trades, the boot and shoe industries, cabinet-making, the tobacco trades, and a miscellany of smaller occupations.[111] In some cases, where Jewish workers joined existing unions, specifically Jewish branches were formed, usually to cope with language difficulties. Thus there existed in London and Manchester Jewish branches of the National Amalgamated Furnishing Trades Association, complete with Yiddish rule-books.[122] A special Jewish branch of the National Union of Boot and Shoe Operatives was established in 1890. But, certainly in the clothing trades, the preference at this time was for separate Jewish unions: the Manchester Jewish Tailors', Machinists' & Pressers' Trade Union (formed at the end of 1889), which by 1903 could claim to have recruited 60 per cent of Jewish tailors in the city;[113] the Leeds Jewish Working Tailors' Trade Society, which had some 3,000 members on its books by 1888;[114] in London the Jewish Boot Finishers' Society (formed early in 1886), the Hebrew Cabinet Makers' Union (founded 1887), the London Tailors' & Machinists'

[109] *JC* (25 Feb. 1887), 7.

[110] Gartner, *Jewish Immigrant*, 114–15; Fishman, *East End Jewish Radicals*, 155–7.

[111] Lipman, *Social History*, 116–17, lists the major Jewish trade unions founded at this time.

[112] Royal Commission on Alien Immigration, Minutes of Evidence, *PP* 1903, ix [Cd. 1742], qq. 13,968–9.

[113] *Manchester Evening News* (28 Jan. 1903), 4.

[114] J. Buckman, 'The Economic and Social History of Alien Immigration to Leeds, 1880–1914', Ph.D. thesis (Strathclyde, 1968), 26–7, 261–73.

Society (1886), the United Ladies' Tailors & Mantle-makers (1889) and the Independent Tailors Machinists & Pressers.[115]

The examples given here are merely the most prominent. In London alone the first issue of the *Jewish Year Book*, in 1896, listed thirteen Jewish unions; in 1902 the German writer Georg Halpern counted no less than thirty-two.[116] The observation was frequently made, however, that the history of Jewish unions was one, not of steady linear progress, but of formation, growth, decay, and—perhaps—renewed growth.[117] The experience of the London Jewish garment-workers was a case in point. In 1889 these workers found a new leader in Lewis Lyons (1862–1918) an English-born machinist who had once been a contributor to the *Arbeter Fraint*, but who had fallen out with mainstream Jewish socialists because he had suggested a combination of workers and small master tailors (whose situation was often no better than that of their employees) against the wholesalers.[118] In January 1889 Lyons and Philip Krantz formed a Committee for Jewish Unemployed and tried, unsuccessfully, to enlist the aid of Hermann Adler in their campaign against sweating; the Delegate Chief Rabbi, though acknowledging the evils complained of, would do nothing that might have linked his name with those of Jewish socialists.[119] In the early summer Lyons and Wolf Wess, a Jewish immigrant from Libau who was also a prominent member of the Socialist League, organized a strike for a twelve-hour day. There was much public sympathy for the strikers, who received financial assistance from non-Jewish trade unions as well as from Montagu and Lord

[115] Gartner, *Jewish Immigrant*, 122; H. Pollins, *Economic History of the Jews in England* (London, 1982), 155; Black, *Social Politics*, 206; Lipman, *Social History*, 116.

[116] G. Halpern, *Die Jüdischen Arbeiter in London* (Berlin, 1903), 66–8.

[117] H. Burgin, *Die Geshichte fun der Idisher Arbayter Bavegung in America, Rusland un England* (Yiddish; *The History of the Jewish Labour Movement in America, Russia and England*) (New York, 1915), 43.

[118] R. Rocker, *The London Years*, trans. J. Leftwich (London, 1956), 130, called him 'an opportunist'. On Lyons see W. Fishman, *East End 1888* (London, 1988), 277, and A. J. Kershen, 'Trade Unionism amongst the Jewish Tailoring Workers of London and Leeds, 1872–1915', in Cesarani (ed.), *Making of Modern Anglo-Jewry*, 48.

[119] Tcherikower, *Early Jewish Labour Movement*, 196–7. For later examples of Hermann Adler's hostility to trade unions, and of his tactlessness in refusing requests for support from sections of the Jewish proletariat in East London, see Tower Hamlets Central Library, Stepney, Local Collection, file 430 (1890); *JC* (27 May 1892), 9, and (1 Nov. 1895), 16–17; and P. Melnikoff, 'The Siege of Duke's Place', *JC* (12 Mar. 1971), 25.

Rothschild.[120] Montagu put himself forward as an arbitrator, and persuaded the masters to agree to the demands of the men, on condition that the latter did not bring up the question of wages for one year.[121] At the same time, a Jewish tailors' strike in Manchester was similarly successful.[122]

But these victories were short lived. By the spring of 1890 it was generally acknowledged that the London settlement had broken down; even the *Arbeter Fraint* warned against any early resumption of the struggle, pointing out that the workers lacked funds as well as organization; the paper had already revealed that Rothschild and Montagu had had to clear the debts incurred by the strike committee the previous year.[123] In the boot and shoe trade there had been a similar sequence of events; Jewish workers had attempted to obtain the abolition of 'outwork' in 1890, but had been locked out in 1891, when outdoor work was reintroduced with a vengeance.[124] The immigrants formed a new union, the International Boot & Shoe Workers' Union, in 1900. By 1901 it was said to have enrolled 1,200 members. By November 1902 it had collapsed.[125]

Reference to the trade cycle will not adequately explain these extreme peaks and troughs. Dr Lipman has pointed to 'the distribution of workers between many small workshops', and to 'the seasonal nature of the work and the necessarily irregular hours'.[126] These factors were to be found in many employments in Britain—for example in the engineering and shipping sectors—but they did not inhibit the formation of durable trade unions. No doubt a large amount of time was, as Dr Lipman also observed, 'spent on ideological disputation'. There is no evidence that this stunted or frustrated trade-union development; it may, in fact, have helped to sustain interest at times of depression. Neither is it sufficient to point to the alleged inability of Jewish immigrants to organize: the multiplicity of *chevrot* and the flowering of friendly societies gives the lie to this particular charge. Isidore Solomons, secretary of the Capmakers' Union, explained to the

[120] Gartner, *Jewish Immigrant*, 124; *JC* (6 Sept. 1889), 4.

[121] *JC* (4 Oct. 1889), 7–8.

[122] Gartner, *Jewish Immigrant*, 126.

[123] Ibid. 129; Feldman, 'Immigrants and Workers', 127–8.

[124] A. Fox, *A History of the National Union of Boot & Shoe Operatives 1874–1957* (Oxford, 1958), 106–15.

[125] Feldman, 'Immigrants and Workers', 135–7.

[126] Lipman, *Social History*, 118.

Royal Commission on Alien Immigration that Jewish immigrant workers 'do take readily to Trades Unions; and, in fact, no sooner do they get into work than the first thing they inquire after is the Trades Union'.[127]

In 1892 the *Arbeter Fraint* estimated that of some 30,000 immigrant Jewish workers in London, only about 1,200 were members of Jewish trade unions.[128] Membership of Jewish socialist organizations was, and remained for some considerable time, minute. In 1907 the Marxist Jacob Lestschinsky gave it as his opinion that the number of Jewish socialists in London amounted to no more than about 200, in a community—he claimed—of some 130,000 persons.[129] To some extent the weaknesses apparent in the Jewish labour movement in Britain at the end of the nineteenth century and the beginning of the twentieth constituted no more than an extreme case of the general experience of trade unionism and socialism in Britain at this time: only a minority of British workers were unionized; hostility to socialism was very strong—especially within the Trades Union Congress; socialism itself was hardly a growth industry.

There were, however, a number of factors which affected the Anglo-Jewish working classes in a unique and uniquely adverse manner. The first was that their outlook differed fundamentally from the British craft tradition; they saw themselves, as we have already observed, as potentially upwardly mobile, not as perpetual members of the proletariat. In the second place, they had to contend with a special blend of lay and ecclesiastical opposition, at one and the same time brutal and subtle; had Hermann Adler championed the London Jewish tailors as Cardinal Manning had the London Gentile dockers, the course of Anglo-Jewish labour history might have been very different. The third factor, so obvious that it can be easily overlooked, was that the continued influx of fresh waves of immigrant labour created, as Lestschinsky observed, a 'reserve army' of Jewish workers, all seeking work in a very narrow range of employments. Fourthly, some of the most energetic and talented leaders of Jewish trade unions in Britain were

[127] Royal Commission on Alien Immigration, Minutes of Evidence, *PP* 1903, ix [Cd. 1742], q. 20,524.

[128] *Arbeter Fraint* (16 Dec. 1892), 3.

[129] J. Lestchinsky, *Der Idisher Arbayter (in London)* (Yiddish; *The Jewish Worker (in London)*) (Vilna, 1907), 31–2.

attracted to the United States. Under the secretaryship of David Policoff, the Manchester Jewish Tailors' Machinists' & Pressers' Union grew to embrace about three-quarters of all the Jewish tailors in that city. In 1905 Policoff emigrated to the United States. For the first time in a decade his union was not represented at the TUC, and it collapsed shortly afterwards.[130] Finally, we need to remember that the mass of Jewry was concentrated in London; London, certainly until the First World War, was an area of trade-union weakness. If we examine the development of Jewish trade unionism in Leeds, the picture that emerges is far less depressing.[131]

The story of Jewish trade unionism in the Leeds ghetto exemplifies the points which have just been made. The Jewish Working Tailors' Trade Society had been formed as long ago as 1876, but was unable to take effective action to force the Jewish masters to comply with the Factory Acts until the immigrant influx. Both orthodox and socialist Jewish workers supported its campaign. In 1885 it conducted a successful two-weeks' strike for a one-hour reduction in the length of the working day, without loss of pay.[132] Three years later, however, another strike, to achieve the closed shop, was defeated by the masters and the Society, then numbering around 3,000 members, collapsed.[133] This outcome might have spelt the end of Jewish trade unionism in the Leeds clothing industry, more particularly as the employers drew up a blacklist to isolate potential trouble-makers. But Leeds was not London. In Leeds the writ of Samuel Montagu did not run, and the presence of Hermann Adler was less strongly felt. Nor were there a number of competing unions, as were to be found in the capital. Prominent members of William Morris's Socialist League made it their business to involve themselves in Jewish labour problems in Leeds, and to make friends with the Jewish socialists, such as Lewis Frank and Morris Kemmelhor, who were now to be found dominating the

[130] Pollins, *Economic History*, 162; Garrard, *The English and Immigration*, 170. See also *JC* (10 Jan. 1902), 23, and A. S. Reutlinger, 'Reflections on the Anglo-American Jewish Experience: Immigrants, Workers, and Entrepreneurs in New York and London 1870–1914', *American Jewish Historical Quarterly*, 66 (1977), 473–84.

[131] See generally Kershen, 'Trade Unionism', in Cesarani (ed.), *Making of Modern Anglo-Jewry*, 34–52.

[132] Buckman, 'Alien Immigration to Leeds', 247–8, 256–7.

[133] Ibid. 261–73; C. Holmes, 'The Leeds Jewish Tailors' Strikes of 1885 and 1888', *Yorkshire Archaeological Journal*, 45 (1973), 161–4; Burgin, *Die Geshichte fun der Idisher Arbayter Bavegung*, 57–62.

organization of the Leeds Jewish tailors. In February 1890 a most remarkable alliance was formed between the Jewish tailors in the city and the English gasworkers, united to fight for shorter hours; in August the tailors struck, and by the end of that month had won a uniform twelve-hour day.[134]

The union of Jewish tailors and English gasworkers in Leeds came to an end in 1891. But in 1893 the entire Jewish branch of the Leeds tailoring trade was reorganized as the Leeds Jewish Tailors' Machinists' & Pressers' Union, with (from 1895) a full-time paid General Secretary, Sam Freedman. The union was regularly represented at the TUC and became an early affiliate of the Labour Representation Committee.[135] Membership rose from 1,180 in 1902 to 4,465 in 1913. With its social clubs and schemes of sickness and unemployment benefit the union became 'in the public mind, more than any religious or charitable institution, the representative communal body' in the city.[136]

In 1902 the Leeds union boasted an income of £615, a reserve fund of £664, and expenditure of only £534.[137] When a London Jewish branch of the Amalgamated Society of Tailors took strike action in 1906, its funds amounted to precisely £3. 12*s.* 9*d.*[138] During 1906, following a revival in trade after a depression dating from 1903, a number of Jewish unions resorted to industrial action; the London tailors won a reduction in the working day from thirteen hours to twelve, the replacement of piece-work by day wages, and a conciliation board.[139] In the spring of 1911 the Leeds' tailors—now part of a federation of Jewish tailors' unions in the Midlands and the North of England—successfully fought a lock-out, and brought subcontracting to an end.[140] In the summer of 1912 the Jewish tailors of London's East End struck in sympathy with the tailors and tailoresses of the West End, initially to prevent strike-breaking; the dispute in the East End lasted for thirty-six days, and resulted in the recognition of the closed shop and a 10 per cent increase in wages.[141]

134 Buckman, 'Alien Immigration to Leeds', 256–8, 282, 291–2.

135 Ibid. 322; Holmes, 'Leeds Jewish Tailors' Strikes', 165.

136 Buckman, 'Alien Immigration to Leeds', 343–6.

137 *JC* (27 Mar. 1903), 28.

138 Gartner, *Jewish Immigrant*, 139.

139 Pollins, *Economic History*, 162.

140 Ibid.; J. Buckman, *Immigrants and the Class Struggle: The Jewish Immigrant in Leeds 1880–1914* (Manchester, 1983), 115.

141 Fishman, *East End Jewish Radicals*, 294–9.

The face and fate of Jewish trade unionism had been immeasurably improved by the passage of the Trade Boards Act of 1909, which, for example, established a single wages board covering the wholesale tailoring employments. The Act stimulated the amalgamation of small unions, and called into question the continued existence of separate unions for Jewish workers, whose linguistically based rationale was, in any case, much less secure now that a generation of British-born Jewish workers had entered the labour market. The Jewish tailoring unions in London amalgamated with the national Tailors' & Garment Workers' Trade Union; in 1915 the Leeds Jewish tailors followed suit.[142]

In connection with the immediate pre-1914 history of Jewish labour organization in London, a myth has arisen from the career of a charismatic radical, the Yiddish-speaking German Gentile anarchist Rudolf Rocker (1873–1958). On being taken over by the anarchists in 1891, the International Workers' Educational Club had left its Berner Street premises, to begin 'a period of wandering through the meeting rooms of London'.[143] Rocker took over the editorship of the *Arbeter Fraint* in October 1898; the paper became the outlet for the considerable intellectual abilities both of Rocker himself and of a highly talented group of Jewish admirers, friends, and collaborators, chief among whom was Abraham Frumkin (1872–1940), a libertarian born into a family of rabbinical scholars and early Zionists in Jerusalem.[144]

On Saturday, 3 February 1906 (the choice of the Sabbath was not a coincidence), Rocker presided at the opening of the Workers' Friend Club on premises leased in Jubilee Street, Whitechapel; the elder statesman of anarchism, Peter Kropotkin, made a surprise appearance to bless the new venture.[145] For the next eight years the Jubilee Street Club acted as an important forum for radical activities and debate in London, but also as a centre of adult education, where the Jewish masses could acquire, through the medium of Yiddish, a thorough grounding in the humanities and the fine arts. The anarchists—and Rocker in particular—came to act as sponsors and leaders of working-class movements, and they figured prominently in the East End garment-workers' strikes of

142 Alderman, *Jewish Community*, 64.
143 Gartner, *Jewish Immigrant*, 132.
144 On Frumkin see above, n. 97.
145 Fishman, *East End Jewish Radicals*, 262.

1906 and 1912.[146] Rocker was a 'gentle' anarchist, opposed to the philosophy of terrorism which characterized anarchist activities elsewhere in Europe, and which, inevitably, had an adverse effect upon the reputation of the Jubilee Street endeavour.[147] He did indeed become something of a legend in his own lifetime, admired even by orthodox Jews.[148] But he was unable to raise anarchism from a clique into anything approaching a movement. When the First World War broke out he was arrested, interned, and repatriated to Germany in 1918; the Jubilee Street Club was closed by the police. Of East End Jewish anarchism nothing remained. But a great many members and friends of Jubilee Street, as of Berner Street a generation earlier, were drawn thereby into the business of running trade unions and, thence, into the wider politics of working-class Britain.[149] This, rather than indoctrination into any particular brand of radical dogma, was the ultimate legacy of the Jewish socialist and anarchist experience in the age of immigration.

It was pre-eminently in and through the world of trade unions that British Jewry found a place for itself within the British labour movement. It would be an exaggeration to say that this would never have happened but for the great immigration. The decline and fall of the old Liberal Party in the first quarter of the twentieth century would have affected Anglo-Jewish politics irrespective of other circumstances. There were, however, matters of peculiar interest to the Jews that impinged upon the Jewish view of Liberalism, as of Conservatism at this time.

We noted in the previous chapter how issues of foreign policy

[146] Fishman, *East End Jewish Radicals*, 277, 281–2, 294–300; Lestchinsky, *Der Idisher Arbayter*, 23–8.

[147] Public hysteria over the alleged activities of anarchist terrorists in London reached its apogee at the time of the 'siege' of Sidney Street, Whitechapel, in 1911. This was a purely criminal affair, involving a shoot-out between the police and a gang of robbers, but it was linked, in the popular mind, with anarchist activity. See Gartner, *Jewish Immigrant*, 137, and C. Holmes, 'In Search of Sidney Street', *Bulletin of the Society for the Study of Labour History*, 29 (Autumn 1974), 70–7.

[148] Fishman, *East End Jewish Radicals*, 301.

[149] Two examples are J. L. Fine (1883–1971), who became Secretary of the United Ladies' Tailors' Trade Union, and A. R. Rollin (1887–1972), subsequently London Organizer of the National Union of Tailors & Garment Workers. See Fishman, *East End Jewish Radicals*, 254, 256; E. R. Smith, 'Jews and Politics in the East End of London, 1918–1939', in Cesarani (ed.), *Making of Modern Anglo-Jewry*, 156–7; L. Samuels, 'The Jewish Labour Movement', *Jewish Quarterly*, 11/3 (Winter 1956), 35–6. On Fine see *JC* (28 May 1971), 24; on Rollin see *JC* (15 Sept. 1972), 50.

broke the spell which seemed to have bound Jewry to the mid-Victorian Liberal Party, and how, in addition, sociological and ideological factors had, by the end of the century, facilitated a rapprochement with Conservatism. This identity became closer still following the passage, by Balfour's Government, of the Education Acts of 1902 and (for London) 1903; the School Boards were wound up, and responsibility for elementary, secondary, and technical education was henceforth placed with local authorities—generally the county councils. Nonconformist fury at the application of the principle of the use of moneys derived from the local rates to support schools dedicated to denominational religious instruction knew no bounds; there were 'passive resisters' who refused to pay rates on this basis and, led by David Lloyd George, Liberal politicians promised that the Acts of 1902–3 would be repealed.

The Jewish reaction was quite different. The Act of 1902 was greeted by the four Jewish voluntary schools then in operation in the provinces (Birmingham, Hull, Liverpool, and Manchester) with quiet satisfaction, for they were only too pleased to have the costs of secular education at their establishments paid for by the State, thus enabling their limited endowments to be used to pay better salaries to teachers of religion.[150] In London the situation was more complex, because by the terms of the 1903 Act financial responsibility lay with the LCC while day-to-day management of elementary schools rested with the borough councils, some of which (notably Stepney) were controlled by anti-alien majorities.[151] The former practice of appointing Jewish headmasters in 'Jewish' Board schools was abandoned, while persons appointed by the LCC to the managing committees of Jewish voluntary schools tended to be Christians.[152] None the less, Jewish spokesmen conceded at once that the community was bound to benefit from the proposal that the administration of the eight Jewish voluntary schools in London be shared with the LCC; the considerable annual expenditure thus saved could be diverted to improve standards of Hebrew and religious instruction.[153]

[150] C. Hershon, 'The Evolution of Jewish Elementary Education in England with special reference to Liverpool', Ph.D. thesis (Sheffield, 1973), 129; *JC* (6 May 1904), 8.

[151] *JC* (10 Apr. 1903), 19–20; (1 May), 20.

[152] Hershon, 'Jewish Elementary Education', 133–4; *JC* (28 Oct. 1904), 8.

[153] *JC* (1 May 1903), 20.

The education controversy at the beginning of the twentieth century drove a deep and lasting wedge between British Jewry and the Liberal Party, whose 'Progressive' arm had controlled the London County Council since its inception. The LCC elections of March 1904 were dominated by the Nonconformist crusade against Balfour's enactments. At Whitechapel a champion of the Jewish view was found in the person of Henry Herman Gordon (1873–1939), second son of the Reverend A. E. Gordon, cantor of the Great Synagogue. Gordon was a Progressive member of the first Stepney Borough Council, and had been in the forefront of the fight against anti-alienism. But in 1904, with the support of a galaxy of Jewish religious and lay leaders, led by Lord Rothschild and two *Dayanim* of the Chief Rabbi's *Beth Din* (Moses Hyamson and Susman Cohen), and with the support also of the local Catholic clergy, Gordon stood as an Independent candidate on a platform which had as its central plank the sanctity of the 1903 Education Act. Armed, according to one local newspaper, with 'the great bulk of the Jewish and the whole of the Roman Catholic vote', Gordon's position was unassailable, and he topped the poll.[154]

Nationally, in its opposition to the Education Acts of 1902 and 1903, the Liberal Party believed that it was backing a winner. Liberal opposition to the abortive Aliens Bill of 1904 and to the passage of the Aliens Act in 1905 undoubtedly did it some good in Jewish eyes. By the early years of the new century, small 'immigrant' Jewish electorates had come into existence, especially but not only in London, either through naturalization, the natural progression of years, or because aliens found it possible to be included illegally on electoral registers.[155] At the general election of 1906 (as I have shown elsewhere) these electorates wreaked a terrible vengeance upon those politicians who had supported the passage of the Aliens Act. The Jewish vote was neither centrally

[154] *East London Advertiser* (12 Mar. 1904), 8; *East London Observer* (12 Mar. 1904), 5.

[155] These issues are discussed in Alderman, *Jewish Community*, 74. The complaint that aliens managed to find their way on to the electoral registers was frequently made at this time: see *East London Advertiser* (5 Sept. 1885), 3. For a Conservative complaint that unnaturalized Jews were included on the register at Mile End in 1905, see *East London Observer* (26 Aug. 1905), 7. In 1914 there were apparently only a handful of non-Jewish names on the register for Rothschild Buildings. It is a safe assumption that some at least of those tenants who were on this register had not been naturalized: J. White, *Rothschild Buildings* (London, 1980), 271.

directed nor nationally organized; but it bore a major responsibility for, *inter alia*, Bertram Straus's victory at Mile End, the defeat of the Jewish anti-alienist Harry Samuel at Limehouse, the failure of Gerald Balfour (Arthur's brother) to retain Central Leeds (where a 'Leeds Jewish Electoral League' worked against him, aided by *Haham* Gaster), and the capture of North-West Manchester by Winston Churchill, who had now become a Liberal.[156]

On the morrow of the 1906 election the *Jewish Chronicle* was ecstatic in its celebration of the Liberal victory which, it claimed, had installed in power 'a Ministry which is thoroughly friendly to our people'.[157] Within four years this euphoria had been replaced by anger and disillusion. The Aliens Act had not been repealed. The naturalization fee had not been lowered. The obsessive determination of the Liberals to undo the educational reforms of 1902–3 turned out to be very real. The central theme of their Education Bill of 1906 was, in Asquith's words, a refusal 'to recognise what was called the inalienable right of the parent to have his child taught a particular creed at the expense of the state'; Jewish susceptibilities were thoroughly aroused, and there was audible relief when the proposals were emasculated in the House of Lords and then dropped.[158] Meanwhile, the experience of Progressive interpretation and administration of the 1903 Act in the arena of the London County Council—for example, restrictions on the amount of time allowed for Hebrew and religious instruction in what were now termed the 'non-provided' schools—afforded no grounds for complacency.[159]

At the municipal elections of 1907 the Progressives lost control of the LCC, which from then until 1934 was controlled by the Municipal Reformers—in effect the Conservatives. In East London the Yiddish press—including the *Arbeter Fraint*—had campaigned for a Progressive victory.[160] But it was generally acknowledged that the future of the Jewish voluntary schools was safer in Conservative

[156] Alderman, *Jewish Community*, 75–6.

[157] *JC* (19 Jan. 1906), 27.

[158] *The Times* (11 May 1906), 8. See also *JC* (4 May 1906), 40; BD C13/1/6: Minutes of the Law and Parliamentary Committee, 16 May 1906 (Report on the Education Bill); and J. M. Stevens, 'The London County Council under the Progressives, 1889–1907', MA thesis (Sussex, 1966), 31–2.

[159] G. Alderman, *London Jewry and London Politics, 1889–1986* (London, 1989), 50.

[160] *Arbeter Fraint* (1 Mar. 1907), 1–2; see also *Idisher Ekspres* (20 Feb. 1907), 4.

hands.[161] News of the diplomatic agreement which the Liberal Government concluded with Tsarist Russia later in the year—the Anglo-Russian Entente—weakened Jewish faith in Liberalism still further.[162] The by-election which Winston Churchill had to fight on his elevation to the Cabinet in 1908 furnished the opportunity for an unprecedented display of communal wrath, both against the Liberal Government and against Churchill himself, who had failed to redeem earlier pledges to amend or repeal the Aliens Act. Some of the 900 or so Jewish electors in North-West Manchester voted Conservative; many Jewish Liberals abstained, or switched to the Conservative side; some undoubtedly voted for the candidate put up by the Social-Democratic Federation, which in Manchester had significant Jewish support.[163]

Churchill's defeat (his victorious opponent, the anti-alienist William Joynson-Hicks, had a majority of 429 votes) was in some degree a verdict by Anglo-Jewry upon the Liberal Government. The appointment the following year of Herbert Samuel (1870–1963) as the first professing Jew to sit in the Cabinet was of little consolation; six months later Lloyd George, the Chancellor of the Exchequer, launched a series of attacks on Lord Rothschild which were anti-Semitic in the crudest sense. Rothschild had been one of the architects of the assault by the House of Lords on the 'People's Budget'. Political criticism of him was entirely legitimate, therefore, but not in terms which likened him to Pharaoh and which linked him with 'Philistines, who are not all uncircumcised'.[164] Lloyd George's motive in making these very public remarks is unclear. Perhaps he was doing no more than capitalize, for reasons of political expediency, upon the unmistakeable undercurrent of popular feeling that Jewish 'power', exercised primarily through business and commerce, was undermining British values and British

[161] *JC* (15 Mar. 1907), 8; see also *The Times* (8 Apr. 1908), 12 (speech of Lord Rothschild at a fund-raising dinner for the Jewish Religious Education Board); (27 Nov. 1908), 11 (speech of Chief Rabbi Adler).

[162] *JC* (2 Aug. 1907), 8; (9 Aug.), 8. There is a useful discussion of this episode in M. Beloff, 'Lucien Wolf and the Anglo-Russian Entente 1907–1914', *The Intellectual in Politics* (London, 1970), 111–42.

[163] The by-election is discussed in Alderman, *Jewish Community*, 80–2. In a letter published in the *JC* (12 Apr. 1907), 5, a Jewish member of the local branch of the Social-Democratic Federation had claimed its members were, 'with two exceptions', all Jews; see also *Manchester Guardian* (17 Apr. 1908), 7.

[164] *The Times* (17 Dec. 1909), 8; (18 Dec.), 6.

interests.[165] 'Rich-Jew anti-Semitism', which had thrived during the Boer War, prospered in these circumstances, and was to reach a high-water mark during the Marconi and Indian silver 'scandals' of 1912–13.[166] But it was a feature also of the Limerick 'boycott' of 1904, initiated by a Catholic priest, and of the South Wales riots of 1911, aided and abetted by Nonconformist rabble-rousers.[167]

Lloyd George's attack upon Lord Rothschild, the premier Jewish peer and still, in many ways, the premier British Jew (and President of the United Synagogue), struck deep into the hearts of many Jewish Liberals. The journalist Lucien Wolf (1857–1930; Secretary of the Conjoint Foreign Committee of the Board of Deputies and the Anglo-Jewish Association), who a quarter of a century previously had berated Lionel Louis Cohen for daring to stand as a Conservative, now announced that he would vote Conservative himself.[168] Another prominent Jewish Liberal who announced he would vote Conservative was Sir John Simon's son, Oswald.[169]

But the option of defecting to the Conservatives was not realistically open to most of the immigrants or to their children, whose apprenticeship in political socialization did not include working-class Toryism, and for whom the Conservative Party was too strongly identified with anti-alienism. In the 1880s socialism lacked credibility; twenty-five years later, subsumed within the social reformism of the Labour Party and its parliamentary representatives, it possessed, if not credibility, at least a certain respectability. These momentous political developments, taken alongside the growth of Jewish trade unions and their involvement in the wider trade-union movement, eased the entry of working-class Jews into labour politics and ultimately into the Labour Party. This relationship was not to be fully consummated until the First

[165] Pollins, *Economic History*, 168–9.

[166] The Marconi scandal, in which the Attorney-General, Rufus Isaacs, and other members of the Isaacs family were involved, broke in the autumn of 1912; as a result of the 'little Marconi case', or 'Indian silver scandal' (1912–13), Sir Stuart Samuel, who had succeeded his uncle Samuel Montagu as Liberal MP for Whitechapel in 1900, was disqualified from sitting in the Commons, but was re-elected a few weeks later (Apr. 1913): see Holmes, *Anti-Semitism in British Society*, 70–82.

[167] On the Limerick boycott of Jewish businesses, initiated by Father John Creagh, see ibid. 97–9, and L. Hyman *The Jews of Ireland from Earliest Times to the Year 1910* (Jerusalem, 1972), 212–17. On the South Wales riots of 1911, and their antecedents, see G. Alderman, 'The Jew as Scapegoat? The Settlement and Reception of Jews in South Wales before 1914', *TJHSE* 26 (1974–78), 62–70.

[168] *The Times* (10 Jan. 1910), 15.

[169] *JC* (14 Jan. 1910), 26.

World War. But, in the immediate pre-war period, signs of its growth can already be observed. For example, in 1912 Lewis Lyons was put up by Labour as a candidate for election to the Stepney Borough Council.[170] By 1919 Jewish Labour candidates were commonplace in East London: ten of the candidates put up by Labour at Stepney that November were Jews.[171]

In the sphere of political allegiance, no less than in those of religious identity and communal organization, therefore, the great immigration brought about changes of a far-reaching and fundamental nature within the Jewish communities of Britain. The cultural horizons of British Jewry also underwent a radical reorientation. Until the 1870s the Anglo-Jewish press had been dominated—almost monopolized—by the *Jewish Chronicle*. In February 1873 the journalist George Lewis Lyon (1828–1904), a literary figure with a distinct anti-establishment streak, launched a rival weekly, the *Jewish World*; it was with this newspaper that Lucien Wolf obtained, at the age of 17, his first journalistic employment.[172] In 1898 the Zionist Jacob de Haas (1872–1937) became editor, and after the turn of the century the position, coupled with that of managing director, fell to Wolf himself.

For the first and only time in its history, the *Jewish Chronicle* had a serious rival. Indeed, there was a moment, in 1906, when it seemed more probable than possible that the syndicate which owned the *World*—led by the banker Meyer Spielman (1856–1936)—would take over the *Chronicle*. In fact the *Chronicle* itself was bought, for £13,000, by Leopold Greenberg (1862–1931), an experienced journalist and publisher who had helped found the English Zionist Federation and had been a close personal friend of Theodor Herzl.[173] Under Greenberg, who also edited the paper, the *Chronicle* became a Zionist organ, but it was equally radical in its approach to other issues (for example, Greenberg was an enthusiast for the use and exploitation of the Jewish Vote) and was not squeamish in attacking the establishment on a range of domestic

[170] *East London Observer* (9 Nov. 1912), 2. Lyons stood in the Central ward and came bottom of the poll; a Philip Kalisky, who may have been Jewish, stood unsuccessfully in the St George's North ward in the same election.

[171] The 10 included Alfred Valentine, President of the Whitechapel & Spitalfields Costermongers' Union: Alderman, *London Jewry*, 78.

[172] [C. Roth], *The Jewish Chronicle 1841–1941* (London, 1949), 159. See Lucien Wolf's obituary of Lyon in the *Jewish World* (19 Feb. 1904), 418–19.

[173] [Roth], *Jewish Chronicle*, 124–8.

issues, such as its lukewarm approach towards the Aliens Act.[174] The *Jewish World* could not survive competition on such a scale. In April 1913 the *World* was bought by the *Chronicle*, and relaunched as a mid-weekly of limited appeal; it ceased publication entirely in 1934.

But the *Chronicle*, no less than the *World*, could only reach an English-speaking audience, a fact which had caused the *World* to launch a short-lived (1906–8) Yiddish-language supplement, the *Yiddisher Velt* ('Jewish World') edited by Jacob Hodess.[175] The first Yiddish newspaper to be published in any English-speaking country, the *London Yiddish-daytshe Tsaitung* ('London Yiddish Newspaper') had made a brief appearance in 1867, and a few issues of the *Londoner Israelit* ('London Israelite') were published in 1877. It was the great immigration that provided the market for a viable Yiddish press in Britain.[176] Some of the radical newspapers produced to satisfy this demand have already been mentioned. The *Yidisher Observer* ('Jewish Observer') appeared in London in 1884, first as a weekly and then (retitled the *Advertiser*) as a daily, to provide a voice for the most orthodox sections of the immigrant community.[177] In time this paper was absorbed within another, the *Idisher Ekspres* ('Jewish Express'), which had begun life as a radical weekly in Leeds in 1895.

Publication of the *Ekspres* was transferred to London in 1899, and by the early years of the twentieth century there were several Yiddish daily as well as weekly newspapers circulating in the capital and the major provincial centres.[178] In the main they offered

[174] *JC* (17 Jan. 1908), 7; (17 July), 8.

[175] See J. Hodess, 'Zu der Geshichte fun der English-Yiddish Press' ('The History of the Anglo-Yiddish Press'), in *Jews in England* (New York, 1966), 50–2.

[176] This brief survey of the Yiddish press in England is based on Hodess, 'History of the Anglo-Yiddish Press', 40–71; Lipman, *Social History*, 131–2; Gartner, *Jewish Immigrant*, 256–60; [Roth], *Jewish Chronicle*, 162–3; and L. Prager, 'A Bibliography of Yiddish Periodicals in Great Britain (1867–1967)', *Studies in Bibliography and Booklore*, 10/1 (Spring 1969), 3–32.

[177] Isaac Wolf Metchik (1849–1953), a founder of the *Machzike Hadath* society, was the publisher of the short-lived religious paper *HaZofeh* (*Observer*) in 1894–5: Gartner, *Jewish Immigrant*, 258.

[178] Among these other papers may be mentioned the *Yudisher Zhurnal* (*Jewish Journal*), founded in 1907 by Anshel Levy and edited by him until 1913, when the experienced radical journalist and author Morris Myer (1879–1944) took over the editorship. That same year Myer began publication of *Di Tsait* (*Jewish Times*), the largest circulating Anglo-Yiddish daily newspaper, which survived until 1950. In 1902 and 1903 Glasgow boasted its own Yiddish paper, *Idisher Tsaitung* (*Jewish Newspaper*); see Gartner, *Jewish Immigrant*, 260.

a left-wing perspective, and, understandably, their coverage was orientated largely to reporting developments in the *heim* ('home') in eastern Europe. Professor Gartner asserts that this Yiddish press 'kept a prudent distance from contentious social and economic questions'.[179] In fact the most popular, and in particular the *Arbeter Fraint* and the *Idisher Ekspres*, paid much attention to industrial relations, both in London and the provinces, and to more general political matters; *Di Tsukunft* (*The Future*), the renamed *Polisher Yidl*, campaigned for Samuel Montagu in 1885 and 1886 partly as a result of its view that it was the duty of Jews to support Irish Home Rule.[180] Yiddish newspapers also acted as a channel through which immigrant resentment at their treatment at the hands of the established community could be articulated. The *Ekspres*, for example, condemned the system operated by the Board of Guardians as 'rotten', and contrary to rabbinic maxims governing the disbursement of charity.[181] Criticizing the failure of the Board of Deputies to demand better terms on which Jews might trade on Sundays, the *Ekspres* (1905) spoke of rights, not of privileges—a formulation indicative of the more strident tone that had infected immigrant discourse in the wake of the campaign against restriction of alien immigration.[182]

London was also, if not the birthplace, then certainly the proving-ground of Yiddish theatre, the development of which in Russia in the 1870s had been brought to an abrupt end by Tsarist decree in 1883.[183] With actors and actresses no less than with socialists and trade-union leaders, America remained the ultimate destination of the Jewish refugee. When the actor-manager Jacob Adler (1855–1926), his wife Sonia, and their companions arrived in London from Riga in December 1883, they found that a vibrant but more or less amateur immigrant theatre was already in existence, the artistry of which was acknowledged by the *Jewish Chronicle* even if the medium of expression—Yiddish—was despised.[184] Adler and his troupe established the Russian Jewish Operatic Company, performing the original works of Abraham

[179] See Gartner, *Jewish Immigrant*, 260.

[180] *Di Tsukunft* (20 Nov. 1885), 153; (1 July 1886), 1–2, 5–6.

[181] *Idisher Ekspres* (11 May 1900), 4.

[182] Ibid. (26 Apr. 1905), 4; the *Ekspres* was a frequent critic of the restrictionists.

[183] M. J. Landa, *The Jew in Drama* (London, 1926), 282–4.

[184] D. Mazower, *Yiddish Theatre in London* (London, 1987), 11; *JC* (26 Mar. 1880), 13.

Goldfaden and N. M. Shaikevitch, as well as those of classical playwrights in translation, in clubs and halls both in the East End and in the North of England.[185]

In March 1886 Adler's company found a permanent home at the Hebrew Dramatic Club, in Princes Street, Spitalfields, London's first purpose-built Yiddish theatre, which soon became 'the leading venue for Yiddish theatre in Western Europe'.[186] Tragically, its activities were brought to a sudden halt in January 1887, when seventeen people died in a panic mass exodus triggered, it would seem, by an ill-founded rumour of a gas leak. Adler left for what became a glittering career in New York. But the Yiddish stage continued to flourish in a number of halls and theatres in London's East End, notably the York Minster Music Hall in Philpot Street and the Pavilion Theatre at the corner of Vallance Road and the Whitechapel Road. The Pavilion was a large Victorian theatre whose fortunes had been revived in the 1870s and 1880s under the management of Morris Abrahams; its reputation for high quality Yiddish productions was grounded in the work of four illustrious actor-managers, Sigmund Feinman (1862–1909), Maurice Moscovitch (1871–1940; later a character actor in Hollywood, United States), Joseph Kessler (1881–1933), and Fanny Waxman (1878–1958).[187]

The presence of women in Yiddish theatrical productions is a striking reminder of an aspect of the great immigration so obvious that its significance and impact are easily overlooked: the immigration resulted in a revolution in the role of women in Jewish life in Britain. In the established Anglo-Jewish community, the role of women more or less mirrored that which was to be found in society at large: man was the breadwinner, while the tasks of woman were

[185] The immigrant presence in London did not at this time result in the development of an original Anglo-Yiddish dramatical form, even though many Yiddish writers of world renown, including Goldfaden (1840–1908) and 'Sholem Aleichem' (the pen-name of Sholem Rabinowitz, 1859–1916) lived in Britain for short periods. The work of Isaac Stone (1855–1916) and Nathan Berlin is examined in L. Prager, 'The Beginnings of Yiddish Fiction in England', in D. Noy and I. Ben-Ami (eds.), *Studies in the Cultural Life of the Jews in England* (Jerusalem, 1975), 245–310.

[186] Mazower, *Yiddish Theatre*, 13.

[187] See generally M. Myer, *Idish Teater in London 1902–1942* (Yiddish; *Yiddish Theatre in London 1902–1942*; copy in Yivo Library, New York). On Abrahams, a 'Moderate' (Conservative) member of the LCC, see *JC* (26 July 1895) 17 and the *Stage* (21 Oct. 1915), 16.

to bear and bring up children, supervise the running of the domestic household, and generally 'to make home happy . . . and, in her own person, to upraise the holy cause of . . . religion'.[188] Orthodox Judaism accords almost no role in *formal* acts of worship to the female sex, and because of the rabbinic prohibition on women being placed in positions of authority over men, they have no part to play in the direction of synagogal affairs in orthodox communities.[189] Attempts to enfranchise widows and single women in synagogue elections in the United Synagogue were unsuccessful.[190] In the Federation of Synagogues such enfranchisement was out of the question. Women were not elected as members of the Board of Deputies until, as part of the wide-ranging reform of the Board in 1919, the Union of Jewish Women was accorded representation.[191] But in the running of the *kosher* household the wife reigned supreme, and by extension of the task of child-rearing, women were expected to play a leading role in Jewish education. Explaining the difference between a 'Conference of British Congregations' and a 'Conference of Jewish Women', both held in 1902, the *Jewish Chronicle* pointed out that the latter would be concerned with 'the religious and educational needs of our people' while the former would busy itself with 'matters of more secular concern'; 'The division of labour [it added] is not unnatural.'[192]

The tenets of Anglo-Jewish orthodoxy thus reinforced British social custom, certainly in relation to middle-class households. At the end of the nineteenth century and the beginning of the twentieth these norms came under attack from two utterly distinct sources. The immigrants arrived with a view of the female role which was quite different from that generally accepted within and by the Anglo-Jewish gentry. In the orthodox Jewish communities of eastern Europe, 'male status was closely bound up with religious

[188] G. Aguilar, *The Women of Israel* (London, 1870), 570.

[189] *Sifrei* to Deutoronomy 17: 15, *pisqa* 157 (Edition Finkelstein, 208–9).

[190] *JC* (17 Nov. 1899), 8–9; (26 Apr. 1901), 19. See also S. Bayme, 'Claude Montefiore, Lily Montagu and the Origins of the Jewish Religious Union', *TJHSE* 27 (1978–80), 63. But as early as 1872 the Spanish & Portuguese congregation had decided to allow married women to serve as *Yehidim* (communal officials): N. Laski, *The Laws and Charities of the Spanish and Portuguese Jews Congregation of London* (London, 1952), 45–6.

[191] A. Newman, *The Board of Deputies of British Jews 1760–1985* (London, 1987), 22; *JC* (27 June 1919), 17–21.

[192] Ibid. (25 Apr. 1902), 14.

scholarship'.[193] To attain that status it might be necessary for the bridegroom to spend much time studying in *yeshivot*; the family would exist either on the dowry provided by the bride, or on the income which the wife generated by taking on the role of breadwinner. It was not at all unusual, therefore, for immigrant wives to expect to have to fulfil this role, and this expectation was reinforced, and given a sense of urgency, by the general poverty in which immigrant families lived. Where (as was not infrequently the case) husbands died prematurely from the diseases of the sweatshop, the expectation became an imperative.

A study of Jewish women in Manchester between 1890 and 1920 suggests that many immigrant wives were either principal breadwinners or made substantial contributions to the domestic budget, perhaps by helping their husbands or by working independently.[194] Immigrant wives might themselves seek employment in sweatshops, or take in work, such as buttonholing and cap-making, which could be completed at home. Dressmaking was of course a common form of Jewish female employment. In an age when planning regulations were virtually non-existent, parlours fronting on to the street could be turned into shops, in which Jewish housewives sold groceries, milk, and food cooked on the premises.[195] Jewish women in Manchester acted as credit drapers and market traders; one became the owner of a small tailoring factory. 'Contrary to the middle-class view held at the time', their historian writes, 'immigrant [Jewish] women seem not only to have engaged in paid work, but also to have derived considerable satisfaction from it.'[196]

Within the established community, too, the role of women was undergoing a transformation, itself part of a much wider, secular trend affecting middle-class women in late Victorian and Edwardian England, and which culminated in the suffragette movement. The daughters of the emancipation, such as Constance, Lady Battersea, and Mrs N. S. Joseph, were content to confine their public roles to the educational and social spheres; voluntary, philanthropic work

193 R. Burman, 'Women in Jewish Religious Life: Manchester 1880–1930', in J. Obelkevich, L. Roper, R. Samuel (eds.), *Disciplines of Faith: Studies in Religion, Politics and Patriarchy* (London, 1987), 38.

194 R. Burman, 'Jewish Women and the Household Economy in Manchester, *c.*1890–1920', in Cesarani (ed.), *Making of Modern Anglo-Jewry*, 58.

195 The author's maternal great-grandmother, Annie Miriam Pollock (d. 1919) kept a greengrocery shop in her home at 105 Old Montague Street, Whitechapel.

196 Burman, 'Jewish Women and the Household Economy', 62.

on behalf of their less fortunate co-religionists ('slumming') seems to have been a favourite pursuit. Women played an important though subordinate part in the work of the Jewish Board of Guardians. But the granddaughters of the emancipation found this vision of their future much too constricted. Well educated, but excluded from taking anything more than a peripheral part in communal and religious affairs, they looked elsewhere for self-fulfilment.[197] The Conference of Jewish Women held in London in May 1902, attended by over 800 women, provided an occasion for these dissatisfactions to be aired; out of it came the Union of Jewish Women, created to form 'a network of Jewish women workers' who might thereby co-operate and pool information regarding educational and career-training possibilities.[198]

For those Jewish women with enough ambition, motivation, and (it must be said) money, the early years of the twentieth century provided two novel outlets, each of them controversial in its own way. One was to go into politics; the other, to find religious fulfilment outside mainstream orthodoxy. The careers of two women of roughly similar ages, both born into orthodox households and neither of whom ever married, exemplify in a remarkable way the opportunities thus provided.

Henrietta ('Nettie') Adler (1868–1950) was the elder daughter of Chief Rabbi Hermann Adler.[199] In 1894 she fell in love with Isaac Friedner of Liverpool, but her father forbade the match and intercepted their letters.[200] Nettie never married. She remained all her life within the orthodox fold, but struck out on a path of which her father was bound not to approve. Her positions as a manager of East London schools under the London School Board and as a member of the Visiting Committee of the Board of Guardians and of the Jewish Religious Education Board were uncontroversial; but

[197] See generally Elizabeth De Bruin, 'Judaism and Womanhood', *Westminster Review* (Aug. 1913), 124–30, and Gertrude Spielmann, 'Women's Place in the Synagogue', *Jewish Review*, 4 (May 1913), 24–36.

[198] E. M. Umansky, *Lily Montagu and the Advancement of Liberal Judaism: From Vision to Vocation* (New York, 1983), 35. On the foundation and early history of the Union see L. G. Kuzmack, *Woman's Cause: The Jewish Woman's Movement in England and the United States, 1881–1933* (Columbus, Ohio, 1990), 48–50, 81–3, 165–9.

[199] On Nettie Adler, see *The Times* (17 Apr. 1950), 7, and *JC* (21 Apr. 1950), 16.

[200] Elkan Adler Papers, Jewish Theological Seminary, New York: Arch 3–3/2–1: Friedner to Miss Ethel Montagu, 21 Nov. 1895. Friedner was then being considered for a position at the New Synagogue; Ethel Montagu was a daughter of Sir Samuel.

her decision to join the Progressive Party, and, in that capacity, to campaign against Henry Gordon on the education issue at the LCC election of 1904, caused a minor sensation. Her father let it be known that she was working 'without his authority and without his consent'.[201]

In 1905 Nettie was rewarded by the Progressives by being co-opted on to the LCC's Education Committee. At the LCC election of March 1910 it became for the first time possible (following legislation passed in 1908) for women to stand in the knowledge that, if successful, their election to the Council could not be challenged on the grounds of their sex. Nettie was adopted by the Progressives in Central Hackney. In what might otherwise have been a lacklustre contest (coming hard on the heels of the January general election), Nettie's candidature provided a centre of interest, for she brought into the division a glittering array of Jewish Liberals, including Herbert Samuel and Rufus Isaacs (1860–1935; appointed in 1913 the first Jewish Lord Chief Justice), as well as Sidney Webb and Sir J. W. Benn, the Progressive Leader at County Hall.[202] She made no secret of her Jewish identity, refused to campaign on the Saturday of the poll, and won a very comfortable victory, thus becoming one of the first two women to sit as of right on the London County Council, of which she became Deputy-Chairman in 1922–3.

The chronicle of Nettie Adler's tenure of the Central Hackney division (1910–25 and 1928–31) is, primarily, a testament to the remarkable abilities of an outstanding Jewess—the first Jewess to achieve national prominence in a political sphere in Britain, and internationally known as a social worker and educationalist.[203] The life of her contemporary Lily Montagu (1873–1963) presents a somewhat similar theme, though in its detail and application the contrast could not be greater.

Lily Montagu was the sixth of Samuel Montagu's ten children; she of all his offspring was most affected by the oppressive orthodox observance which her father visited upon his household, but this in turn was due to the fact that she was the most spiritually inclined of all his sons and daughters.[204] Louis, his eldest son

[201] Alderman, *London Jewry*, 48.
[202] *Hackney Gazette* (16 Feb. 1910), 6; (23 Feb.), 5; (25 Feb.), 1.
[203] Alderman, *London Jewry*, chs. 2, 3.
[204] Bermant, *Cousinhood*, 208–9.

(1869–1927) wore his orthodoxy lightly while conducting a campaign of slander and libel against the immigrants with whom his father had identified so closely. Edwin (1879–1924), who became Secretary of State for India during the First World War, would have liked to have turned his back on orthodoxy and marry out, but felt he could not do so on account of the disinheritance clause in his father's will.[205] He exacted his revenge by attempting to sabotage the Zionist movement, against which, in any case, he had harboured a long-standing aversion. Lily was too honest and too conscientious to treat her Jewish heritage with such disdain. She was attracted by Jewish ethics, but found the ritual of orthodox Judaism empty and off-putting; the failure of orthodoxy to provide a formal role for women in its ecclesiastical organization was, if anything, an even greater source of complaint.[206]

No one who reads Lily Montagu's letters and sermons can fail to be struck by her intense desire to be of spiritual service to Jewry, and in particular to reach out to the many British Jews (both 'native' and immigrant) who had lost or were losing their sense of religious commitment as a result of alienation from orthodox practice and the counter-attractions of secular society:

> I came from a home [she recalled in 1950] in which Judaism was a reality . . . My father saw all around him the lax Jews, and considered them dead leaves which would drop off, and the faithful would remain and pass on true religion to the next generation.
>
> I began to worry about the so called dead leaves.[207]

At the age of 15 Lily suffered a mental crisis, from which she emerged with the conviction that it was her destiny to minister to the Jewish community.[208] Had she been a man she would almost certainly have entered the rabbinate. Within orthodoxy this was of course impossible. So she immersed herself in social work in the

[205] T. M. Endelman, *Radical Assimilation in English Jewish History 1656–1945* (Bloomington, Ind., 1990), 106–7: Edwin fell in love with Venetia Stanley, a society beauty, whom he took care to persuade both to marry him and to convert to Judaism.

[206] Umansky, *Lily Montagu*, ch. 7.

[207] Liberal Jewish Synagogue Archives, American Jewish Archives, Cincinnati, United States: Microfilm Reel 2717: speech given by Lily Montagu, entitled 'What I owe to the Synagogue', at a reception, 18 Oct. 1950.

[208] Umansky, *Lily Montagu*, 141.

Jewish East End.[209] She was also drawn to the pronouncements and personality of Claude Goldsmid Montefiore (1858–1938), a great nephew of Sir Moses. Claude Montefiore was a gentleman scholar, whose ambition to become a rabbi had been deflected at Oxford through the influence of liberal ideas, particularly those purveyed at his college, Balliol, by Benjamin Jowett.[210] To complete his education he had in 1882 brought to England a German academic of great brilliance, Solomon Schechter (1847–1915), later Reader in Rabbinic and Talmudic Literature at Cambridge, and the only world-class rabbinic scholar resident in England at the end of the nineteenth century.[211]

Schechter grew progressively disenchanted with the lack of importance attached by British Jewry to the rabbinate in general and to his own work in particular.[212] In 1902 he left to become President of the Jewish Theological Seminary in New York. Perhaps, too, he had become disappointed—even upset—by the activities of his former pupil. In 1904 he wrote to his future biographer, Herbert Bentwich, to express his fear that there might be an 'amalgamation of Liberal Judaism with Liberal Christianity'.[213] Some years later Claude Montefiore did indeed confess, in print, that he, Montefiore, was 'in more religious sympathy with Lib[eral] Christians and Unitarians than with many (not all) Orthodox Jews'.[214]

Claude Montefiore had evolved, on an intellectual plane, a theology of Judaism which was entirely de-nationalized and de-ritualized. He rejected the claim of orthodoxy that the Hebrew Bible was the revealed Word of God, and he rejected the claim of the rabbis of old, more especially as set out in the *Talmud*, to be the ordained interpreters of that Word. What was left was a system of

[209] E. M. Umansky, 'Lily H. Montagu: Religious Leader, Organizer and Prophet', *Conservative Judaism*, 34/6 (July/Aug. 1981), 19.

[210] On Montefiore see Bermant, *Cousinhood*, ch. 24, and W. R. Matthews, *Claude Montefiore: The Man and his Thought* (Southampton, 1956).

[211] On Schechter, see N. Bentwich, *Solomon Schechter: A Biography* (Cambridge, 1938).

[212] Such disillusion is expressed in S. Schechter, *Four Epistles to the Jews of England* (reprinted from the *Jewish Chronicle*, London, 1901), especially 12–13. Compare S. Daiches, *Judaism in England* (sermon delivered in Sunderland, 16 Feb. 1907).

[213] Solomon Schechter Papers, Jewish Theological Seminary, New York: 101:1: Schechter to Bentwich, 30 Nov. 1904.

[214] L. Cohen, *Some Recollections of Claude Goldsmid Montefiore: 1858–1938* (London, 1940), 106.

ethics based on a vague monotheistic doctrine. To be a good Jew was to be a good citizen, and the task of the good Jew was simply and exclusively to bear witness to 'righteousness in action and truthfulness of the heart'.[215]

Such, in essence, was the conceptual origin of Liberal Judaism, the tenets of which Montefiore proclaimed from the pulpit of the West London Reform Synagogue on 1 February 1896.[216] It dovetailed perfectly with the conclusions at which Lily Montagu had arrived by a more practical and a more painful route. From 1890 she had conducted, at the New West End Synagogue, a children's service based upon an English liturgy, and with an order of service which was remarkably flexible.[217] She had also (1893) established the West Central Girls' Club, for the members of which she composed *Prayers for Jewish Working Girls.* In the January 1899 issue of the *Jewish Quarterly Review*, of which Montefiore was co-editor, she published an essay condemning the 'materialism and spiritual lethargy' into which she and Montefiore both (as it happened) believed Anglo-Jewry had lapsed, and calling upon those of like mind to join with her in establishing a new form of Judaism, in which 'all that was valuable and lovely in the ancient faith' would be preserved in 'forms acceptable to emancipated minds'.[218] The eventual result of this call was the establishment, on 16 February 1902, of the Jewish Religious Union (JRU), known from 1909 as the Jewish Religious Union for the Advancement of Liberal Judaism. The change of title was significant, and denoted nothing less than the failure of the JRU to evolve in the way Lily Montagu had planned.

Claude Montefiore became President of the JRU on its foundation; Lily Montagu was one of the three Vice-Presidents. As Montefiore was gracious enough to admit some years later, 'The Union was founded . . . by Miss Montagu . . . [who] brought together, as the first members of a Committee or Governing Body of the Union, a number of persons by no means all of the same

[215] C. G. Montefiore, 'Mystic Passages in the Psalms', *Jewish Quarterly Review*, 1 (Jan. 1889), 152; see also the same author's *Liberal Judaism: An Essay* (London, 1903), 92–4, and his 'The Liberal Movement in English Jewry', *Yearbook of the Central Conference of American Rabbis*, 20 (1910), 180–4.

[216] *JC* (14 Feb. 1896), 19–20.

[217] Umansky, 'Lily H. Montagu', 21.

[218] L. H. Montagu, 'Spiritual Possibilities of Judaism Today', *Jewish Quarterly Review*, 11 (Jan. 1899), 216, 228.

views'.[219] Lily wanted the JRU to act as a catalyst for change. She naïvely assumed that its Saturday afternoon services, mainly in English (the musical portions 'with instrumental accompaniment'), and with men and women sitting together, could achieve this. It does not seem to have occurred to her that the JRU would and was bound to become a separate synagogal body, with a distinct faith of its own—a force for division rather than for unity. Why was she blind to this evident possibility?

There are two answers to this question; they are not mutually exclusive. We have already noted the movement for liturgical change within the United Synagogue, which Hermann Adler went some way to appease. In 1888 the West London Reform Synagogue had agreed to shorten its service, omit the prayer for the restoration of sacrifices, and read in English rather than in Hebrew a portion from the Prophets on every Sabbath.[220] But further modifications of service—especially the extension of the use of the vernacular—were resisted. In a number of respects, indeed, the Reform and the United Synagogues moved closer to each other as the century drew to a close. In 1890 the Reform congregation was invited (but declined) to be represented at the Chief Rabbinate Conference, and two years later the United Synagogue Council voted to permit the burial of Reformers in United Synagogue cemeteries.[221] Hermann Adler refused to attend in person the Reform Synagogue's jubilee service (1892), but in fact all the principal orthodox synagogues were represented, and in 1905 Adler dared to set foot in the Reform Synagogue himself for the memorial service to F. D. Mocatta.[222] Reform and United Synagogue ministers were known to exchange pulpits: Simeon Singer preached to the Reform congregation in Manchester.[223]

The fact, therefore, that Lily Montagu managed to persuade a number of leading members of the United Synagogue to join the governing body of the JRU (including Rabbi Singer and the Revds A. A. Green of Hampstead and J. F. Stern of the East London) did not seem so remarkable at the time; if anything, it appeared to be a

219 Montefiore, 'The Liberal Movement in English Jewry', 193.

220 *JC* (4 May 1888), 7; (11 May), 11; (1 June), 9; (15 June), 6–7; (13 July), 8.

221 S. Sharot, 'Reform and Liberal Judaism in London: 1840–1940', *JSS* 41 (1979), 217.

222 Ibid.; D. Philipson, *The Reform Movement in Judaism* (2nd edn., New York, 1931), 305.

223 *JC* (27 Oct. 1893), 5–6.

confirmation that the establishment of the JRU was not regarded as schismatic. But Lily was determined to have Claude Montefiore as its President. Montefiore's first wife had died in childbirth in 1889. Lily formed an emotional attachment to him, but was rebuffed; in 1902 he married his first wife's former tutor at Girton College, Cambridge, Florence Ward, who converted to Judaism.[224] Like other women in this position, Lily seems to have decided that if she could not be married to Montefiore, she would remain unwed.[225] She dedicated herself to a life of distinguished service (both to British Jewry, world Jewry, and British society) but determined to bring about a situation in which she and Montefiore worked closely together. She was, in fact, prepared to spend the better part of three years (1899–1902) persuading him to agree to become the JRU's President.

The most distinctive feature of Reform Judaism in Britain at this time was that it had no discrete theology. Membership of the West London Synagogue had declined; attendances were poor, and dominated by female worshippers.[226] Given the remarkable similarity in social class between the membership of the West London congregation and that of the larger United synagogues, coupled with the high degree of social and professional contact between the lay and ecclesiastical leaderships of both, and with the modest convergence in their forms of service, the weakness of British Reform—certainly in London—is easily understood. Attempts to establish Reform congregations elsewhere in the capital had been unsuccessful.[227] In the face of the immigration of orthodox Jews from eastern Europe, and the problems to which this immigration gave rise for 'native' Jews of both orthodox and Reform persuasions, the desire for a rapprochement was strong on both sides. Hermann Adler's appeal to the Reformers to help put down Liberal Judaism did not fall on deaf ears.[228] In 1903 the West London synagogue agreed to put its premises at the disposal of the JRU for its Saturday afternoon services, but laid down a set of conditions—including the

[224] Bermant, *Cousinhood*, 210, 324.

[225] Umansky, *Lily Montagu*, 238. Lily apparently received a proposal of marriage from the anti-Zionist Laurie Magnus (1872–1933), but it is unclear whether this preceded or followed Montefiore's second marriage in 1902: Liberal Jewish Synagogue Archives, American Jewish Archives, Cincinnati, United States: Microfilm Reel 2718: Philip Magnus-Allcroft (Laurie's son) to Lily Montagu, 10 Aug. 1962.

[226] Sharot, 'Reform and Liberal Judaism', 215–16.

[227] Ibid. 215.

[228] Philipson, *The Reform Movement*, 305.

separation of sexes, the inclusion of a number of Hebrew prayers of central importance in the orthodox liturgy, and a prohibition on the use of hymns and psalms not composed by Jews—which at the urging of Montefiore and Montagu the JRU rejected.[229]

Hermann Adler could fairly claim that he had succeeded in bringing the United Synagogue and the Reformers closer together; at the time of his visit to the West London in 1905 one might have argued that the West London was almost in the position of being merely on the radical wing of mainstream native orthodoxy. But in order to maintain some vestige of credibility with the *chevrot*—if for no other reason—Adler was obliged to condemn the JRU, for which Claude Montefiore had, so to speak, through his writing and speeches, created a theological prospectus. The Chief Rabbi was joined in this condemnation by Samuel Montagu, who became estranged from Lily and from her sister, Marian, who had joined in her venture; in his will Montagu stipulated that each was to lose three-quarters of her share of his estate should she persist in the promotion of 'a movement known as "Liberal Judaism" the objects of which I strongly disapprove'.[230]

The inheritance was forfeited. In urging the members of the JRU to reject the West London's terms for the use of its synagogue, Lily had pleaded for a commitment to repudiate the outmoded 'oriental custom' of separate seating.[231] The JRU was not to be merely a rather exotic and genteel dilution of United Synagogue Judaism, but was to strike out on a path of its own. It had, in the words of those who argued in vain against rejecting the West London's offer, raised a 'flag of defiance'.[232] Ministers of orthodox congregations, and leading lay members of the United Synagogue who had identified with the JRU, were pressured by the United Synagogue Council into resigning from it after Adler had declared its form of services to be contrary to Jewish law.[233] Lily Montagu had envisaged the Union as a force that would bring together the

[229] *JC* (10 Apr. 1903), 11–14.

[230] Bermant, *Cousinhood*, 207.

[231] Umansky, 'The Origins of Liberal Judaism in England', 318; *JC* (10 Apr. 1903), 12, 19. Underlying this insistence on the equality of the sexes at prayer Lily Montagu and Claude Montefiore nurtured a profound view of the part that the JRU was to play in the emancipation of the Jewish woman: see Umansky, *Lily Montagu*, 154–9, and Bayme, 'Claude Montefiore, Lily Montagu and the Origins of the Jewish Religious Union', 62.

[232] Umansky, 'The Origins of Liberal Judaism in England', 318.

[233] Sharot, 'Reform and Liberal Judaism', 220; Umansky, 'Lily H. Montagu', 24.

orthodox and the non-orthodox, and attract the apathetic back into a meaningful relationship with Judaism. What she and Montefiore created was an entirely separate movement.

The change of title of the JRU in 1909 has already been noted. The Union had till then been using the Steinway Hall for its Saturday afternoon services. In 1909 it was decided to hold services on Friday evenings and Saturday mornings as well, and on two weekdays each month. A former chapel in Hill Street, Marylebone, was acquired for this purpose. The Liberal Jewish Synagogue, as it was called, began to function in 1911, and acquired its first minister, Israel Mattuck (1883–1954, an American Reform rabbi) the following year. Some parts of the service were in Hebrew, but most were in English. A few verses were chanted from the *Torah* scroll, but no one was 'called' to the Reading of the Law, as in orthodox synagogues. There was an organ and a mixed choir; men and women sat together.[234]

Before the First World War Liberal Judaism in Britain was still a very small plant. A branch of the JRU had been established in East London in 1903, but had had to close down in 1911. The Hill Street synagogue could boast, in 1915, that all its 446 seats had been let; yet attendances at services were still low.[235] In 1913 Lily's West Central Jewish Girls' Club had been reorganized as the West Central Section of the JRU (fifty-one members); a Golders Green & District branch had a membership of forty-four by the end of the following year.[236] Lily herself remained in some respects brazenly orthodox; she adhered throughout her life to the orthodox dietary laws, recited (at the New West End Synagogue) the memorial prayers for her parents, and was buried next to them at the Edmonton Federation cemetery.[237] But the flame of rebellion that had been kindled in her was never extinguished. In 1918, at Mattuck's insistence, she preached her first sermon at Hill Street; in 1944 she was formally inducted there as a lay minister.[238] By then the membership of the Liberal Jewish Synagogue (which had moved to larger premises in St John's Wood Road in 1925) exceeded that to be found at the West London Reform, Berkeley Street. For those who could see it, a revolution was in the making.

[234] Sharot, 'Reform and Liberal Judaism', 221. [235] Ibid. [236] Ibid.

[237] Bermant, *Cousinhood*, 214; Marian, who also remained unmarried, and who dedicated her life to helping her sister, is buried next to her.

[238] Umansky, *Lily Montagu*, 85, 177. Britain's first woman, rabbi, Jackie Tabick, was ordained in London in 1975.

5
The End of Consensus

THE underlying theme of the communal politics of British Jewry in the late nineteenth and early twentieth centuries was the tension created by the desire of the established, Anglicized ruling élites to maintain their control of communal organization and leadership, and the determination of the newer arrivals that these should ultimately fall under their sway. Oligarchy was confronted by democracy; laxity by orthodoxy; political conservatism by social radicalism; synagogal centralism by the independency of the *chevrot*; the numerical dominance of London by the jealous independence of provincial Jewries; the institutionalized charity of the Boards of Guardians by the communal self-help of the friendly societies. At some times the drama was played out through explicit issues, such as *kashrut*. At others, issues of great importance in themselves were none the less used for ulterior purposes: everyone knew what was ultimately at stake, but it suited both sides not to say so. Of these, by far the most fundamental was that of Zionism, the movement having as its goal the national self-determination of the Jewish people, expressed through the re-establishment of the Jewish State.

In 1880 British Jewry was remarkably centralized as well as self-disciplined. By 1914 this was quite clearly no longer the case. In addition to specific areas of communal divergence, social and even geographical factors had come to play a part in dissolving the ties between those who were expected to lead and those who were expected to follow. Extremes of wealth and poverty within British Jewry were at their starkest during the early years of the twentieth century. Professor Rubinstein has calculated that 'the Jewish percentage of top [British] wealth holders rose to a peak of 23 per cent of those non-landed millionaires deceased during the decade 1910–19'.[1] Some of these deceased millionaires, their fortunes

[1] W. D. Rubinstein, 'Jews Among Top British Wealth Holders, 1857–1969: Decline of the Golden Age', *Jewish Social Studies* 34 (1972), 76.

typically made in the finance and banking sectors, and on the stock market, had played key roles in the arrangement of communal affairs during the late Victorian and Edwardian periods; a few, notably Samuel Montagu, Sydney Stern (1845–1912), and his cousin Hubert Stern (1851–1919), had used their wealth to acquire peerages.[2]

Edward VII, when Prince of Wales, had defied convention by deliberately seeking out the company of wealthy and cultured Jews, particularly if they shared his passion for the turf—the Rothschilds, the Sassoons, above all Baron Maurice de Hirsch and Sir Ernest Cassel, 'the King's greatest friend'.[3] These so-called 'Court Jews' no doubt formed a glittering top tier to the social hierarchy of British Jewry, and may have been a source of communal pride.[4] But they were, in the main, irreligious and took little part if any (other than in a formal sense) in communal affairs—an inevitable consequence of their marginal status as professing Jews, which was in turn an outcome of their having been educated exclusively at sectarian public schools. 'Wealthy Jews', Hermann Gollancz noted in 1907, 'and men of note among us send their sons to the public schools of the land and permit them to join hypocritically in the religious services held in church or chapel.'[5]

None the less, there was no denying that the progression of Jews into institutions of higher education had also had beneficial results. By the time of the First World War there was a significant Jewish undergraduate presence at Oxford and Cambridge and at other English universities.[6] A small but growing number of Jews had

[2] W. D. Rubinstein, 'Jews Among Top British Wealth Holders, 1857–1969: Decline of the Golden Age', *Jewish Social Studies* 34 (1972), 82. On Sydney Stern, a Liberal MP who was created Lord Wandsworth, see *JC* (16 Feb. 1912), 10; and on Hubert (Lord Michelham), brother-in-law to Sir David Salomons but a Conservative none the less, see ibid. (10 Jan. 1919), 7; both the Sterns were bankers.

[3] Sir S. Lee, *King Edward VII*, 2 vols. (London, 1927), ii. 60. On the philo-Semitism of the Prince of Wales see Hermann Adler Papers, Jewish Theological Seminary, New York, Box 3–3: Arthur Sassoon to Adler, 14 Dec. 1898.

[4] M. Simon, 'Anti-Semitism in England', *Jewish Review* (Nov. 1911), 299. See generally A. Allfrey, *Edward VII and his Jewish Court* (London, 1991).

[5] H. Gollancz, *Sermons and Addresses* (London, 1909), 262. And see David Philipson Papers, American Jewish Archives, Cincinnati, MS Collection 35, 1/1: Israel Abrahams (Cambridge, England) to Philipson, 1 Mar. 1903: 'The lay leaders who denounce reform do not themselves obey one per cent of the ritual laws.'

[6] R. Loewe, 'The Evolution of Jewish Student Feeding Arrangments in Oxford and Cambridge', in D. Noy and I. Ben-Ami (eds.), *Studies in the Cultural Life of the Jews in England* (Jerusalem, 1975), 165–84.

flourished in the professions, including the armed forces and the civil service; Sir Lionel Abrahams (1869–1919) rose to become Assistant Under-Secretary at the India Office in 1911. The placing of Selig Brodetsky (1888–1960) as Senior Wrangler at Cambridge in 1908 showed that foreign-born children of recent immigrants were also capable of taking advantage of the educational opportunities open to them.[7] The cultural milieu of Edwardian England provided a fertile soil in which Jewish artistic and literary talents could flourish. Frequently, it is true, a Jewish dimension was not very evident in the work produced; Sir Sidney Lee (1856–1926), editor of the *Dictionary of National Biography*, had little contact with the community and little impact on its literary output. The pre-Raphaelite painter Simeon Solomon (1840–1905) produced some very fine depictions of Jewish religious ceremonial, yet in later life moved away from Jewish themes.

But it was in the visual arts that the late nineteenth and early twentieth centuries witnessed a flowering of talent, much of which was very Jewish in its focus. Most notable were the painters Solomon J. Solomon (1860–1927), only the second professing Jew to be appointed a Royal Academician (the first was Solomon A. Hart, 1806–81), and Mark Gertler (1891–1939), born in Spitalfields to poor immigrants from Galicia. Gertler, the protégé of the baptized Jew Sir William Rothenstein, became a pupil at the Slade School of Art at the close of the Edwardian period; his fellow pupils included David Bomberg (1890–1957), born to Polish-Jewish immigrants in Birmingham, Jacob Kramer (1892–1962), born in the Ukraine but living in Leeds from 1900, and the future 'war poet' Isaac Rosenberg (1890–1918). The sculptor Sir Jacob Epstein (1880–1959), born to Polish-Jewish immigrant parents in New York, came to Paris in 1902 and settled in London three years later.[8]

In 1914 the Rothschilds could still claim to possess an undisputed primacy as the lay leaders of British Jewry; Nathan Mayer ('Natty'), the first Lord Rothschild, was President of the United Synagogue from 1879 to his death in 1915, and the Presidency remained in Rothschild hands until 1942.[9] But from their palatial

[7] H. Pollins, *Economic History of the Jews in England* (London, 1982), 180–2.

[8] See appropriate entries in G. Abramson (ed.), *The Blackwell Companion to Jewish Culture* (Oxford, 1989).

[9] A. Newman, *The United Synagogue 1870–1970* (London, 1977), 212.

homes in the Buckinghamshire countryside it was difficult for the Rothschilds to maintain a close rapport with the Jewish masses, into whose midst they consented to make occasional, semi-regal forays and for whom they became little more than distant sources of financial subsidy. Beneath such an Anglo-Jewish aristocracy there had grown into maturity a self-satisfied *haute bourgeoisie*, whose material preoccupations acquired a bizarre but entirely appropriate symbolism through its obsession with card-playing, which had by the end of the nineteenth century become something of a communal joke.[10] It was this middle class, migrated to Maida Vale in north-west London and Cheetham Hill and Crumpsall in north Manchester, that supervised the day-to-day running of communal institutions, assisted by the more prosperous of the newest immigrant generations, who moved as quickly as they could from Whitechapel and Bethnal Green to Hackney and Stamford Hill in North London, from Strangeways to Cheetham, and from The Leylands to Camp Road and Chapeltown, in Leeds.[11] In 1918 The Leylands had housed nine synagogues, Chapeltown only one; twenty years later Chapeltown boasted no less than six, Camp Road eight, but The Leylands only two.

The rise of 'Jewish suburbia' is often thought of as a phenomenon of the inter-war period. In London this was not the case. The United Synagogue at Stoke Newington was admitted to constituent status as early as 1903. In 1913 the decision was taken to close the New Synagogue at Great St Helens, and to rebuild it at Stamford Hill, where it was reopened in 1915.[12] Further west, Jewish migration from inner London followed the expansion of the underground railway network, which reached Hampstead and Golders Green (then in the final stages of transition from a rural village to a London suburb) in 1907. Jews living in Golders Green began holding services together in 1913; a synagogue was established in 1916, and admitted to 'Associate' status by the United Synagogue the following year.[13] By then, a nucleus of

[10] T. M. Endelman, *Radical Assimilation in English Jewish History 1656–1945* (Bloomington, Ind., 1990), 93–4.

[11] V. D. Lipman, 'The Rise of Jewish Suburbia', *TJHSE* 21 (1962–7), 87; E. Larsen, 'Death of a District', *JC Colour Magazine* (26 Nov. 1969), 70–6; E. Krausz, *Leeds Jewry: Its History and Social Structure* (Cambridge, 1964), 23–4.

[12] Newman, *United Synagogue*, 73; Lipman, 'Suburbia', 87.

[13] G. Alderman, *The History of the Hendon Synagogue 1928–1978* (London, 1978), 1.

Jewish families had established itself also in Finchley, and more especially in Hendon, served by the railway line which, partly in response to the wave of speculative house-building which was a marked feature of the immediate post-war period, was extended from Golders Green to Edgware in 1924.[14]

Such were the origins of the Jewish concentration in what became north-west London, but which was then still the County of Middlesex. The families who moved there were attracted by relatively cheap housing, acquired with mortgages which were well within the means of those who had prospered in East London. But they were also encouraged to look beyond the administrative borders of the London County Council by an anti-alien housing policy, enforced by the Conservative-controlled LCC in 1923, which, as we shall see, had a dramatic impact upon alien applicants for LCC accommodation.[15] The 'Associated Synagogues' scheme, which the United Synagogue had implemented in 1899, gave grants to outlying communities, without imposing the burdens of communal taxation which full constituent status would have entailed. The scheme was intended to stimulate the dispersion of Jews from the East End; by 1928, when it was superseded by the District Synagogues scheme, fourteen outlying congregations had been admitted to Associate status.[16] Between 1913 and 1939 six full constituents of the United Synagogue were established (Brixton, Golders Green, Cricklewood, Hendon, Willesden, and Hampstead Garden Suburb), and a further fourteen congregations, many of which (such as Wembley, Finchley, and Edgware) were eventually to achieve constituent status, joined the parent body as District Synagogues.

After the First World War the historic focus of the United Synagogue continued to be located in the City of London; but the membership was fast on the way to removing itself thence, and the destruction of the Great (and the Central) by enemy bombing during the Second World War marked in dramatic fashion the end

[14] Ibid.; H. S. Levin and S. S. Levin, *Jubilee at Finchley: The Story of a Congregation* (London, 1976), 2–3.

[15] BD C13/9: Memorandum, undated but *c.*Jan. 1933. It was the view of Nettie Adler that this housing regulation was one factor pushing Jews who sought better housing in the inter-war period to look beyond the boundaries of the administrative County of London: N. Adler, 'Jewish Life and Labour in East London', in H. L. Smith (ed.), *New Survey of London Life and Labour* (London, 1934), vi. 272–3.

[16] Newman, *United Synagogue*, 75, 115–16.

of an era. The United Synagogue had become, in the nicest sense of the word, a business enterprise; it could be run, Israel Zangwill had declared in *Children of the Ghetto*, 'as a joint-stock company . . . [and] . . . there wouldn't be an atom of difference in the discussions . . . Long after Judaism has ceased to exist, excellent gentlemen will be found regulating its finances.'[17] 'Head Office'—located from 1932 at Woburn House, Euston—handled every aspect of property building, acquisition, and management; maintained and operated burial grounds and burial facilities; superintended a variety of bequests and trusts for charitable purposes; helped fund, through the Jewish Religious Education Board, a network of religion classes; centralized the payment of Ministers, Readers, and other synagogue officials; and contributed very heavily to many metropolitan and national Jewish bodies, including, of course, the Chief Rabbinate.[18]

By the end of the First World War the United Synagogue had acquired a centrality in the affairs of London—and therefore of British—Jewry which it could not honestly have claimed twenty years before. Social and communal circumstances had worked and were to continue to work in its favour. Concerning the fortunes and misfortunes of the Federation of Synagogues more will be said in due course. Here it must be noted that whereas the United Synagogue had failed to attract the immigrants of the 1880s and 1890s, their more assimilated and less observant children and grandchildren were drawn to it both on account of its willingness to subsidize the establishment and building of synagogues in the suburbs (which the Federation was unable to do until after the Second World War), and by reason of the much less rigorous varieties of orthodoxy which it encouraged and embraced.

Concerning the degree of religious observance of these suburbanites it is impossible to generalize. Save in times of emergency, or under very special circumstances, practising orthodox Jews, particularly if they have young families about whose religious education and socialization they are concerned, are unlikely to settle in areas remote from Jewish communal organization. This must not be taken to imply that the Jews who moved to the suburbs

[17] I. Zangwill, *Children of the Ghetto* (London, 1972), 241–2.

[18] On the administrative organization of the United Synagogue at this time see Newman, *United Synagogue*, ch. 11. On Woburn House see *JC* (8 Apr. 1932), 23–5.

of London were irreligious. Rather, the religious outlook of many of them was easy-going, and dovetailed perfectly with the then existing requirements of United Synagogue Judaism.[19] The founders of the Hendon community, mainly small shopkeepers and businessmen, took great pride in their Jewishness; but relatively few were meticulously orthodox.[20] One of the early promoters of what became the United Synagogue at Finchley, A. King-Hamilton, was himself 'a distinguished member' of the West London Reform Synagogue.[21] The Hendon Synagogue, when it was removed to purpose-built premises in Raleigh Close in 1935, was constructed along Reform lines, with the *bimah* (reading desk) immediately in front of the Ark; a mixed choir was permitted at weddings, and silk *tallesim* (prayer-shawls) were more in evidence than the traditional woollen ones.[22]

Jews who settled in the suburbs in the inter-war period were not, it must be stressed, seeking to escape from Judaism, and certainly not from their identity as Jews. Rather, they were seeking to escape from a particular form and intensity of Judaism and of Jewish life, which had suited their grandparents and parents, but which did not suit them. The world of the immigrant Jew was introspective; the popular abuse to which the immigrant was subject made it more so. In the suburbs, the Jew could face his Gentile neighbour on more equal terms:

> Whatever the strength of his Judaism [a writer in *The Times* observed in 1924] the middle class Jew who settles outside the largely Jewish areas is bound to see more of the Gentile, and I think it would be rather an exception to find a Jewish family established for more than a few years in London outside the Jewish areas of East London and a few smaller settlements who had not Gentile friends as well as acquaintances.[23]

Viewed from this perspective, what Chief Rabbi Dr Hertz referred to (using unfortunate phraseology) in 1931 as the 'Progressive Conservatism' of the United Synagogue undoubtedly helped retain within the formal framework of orthodoxy many

[19] Professor Krausz makes a similar point in relation to the dispersal of Leeds Jewry: 'The aim is to move to a *better* area and not to a *non-Jewish* area': Krausz, *Leeds Jewry*, 26.

[20] Alderman, *Hendon Synagogue*, 3; private information.

[21] Levin and Levin, *Finchley*, 3.

[22] Alderman, *Hendon*, 9, 11–12.

[23] *The Times* (8 Dec. 1924), 15.

who might otherwise have drifted away.[24] On this subject the United Synagogue itself was commendably frank. A committee which reported in June 1929 on the provision of synagogue and classroom facilities in north and north-east London observed that 'the younger men and women who are born and bred in London often prefer, if they join a synagogue at all, to join a United Synagogue type of synagogue'.[25]

It must not be thought that practising orthodox Jews ceased identifying with the United Synagogue: many continued and were proud to do so. But the relationship was uneasy and at times embarrassing. The United Synagogue acquired—perhaps had been born with—a species of religious schizophrenia, and deliberately so. Within and through it, orthodoxy survived, but usually in a much diluted form, supported by businessmen and their wives who reached an accommodation with a religious creed they themselves no longer practised to the full, or even fully understood. An incident in November 1923 illustrates its outlook. The Bayswater synagogue requested a contribution from Head Office towards the cost of maintaining its *mikvah*. There were probably not many married couples in membership of the United Synagogue who bothered with the rules of family purity. The United Synagogue's Council declared that it was 'no part of its functions to provide or maintain Mikvahs for the London Community'—but none the less voted the sum of £25 to satisfy the requirements of piety.[26]

The man who was effectively in charge of the United Synagogue throughout the inter-war period exemplified and typified this approach. Sir Robert Waley Cohen (1877–1952), a nephew of Lionel Louis, was neither an observant Jew nor, at the time of his election as Treasurer of the United Synagogue in 1913, had he any experience of service on its Council. A scientist who had become, at the age of 26, assistant manager of The Asiatic, a marketing company owned jointly by the Shell and Royal Dutch petroleum companies, Waley Cohen 'did not keep the dietary laws, worked,

[24] *Joint Celebration of the seventy-fifth Anniversary, Jews' College, the seventieth Anniversary, Jewish Religious Education Board, and the sixtieth Anniversary, United Synagogue* (London, 1931), 11.

[25] Quoted in Newman, *United Synagogue*, 120.

[26] United Synagogue Council Minute Book No. 6: minutes of 13 Nov. 1923 (microfilm roll 8). In 1912 Lord Rothschild had announced that he did 'not consider it the part of an orthodox Jew to discuss the shape and size of a mikvah': *JC* (19 Jan. 1912), 24.

hunted [*sic*] and played on the Sabbath, and was rarely seen in synagogue'.[27] Why, then, did he consent to become Treasurer of the United Synagogue, and why was he elected as its Vice-President five years later, holding the post until 1942, when he succeeded to the Presidency? The idea was not his, but came from his cousin, Albert Jessel. The administration of the United Synagogue, Jessel explained, needed 'the presence of a practical businessman'; through Waley Cohen this expertise would be provided, moreover, by someone who was bound to it by 'family ties'.[28]

Waley Cohen proved to be a tireless and selfless worker, who gave yeoman service to the United Synagogue and to many other Jewish institutions, not merely in Britain but more especially in Palestine, where he helped promote a number of industrial and commercial ventures of supreme importance to the development of the *Yishuv*, including the oil-refining complex at Haifa. But whilst believing fervently that the needs of those Jews who had settled or who were compelled to settle in Palestine had to be supported, he was far too English, and much too convinced of his British loyalties, to even contemplate espousing the view that there was merit in the reinstatement of Jewish nationhood, less still in the re-establishment of the Jewish State. He refused to support the political aims of the World Zionist Organization and he battled ferociously against those who demanded that the United Synagogue identify itself with the Zionist movement.

Albert Jessel did not—to the best of our knowledge—put it to Waley Cohen that the United Synagogue might be well served by having a non-Zionist effectively in charge of its affairs. But it is difficult to believe that the circumstance was entirely coincidental. At the beginning of 1913 the United Hebrew Congregations of the British Empire (in effect, the United Synagogue) had elected a new Chief Rabbi. The choice had been particularly difficult since the point had been well taken in United Synagogue circles that Hermann Adler's successor had to be as acceptable to East End as to West End Jewry.[29] Dr J. H. Hertz was as near perfect a fit as could be imagined. His educational background, in New York, had

[27] Bermant, *Cousinhood*, 368.

[28] R. Henriques, *Sir Robert Waley Cohen, 1877–1952* (London, 1966), 179.

[29] *JC* (17 Jan. 1913), 9–10. Hermann Adler had himself recognized and made this very point in the 'Message' he had drafted to be read after his death: Hermann Adler Papers, Jewish Theological Seminary, New York, Box 3–1.

instilled in him a 'cultured Orthodoxy'.[30] He had obtained rabbinical ordination both in the traditional orthodox mode and as a student at the Jewish Theological Seminary (JTS) Manhattan, the foundation of which, in 1887, had resulted from a coalition between 'those who desired to perpetuate the [Jewish] tradition but could not themselves observe the details of [orthodox] Jewish practice . . . and those who accepted and desired to observe Judaism as prescribed and codified' by the *Shulchan Aruch*.[31]

A rabbi destined to fill the position of ecclesiastical authority of the mid-twentieth century United Synagogue could hardly have wished for a more appropriate apprenticeship. The fact that the ethos of the JTS was emphatically opposed to the preservation of any Yiddish-based culture was an added bonus, for Lord Rothschild, in stressing that Hermann Adler's successor would have to 'be acquainted with English life and English laws and be able to speak English' had added that the person appointed would be expected to 'do all in his power to prevent the teaching and the spread of slang and jargon like Yiddish'.[32] Hertz's acquaintance with English life was decidedly limited, but it possessed a unique and singular dimension. In 1898 he had accepted a call to minister to the Jews of Johannesburg, whence the Boers had expelled him the following year on account of his pro-British sympathies; he had shared the cattle train bound for Portuguese East Africa with a young British war correspondent, Winston Churchill, and his experiences and sufferings had come to the attention of Sir Alfred Milner, the British High Commissioner in South Africa (and a friend of Lord Rothschild), who subsequently appointed Hertz to his advisory council.[33] Hertz had spent a short time in England on his way from New York to Johannesburg. Following his expulsion he had come to England once more, and had made the acquaintance of Solomon Schechter, upon whom he made a deep and lasting impression.

There can be no doubt that Milner's commendation of Hertz boosted his candidature for the British Chief Rabbinate in 1912.[34] But the story that this rather obscure Hungarian-American rabbi

[30] S. Temkin, 'Orthodoxy with Moderation: A Sketch of Joseph Herman Hertz', *Judaism*, 24 (Summer 1975), 279.

[31] M. Davis, *The Emergence of Conservative Judaism* (Philadelphia, 1963), 231.

[32] *JC* (19 Jan. 1912), 25.

[33] Temkin, 'Orthodoxy with Moderation', 285–6.

[34] A. Newman, *Chief Rabbi Dr Joseph H. Hertz* (London, 1973), 6; P. Paneth, *Guardian of the Law: The Chief Rabbi Dr J. H. Hertz* [London, 1943], 7.

(who by then had returned to New York) became Chief Rabbi of the British Empire largely on account of Milner's friendship with Rothschild is a piece of romanticized over-simplification.[35] The contest in 1912 resolved itself into a choice between Hertz, *Dayan* Moses Hyamson, and Rabbi Dr Bernard Drachman (1851–1945), Hertz's teacher.[36] Schechter, through Albert Jessel, was able to persuade the electoral college that had been established to appoint Hermann Adler's successor that Hertz was a better scholar than Drachman, who withdrew rather than face a formal contest.[37] Hyamson's candidature was compromised by the hostility he faced in London's East End. At the formal election, on 16 February 1913, Hyamson obtained 39 votes, and Hertz 298.[38]

Throughout what had been a very public contest, Hertz had had the support of Leopold Greenberg, whom Schechter supplied with background information for use in the *Jewish Chronicle*, and whose correspondence with Jessel the *Chronicle* reproduced.[39] But the reason for Greenberg's intense desire to see Hertz installed as Chief Rabbi undoubtedly had little to do with his treatment at the hands of the Boers, his love of things British, or even his academic potential. Hertz was indeed a good rabbinical scholar. He was not a great *Talmudist*, in the sense of being an original thinker, but he was thoroughly read in *Talmudic* and rabbinical literature, and subsequently produced three highly competent works of synthesis, a *Book of Jewish Thoughts* (compiled for Jewish soldiers serving in the First World War), an annotated edition of Simeon Singer's prayer-book, and a brilliantly composed edition of the *Pentateuch and Haftorahs*, with commentaries derived from all manner of Jewish and non-Jewish sources, which since its completion in 1936 has become a standard work of reference and use throughout the English-speaking Jewish world.

As Chief Rabbi from 1913 to his death in 1946 Hertz was also a most conscientious pastoral worker. He undertook (1920–1) the

[35] See Bermant, *Cousinhood*, 371, who follows Henriques, *Waley Cohen*, 179. Newman, *United Synagogue*, 99–101, offers a full account of the manner in which Hertz came to be elected Chief Rabbi.

[36] Temkin, 'Orthodoxy with Moderation', 282.

[37] Solomon Schechter Papers, Jewish Theological Seminary, New York: 101:3: Schechter to Jessel, 5 Aug. 1912 and 31 Jan. 1913.

[38] *JC* (17 Jan. 1913), 13; (21 Feb. 1913), 32.

[39] Solomon Schechter Papers, Jewish Theological Seminary, New York: 101:3: Schechter to Greenberg, 15 Aug. 1912; *JC* (14 Feb. 1913), 13.

first tour of the Jewish communities of the Empire by a holder of his office, laboured and lobbied long and hard—and successfully—against a movement within the League of Nations to effect a reform of the calendar which would have resulted in the Jewish Sabbath falling on weekdays rather than regularly on Saturdays,[40] and, as we shall see, did his best to prevent or at least postpone the religious polarization of British Jewry. But what interested Leopold Greenberg about him was neither his claims to scholarship, nor his obvious potential as a religious leader firmly planted within orthodoxy yet relatively free from traces of an intolerant and narrow-minded bigotry.

Joseph Herman Hertz was a Zionist. It is true, as Professor Cohen has observed, that at the time of his candidature for the Chief Rabbinate he had been careful to reduce public awareness of his Zionist commitment to the lowest of profiles.[41] Given the hostility to the idea of Jewish nationalism evinced by many of the leading lights in the United Synagogue, this reticence is perfectly understandable.[42] In fact, Hertz had proclaimed his support for the political Zionism of Theodor Herzl within a few months of the summoning, by Herzl, of the First Zionist Congress at Basle in 1897. He had played his part in the foundation of the Federation of American Zionists; from 1899 to 1904 he had filled the office of Vice-President of the South African Zionist Federation; in 1904 he had been a participant at the London deliberations of the Fourth Zionist Congress.[43] He had told a *Jewish Chronicle* reporter in April 1911 that he was 'a convinced Zionist'.[44] So he was.

In this respect, the change of direction signified by Hertz's election could not have been more radical, though even Leopold Greenberg could hardly have realized its ultimate potential. Some reference was made in the last chapter to the weakness of Zionism,

[40] Solomon Schechter Papers, Jewish Theological Seminary, New York: 101:3: Schechter to Greenberg, 15 Aug. 1912; *JC* (14 Feb. 1913), 9; J. H. Hertz, *Sermons, Addresses and Studies* (London, 1938), ii. 324–52; J. H. Hertz, 'The First Pastoral Tour to the Jewish Communities of the British Overseas Dominions', *TJHSE* 10 (1921–3), 149–68.

[41] S. A. Cohen, *English Zionists and British Jews: The Communal Politics of Anglo-Jewry, 1895–1920* (Princeton, NJ, 1982), 145, 190–1.

[42] Professor Cohen, *English Zionists*, is too restrained in his treatment of this point. The fact that Hertz's interview with the *Idisher Ekspres* (14 Aug. 1912), 1, made no mention of his Zionism may tell us more about the newspaper than about the man.

[43] Sir I. Jakobovits, *The Attitude to Zionism of Britain's Chief Rabbis as Reflected in their Writings* (London, 1981), 6–7.

[44] *JC* (7 Apr. 1911), 22.

in its specifically socialist mode, in Britain before the First World War. This weakness needs to be stressed, and understood, if the part played by Zionism in the communal affairs of British Jewry at this time is to be correctly appraised.

The visit which Theodor Herzl made to Israel Zangwill in London on 21 November 1895 marked a turning-point in the history of the Zionist movement.[45] Herzl neither invented Zionism nor did he contribute anything original to its philosophical dimensions. As a specifically Jewish contribution to the nationalisms that characterized European history in the nineteenth century, Zionism was late on the scene, and its proponents, galvanized by the failure of Emancipation to truly emancipate in central and even western Europe, and more especially by the failure of Emancipation to take root at all in Russia, searched desperately for ways in which the aims of Jewish nationalism (which had cultural and social as well as territorial dimensions) might be realized. Herzl was an irreligious and totally assimilated Viennese Jew. His conversion to Zionism was rooted in pragmatism, not idealism. At bottom, he did not care whether a Jewish State was established in Palestine, El Arish, Cyprus, or East Africa; only after his death did the leadership of the movement he founded pass to those for whom a Jewish State elsewhere than in the Holy Land was unthinkable. Herzl's brilliance lay in his accomplishments as a publicist. Like all journalists, he dealt in ideas second-hand. Deeply disturbed by anti-Semitism in Russia, and shocked by its recrudescence in France at the time of the Dreyfus Affair, he took hold of Zionist thinking and gave it political momentum.[46]

At first sight, British Jewry at the end of the nineteenth century might not have appeared a very fertile soil in which Jewish nationalism might grow. Wealthy English Jews of course gave generously towards the maintenance of the impoverished Jewish communities which were permitted to exist in Ottoman Palestine, and which Sir Moses Montefiore had visited no less than seven times between 1827 and 1874.[47] During the 1880s a number of what might be termed Palestine support groups enjoyed a meteoric

[45] J. Fraenkel, 'The *Jewish Chronicle* and the Launching of Political Zionism', in R. Patai (ed.), *Herzl Year Book*, 2 (New York, 1959), 218.

[46] S. Avineri, *The Making of Modern Zionism* (London, 1981), 88–100.

[47] T. Parfitt, 'Sir Moses Montefiore and Palestine', in V. D. Lipman (ed.), *Sir Moses Montefiore* (Oxford, 1982), 29–42.

existence in London and some major and minor provincial centres, their establishment (through the efforts of recent immigrants) triggered by the 'Love of Zion' movement which took hold in eastern Europe following the Russian pogroms of 1881–2. This movement led eventually to the summoning of a conference at Kattowitz, Silesia, in 1884, which resulted in the foundation of an international endeavour—*Chovevi Zion*—dedicated to the maintenance and strengthening of Jewish settlements in Palestine.[48]

The *Chovevi Zion* Association of England was not founded until 1890. Its inaugural public meeting was held at the Jewish Working Men's Club on 31 May; but it was by no means an entirely proletarian or even immigrant body. Its 'chief' was Colonel A. E. W. Goldsmid; its supporters and patrons included Lord Rothschild, Samuel Montagu, Benjamin Louis Cohen, Simeon Singer, and Rabbi Dr Moses Gaster (1856–1939), the brilliant if volcanic Romanian-born scholar who had settled in England in 1885 and been appointed *Haham* two years later.[49] Hermann Adler, soon to succeed his father as Chief Rabbi, also (as we noted in the previous chapter) graced the *Chovevi Zion* with his support. Gaster was to become one of Herzl's earliest English supporters.[50] Samuel Montagu confided to Herzl that 'he felt himself to be more an Israelite than an Englishman'—though the two were later to become estranged as a result of Herzl's irreligiosity.[51] Hermann Adler was to condemn the First Zionist Congress as 'an egregious blunder' and to denounce the idea of a Jewish state as 'contrary to Jewish principles'.[52] All, however, could support the broad aims of *Chovevi Zion*, which found practical expression in the 'adoption' of two Palestinian–Jewish settlements and the petitioning of Her Majesty's Government with the aim of effecting improvements in the conditions under which these and other settlements might operate.

Exaggerated statements [a circular explained in 1894] have . . . been put forward as to the aims of the Chovevei Zion societies . . . that their object is

[48] W. Laqueur, *A History of Zionism* (London, 1972), 75–83.

[49] *JC* (6 June 1890), 14. On Gaster see A. Hyamson, *The Sephardim of England* (London, 1951), 362–3, L. Stein, *The Balfour Declaration* (London, 1961), 286–7, and *JC* (10 Mar. 1939), 14–15.

[50] *JC* (6 Aug. 1897), 11; see also D. Vital, *The Origins of Zionism* (Oxford, 1975), 305–8.

[51] M. Lowenthal (trans. and ed.), *The Diaries of Theodor Herzl* (London, 1958), 81: 24 Nov. 1895.

[52] *JC* (16 July 1897), 13.

to anticipate the fulfilment of prophesy by encouraging a wholesale immigration of Jews to Palestine. Such is not the aim or idea of the Chovevei Zion.[53]

The visit which Herzl made to London in 1895 was to set in motion a train of events that quickly undermined the alliance upon which *Chovevi Zion* rested. It has been truly said that 'Modern Zionism in London began when Herzl entered Zangwill's study'.[54] Zangwill was not—as yet—convinced about the merits of Zionism, but he was sufficiently impressed by Herzl to introduce him to a range of notables, of whom the most important (as it turned out) were the artist Solomon J. Solomon, who had in 1891 become the first President of the Maccabaeans, and Asher Myers (1848–1902), Treasurer of the Maccabaeans and the then editor of the *Jewish Chronicle*. The Maccabaeans, a society of young Jewish professionals (many of them disciples of Schechter) who made a habit of dining together, had been instrumental in fostering a modest revival of interest in the Jewish cultural heritage; it was at a meeting of the society in May 1893 that the idea of establishing the Jewish Historical Society of England had taken shape.[55] On 24 November 1895 the Maccabaeans hosted a reception at which Herzl expounded (to an audience numbering no more than thirty) his view that the painfully slow penetration of Palestine by Jews dependent on outside support must be superseded by the establishment of a Jewish State.[56] Myers commissioned from Herzl an essay, 'A "Solution of the Jewish Question"', which appeared in the *Jewish Chronicle* on 17 January 1896. The article 'caused a sensation'.[57]

Herzl returned to London in July 1896. By then, he had expounded his views more formally in a thin volume, *Der Judenstaat*, published in Vienna on 14 February, the English translation of which went on sale in London two months later.[58] Herzl's July visit was a much grander affair than that of the previous year. On 14 July he attended the Headquarters 'Tent' of the *Chovevi Zion* Association; the previous day he had made his

[53] CZA, Jerusalem: Files of the *Chovevi Zion* Association in England: A2/7(i): circular dated Feb. 1894.

[54] J. Fraenkel, *Theodor Herzl* (London, 1946), 93.

[55] R. A. Goodman, *The Maccabaeans* (London, 1979), 18.

[56] Cohen, *English Zionists*, 26.

[57] Fraenkel, 'The Launching of Political Zionism', 220; *JC* (17 Jan. 1896), 12–13.

[58] Fraenkel, 'The Launching of Political Zionism', 223.

first public speech on political Zionism, to a vast, adulatory audience, chaired by *Haham* Gaster, at the Jewish Working Men's Club.[59] Gaster ostentatiously identified himself with political Zionism, the progress of which (both in Britain and in Europe) now gathered momentum at a remarkable speed. In Britain, and in the wake of the success of the Basle Congress, *Chovevi Zion* split. Under the influence of militant 'Herzlites' led by Jacob de Haas, (who acted as secretary to the English delegation at Basle), there was a concerted effort to push the Lovers of Zion into an identity of interest with the World Zionist movement.[60] At the end of 1897, and in an attempt to restore unity, it was agreed that *Chovevi Zion* would host a 'Conference of English Zionists' at the Clerkenwell Town Hall, London, on 6 March 1898. At that meeting a series of resolutions was passed espousing 'The National Idea . . . a legally safeguarded re-settlement of the Jewish Nation in Palestine' and asking, in effect, for affiliation to the World Zionist Organization which Herzl had called into being.[61]

Chovevi Zion could have become the English expression of World Zionism. Some of its adherents feared that its separate identity would be lost thereby. Others were opposed to 'the national idea' root and branch. At the beginning of October 1898 Herzl paid another visit to London, primarily to explore the possibility of establishing there a Jewish Colonial Trust, the financial arm of the Zionist movement. The Herzlites had already decided upon a split. On 6 October Herbert Bentwich, Moses Gaster, Jacob de Haas, and Leopold Greenberg addressed a public appeal 'To the Zionists of the United Kingdom':

> For years past, Zionism in England has been represented in the main by an organisation which . . . has failed to realise the expectations of its members and constituents, has worked in an irresolute spirit, and has shown itself incapable of identifying itself with the greater movement. . . . It is imperatively necessary that an end should be put to all this feebleness and uncertainty.[62]

At the Great Assembly Hall, Mile End, Herzl addressed a monster rally. Gaster was again in the chair; other speakers

[59] *JC* (17 July 1896), 8.

[60] Cohen, *English Zionists*, 39–40.

[61] CZA: Files of the *Chovevi Zion* Association in England: A2/122: 'Report of the Zionist Conference Committee 1898'.

[62] Ibid.: 'English Zionist Federation. To the Zionists of the United Kingdom'.

included de Haas, Herbert Bentwich (who had recently resigned as 'Vice-Chief' of *Chovevi Zion*), and Rabbi Werner of the *Machzike Hadath*. 'The East End', Herzl proclaimed, 'is ours.'[63] The attempt to affiliate *Chovevi Zion* to the World Zionist Congress was abandoned. Having apparently captured the East End, the Herzlites dined together at the Trocadero Restaurant, in the West End, on 22 January 1899, and there inaugurated the English Zionist Federation (EZF), of which Sir Francis Montefiore, the handsome and ineffective great-nephew of Sir Moses, was graciously pleased to accept the Presidency.[64] *Chovevi Zion* died an inevitable but slow death. Its members defected to local Zionist societies, its 'Tents' were gradually wound up, its income fell. Its demise was announced in a one-page circular issued on 1 December 1902.[65]

By then the EZF could claim, through its various affiliates, an individual membership of over 7,000, almost two-thirds of whom lived—significantly—in the provinces. The support of immigrant rabbis, such as Gaster, Werner, S. Y. Rabbinowitz, I. H. Daiches, and Israel Joffey of Manchester, imparted a strong sense of religious respectability.[66] Herzl's almost annual addresses to the immigrant masses in Whitechapel after 1898 drew large and rapturous audiences. At the end of 1903 *Dayan* Asher Feldman could write of the Zionist movement in East London in the following terms:

> Zionism has become a strong factor in East End life. It has rallied round it the intellectual forces of East End Jewry. The national idea . . . has taken a strong hold upon the greater bulk of the Jewish population. It has attracted the flower of Jewish youth. The [Zionist] ideal has given rise to numerous associations, nearly every one of which has its literary programme.[67]

But the reality was very different. Certainly before the First World War, Zionism in Britain could claim—on the EZF's own figures—the support of fewer than 6 per cent of the Jewish population of Great Britain.[68] The majority of societies affiliated to the EZF seem to have consisted of little more than miniscule committees armed

[63] *JC* (7 Oct. 1898), 12.
[64] Bermant, *Cousinhood*, 243; *JC* (27 Jan. 1899), 12–13.
[65] CZA: Files of the *Chovevi Zion* Association in England: A2/158.
[66] L. P. Gartner, *The Jewish Immigrant in England, 1870–1914* (London, 1960), 265.
[67] Quoted ibid. 265.
[68] Cohen, *English Zionists*, 107.

with a supply of notepaper.[69] Entranced by the welcomes he received from immigrant audiences, Herzl suggested that an independent Zionist candidate be put up in Whitechapel in the 1900 parliamentary election; de Haas, and Joseph Cowen (1868–1932) a friend of Zangwill's who later became President of the EZF, wisely dissuaded him from pursuing such a scheme.[70] The circular which the Zionists eventually put out had no discernible effect; neither did that which was produced for the general election of 1906.[71] The EZF itself suffered grievously in its early years from an accumulation of ills: from organizational weakness following de Haas's departure for the United States (in 1902) to become the first paid official of the Federation of American Zionists; from the dispute that had split the World Zionist movement (1902–3) over the British offer of a Jewish colony in East Africa;[72] from Zangwill's defection (in 1905) to found the Jewish Territorial Organization, 'dedicated to the creation of a Jewish territory in some country that need not necessarily be Palestine';[73] and from a bitter and protracted quarrel between Greenberg and Gaster (and their respective seconds) which was rooted partly in a genuine difference of approach to the realization of Zionist ambitions, but partly also in a fatal clash of temperament and—perhaps—of ambition.

Greenberg and Cowen were 'politicals', insisting that Zionism's first priority must be recognition by the international community of the Jewish claim to Palestine. The 'practicals' laid much greater stress on physical settlement—the creation of facts which world opinion would have to recognize in due course.[74] Chief among Gaster's lieutenants was Dr Charles (Chaim) Weizmann (1874–

[69] *Idisher Ekspres* (5 Nov. 1902), 4.

[70] CZA: Records of the Central Zionist Office, Vienna: Z1, file 236: de Haas to Herzl, 27 Sept. 1900; Cowen to Herzl, 28 Sept. On Cowen see *JC* (27 May 1932), 9–10.

[71] G. Alderman, *The Jewish Community in British Politics* (Oxford, 1983), 93.

[72] On the so-called 'Uganda' offer see R. G. Weisbord, *African Zion: The Attempt to Establish a Jewish Colony in the East Africa Protectorate, 1903–1905* (Philadelphia, 1968).

[73] M. Simon (ed.), *Speeches Articles and Letters of Israel Zangwill* (London, 1937), 232; the Jewish Territorial Organization was wound up in 1925, a year before Zangwill's death. Zangwill's evolving scepticism about the value of the Organization is reflected in his letter to Dr David Jochelman (London Manager of the Volga Insurance Company) preserved in the Jochelman Papers, Jabotinsky Institute, Tel Aviv, 105F, 18 Nov. 1918.

[74] Cohen, *English Zionists*, 114.

1952), a native of Russia who had arrived in England, and Manchester, in the summer of 1904 to take up a lectureship in chemistry at Manchester University; later that year he was appointed a part-time researcher with the Clayton Aniline Company, the managing director of which, Dr Charles Dreyfus (1848–1935), was President of the Manchester Zionist Society, a member of Manchester City Council, and a leading light in the East Manchester Conservative Association.[75] The Member of Parliament for East Manchester was the Prime Minister, Balfour, and it was at a constituency meeting which Balfour addressed on 27 January 1905 that Weizmann and Balfour met—briefly—for the first time.[76]

Following the collapse of Balfour's Government over the issue of Tariff Reform at the very end of 1905, Weizmann, who was by then clearly marked out as the rising star of Manchester Zionism, and had become its delegate to the EZF, found himself the object of attention from both the Liberal and Conservative camps in Manchester party politics, each side wishing to gain, through him, the adhesion of the Jewish vote in the 1906 general election.[77] It was as a result of these machinations that the second meeting between Balfour and Weizmann took place, in the privacy of the Queen's Hotel, Manchester, on 9 January 1906. For over an hour the two men talked about Zionism; Balfour told Weizmann that he saw 'no political difficulties in the attainment of Palestine—only economic difficulties'.[78] The two did not meet again until 12 December 1914; on that occasion Weizmann found the Conservative statesman 'much more than sympathetic'.[79]

By then Weizmann, who had served as Provincial Vice-President of the EZF under Gaster, had taken care to distance himself from the irascible *Haham*, whose support, in truth, he no longer needed. He had also widened his political contacts, especially with the Liberal Party, and had formed his own circle of disciples, chief

[75] C. Weizmann, *Trial and Error* (London, 1949), 125–33.

[76] Stein, *Balfour Declaration*, 147; see also M. M. Weisgal (gen. ed.), *The Letters and Papers of Chaim Weizmann* (London, 1968–), iv. series A, 19: Weizmann to Vera Chatzman (his fiancée), 28 Jan. 1905.

[77] Alderman, *Jewish Community*, 95.

[78] *Letters and Papers of Chaim Weizmann*, iv. series A, 219: Weizmann to Vera Chatzman, 9 Jan. 1906. This letter is the only contemporary record of what took place; the account it gives differs considerably from that presented by Weizmann in *Trial and Error*, 142–5.

[79] Stein, *Balfour Declaration*, 153–4. Balfour's motives in supporting Zionism are examined ibid. 157–65.

among whom were the celebrated Hebrew writer Asher Ginzberg (1856–1927; known by his pen-name 'Ahad Ha'am' ('One of the People'); the London representative of the Wissotsky Tea Company from 1907 to 1922), Leon Simon (1881–1965; the son of a Manchester rabbi; a civil servant and Ginzberg's translator), the Manchester business partners and brothers-in-law Simon Marks (1888–1964) and Israel Sieff (1889–1972), and another brother-in-law Harry Sacher (1881–1971), a journalist who from 1905 to 1909 had worked on the editorial staff of the *Manchester Guardian*.[80]

It was, in fact, as the acknowledged leader of a quite unofficial caucus of mainly Manchester Zionists (in his own words, 'a small band of workers . . . out of contact with Jewry at large')[81] that on the outbreak of war in 1914 Weizmann found himself in a position to outflank both the EZF and the World Zionist Organization. In September a chance meeting with C. P. Scott, editor of the *Manchester Guardian*, led to dialogues with David Lloyd George and also with Herbert Samuel, who, unknown to any of the English Zionists with the exception of Samuel's confidant, Moses Gaster, was already sympathetic to the Zionist cause.[82] These meetings were to be crucial in the chain of events which led to the promulgation of the Balfour Declaration on 2 November 1917.

Weizmann's election as President of the EZF in February 1917 was neither more nor less than the purely formal recognition of the fact that he was already the undisputed leader of British Zionism. But, as he himself recognized, he was by no stretch of the imagination the leader, therefore, of a mass movement. Indeed, as the many historians of Zionism have come to know, the story of the essentially diplomatic struggle for the Balfour Declaration can be told in more or less conventional diplomatic terms: a series of private negotiations, both domestic and international, which had as their backcloth the progress of the British expeditionary force across the Sinai peninsula in late 1916, and the British invasion of Palestine proper the following March.

[80] Alderman, *Jewish Community*, 96; Stein, *Balfour Declaration*, 124.

[81] Quoted in Stein, *Balfour Declaration*, 124.

[82] Ibid. 103–7, 131, 137. Samuel had become intellectually converted to Zionism after reading *Der Judenstaat*: J. Fraenkel, 'Lucien Wolf and Theodor Herzl', *TJHSE* 20 (1959–61), 168. See also J. Bowle, *Viscount Samuel* (London, 1957), 170–8.

The earliest evidence we have of genuine widespread support for Zionism amongst British Jewry is the petition of 1915 calling for the establishment of a 'publicly recognized, legally secured home for the Jewish people in Palestine', signed by some 50,000 members of the British–Jewish community.[83] By then, of course, what had seemed wellnigh impossible but a few years before—British control of the Holy Land—had acquired an air of startling credibility. But the failure of pre-war Zionism to evoke mass support in Britain sprang from a variety of causes much deeper than considerations arising merely from the practicality of its aims and objectives. At the spiritual level there is no doubt that Zionism, like Love of Zion, struck sharp chords with the immigrant masses. But its relevance to the immediate and severely practical problems which they faced was hardly apparent. Both religious 'Love of Zion' and Herzlian Zionism were the targets of savage attacks in the columns of the *Arbeter Fraint*, the former on account of its alleged desire to support and preserve in Palestine an essentially religious society founded upon charity, the latter as a plot hatched by the bourgeoisie to undermine the proletarian class struggle.[84] The weakness of *Poale Zion* in pre-war days has already been noticed. Much more serious, however, was the company the EZF chose to keep at this time. For it was a fact that some of the parliamentary candidates whom the EZF supported in 1900—such as David Hope Kyd at Whitechapel—were out-and-out anti-alienists, only too happy to favour any scheme that would (in the words of the EZF itself) 'divert the tide of emigration which now takes place to Western countries'.[85] Liberals who were sympathetic on the aliens' question were opposed by the EZF none the less.[86]

[83] Laqueur, *History of Zionism*, 158.

[84] *Arbeter Fraint* (Aug. 1886), 11–12; (Sept.), 18–19; (7 July 1899), 5–6; (14 July), 5–6.

[85] *English Zionist Federation. General Election, 1900* (London, 1900), 2 (copy in CZA).

[86] It is worth recording that the anti-alienism of leading British Conservatives at this time struck many Zionists as wholly understandable; the fact that it was a Conservative Government that had passed the 1905 Aliens Act did not prevent Weizmann from meeting and making friends with Balfour, or from retaining, until the very end of his life, a sympathetic attitude towards Major Evans-Gordon, of whom he wrote apologetically in *Trial and Error*, 118–19. 'The fact is inescapable [writes Professor M. Scult of Vassar College] that many Zionists and anti-Semites share in common the conviction that integration into non-Jewish society is impossible and that basically the Emancipation was a mistake': in J. Katz (ed.), *The Role of Religion in Modern Jewish History* (Cambridge, Mass., 1975), 144.

In any case, those who put themselves at the head of the Zionist movement in Britain at this time had impeccable middle class credentials. In this sense the accusation of the *Arbeter Fraint* had—or at least appeared to have—a ring of truth about it. The founders of the EZF were only too well aware of the need to prevent the movement falling into the hands of the proletariat, to be used, perhaps, as an instrument of class war. Gaster had warned in 1898 against the possibility of precipitating a 'social crusade'; de Haas wrote to Herzl in disparaging terms about the 'Jargon element', and justified his resignation from the EZF (November 1901) in terms of his fear that it might become 'wholly . . . East End' in character.[87]

There was an irony here. Those who had given Herzl his most rapturous London ovations were precisely those whom the official leaders of English Zionism took care to distance from anything approaching control of the movement. Yet at the same time the official leadership used Zionism as an instrument with which to challenge the Anglo-Jewish gentry then to be found in positions of communal authority. It was precisely because of its weakness 'on the ground' that English Zionism had to pursue instead a policy of entryism, by which its spokesmen obtained for themselves—and hence, it was argued, for the movement as a whole—positions of influence on established communal bodies. In this way, using Zionism as a pretext, one middle class élite challenged another for the mastery of British Jewry.[88]

This motif was at its most transparent in the case of Gaster, who risked (and enjoyed) confrontation with the lay leaders of the Spanish & Portuguese congregation through his very public espousal of Jewish nationalism.[89] Greenberg and Bentwich, Cowen and Zangwill, and a host of less well-known Zionist devotees deliberately exploited, for reasons both personal and political, existing and developing communal tensions: the growing self-confidence of provincial Jewries; the silence of the communal grandees over the Aliens legislation; the reluctance of the Board of Deputies and the Anglo-Jewish Association to engage in a public

[87] CZA: Gaster Papers: A203/113: Gaster to Samuel Bensusan (1872–1958; editor of the *Jewish World*), 29 June 1898; Herzl Papers, H VIII 315: de Haas to Herzl, 5 Nov. 1901.

[88] The Manchester dimension to this dialectic is examined in B. Williams, '"East and West": Class and Community in Manchester Jewry, 1850–1914', in D. Cesarani (ed.), *The Making of Modern Anglo-Jewry* (Oxford, 1990), 26–7.

[89] Cohen, *English Zionists*, 48, 191–2.

display of anger at the time of the Kishineff pogrom.[90] In the furtherance of Zionist aims narrowly defined, British Zionists could do very little. But as the proponents of a strident brand of Anglo-Jewish anti-assimilationist self-assertiveness they became genuine heroes. Whenever the establishment needed to be chastised, the Zionists could be relied upon to administer the punishment. The fact that—with few exceptions—the establishment was anti-Zionist was an additional source of comfort and of consolation.

The anti-Zionism of the old-established communal leadership sprang directly from its perception of the grounds upon which Emancipation had been granted, and the obligation which British Jewry had (if not in so many words) taken upon itself as a result. Hermann Adler's opposition to political or Herzlian Zionism claimed to be rooted in religious orthodoxy:

> It is not declared in the prophetic books [Adler told his audience at the North London Synagogue, 12 November 1898] that our return to Palestine is to be accomplished by our instrumentality and at the period we desire. It is distinctly announced that our redemption is to be effected by Divine interposition at such time as seemeth good in God's sight.[91]

Adler thus appeared to align himself with that strand of religious orthodoxy which inveighed against political Zionism because of its presumption to do what the Almighty had apparently decreed He alone, at a time of His choosing, would accomplish; indeed, Adler was the only western European rabbi to contribute to a collection of anti-Zionist articles, by many leading Jewish ecclesiastics, published in Warsaw in 1900 under the title *Or Layesharim* (*Light unto the Righteous*).[92] International rabbinic opinion was divided as to the religious merits of Herzl's schemes. In Britain Herzl's efforts, from the start, attracted clerical support, both from rabbis who ministered to immigrant flocks and from those who were identified with the native, Anglicized community: for example, Simeon Singer in London and the Revd John Harris in Liverpool.[93]

[90] *JC* (29 May 1903), 12, 14; (19 June), 25.

[91] Ibid. (25 Nov. 1898), 13.

[92] S. Z. Landau and J. Rabinowitz (eds.), *Or Layesharim* (Warsaw, 1900), 62–8 (copy in the Library of the Jewish Theological Seminary, New York); Adler's contribution was his own Hebrew translation of his sermon of Nov. 1898 at the North London Synagogue.

[93] On Singer's relationship with Herzl see I. Finestein, 'The New Community 1880–1918', in V. D. Lipman (ed.), *Three Centuries of Anglo-Jewish History*

The major thrust of Hermann Adler's attack upon the summoning of the First Zionist Congress was, indeed, not religious at all, but political. Herzl's plan for a Jewish state, he warned, 'might lead people to think that we Jews are not fired with ardent loyalty for the country in which it is our lot to be placed'.[94]

In April 1909 twenty-five Jewish university graduates signed a letter to the *Jewish Chronicle* criticizing the growth of Zionist societies at both the ancient and civic universities of Britain; such societies, they argued, compromised the status of Jewish university students.[95] Later that month Adler supported them. In a statement to a Manchester newspaper he presented the manifesto, so to speak, of those British Jews who, long after his death, were to oppose the Zionism of the EZF and the World Zionist Organization:

> Since the destruction of the Temple and our dispersion, we no longer constitute a nation; we are a religious communion. We are bound together with our brethren throughout the world primarily by the ties of a common faith. But in regard to all other matters we consider ourselves Englishmen and we hold that in virtue of being Jews it is our duty and privilege to work as zealously as possible for the welfare of England.[96]

Adler's extreme patriotism lent weight to these sentiments; the welcome which Zionists gave to his successor, Hertz, is thus easily understood. Adler had, however, made a telling point. Political Zionism, embracing as it must the notion of Jewish statehood and thus of Jewish nationality, struck at the very heart of the process of social, cultural, and political assimilation of which the Anglo-Jewish leadership was so proud. The question was indeed posed by Claude Montefiore (then President of the Anglo-Jewish Association) in November 1916. 'How [he asked] can a man belong to two nations at once? . . . No wonder that all anti-Semites are enthusiastic Zionists.'[97]

(Cambridge, 1961), 116. On Harris, see N. Kokosalakis, *Ethnic Identity and Religion: Tradition and Change in Liverpool Jewry* (Washington, DC, 1982), 140–1, and E. Wilcock, 'The Revd John Harris: Issues in Anglo-Jewish Pacifism, 1914–18', *TJHSE* 30 (1987–8), 167.

[94] *JC* (16 July 1897), 13.

[95] Ibid. (9 Apr. 1909), 6.

[96] Quoted ibid. (23 Apr. 1909), 11. Compare this declaration with the article which Adler wrote in the *Nineteenth Century* (July 1878), cited in Ch. 2 above, n. 155.

[97] 'An Englishman of the Jewish Faith' [C. G. Montefiore], 'Zionism', *Fortnightly Review* (Nov. 1916), 823. See also the useful discussion by V. D. Lipman, *History of the Jews in Britain since 1858* (Leicester, 1990), 127–30.

Whatever the motives of the British Cabinet in authorizing the Balfour Declaration, its condemnation by the older ruling élites in Anglo-Jewry, and by all those who declared themselves English men and women of the Jewish persuasion, was assured. So too was its welcome in immigrant circles, and its exploitation by provincial Jewries anxious to cock a snook at the dominance enjoyed in communal affairs by the London grandees, as well as by the miscellany of aspiring communal leaders who found their road to advancement blocked by existing oligarchies. Zionism, in short, became the battleground upon which a number of smouldering and pre-existing conflicts were fought out. But the First World War itself intensified and gave added urgency to these debates, principally in two directions: through its effect upon the immigrants; and by the encouragement it gave to those—nationally and within British Jewry—who sought a more democratic structure and more popular participation in the ordering of public affairs.

Sociology and politics coalesced, forming a highly volatile mixture. Nowhere was the pressure more intense than in London, where, in the years immediately preceding the war, affluence and poverty affected the immigrants and their offspring in a predictable way: economic inequality resulted in geographical separation. In the period 1910–30 London Jewry relocated itself. At the beginning of the century well over 80 per cent of the Jewish population of the County of London lived in the boroughs of Stepney, Bethnal Green, and Poplar. Twenty years later, when Jews in London numbered perhaps 200,000, only 46 per cent were still living in the East End boroughs.[98] Hackney was by far the most popular area of resettlement; at the time of the First World War its Jewish population had risen to almost 15,000 persons.[99]

In the material which she collected in order to write her contribution to the *New Survey of London Life and Labour*, Nettie Adler prepared a table showing the working- and middle-class proportions among the Jews of East London; the category 'middle class' was primarily an occupational one, and included professional

[98] V. D. Lipman, *Social History of the Jews in England 1850–1950* (London, 1954), 168–9. H. L. Trachtenberg, 'Estimates of the Jewish Population of London in 1929', *Journal of the Royal Statistical Society*, 96 (1933), 96. See also the discussion in V. D. Lipman, 'Social Change in Anglo-Jewry 1918–1939', *Yahadut Zemanenu (Contemporary Jewry)*, 3 (1986), 51–3.

[99] B. A. Kosmin and N. Grizzard, *Jews in an Inner London Borough* (London, n.d. [1975]), 31.

and clerical workers, shopkeepers, supervisory staff, and the self-employed; but it also comprised households enjoying an income of at least £250 per annum, regardless of occupation. Using these definitions, Nettie calculated that in the boroughs of Stoke Newington and Hackney at the end of the 1920s there were almost twice as many middle-class as working-class Jews; indeed, even in Stepney and Bethnal Green more than a fifth of the Jews were middle class by this time.[100]

These developments were also to be observed in the outlying areas. The Jews who established themselves in Palmers Green, and Chingford, to the immediate north of the LCC boundary, and in Golders Green, Hendon, and Finchley to the north-west, were not 'refugees' from Maida Vale or Hampstead, but true *nouveaux riches* from the East End; one of the first Jews to settle in Golders Green had come there from Bow Road (Bethnal Green) in 1910.[101] The very fact of Jewish settlement in these areas, as of Jewish migration to Hackney and Stoke Newington, was of course a sign of upward social mobility, assisted by a decline in the birth rate and a consequent fall in the average size of Jewish families.[102] These trends, which mirrored those experienced in British society as a whole, were bolstered by the virtual cessation of immigration to Britain of poor working-class Jews in the inter-war period; indeed, apart from a relatively small influx of Polish Jews in the early 1920s, and of a small immigration of *Sephardic* Jews from Salonika, Smyrna and Bukhara around the same time, there was no further Jewish immigration to Britain until the influx of refugees from Nazism in the 1930s.[103]

[100] V. D. Lipman, 'The Booth and New London Surveys as Source Material for East London Jewry (1880–1930)', in A. Newman (ed.), *The Jewish East End 1840–1939* (London, 1981), 46–7.

[101] Levin and Levin, *Finchley*, 3.

[102] See generally H. Neustatter, 'Demographic and Other Statistical Aspects of Anglo-Jewry', in M. Freedman (ed.), *A Minority in Britain* (London, 1955), 55–108.

[103] There has been no systematic study of the Jewish immigrations of the 1920s. That from Poland is noted in passing in G. Alderman, *The Federation of Synagogues 1887–1987* (London, 1987), 87; Hyamson, *The Sephardim*, 412–13, briefly mentions the influx from Salonika, which resulted in the erection of a synagogue in Holland Park, West London, in 1928; this community accepted the jurisdiction of Bevis Marks in ecclesiastical affairs, and in 1932 was given representation on the Board of Elders of the Bevis Marks synagogue. The immigrations from Salonika, Smyrna, and Bukhara are also noted briefly by R. D. Barnett, 'The Sephardim of England', in R. D. Barnett and W. M. Schwab (eds.), *The Sephardi Heritage*, ii (Grendon, Northants, 1989), 21. All these exoduses were the result of political upheaval and persecution during and immediately after the First World War.

By the early 1930s slightly over 12 per cent of the entire working population of East London lived in what the *New Survey* considered to be poverty; for working-class Jews the proportion was 13.7 per cent.[104] The centrifugal forces that played upon London Jewry in the war and inter-war years had left, in the East End, a residuum of poor Jews, many of them still aliens in the legal sense. At the same time it resulted in the emergence of a new middle class. Both searched for ways of making their presence felt. Both found in Zionism a means by which this might be achieved.

The outbreak of war in 1914 led to a deterioration in the social position of Jews, and especially of Jewish aliens, in Britain. The Jewish leadership took very public steps to advertise the supposed support of all sections of British Jewry for the war effort. Religious services themselves were turned into manifestations of patriotic fervour.[105] The number of Jews who served in the armed forces during the First World War totalled 41,500, or about 13.8 per cent of British Jewry; the proportion of the general population of Great Britain who served in the armed forces amounted to only 11.5 per cent.[106] Those few Jews who had the temerity to take an anti-war stance were quickly disowned by the leadership; the Liverpool Old Hebrew Congregation dismissed the Revd John Harris after he refused to give an undertaking that he would cease supporting Jewish conscientious objectors before recruiting tribunals.[107]

At the same time, the ultra-patriotism and violent anti-German hysteria that swept the nation did not bother to differentiate much between Germans and Jews, and, inevitably, soon gave way to a general xenophobic atmosphere from which Jews suffered disproportionately, whether or not they were indeed of German origin. The campaign against prominent persons of German birth, who were challenged to write 'loyalty letters' to *The Times*, is a case in point. Many of those who were the targets of this campaign, such as the laryngologist Sir Felix Semon (1849–1921) and the banker

[104] H. L. Smith (ed.), *The New Survey of London Life and Labour*, vi (London, 1934), 22.

[105] *JC* (14 Aug. 1914), 4; (1 Oct. 1915), 6.

[106] B. A. Kosmin and N. Grizzard, 'The Jewish Dead in the Great War as an Indicator for Anglo-Jewish Demography and Class Stratification in 1914' (London, Board of Deputies mimeo., 1974), 2.

[107] *JC* (17 Mar. 1916), 23; see also S. G. Bayme, 'Jewish Leadership and Anti-Semitism in Britain, 1898–1918', Ph.D. thesis (Columbia, New York, 1977), 25. On Harris see above, n. 93.

Sir Edgar Speyer (1862–1932) were Jews or of Jewish origin. Their sufferings might be said to have taken place on account of their German roots; but the charge made against them, of being 'cosmopolitans, wanderers on the face of the earth', was in fact a barely concealed form of anti-Jewish prejudice.[108] 'Hundreds of families', Jewish and of German-Jewish origin, anglicized their names and did their best in other ways to merge into anonymous non-Jewish surroundings.[109]

On the face of it, the position of Russian Jews ought to have been much easier; Russia and Britain were allies, and although the many non-naturalized Jews in this category (estimated in 1916 to number between 25,000 and 30,000 males of 'military' age) were aliens, they were not *enemy* aliens.[110] In practice this status was of no help. In Stepney, in the autumn of 1914, Jews applying for relief under the Poor Law were subject to discrimination.[111] The sinking by a German submarine of the *Lusitania* (7 May 1915) led to extensive rioting in East London, in which no attempt appears to have been made to distinguish between Germans and Jews. But the most serious incidents of wartime hostility to Jews took place in Leeds, where, at the beginning of June 1917, several thousand people took part in attacks on the Jewish 'ghetto'. Evidence of Jew-baiting was overwhelming.[112]

In his report to the Home Office on these disturbances, the Chief Constable went to the heart of the matter. There were in Leeds roughly 1,400 Jewish aliens, mostly Russian Jews; he observed that of these only twenty-six had joined the armed forces, while 'a large number of Jews of military age' were believed to have fled to Ireland rather than face the prospect of military service.[113] The same issue surfaced also in London. On 23 January 1917 a meeting

108 C. Holmes, *Anti-Semitism in British Society 1876–1939* (London, 1979), 123–4. On Speyer, who was in effect forced to leave Britain for the United States, see *Dictionary of National Biography 1931–40*, 828–9. On Semon see H. C. Semon and T. A. McIntyre, *The Autobiography of Sir Felix Semon* (London, 1926), 294–323. See also, generally, C. C. Aronsfeld, 'Jewish Enemy Aliens in England during the First World War', *JSS* 18 (1956), 275–83.

109 Endelman, *Radical Assimilation*, 142.

110 *House of Commons Debates*, 5th ser., lxxxv. 1839 (16 Aug. 1916).

111 J. Bush, *Behind the Lines: East London Labour 1914–1919* (London, 1984), 168.

112 N. Grizzard, *Leeds Jewry and the Great War 1914–1918* (Leeds [1982]), 8–11.

113 PRO HO45 10810/311932/43: letter dated 18 June 1917.

at Bethnal Green Town Hall passed a series of resolutions drawing attention to the inequity of aliens being permitted to earn good wages while English conscripts were dying for their country.[114] A Foreign Jews Deportation Committee was set in motion, and MPs were lobbied.[115] Later that year, in September, serious disturbances took place in Bethnal Green, certainly triggered by the issue of military enlistment.[116]

The related issues of military service and conscription brought to a head two interconnected sets of tensions: between Jews and non-Jews, and between native and immigrant Jews. However just Britain's quarrel with Germany might have seemed, it was not perceived in immigrant circles as a Jewish quarrel; for Jew to kill Jew appeared particularly profane.[117] Immigrant Jews had not escaped from Tsarist Russia only to be told that in the Anglo-Jewish communal interest they must volunteer to lay down their lives for its preservation. Yet this was precisely what the Anglo-Jewish leadership demanded of them. And the demand became ever more insistent as the resistance to it grew more determined. Jews liable for conscription who pleaded before military tribunals that they should be exempted because they did not wish to fight for the Tsar, or because they feared that they would not be able to practise their religion in the armed forces, obviously created a bad impression. A press campaign was whipped up against them and—by extension—against 'foreign' Jews in general.[118]

Jews who were not naturalized were in a difficult situation, because the conscription laws did not apply to them. When it became clear that the proportion of unnaturalized Jews volunteering was small, and after conscription had been introduced for British subjects, Herbert Samuel, then Home Secretary, told the House of Commons that Russians of military age were 'expected either to offer their service to the British Army or to return to Russia to fulfil

[114] Holmes, *Anti-Semitism*, 135. This type of accusation was not groundless. 'Jewish' occupations benefited from army contracts for uniforms, boots, and so on, so that between 1915 and 1917 there was 'an unprecedented rise in the wages and living standards of Jewish workers': D. Cesarani, 'An Embattled Minority: The Jews in Britain during The First World War', *Immigrants & Minorities*, 8 (1989), 73.

[115] *East London Observer* (3 Mar. 1917), 4.

[116] Bush, *Behind the Lines*, 181–2.

[117] Ibid. 167.

[118] See e.g. *East London Observer* (5 Aug. 1916), 4: 'The misbehaviour of any offensive foreign bounder, or the impertinence of a Whitechapel Jew boy, may light the smouldering flames of native feeling.'

their military obligations there'.[119] There was a hint of involuntary repatriation. 'If the mass of Russian Jewry in this country', Samuel wrote to Lucien Wolf in August, 'refuse to lift a finger to help when this country is making immeasurable sacrifices in a war in which the cause of Liberty all over the world is bound up, the effect on the reputation of the Jewish name everywhere will be disastrous.'[120] To fight against conscription, and to preserve the right of asylum in Britain, a Foreign Jews Protection Committee (FJPC) was established in East London by a miscellany of Jewish socialist groups, trade unions, and friendly societies. Branches were established in other parts of London, and in all the major provincial centres of Jewish settlement.[121]

The activities of the FJPC were anathema to the generality of the Anglo-Jewish leadership. Herbert Samuel refused to meet its representatives (even though Israel Zangwill was numbered amongst its supporters); the following year its secretary, Solly Abrahams ('Abraham Bezalel') was sent back to Romania.[122] Behind the scenes and occasionally in public the communal leadership—pre-eminently Lucien Wolf—urged the Government to move against their Russian co-religionists who refused to join up.[123] In July 1917 the British and Russian Governments signed a Military Service Convention, one consequence of which was that males of Russian nationality who declined to be conscripted into the British forces were made liable to deportation; in August deportations actually began, but a month later the Bolshevik Revolution took Russia out of the war, and it is unlikely that many Jews so repatriated ever saw active service in the Russian army.[124]

[119] *House of Commons Debates*, 5th ser., lxxxiii. 1084 (29 June 1916).

[120] Stein, *Balfour Declaration*, 489.

[121] *East London Observer* (19 Aug. 1916), 4; Lucien Wolf Papers in the David Mowshowitz Collection, YIVO Institute, New York, folder 87: materials concerning Russian refugees in England, 1916.

[122] *JC* (9 Nov. 1917), 18. The best treatment of the FJPC is by S. Kadish, 'Bolsheviks and British Jews: The Anglo-Jewish Community, Britain and the Russian Revolution', D.Phil. thesis (Oxford, 1987), 251–80; see also S. Almog, 'Antisemitism as a Dynamic Phenomenon: The "Jewish Question" in England at the End of the First World War', *Patterns of Prejudice*, 21 (1987), 7–8, and I. Wassilevsky, *Jewish Refugees and Military Service: The Ethical Aspects of Compulsion under Threat of Deportation* (National Labour Press, Manchester, n.d. [1916]) (copy in Yivo Library, New York).

[123] Kadish, 'Bolsheviks and British Jews', 277.

[124] The fullest treatment of this episode is in Holmes, *Anti-Semitism*, 126–31.

The total number of Jews 'returned' to Russia in this way is uncertain. It is clear from surviving evidence that the popular notion that many thousands of Jews were compelled to return was a gross exaggeration; the true figure was probably no more than 3,000 at most.[125] Some of these, fervent supporters of the Bolshevik cause, were certainly willing participants in their free passage back to their 'liberated' Russian homeland. It is worth recalling, in this connection, that events in Russia in the autumn of 1917, and subsequently, excited great interest among alien Jewish refugees in Britain, and that many Bundists eventually returned to what became the Soviet Union, Joe Fineberg, who had in 1914 been a member of the Executive Committee of the London Labour Party, resigned his position as secretary of the Stepney Branch of the British Socialist Party in order to take up employment in Lenin's administration.[126] But if the number of 'returnees' was relatively small, and if some of them were not entirely involuntary, it is equally true that the plight of the families they left or were forced to leave behind evoked widespread sympathy, and that the deliberate refusal of the Jewish Board of Guardians to ease the plight of these unfortunates, and of the Board of Deputies to plead their cause, left their own bitter memories.[127]

These events played into the hands of the Zionists, though in a somewhat complicated fashion. The FJPC had no overt Zionist connections. At a meeting which it called in July 1916, a spokesman from the EZF (Joseph Cowen) who was known as a supporter of the recruitment of alien Jews was shouted down.[128] The Zionists, for very obvious diplomatic reasons, needed the friendship of the British Government, and were certainly not prepared to jeopardize the relationship they were developing with it by supporting the anti-enlistment lobby. The *Jewish Chronicle*, now under Greenberg's editorship, eventually came out in support of the Anglo-Russian Convention[129] But a few prominent Zionists, in an individual capacity, did identify with the broad humanitarian activities and objectives of the FJPC; chief among these was (of

125 Kadish, 'Bolsheviks and British Jews', 267–8.

126 Bush, *Behind the Lines*, 186.

127 *JC* (21 Sept. 1917), 5; (12 Oct.), 5; Cohen, *English Zionists*, 217–18, 252–4. See also Felix M. Warburg Papers, American Jewish Archives, Cincinnati, 184/16: Israel Zangwill to Jacob H. Schiff (New York), 8 Jan. 1919.

128 *East London Observer* (29 July 1916), 7–8.

129 *JC* (27 July 1917), 5.

course) *Haham* Gaster, whose increasingly fraught relationship with the gentlemen of Bevis Marks was to reach new depths over a letter of his, supporting the FJPC, which appeared in the *Manchester Guardian*.[130]

Gaster's eccentricities were well known, as was his propensity for using any communal organization with which he happened to come into contact as a vehicle for his own advancement in communal ranks. But during the course of 1916 he had had the good fortune to be chosen as successor to Lucien Wolf as President of the National Union for Jewish Rights, a federation of some thirty or so East London groups, with a combined male membership of about 15,000, which had come together at the end of 1915, and which Wolf had agreed to lead in the fantastic hope that it might be turned into an instrument of anti-Zionist propaganda.[131] The goal which united the members of the National Union had nothing to do with Zionism or anti-Zionism, but concerned the desire to secure an enlargement of the Board of Deputies in order to permit the immigrant communities and their leaders a much greater say in the Deputies' activities.[132] But, although neutral on the issue of Jewish nationalism, the National Union managed to recruit into affiliation nine societies affiliated to the EZF.[133] Wolf resigned from it. Gaster was put in charge, and soon brought it into a working arrangement with the FJPC. Both bodies had, in fact, become focal points of what had by then become an unmistakeable and genuine movement 'at the grass roots' against the communal grandees. This movement coincided with a desperate political struggle between the Zionists and the anti-Zionists for the ear of the British Government; it was, therefore, a movement of which the Zionists took every advantage.

The institutions which surmounted and purported to govern British Jewry in 1914 were intensely oligarchical in character, incestuous in their reliance upon a coterie of wealthy and interrelated families, and additionally protected from the depredations of democracy by actual or indirect considerations of wealth. The issues of conscription and deportation had galvanized the immigrant cohorts, but their implications were not lost on other

[130] *Manchester Guardian* (26 Mar. 1917), 6.

[131] Cohen, *English Zionists*, 254–5. E. C. Black, *The Social Politics of Anglo-Jewry 1880–1920* (Oxford, 1988), 373, is unhelpful in implying that Wolf actually founded the National Union.

[132] *JC* (28 Jan. 1916), 18.

[133] Cohen, *English Zionists*, 256.

sectors of Anglo-Jewry. The failure of the Board of Deputies (June 1915) to take any action to challenge the Government's decision to intern Jewish 'enemy aliens' had set a tone which it was to follow throughout the war: the preservation of image was to override that of religious or ethnic solidarity.[134] But if that sin of omission could be justified on the grounds that the Jewishness of an enemy alien was immaterial in the context of a war for national survival, what excuse could be offered for the decision of the Jewish Soup Kitchen, in London's East End, to refuse to make its facilities available to Russian Jews (and their families) who refused to volunteer for service in the British Army?[135]

The emergence of the FJPC amounted to a vote of no confidence in the existing representative institutions. This antipathy was by no means confined to aliens, immigrants or even to the Jewish working classes as a whole. The National Union was, in broad terms, a proletarian body with a middle-class leadership. Because of the deliberate failure of the Board of Deputies to extend help to those who appealed against repatriation or internment, or to their families, the task had fallen upon the friendly societies and upon some other organizations of much younger vintage. Pre-eminent among these was *B'nai B'rith* ('Children of the Covenant'), an American philanthropic fraternity (bearing a certain but limited resemblance to the Freemasons), the 'First [English] Lodge' of which had been established in London in 1910 following a visit by a member of the American Grand Lodge the previous year.[136] The doubts of those who argued that another communal organization was not wanted were overcome by the eagerness of a section of the newer middle classes to forge an instrument capable of challenging the 'oligarchy, autocracy, traditionalism and narrow insularity'

[134] *JC* (18 June 1915), 12; (25 June), 13; (2 July), 13. The vote in favour of doing nothing was almost unanimous. This neurosis reached an extreme form in the wake of the Government's announcement (28 July 1917) that a specifically 'Jewish' fighting unit would be formed, which Russian Jews could join; even Chief Rabbi Hertz stayed aloof from the plan, which was championed by Weizmann and the Polish Zionist leader V. Jabotinsky. In an attempt to placate the assimilationists the unit, when formed, was merely a battalion of the Royal Fusiliers; only later did it and other similar 'Jewish' units become the Judean Regiment: see Lipman, *History*, 147–9, and Cesarani, 'An Embattled Minority', 69–72.

[135] Alderman, *Jewish Community*, 102.

[136] On the origins of *B'nai B'rith* see *Encyclopaedia Judaica*.

which, they claimed, characterized the communal leadership at that time.[137]

In the years immediately preceding the outbreak of war, the First Lodge busied itself with a number of matters that ought properly to have been the sole concern of the Board of Deputies: the 1911 Slaughter of Animals Bill (in respect of which *shechita* had to be safeguarded); a Sunday Closing of Shops Bill (in which concessions were eventually extracted from the Government for London, West Ham, and parts of Leeds, Liverpool, and Manchester); the 1911 National Insurance Bill (in which the position of the Jewish friendly societies required protection).[138] Significantly, too, the First Lodge took an interest in the question of legal representation for Jewish aliens and that relating to the difficulties encountered by Jews wishing to visit Russia in obtaining the necessary legal permissions from St Petersburg. The success of *B'nai B'rith* in opening dialogues on all these matters with the relevant departments of the British Government was such that in 1912 the Board of Deputies was forced to agree to the establishment of a joint committee, through which the responsibility for dealing with such matters was, in effect, to be shared with the *B'nai B'rith* movement.[139]

For the moment, the theatre of operations of *B'nai B'rith* was largely confined to London; a Manchester Lodge was not inaugurated until November 1912. But in the provinces, during the same pre-war period, a different type of communal organization grew up, the Representative Council. The precise circumstances which resulted in the establishment of a Representative Council were different in the case of each provincial community. In Leeds an attempt to form such a Council, to act as a point of unity at the local and at the lay levels, and to function as an instrument of communal defence, was made as early as 1907; a more permanent body was in existence in Leeds from 1913 until about 1928.[140] In Glasgow the impetus to the formation of a Representative Council was provided by the

[137] W. M. Schwab, *B'nai B'rith: The First Lodge of England: A Record of Fifty Years* (London, 1960), 16.

[138] *JC* (7 July 1911), 3; (14 July), 17–19; (28 July), 11; (27 Oct.), 16–17; (24 Nov.), 16; House of Lords Record Office Historical Collection 97: Sir Stuart Samuel Press Cuttings Book 1911–20, 6–9.

[139] BD Minute Book, vol. 16, 21 Jan. and 14 July 1912; Schwab, *B'nai B'rith*, 25.

[140] *JC* (25 Oct. 1907), 31; (31 Oct. 1913), 21; (19 Dec.), 10; and see E. C. Sterne, *Leeds Jewry and the Great War 1914–1918: The Home Front* (Leeds [1982]), 12, and *Leeds Jewry 1919–1929* (Leeds, 1989), 28. The Leeds Representative Council was not revived until 1938.

notorious 'blood libel' trial, in Kiev in 1913, of Mendel Beilis. The Glasgow Council was formally inaugurated in February 1914; significantly, much of its work, during the war years, was focused upon the plight of unnaturalized Jews and internees.[141] In Manchester a Representative Council came into being during the war, again largely in response to the needs of communal defence and of Jewish aliens.[142]

A number of common themes run through the histories and pre-histories of the early Representative Councils: the feeling that local needs were best dealt with at local level by local people; the conviction that the provincial Jewries had come of age; above all, dissatisfaction with the performance of London-based and London-dominated communal organs. Nowhere were these sentiments more strongly felt than in Manchester. As early as 1906 there were signs of public annoyance from the Manchester Jewish bourgeoisie with the lack of adequate representation on the Board of Deputies.[143] In 1912 the Manchester Deputies, under the leadership of Louis Kletz, began agitating for greater provincial representation on the Board's most important committees.[144] As a result, in the autumn of 1913, some reforms were agreed: in particular, Board meetings were to be held on Sundays, when it would be easier for provincial Deputies to attend, and there were to be regular reports from the Conjoint Foreign Committee.

But these essentially procedural changes were minimal, and grudgingly made. The Board leadership resented the status and influence of the Representative Councils, and, for the moment at least, held them at arm's length.[145] The reluctance of the leadership to make further major concessions in the direction of more representative and open communal government was doubly dangerous,

[141] *JC* (19 Dec. 1913), 10, 30; (13 Feb. 1914), 27.

[142] Ibid. (21 May 1915), 5; (28 May), 16; (23 Mar. 1917), 24; (6 Apr.), 15. B. Williams, *Manchester Jewry: A Pictorial History 1788–1988* (Manchester, 1988), 75, errs in suggesting that the Manchester Council was formed in 1919. See also D. Cesarani, 'The Transformation of Communal Authority in Anglo-Jewry, 1914–1940', in D. Cesarani (ed.), *The Making of Modern Anglo-Jewry* (Oxford, 1990), 119. A Representative Council in Birmingham was not formed until 1937: *JC* (23 Apr. 1937), 42.

[143] Ibid. (2 Mar. 1906), 21; (16 Mar.), 26; (11 May), 23–4 (letters from Barrow Belisha); (6 July), 29 (letter from Joseph Dulberg).

[144] Ibid. (9 May 1913), 20; Cohen, *English Zionists*, 142–3.

[145] See e.g. BD B3/34 (letter book): C. H. L. Emanuel (Secretary, Board of Deputies) to A. Goldstone (Secretary, South Manchester Synagogue), 23 May 1917.

because there were by then unmistakeable signs of an alliance between disaffected provincials and rebellious Londoners on these matters. Between 1904 and 1909 the number of Deputies supporting moves to disband the Conjoint had risen from two to twenty-three.[146] The prime agitator, the statistician Simon Rosenbaum (later Rowson; 1877–1950) was not a Zionist; but he was the Deputy for Exeter (though a member of the Hammersmith Synagogue) and he was to become in 1915 the President of *B'nai B'rith*.[147] Rowson's attacks upon the unrepresentative nature of the Board became ever more strident; perhaps as a result, the Board's President, David Lindo Alexander, conceded a role for *B'nai B'rith* in meeting the needs of Jewish internees in 1915.[148] During the course of 1916 Deputies who represented congregations held two conferences to discuss the reform of the Board's constitution.[149] More ominously, Deputies who were members of *B'nai B'rith* formed an 'Actions Group', while the First Lodge set in being a 'Jewish Emergency Committee' to shadow the activities of the Conjoint Foreign Committee.[150]

It was here, in the matter of the Conjoint, that the interests and preoccupations of the constitutional reformers and the provincial leaders fused with those of the Zionists. Zionism had made some headway in Britain during the early years of the war, partly no doubt owing to the patronage of the Chief Rabbi and partly through the opportunities it offered to Jewish aliens whose situation as residents of the United Kingdom looked increasingly precarious. But as the negotiations which Weizmann and others conducted with the British Government took a serious turn, the opposition of anti-Zionists to any move in the direction of Jewish nation- or statehood became more entrenched. 'Unable to conquer the community with their own program, or even by their own efforts', Professor Cohen writes, 'the members of the EZF felt themselves to be increasingly dependent upon the enthusiasms engendered by other, non-Zionist interests that were better placed to embody native Anglo-Jewry's abstract feelings of unease and better equipped to serve as vehicles for its expression.'[151] Zionists

146 Cohen, *English Zionists*, 134.
147 On Rosenbaum see *JC* (30 June 1950), 17.
148 Ibid. (18 June 1915), 13; *Di Tsait*, (25 July 1915), 4.
149 *JC* (14 Jan. 1916), 13–14; (28 Jan.), 13.
150 Cohen, *English Zionists*, 270.
151 Ibid. 273.

began joining provincial representative councils. Weizmann, Israel Sieff, and other colleagues took steps to have themselves enrolled in *B'nai B'rith*, of which Paul Goodman (1875–1949), already secretary of the EZF, became the secretary also.[152]

The claim of the fourteen members of the Conjoint Foreign Committee of the Board of Deputies and the Anglo-Jewish Association to represent the views of British Jewry on foreign affairs had hitherto been unquestioned.[153] But its secretive nature and self-appointed role as communal 'cabinet' had caused increasing resentment. In January 1915 *Haham* Gaster had attempted to persuade the Anglo-Jewish Association to allow Zionist representation on the Conjoint. The proposal was voted down and, to make matters worse, almost at once Lucien Wolf became the Conjoint's secretary.[154] Wolf was not merely a leading anti-Zionist, who shared with Claude Montefiore, the President of the Anglo-Jewish Association, the conviction that Zionism was 'dangerous and provoking anti-Semitism'.[155] He was also *persona grata* with the Foreign Office; through his good offices, the Conjoint was thus enabled to deal with the Foreign Office under a veil of secrecy which Lindo Alexander, at the Deputies, made clear he was not prepared to lift.[156]

Wolf rejected out of hand attempts by Zionists to formulate a common approach to the British Government on the Palestine question. During 1916, as the split between Zionists and anti-Zionists grew ever wider, Weizmann and his friends took steps to bypass the Conjoint and deal directly with the British Government in the matter of a declaration of British policy as to the nature of future Jewish settlement in a Palestine under British control. From the Zionist point of view, the dissolution of the Conjoint became an imperative. Since this could obviously not be achieved through the self-elected Anglo-Jewish Association, it would have to be achieved

[152] On Goodman, see *JC* (19 Aug. 1949), 6.

[153] *JC* (26 Feb. 1915), 17. See also M. Levene, 'Anglo-Jewish Foreign Policy in Crisis—Lucien Wolf, the Conjoint Committee and the War, 1914–18', *TJHSE* 30 (1987–8), 182–3.

[154] *JC* (15 Jan. 1915), 11–13; (22 Jan.), 13.

[155] Wolf to N. Sokolow, 15 July 1915, quoted in Weizmann, *Trial and Error*, 201. Sokolow, a member of the Executive of the World Zionist Organization, had come to London to assist Weizmann in his negotiations with the British Government. See also Cyrus Adler Papers, American Jewish Archives, Cincinnati: Wolf to Cyrus Adler, 18 June 1920.

[156] *JC* (26 Feb. 1915), 16–17; (26 Mar.), 17; (22 Oct.), 9.

through the Deputies. Events and circumstances played into Zionist hands.

To begin with, Wolf made an ill-judged attack upon the immigrant Jews, not bothering even to distinguish between those who were aliens and those who had taken the trouble to become naturalized. He was adamant that he was not prepared to permit the Conjoint to be enlarged so as to 'submerge the English-born elements in the community'. To a meeting of the Anglo-Jewish Association in April 1916, the *Jewish Chronicle* revealed, he 'proceeded to make some observations concerning our brethren in the East End which we think it not in the general interest to reproduce'.[157] As if by way of rejoinder there was published, in July 1916, *Zionism and the Jewish Future*. Its appearance caused an uproar in anti-Zionist circles. Edited by Harry Sacher, it contained an essay by Weizmann in which the argument was advanced that Jews remained aliens however emancipated they might be in the countries in which they lived, and another by Moses Gaster in which 'The claim to be Englishmen of the Jewish persuasion' was condemned as 'an absolute self-delusion'.[158] Thus began a literary and pamphlet war which carried on through to 1917: at its heart was the clash between two views of Jewish identity and two views of what Emancipation (more especially in Britain) actually meant.[159]

In late 1916, as the British Expeditionary Force proceeded to occupy the Sinai Peninsula, the anti-Zionists showed signs of panic. Lord Rothschild (who was not a Zionist) refused to lead them. Montefiore and Lindo Alexander did so instead. In October Lindo Alexander told the Deputies that co-operation between the Conjoint and the Zionists could not take place 'on an overt or official assumption of the existence of a Jewish nationality for the Jews all over the world'.[160] In March 1917 the British invasion of Palestine began. Wolf had had an interview with Balfour, the Foreign Secretary, in January, and knew that some form of British declaration concerning the Jewish future in Palestine was contemplated. But he did not know when, or in what manner, such a definitive statement might emerge.[161] A counterblast was prepared,

[157] Ibid. (7 Apr. 1916), 16.

[158] M. Gaster, 'Judaism—A National Religion', in H. Sacher (ed.), *Zionism and the Jewish Future* (London, 1916), 93.

[159] Cohen, *English Zionists*, 234–5.

[160] *JC* (27 Oct. 1916), 16.

[161] Laqueur, *History of Zionism*, 193.

a manifesto against the Zionist movement, and it appeared, in the form of a letter over the signatures of Lindo Alexander and Montefiore, in *The Times* of 24 May.[162]

There have been few watersheds in the history of British Jewry since the Resettlement as dramatic and as well defined as that represented by the appearance and reception of this document. There have been few events in Anglo-Jewish history so widely misunderstood. The contents of the letter—'a venomous stab at the Zionist movement' was how Greenberg condemned it—were much less important than the manner in which it had appeared.[163] In pleading that 'emancipated Jews in this country . . . have no separate aspirations in a political sense', that the Jews were not 'a homeless people', that they had 'no separate national aspirations', and that they were simply a 'religious community' Montefiore and Lindo Alexander were saying nothing new. Lucien Wolf had condemned Zionism in much more vitriolic terms in a well-publicized speech at the Liberal Jewish Synagogue a week before;[164] indeed Chief Rabbi Adler had said as much in 1897. The attack upon Zionism was not the point at all. The letter of 24 May purported to represent the views of British Jewry. Yet its contents—indeed its very existence—had neither been discussed nor disclosed at the Board of Deputies.[165] Repudiations of the letter quickly appeared from Weizmann, Chief Rabbi Hertz, and even from Lord Rothschild.[166] More significantly, every accusation that had ever been made about the secretiveness of the Conjoint, about the lack of democracy at the Board, and about the oligarchic rule there of a handful of arrogant London grandees, was now (it was argued) proved beyond doubt.

At the Anglo-Jewish Association Montefiore was sure of support. At the Board Lindo Alexander appeared unmoved. But on 17 June 1917, by the narrow margin of fifty-six votes to fifty-one, the Deputies condemned the letter and passed a vote of censure on the Conjoint, which was wound up. Lindo Alexander resigned.[167] It must be said at once that this was in no sense 'a Zionist revolution'. Within a year of these events Harry Sacher can be found declaring to Simon Marks (by then chairman of Marks & Spencer Ltd.) that

162 *The Times* (24 May 1917), 5.
163 *JC* (25 May 1917), 5.
164 Ibid. (16 Mar. 1917), 7.
165 Ibid. (25 May 1917), 5–6.
166 *The Times* (28 May 1917), 5.
167 *JC* (22 June 1917), 14–19; (20 July), 5.

it was becoming urgent 'to carry through and organise all Zionist forces on the Board of Deputies'.[168] It is not difficult to understand why. The new President of the Board was Sir Stuart Samuel, who was not a Zionist. The Conjoint had been killed off, but it was soon replaced by a 'Joint Foreign Committee' which survived until 1943. Lucien Wolf retained a power base as secretary to this Committee, whose efforts ensured that the official statement of the Board of Deputies to the Peace Conference in April 1919 began with the observation that nothing in the Balfour Declaration 'should be held to imply that Jews constituted a separate political nationality all over the world, or that Jewish citizens of countries outside Palestine owe political allegiance to the Government of that country'.[169] It was hardly surprising, therefore, that within weeks the Zionists should be loud, once more, in their condemnation of the Board's oligarchical structure.[170]

What happened in the summer of 1917 certainly made the Zionist task easier; but it is best understood as 'a revolt against a system of oligarchical repression',[171] a rebellion against the old ruling cliques within the community, and an attack by the provincial communities against the leadership in London.[172] The 1917 vote of censure was followed, not by any resolution placing the Board of Deputies at the disposal of the EZF, but by a revision of the Board's constitution, completed in January 1919, broadening its representative base.[173] Hitherto the right to elect Deputies had been restricted, in general, to Jewish congregations having certified marriage secretaries. Now a second institutional category of 'Jewish Secular Societies and Associations' was introduced, comprising initially six friendly societies, the Council of United Jewish Friendly Societies, and *B'nai B'rith*. The United Synagogue and the

[168] CZA: Papers of the Zionist Organization, London: Z4 file 120: Sacher to Marks, 12 Apr. 1918.

[169] Board of Deputies, *68th Annual Report* (London, 1919), 44.

[170] *Zionist Review* (May 1919), 2; (June 1919), 29; *JC* (9 May 1919), 10, 25.

[171] Ibid. (22 June 1917), 5.

[172] Of the 56 Deputies who voted in favour of the censure of the Conjoint, 42 represented provincial congregations: *JC* (29 June 1917), 14. Nathan Laski, who, following these events, became the Board's new Treasurer, was the first provincial Deputy to be elected to the position of an Honorary Officer of the Board.

[173] *JC* (27 June 1919), 17–21; London Committee of Deputies of the British Jews, *Constitution of the Board*, editions of 1916 and 1919. The deliberations which resulted in the constitution of 1919 may be followed in BD C5: Bye-Laws Committee Minute Book, 30 Jan. 1918–30 July 1919.

Federation of Synagogues were given representation in their own right (twelve Deputies and six Deputies respectively), and the Jewish students at Oxford and Cambridge were allotted one Deputy each. The franchise for the purposes of taking part in the election of Deputies was extended to male and female seat-renters. Women could henceforth be elected as institutional Deputies. As we noted in the previous chapter, the Union of Jewish Women was, later that year, given the right to return its own Deputies. Significantly, a proposal to exclude as Deputies those who were aliens was made, and rejected.[174]

These reforms were, to be sure, not nearly as extensive as radicals and Zionists had demanded. The representation of the Anglo-Jewish Association was actually increased. Zionist organizations remained unrepresented on the Board. So did Jewish trade unions. The major avenue for immigrant representation was through the friendly societies. The Presidency of the Board remained firmly in 'establishment' hands throughout the 1920s: Stuart Samuel was followed by Henry Henriques, Lord Rothschild, and Osmond d'Avigdor Goldsmid. It is also true that the committee structure of the Board was still controlled, in practice, by the old, London-based élites and that these élites remained in command of other institutional heights—notably the United Synagogue and the Board of Guardians.[175] But at least in relation to the Board of Deputies, an opportunity had been created for the entry of new blood; by 1925 no less than eleven individual friendly societies had a Deputy each, and the election that year of Joseph Prag (1859–1929) as Vice-President of the Board proved that a corner had been turned. Prag was an archetypal representative of the new Jewish middle class; a pipe manufacturer who had acted as 'vice-chief' of *Chovevi Zion*, he was lukewarm towards Herzlian Zionism but as a member of the old Conjoint had refused to sanction its anti-Zionist manifesto of May 1917.[176] In the Board of Deputies he distinguished himself as a champion of immigrant rights.[177] From 1919 to 1929

[174] *JC* (17 Jan. 1919), 13–15.

[175] Cesarani, 'The Transformation of Communal Authority', 122–3.

[176] On Prag see Cohen, *English Zionists*, 17, 29, 237; N. Bentwich, *Early English Zionists 1890–1920* (Tel-Aviv [1940]), 240; and *JC* (28 June 1929), 11. See also Prag's letter to Lucien Wolf, 20 Nov. 1917, in the Lucien Wolf Papers in the Mowshowitch Collection, YIVO Institute, New York, folder 35.

[177] Alderman, *London Jewry*, 67–8.

he was a Treasurer of the United Synagogue's Burial Society; that did not make him 'virtually part of the establishment'.[178]

By the mid-1920s we are justified in concluding that a major realignment of communal forces was under way, generated initially by the publication of the Balfour Declaration, but in which Zionism itself played only a part. What was at stake was nothing less than the public status of the Jews in Britain, not so much in a legal sense (though the issue had legal implications) as in relation to the public perception of the British Jew. This image was inevitably dependent, in some measure, upon the profiles and policies of those who led and who were regarded as the communal spokesmen. On all sides of the argument there was at least a broad measure of agreement within British Jewry that the image was intimately related to those who projected it. In consequence, a conflict of even greater severity and bitterness took place on the issue of communal authority and power.

The issue of the Balfour Declaration (2 November 1917) had closed the first phase of this conflict, but had also marked the opening of the second. The letter embodying the Declaration was not addressed to the EZF, but to Lord Rothschild (still acknowledged as the lay leader of British Jewry). Edwin Montagu, now Secretary of State for India, had fought on behalf of the anti-Zionist Jews a grim rearguard action to have it sabotaged; in the event he succeeded in having the text altered in two crucial respects. In the final version, Palestine was referred to as *a* rather than as *the* national home for the Jewish people; there was also inserted a reference to the civic and religious rights of Palestine's existing non-Jewish communities.[179]

The second alteration was of much more tangible concern to the Zionists than the first. But the first was of greater moment to the British-born leadership of Anglo-Jewry than the second. A week after the Balfour Declaration had been published there was formed the League of British Jews, which boasted all the leading Jewish anti-Zionists amongst its founders. The membership of the League never exceeded about 1,300; by the end of the 1920s attendances at its meetings had fallen drastically, and the newspaper which it

[178] This is Dr Cesarani's phrase, in 'The Transformation of Communal Authority', 122.

[179] Weizmann, *Trial and Error*, 256–62. On Edwin Montagu see S. D. Waley, *Edwin Montagu* (London, 1954), 139–41.

launched in 1919, the *Jewish Guardian*, ceased publication in 1931.[180] But what the League lacked in numbers was counterbalanced to some extent by the prestige and social status of its adherents; its President was the Conservative MP Lionel de Rothschild; Sir Philip Magnus was a Vice-President; other members included Claude Montefiore, Lindo Alexander, and Louis Montagu (1869–1927), the second Baron Swaythling, who had succeded his father as President of the Federation of Synagogues.

In dedicating itself to upholding 'the status of British subjects professing the Jewish religion' and to resisting 'the allegation that Jews constitute a separate Political Entity', and in ostentatiously refusing to admit into membership Jews living in Britain who were not British subjects, the League undoubtedly reflected fears as well as prejudices genuinely held by the Anglo-Jewish aristocracy. These fears (which included the utter conviction that 'the Jewish Relief Act of 1858 might be repealed if Zionists convinced anti-Semites that the Jews were a nation in Palestine')[181] became immeasurably greater following the Bolshevik Revolution and the withdrawal of Russia from the Allied war effort. Lenin's peace with Germany (March 1918) was universally regarded in Britain as a betrayal of the Allied cause. More seriously, the advent in Russia of a government committed, apparently, to the notion of world revolution to advance Communism put all Russian immigrants in Britain under popular suspicion. Following the Armistice with Germany, fear of the 'German Menace' gave way to a 'Red Scare', and as the Allied intervention in the Russian civil war developed, the Jewishness of leading Marxists became a common topic of press comment.[182] More particularly, the right-wing press found it easy to make a connection between revolutionary events in Russia (and elsewhere in Europe), the rise of the Labour Party in Britain, the exertions of Zionist diplomacy, and the idea of a world-wide Jewish conspiracy.

Two pieces of evidence appeared to give credence to this macabre synthesis. The first was the Balfour Declaration, subsequently to be embodied in the terms of the Palestine Mandate (agreed upon at

[180] *JC* (22 Mar. 1918), 15–16; (21 Mar. 1919), 9; (28 May 1926), 15. See also L. Magnus, *Old Lamps for New: An Apologia for the League of British Jews* (London, 1918).

[181] *JC* (16 Nov. 1917), 5–6; (7 Dec.), 13; (21 Feb. 1919), 9.

[182] S. Kadish, '"The Letter of the 'Ten'": Bolsheviks and British Jews', in J. Frankel (ed.), *Studies in Contemporary Jewry*, iv (Oxford, 1988), 97.

San Remo in April 1920) which was granted to the British Government. The second was the undoubtedly socialist proclivities of the bulk of immigrant Jewry and their offspring. These proclivities sprang from socio-economic roots, and were reflected in and symbolized by such developments as the formation in June 1918 of the Stepney Central Labour Party, the founder and secretary of which was the formidable Romanian-Jewish political strategist, Oscar Tobin;[183] the Labour victory in the Stepney Borough Council elections of November 1919; Labour's capture of the combined Whitechapel and St George's parliamentary constituency at the general election of 1922;[184] and even the appearance in the House of Commons, as a result of that same election, of the first Jewish Labour MP, Emanuel Shinwell.[185]

But it is important to remember—and the fact was certainly not lost on contemporary observers—that there was an ideological dimension to Jewish support for Labour which did not originate from considerations of class or social dogma. In its *War Aims Memorandum* of August 1917 the Labour Party had included a statement supporting Jewish settlement in Palestine.[186] *Poale Zion* claimed some credit for this insertion, though it is equally true that it was Labour's apparently sympathetic attitude towards Zionism which was to have a positive impact on the war and and post-war fortunes of *Poale Zion*.[187] On the eve of the 1918 general election *Poale Zion* had issued a manifesto urging Jewish electors to vote for the Labour Party, to which it became formally affiliated in 1920.[188] 'Jews have no better friends in this country than the Labour Party',

[183] I deal with Tobin and the Jewish dimension to Stepney politics at this period in 'M. H. Davis: The Rise and Fall of a Communal Upstart', *TJHSE* 31 (1988–90), 251–2.

[184] Alderman, *Jewish Community*, 106; id., *London Jewry*, 79. The old Whitechapel and St George's constituencies had been amalgamated in 1918; the new constituency was probably more thickly populated with Jewish electors than any other parliamentary division at that time.

[185] In Jewish terms, of course, Shinwell's victory, at Linlithgow, Scotland, was purely symbolic.

[186] S. Levenberg, *The Jews and Palestine: A Study in Labour Zionism* (London, 1945), 204–5; J. Gorny, *The British Labour Movement and Zionism 1917–1948* (London, 1983), 7–10.

[187] Cohen, *English Zionists*, 251; G. Shimoni, 'Poale Zion: A Zionist Transplant in Britain (1905–1945)', in P. Y. Medding (ed.), *Studies in Contemporary Jewry*, ii (Bloomington, Ind., 1986), 232–3.

[188] Levenberg, *Jews and Palestine*, 205–6; *JC* (17 Nov. 1920), 25.

Leopold Greenberg told readers of the *Jewish Chronicle*.[189] By 1924, and following the collapse of Liberal political fortunes, support for Labour had become respectable among British Jews.[190]

It is none the less true that the rise of Labour, its displacement of the Liberal Party as the only credible alternative to Conservatism, and the advent, in 1924, of the first, short-lived, Labour Government, were events which profoundly disturbed those who had hitherto regarded themselves as the ruling classes in Britain. Labour's friendship with the Bolshevik regime only served to reinforce these fears. In shaping a popular attitude towards Jews in the immediate post-war period, therefore, the attitude of British Jewry towards Bolshevism was bound to play a part. In the long term, this attitude became predominantly hostile. But in the period 1917–19 it was not so, a fact of which the High Tory *Morning Post* took due note. The portrayal of Russian Jews (whether or not they were naturalized was immaterial) as emissaries of Bolshevism had been a feature of the 1918 general election; the *Morning Post* saw to it that this portrait was preserved and enhanced as the Allied intervention in Russia got under way.[191]

Anti-Bolshevism—like anti-Zionism (which was loudly heard during the general election of 1922)[192]—was undoubtedly used as a cover for anti-Semitism. But it was true that the overthrow of Tsarism was widely celebrated by the Anglo-Jewish masses and in the Yiddish press, even if few Yiddish journalists had any illusions about the anti-Jewish potential of the Bolshevik take-over.[193] Nor was this euphoria confined to the Yiddish-speaking ghettos. Leopold Greenberg, in particular, invited his readers to view Bolshevism as both a 'menace' and a 'hope'; its methods he found wanting, but its ideals, he claimed, were 'at many points . . . consonant with the finest ideals of Judaism'.[194]

[189] Ibid. (1 Aug. 1919), 7; Greenberg wrote under the pseudonym 'Mentor', for the identification of which see [C. Roth], *The Jewish Chronicle 1841–1941* (London, 1949), 136–7.

[190] Alderman, *Jewish Community*, 105–6. The reputation of the Liberal Party had, additionally, been tarnished in Jewish eyes by Asquith's public hostility to the Mandate: *JC* (3 Nov. 1922), 15.

[191] Ibid. (24 Jan. 1919), 5; *Morning Post* (8 Apr. 1919), 6. The policy of the *Post* is discussed in Holmes, *Anti-Semitism*, 141–2, 147–51, and Lipman, *History*, 151–2.

[192] Alderman, *Jewish Community*, 102–3.

[193] *Idisher Ekspres* (21 Mar. 1917), 4; *Di Tsait* (19 Mar. 1917), 2; (27 May 1918), 2; (31 May), 2; *Manchester Guardian* (2 Apr. 1917), 4. See generally Kadish, 'Bolsheviks and British Jews', 236–51.

[194] *JC* (4 Apr. 1919), 7–9.

It was by way of reprimand for having penned this sympathetic critique, and in furtherance of an eternal quest for respectability in the eyes of the Gentiles, that ten leading members of the League of British Jews, including Claude Montefiore and Louis Montagu, appended their signatures to a letter which appeared in the *Morning Post* of 23 April 1919 accusing the *Jewish Chronicle*, and its sister paper, the *Jewish World*, of aiding and abetting the Bolshevik cause.[195] The letter itself did not refer to Zionism; but in so far as Zionism had gained currency (as it had gained credibility) in immigrant circles, and inasmuch as anti-Zionism rather than anti-Bolshevism was the *raison d'être* of the League, it was rightly interpreted as another attempt to drive a wedge between the indigenous minority and the immigrant majority among British Jewry, to the public detriment of the latter.[196]

There is merit in the argument that 'The Letter of the Ten' had an impact at least as great upon the reshaping of British Jewry in the 1920s as had the Conjoint's anti-Zionist manifesto of May 1917. The signatories of 1919, through their action, fatally compromised themselves and the old ruling families whose claim to hold sway over British Jewry the League of British Jews was taken, in some measure, to personify. Although, therefore, what Dr Cesarani describes as 'the social matrix which supplied the pre-war leadership' continued to exercise authority, we can detect, in the course of the 1920s, a change in the underlying basis of this hegemony, which was increasingly tolerated only on sufferance.[197] Within the United Synagogue and at the Board of Deputies this rule persisted, but came under severe stress. In the Federation of Synagogues the old regime was swept away.

By the mid-1920s Federation synagogues had on their books no less than 12,565 families, representing something in excess of 50,000 souls; even in 1930 male membership of the United Synagogue totalled only 8,310.[198] The Federation was thus at this time the largest synagogal body in the country. Louis Montagu's ill-judged arrogance in signing the letter to the *Morning Post*, in utter disregard of his position as titular lay leader of East End Jewry,

[195] *Morning Post* (23 Apr. 1919), 6.

[196] *Jewish World* (30 Apr. 1919), 7–10; (7 May), 4–6; *Di Tsait* (2 May 1919), 'Peace Supplement', 4 (editorial).

[197] Cesarani, 'Transformation of Communal Authority', 122.

[198] Alderman, *Federation*, 58; Newman, *United Synagogue*, 216.

accelerated tensions which had been current for some time in Federation circles, relating not so much to Montagu's anti-Zionism (the fact that this was tolerated for so long was itself significant) as to the arbitrary nature of his rule and the faith and authority he placed in Joseph Blank, Secretary of the Federation since its inception and who regarded the Federation as his personal fiefdom.

Montagu lacked his father's devout orthodoxy; he was tolerated within the Federation mainly out of respect for his father's money and memory.[199] The appearance of his name under the *Morning Post* letter provided the occasion for the entry into Federation politics of Morry Davis, the Whitechapel-born son of Russian immigrants, who was already active in creating a role for himself as Oscar Tobin's protégé. Davis was a Zionist and a socialist. By 1922 he had become Vice-President of the Stepney Labour Party; in 1924 he became a Stepney Councillor, and the following year was elected to the LCC; by then he had also put himself at the head of growing opposition within the Federation to the rule of Montagu and Blank.[200] Enquiries into the financial misdeeds of Blank brought matters to a head. In a series of meetings of the Federation's Board of Delegates during 1925 Louis Montagu took it upon himself to defend Blank, and thus sealed his own fate.

It was in and through Morry Davis that the embittered Yiddish-speaking membership of the Federation's affiliated congregations found the voice to articulate their mounting anger with the English lord who ruled over them. Davis proved equal to the task. At a meeting attended by no less than 172 members of the Board of Delegates on 13 May 1925 (just a few weeks after his election to the LCC) Davis expressed the mood of no confidence in Louis Montagu's leadership, and gave public utterance to the suspicions concerning Joseph Blank, who was dismissed. It was Davis who obtained the largest number of votes in the election of a three-man subcommittee charged with the duty of finding a new secretary.[201] And at the fateful Board meeting of 25 November 1925, the last which Louis Montagu attended, it was Davis who moved and carried a portentous resolution, 'That despite any rule or minute to

[199] Alderman, *Federation*, 43–4, 53.

[200] Ibid. 56; *East London Advertiser* (12 Nov. 1921), 5; (24 June 1922), 6. See also E. R. Smith, 'Jews and Politics in the East End of London, 1918–1939', in Cesarani (ed.), *Making of Modern Anglo-Jewry*, 154.

[201] Federation of Synagogues, Minute Book No. 3.

the contrary . . . at any meeting of the Federation, where any delegate desires to address the meeting in Yiddish, such permission be granted'. Louis Montagu admitted he could not understand Yiddish; his Presidency thus came to an inglorious end.[202]

During 1926 Davis acted as chairman of Federation meetings while, as a newly elected Treasurer of the Federation's Burial Society, he was instrumental (January 1926) in the voting of funds for Zionist causes—the *Keren Hayesod* and the *Keren Kayemet*. The Federation thus became, to the delight of Zionist fund-raisers, the first significant non-Zionist organization in Anglo-Jewry to contribute to the redemption of the National Homeland. In February similar resolutions were approved by the Board of Delegates, and grants of increasing magnitude were made to the *Keren Kayemet* and the *Keren Hayesod* regularly thereafter.[203] In 1928 Davis became the Federation's third President. Its commitment to Zionism was henceforth total, but so was its support of other causes—such as the collection of moneys to relieve distress among the mining communities of Britain—which would have been anathema to the old regime.[204]

The rise to power of Morry Davis within and through the Federation bore witness to the self-confidence and assertiveness of the immigrants and their children. The establishment was put on notice, so to speak, that its unfettered discretion to order the affairs of British Jewry was at an end. Issues which the establishment would rather have kept off the communal agenda were firmly secured there by the actions of the new power-brokers. One set of these related to policy decisions taken by the LCC under Municipal Reform (i.e. Conservative) control. In 1918, taking advantage of the xenophobic and anti-Jewish mood, the Municipal Reformers secured LCC support for a resolution that in order to be eligible, henceforth, for Council scholarships, children would have to be British when applying for the award, *and* be born, or have fathers who were born, in Britain or the Dominions.[205] In 1920 the Council adopted a recommendation that, except in the case of teachers of foreign languages or where it resolved otherwise, no

202 Alderman, *Federation*, 57.

203 Federation of Synagogues, Minute Book No. 3; Cesarani, 'Transformation of Anglo-Jewry', 154.

204 Alderman, *Federation*, 60; Federation of Synagogues Minute Book No. 3: balance sheet for 1929–30.

205 Greater London Record Office, LCC Minutes, 19 Mar. 1918.

persons other than British subjects be taken into the employ of the LCC.[206] Three years later the philosophy embodied in these measures was taken a stage further. Under the provisions of a housing regulation approved in June 1923, preference in the general allocation of accommodation on the Council's housing estates (other than accommodation in respect of displacement through slum clearance) was to be given in future to British citizens. This regulation, originally intended (so it was said) to be of a merely temporary nature, soon acquired a permanent place on housing application forms. Its effect, quite simply and in the words of a Board of Deputies' memorandum, was to exclude alien applicants 'entirely from consideration for any tenancy in the Council's dwellings'.[207]

At the LCC elections of 1925 the Municipal Reformers sought to strengthen the policy adopted in 1923, by holding out the promise that in future no council housing or tenements would be let to aliens at all, even if they happened to be ratepayers.[208] Within British (and not just London) Jewry, those in power at County Hall were now widely regarded as anti-Semitic. But at least among top-tier opinion formers a different view prevailed. The 1920 employment policy had been supported by four Jewish members of the Council (David Davis, Major H. B. Lewis-Barned, Percy Simmons, and Oscar Warburg).[209] Like the housing policy, it was without doubt legal. The 1918 scholarships policy may well have been illegal.[210] But even where the LCC might have been open to challenge in the courts, very influential leaders of the community queried the wisdom of so doing.

When Joseph Prag initiated a debate at the Board of Deputies on the 'blind prejudice' of the LCC, and called for legal action to make 'these London County Council people . . . see the wickedness of their ways', he received some support from Stuart Samuel, but only because 'the educational policy of the LCC was driving the pick of Jewish children into the ranks of the socialists and would possibly be the seed of revolutionary tendencies'. The tone of the Board's

[206] Ibid. 6 July 1920.

[207] BD C13/9: Memorandum, undated but *c.*Jan. 1933.

[208] *JC* (20 Mar. 1925), 19.

[209] Greater London Record Office, LCC Minutes, 6 July 1920.

[210] Such was the conclusion of a legal opinion obtained by the Board of Deputies in 1917; see BD E3/42 (I).

response was set by Sir Isadore Salmon (1876–1941), a member of the League of British Jews, Conservative MP for Harrow from 1925 until his death, a member of the LCC from 1907 to 1925, and a Treasurer of the United Synagogue from 1925 to 1934, when he became a Vice-President.[211] Salmon's view was that, given the temper of the times, it was both foolish and counter-productive for the Board to make a nuisance of itself by campaigning against LCC policy, more especially in the matter of scholarships. Another speaker, Robert Henriques, 'pointed out how necessary it was to exercise tact in cases like this. These were difficult times and there was much prejudice abroad.'[212]

This was not a view which Morry Davis shared. Within a few weeks of his election to the LCC in 1925, Davis entered into a correspondence with the Board of Deputies on the scholarships question.[213] As a member of the Board, and using as examples some of the most blatant cases of hardship and injustice in which the policy had resulted, he began a campaign to swing official Anglo-Jewish opinion into a less docile frame of mind.[214] Although Davis and his allies (prominent among whom was Nettie Adler) were then in a minority at County Hall, at the Board of Deputies they were in a position to carry all before them. Their persistence threatened the position of the Board's leadership, and it is certain that towards the end of 1926 contact was made by this leadership with the London Municipal Society, which co-ordinated the efforts of the Municipal Reform Party in London, with the aim of defusing a situation fraught with danger not so much for London Conservatism as for the ability of anti-socialist and non- and anti-Zionist forces to continue to dominate the Board's proceedings.[215] The result was a double victory of sorts. In July 1928 the LCC agreed to deal with each scholarship case on its merits; the following

[211] On Salmon, who became chairman of the catering firm of J. Lyons & Co., and honorary catering adviser to the British Army, see *The Times* (17 Sept. 1941), 7, and *JC* (19 Sept. 1941), 8.

[212] BD A19: Minutes of Meeting of Board of Deputies, 15 Mar. 1925; *JC* (20 Mar. 1925), 9, 19.

[213] BD E3/42 (I): Davis to the Board, 5 Apr. 1925.

[214] BD A3/2: Minutes of Meeting, 21 Mar. 1926: Joint Report of the Education and Law and Parliamentary Committees.

[215] BD E3/42 (I): Percy Cohen to E. M. Rich (LCC Education Department), 12 Dec. 1926. Cohen (d. 1987), as well as being an official of the Board of Deputies, was employed at Conservative Central Office, of which he became Head of Library and Information in 1928: *JC* (23 Oct. 1987), 14.

December it announced that it would employ naturalized as well as natural-born British subjects.[216]

As I have argued elsewhere, to some extent these policy changes by the LCC were the result of secular pressures quite outside the control of Anglo-Jewry.[217] But the fact that pressure from the Board—albeit in a controlled and to some extent manipulated fashion—had helped bring them about was a straw in the wind. The United Synagogue itself had seemed throughout the 1920s to be impervious to change. But in 1928, too, its leadership made public acknowledgement that the past was dead. Ever since 1921 Robert Waley Cohen had been engaged in a battle of wits with Zionist members of the United Synagogue's Council, and ultimately with an expanding Zionist faction within the United Synagogue membership, whose views these Council members were elected to represent. Using the excuse that Zionism was beyond the remit of the United Synagogue, he refused to accept a motion from the New Synagogue (now relocated in Hackney) that a donation of £100 be made to the *Keren Hayesod*. Attempts to revise the United Synagogue's constitution so as to permit the collection of a voluntary levy for the *Keren Hayesod* were defeated or ignored.[218]

The controversy over this matter assumed an importance that went quite beyond the collection of moneys. Waley Cohen was not a 'Leaguer' (though his President was). But to permit the collection of Zionist funds was to admit that Zionism was a legitimate object of United Synagogue patronage; the British character of the United Synagogue—established by an Act of Parliament—could thus be called into question. By 1926, however, a number of important suburban constituents of the United Synagogue had championed the Zionist proposal, including Hampstead, Hammersmith, and Golders Green, and at a special conference of the Council and representatives from the constituents, the Zionists won by 152 votes to 108.[219] There followed a thoroughly shabby attempt by

[216] Greater London Record Office, LCC Minutes, 17 July 1928; LCC/MIN/3467: Minutes of the General Purposes Sub-Committee of the Education Committee, 30 Jan. 1928; *East London Observer* (8 Dec. 1928), 6; see also the correspondence in BD E3/94, Nov.–Dec. 1928.

[217] Alderman, *London Jewry*, 88. In modifying its employment policy, the LCC had merely fallen into line with the policy of central government in relation to the civil service.

[218] D. Cesarani, 'Zionism in England, 1917–1939', D.Phil. thesis (Oxford, 1986), 51–3; *JC* (26 May 1922), 14–15.

[219] Ibid. (5 Nov. 1926), 17.

Waley Cohen to invoke the help of the Charity Commissioners in depriving the Zionists of their victory.[220] Only after unilateral action by the New Synagogue (in including a Zionist levy in the bills sent to seat-holders) did the Honorary Officers of the parent body relent. In 1928 they agreed to the formation of 'The United Synagogue Central Keren Hayesod Committee', to act as an official fund-raising body.[221]

How justified is the view that these developments reflected a creeping but authentic 'Zionization' of British Jewry? By the end of the 1920s, as the League of British Jews entered upon its final decline, most of the leading communal organizations had adopted, to a greater or lesser extent, a pro-Zionist position. The Board of Deputies had agreed to join the Jewish Agency for Palestine in 1924; in 1928 it decided (against the wishes of its President) that it should be represented at the EZF Annual Conference.[222] Chief Rabbi Hertz had, in 1918, accepted the Presidency of the newly formed British section of the religious Zionist *Mizrachi* movement, in which *Dayan* Asher Feldman also held office.[223] *B'nai B'rith*, though not formally Zionist, elected Zionists as Presidents.[224] The laws governing charities acted as an impediment to overt identification by the Jewish friendly societies with political Zionism; nevertheless, in 1925 the largest of them, the Grand Order of Israel, carried a motion at the Association of Jewish Friendly Societies commending the proposal that individual societies change their rules to permit the imposition of a levy to support Jewish institutions in the Holy Land.[225] The various welfare agencies were of course untouched by Zionist work, and the Liberal Jewish Synagogue, under the influence of Claude Montefiore and Israel

220 Cesarani, 'Zionism in England', 55–7.

221 *JC* (17 Feb. 1928), 20–1; (13 Apr.), 17.

222 Ibid. (22 June 1928), 17. The Jewish Agency for Palestine was set up pursuant to the Palestine Mandate, to promote Jewish immigration to and settlement in Palestine; it brought together Zionist and non-Zionist Jews.

223 P. Goodman, *Zionism in England: English Zionist Federation 1899–1929* (London, 1929), 44–5; *Report of The First Mizrachi Conference in the United Kingdom, 28–9 December 1918* (London, 1919), 17. The *Mizrachi* movement had been founded by Rabbi Y. Y. Reines in Lithuania in 1902. Its British component, established partly in order to dispel the rumour put about by the League of British Jews that religious Jews were opposed to political Zionism, did not affiliate to the EZF. See generally Laqueur, *History of Zionism*, 481–3, and Cesarani, 'Zionism in England', 63.

224 Cesarani, 'Zionism in England', 63.

225 *JC* (25 Sept. 1925), 13.

Mattuck, set its face against Zionist propaganda.[226] But even the Jewish Religious Education Board voted, in 1922, to participate in a conference called by the *Keren Hayesod*.[227]

Faced with the chronic weakness of Zionism as a communal force at the beginning of the century, the leaders of the EZF had chosen 'to sap the bastions of anti-Zionism from within rather than storm them from without'.[228] There can be no question but that this policy of infiltration had paid handsome dividends. But it had been most powerfully assisted by sociological factors, and by developments in communal politics, over which Zionists had no control and only limited influence. On the eve of the Hebron massacre (1929) there was a Zionist dimension to almost every facet of Anglo-Jewish life. But the question must be posed: of what did this Zionism consist? The short if brutal answer must be: little, apart from fund-raising and social events. The reasons why this should have been so must now be briefly addressed.

After the excitement created by the Balfour Declaration, the granting to Britain of the Mandate for Palestine, and the installation there of Herbert Samuel as the first High Commissioner, Zionism in Britain entered a period of decline, if not actual decay. In 1918 the EZF claimed a membership of some 25,000 Jews located in 216 affiliated bodies; in 1919–20 it claimed to have sold 20,000 *shekels*, upon which its representation at the Congresses of the World Zionist Organization was based. These figures—even if accurate—represented less than 10 per cent of all British Jews. But there are strong grounds for believing that the figures themselves were artificially inflated (partly as a result of collusion between the EZF and the World Zionist Organization) in order to raise representation to a respectable level.[229] In November 1918 the EZF's Provincial Advisory Committee warned that from a total of thirty-eight provincial Zionist societies only a very few could be regarded as properly functioning; most 'existed in name only'.[230] The EZF, and Zionism in general, had certainly not become mass movements; working-class Jews developed more powerful loyalties within the trade-union and friendly society movements, and there is some evidence that the harsh provisions of the 1919 Aliens Act may

[226] *JC* (29 Mar. 1929), 11; J. D. Rayner, *Progressive Judaism, Zionism and the State of Israel* (London, 1983), 8–10.

[227] *JC* (2 June 1922), 13.

[228] Cohen, *English Zionists*, 54.

[229] Cesarani, 'Zionism in England', 18–19.

[230] Quoted ibid. 17.

have persuaded Jewish aliens that identification with Zionism was not conducive to their continued stay in Britain.[231] The post-war slump had an inevitable effect upon fund-raising; those who could afford to, donated money, but in Paul Goodman's view they did so without any sense of ideological commitment, and perhaps merely to acquire the communal prestige that large donations apparently guaranteed.[232]

Fewer than 500 British Jews actually settled in Palestine during the first decade of the Mandate.[233] Fund-raising was of course most important, but was not attractive for the less well off, and detracted (in the view of Rabbi Salis Daiches) from propaganda and educational activities.[234] In political terms the EZF found itself cast into the shadows by the World Zionist Organization's London Bureau and by the diplomatic activities of Dr Weizmann. It made its presence felt during the general elections of 1922, 1923, and 1924; these interventions were important, if only because a strong anti-Zionist and pro-Arab lobby had developed within the Conservative Party, while the Labour Party had already begun to take the view that Zionism might—after all—be nothing more than a species of the Imperialism it felt it must condemn.[235] The EZF also played a role in the early attempts (1926) to establish a Zionist group among non-Jewish MPs.[236]

This political work undoubtedly helped Weizmann as he walked the corridors of power. But inasmuch as Zionism of this variety was arguably anti-assimilationist in intent and effect it did not square very comfortably with the desire of the communal leadership to manufacture and project the image of a Jewry entirely integrated

[231] *Unser Weg* (Yiddish; *Our Way*) (1 June 1919), 2–3.

[232] *Zionist Review* (July–August 1922), 270–1.

[233] I. Cohen, *The Zionist Movement* (New York, 1946), 359.

[234] *Zionist Review* (Oct. 1925), 64–5.

[235] The EZF's activities during the elections of 1922, 1923, and 1924 are described in Cesarani, 'Zionism in England', 94–9; see also Alderman, *Jewish Community*, 102–4.

[236] Cesarani, 'Zionism in England', 100; *JC* (29 Oct. 1926), 26; CZA F13, file 56 III; L9, file 256. In view of the mythology surrounding the part alleged to have been played by Barnett (later Lord) Janner in establishing the 'Palestine Parliamentary Committee' (see E. Janner, *Barnett Janner: A Personal Portrait* (London, 1984), 40) it needs to be stressed that the initiative on the parliamentary side came from the Jewish Conservative MP Samuel Finburgh (1867–1935) a Manchester cotton manufacturer, an orthodox Jew, and President of the North Salford Conservative Association; Finburgh sat in Parliament from 1924 to 1929: see Alderman, *Jewish Community*, 109–10, and *JC* (3 May 1935), 10.

into the British social, and political structure; nor, in consequence, did it contribute towards a communal consensus. It was partly out of a desire to meet such criticism that the philosophy of 'Patriotic Zionism' was evolved: according to this view, the re-establishment of the Jewish presence in Palestine accorded with Anglo-Christian values, and with Britain's strategic interests in the Near East.[237] Patriotic Zionism was a powerful propaganda tool, within as well as beyond British Jewry. But its sponsorship inevitably detracted from the wider, political aims of the Zionist movement. These were, as yet, not precisely defined; but as they were bound to evoke widespread hostility from the many millions of Muslims under British control, they could hardly be said to aid and abet the Imperial mission. In the view of *Haham* Gaster the development of Patriotic Zionism reduced the Zionist presence in Britain to 'a philanthropic, charitable movement'.[238] There can be little doubt of the truth of this accusation.

Zionism flourished in Britain as an image to which there was only limited substance. The anti-Zionists were equally concerned to preserve the myth of an image, but one which no longer existed. Anti-Jewish prejudice was widespread in Britain in the 1920s, sometimes disguised as anti-Zionism, anti-Bolshevism, or plain anti-alienism. The appearance at the beginning of 1920 of *The Jewish Peril* (the English translation of the notorious *Protocols of the Learned Elders of Zion*) was a cause of intense concern.[239] But the impact of the *Protocols* (exposed as a forgery by *The Times* in August 1921) was not nearly as immediate or as disheartening—certainly in relation to Jewish aliens—as the rule of William Joynson-Hicks ('the most avowed and determined anti-Semite in the House', and a leading pro-Arabist)[240] as Home Secretary between 1924 and 1929. Joynson-Hicks's anti-Jewish bias, his love of the powers given to him by the Aliens Act of 1919, and his extreme reluctance to grant naturalization to foreign Jews who maintained any semblance of religious or ethnic distinctiveness, struck real fear with foreign and native Jews alike.[241]

[237] Goodman, *Zionism in England*, 74–5.

[238] *JC* (17 Feb. 1922), 11. See also J. K. Goldbloom Papers, CZA A61/21: Minutes of a Special Meeting of the Honorary Officers of the EZF, 12 Jan. 1927.

[239] Alderman, *London Jewry*, 65; Holmes, *Anti-Semitism*, 149. On the *Protocols* see N. Cohn, *Warrant for Genocide* (Harmondsworth, 1970).

[240] *JC* (7 July 1922), 26–30; (3 Nov. 1922), 15.

[241] This aspect of Joynson-Hicks's tenure of the Home Office is admirably treated

Defence of image became, in short, a communal priority in the 1920s. In the following decade, as British Jewry fragmented more deeply along religious, social, and political lines, it was to become a communal obsession.

in 2 essays by D. Cesarani: 'Anti-Alienism in England after the First World War', *Immigrants & Minorities*, 6 (1987), 5–29, and 'Joynson-Hicks and the Radical Right in England after the First World War', in T. Kushner and K. Lunn (eds.), *Traditions of Intolerance* (Manchester, 1989), 118–39.

6

The Defence of an Image

THE period which began with the crisis triggered by the publication of Lord Passfield's White Paper on Palestine (October 1930) and which ended with British recognition of the State of Israel (April 1950) posed for the British Jewish communities problems of unprecedented complexity and severity. Against the background of Nazi persecution of Jews in Germany and later Austria, and then of the unassailable truth of the Final Solution, support for Zionism acquired a grim centrality—and urgency—in Anglo-Jewish affairs which at last made possible that which had not been achieved in 1917 (the Zionist conquest of the Board of Deputies). But it was acquired in an atmosphere in which it was difficult and finally impossible to sustain the myth that Zionism accorded with the interests of Jews as British citizens and as nothing else.

At precisely the same time, the rise of an organized anti-Jewish movement within Britain, deriving transient strength in part from undeniable aspects of the Jewish impact on British society (preeminently in London), made the exercise of communal discipline at once all the more necessary but at the same time all the more difficult to implement. The very traits off which this anti-Jewish prejudice fed were precisely those which were symptomatic of the centrifugal tendencies at work amongst British Jews. In consequence, attempts to reassert central control themselves became new sources of intra-communal friction. In religious terms, we can detect in this period the first signs of the polarization which was to result in such deep cleavages in British Jewry after 1945, but which, already in the 1930s, were to challenge the concept of a Chief Rabbinate as boldly as the national and international political events were to challenge the authority of the Board of Deputies.

The outbreak of anti-Jewish riots by Palestinian Arabs in August 1929, and the subsequent fundamental reappraisal of the Mandate by Ramsay MacDonald's Labour Government, lifted the Zionist movement in Britain out of the doldrums to which it had been consigned ever since the early 1920s. To begin with, even anti-Zionist Jews could find no objection to identifying themselves with the expressions of outrage that greeted the deaths of 133 Jews in the *Yishuv*. Organizations hitherto thought of as remote from if not actually opposed to the politics of Zionism, such as the Union of Jewish Women and the Liberal Jewish Synagogue, rushed to add their names to expressions of communal outrage.[1] A resolution to this effect, proposed by the recently formed Palestine Committee of the Board of Deputies, was accepted by the Joint Foreign Committee of the Board and the Anglo-Jewish Association in spite of the misgivings of the Association's President, Leonard Montefiore.[2]

At the end of May 1930, following publication of the findings of the Shaw report into the causes of the disturbances, the Labour Government announced the suspension of Jewish immigration into Palestine. The Colonial Secretary, Lord Passfield (Sidney Webb), embarked on a basic reassessment of British obligations under the Balfour Declaration. The result was presented as a White Paper the following October: large-scale immigration of Jews to Palestine was to be ruled out, and such further Jewish immigration as was permitted was to take place, in effect, with Arab consent.[3] This policy was broadly in line with the Balfour Declaration taken as a whole; it was, in fact, a desperate attempt to adhere to the terms of the Declaration, and of the Mandate. What is more, it was consistent with the Churchill White Paper of 1922, which had contained an explicit rejection of the notion that Palestine might become 'as Jewish as England is English' and which, in accepting the view that Jewish immigration into Palestine should be determined by that country's 'economic capacity . . . to absorb new arrivals' had declared that Palestine 'as a whole' would not become 'a Jewish national home, but that such a home should be founded *in*

[1] BD E3/111 (a): note of a deputation from the Union of Jewish Women to the President of the Board of Deputies, 23 Oct. 1929; Board Minutes, vol. 23, 8 Sept. 1929.

[2] D. Cesarani, 'Zionism in England, 1917–1939', D.Phil. thesis (Oxford, 1986), 124. On Leonard Montefiore, son of C. G. Montefiore, see L. Stein and C. C. Aronsfeld (eds.), *Leonard Montefiore In Memoriam 1889–1961* (London, 1964).

[3] W. Laqueur, *A History of Zionism* (London, 1972), 492–3; *PP* 1930, xvi [Cmd. 3692].

Palestine', which for this purpose was deemed to exclude Transjordan.[4]

The Executive of the World Zionist Organization had accepted (admittedly without enthusiasm) the 1922 statement of British policy. How are we to explain the very different manner in which the 1930 White Paper was received? One part of the explanation lies within the political dynamics of world Zionism, which had scarcely begun to contemplate the practical possibilities of a Jewish national homeland in 1922, and which nurtured still the hope that the Arabs might be induced to acquiesce in the Balfour Declaration. By 1930 Zionist leaders were much less uncertain about the ultimate goal of a self-governing Jewish national polity (perhaps within the framework of the British Empire), in respect of which hopes of Arab co-operation had generally been abandoned. The Passfield White Paper, from this viewpoint, seemed destined to frustrate ambitions which were current in 1930 but which had not been sufficiently developed in 1922. The Zionists were also exceedingly put out by the fact that they had not been kept informed of what was afoot. In protest, Weizmann resigned from the Jewish Agency, along with Felix Warburg and the industrialist Lord Melchett (Sir Alfred Mond, 1868–1930).[5]

But there were factors domestic to British Jewry which invited a much more robust reponse to Passfield's document, and which held out the prospect that its intentions might indeed be thwarted. The White Paper 'led to the first open political confrontation between the Zionist movement and the British Government'.[6] As such, the highly antagonistic posture adopted by the Zionists amounted to an open repudiation of 'Patriotic Zionism', but the strength of feeling over the massacres of 1929 virtually ensured that this repudiation attracted support (perhaps implicit and perhaps tacit) from elsewhere within British Jewry. The leadership of the Board of Deputies strained every muscle to avoid a public demonstration against the Labour Government, but was eventually manœuvred into a position where it could do no other than agree to support a

[4] G. Shimoni, 'From Anti-Zionism to Non-Zionism in Anglo-Jewry, 1917–1937', *JJS* 28 (1986), 27; *PP* 1922, xxiii [Cmd. 1700], 17–18.

[5] Laqueur, *History of Zionism*, 492; on Mond, who had 'married out' but became converted to Zionism after visiting Palestine in 1921, see H. Bolitho, *Alfred Mond First Lord Melchett* (London, 1933), 368–70.

[6] J. Gorny, *The British Labour Movement and Zionism 1917–1948* (London, 1983), 89.

public protest.[7] This meeting, at the Kingsway Theatre, London, addressed by the Board's President (Osmond d'Avigdor Goldsmid), Chief Rabbi Hertz, Nettie Adler, Professor Selig Brodetsky (1888–1954; then a member of the World Zionist Executive), and the Jewish Labour MP Michael Marcus was followed by others, both in London and in the provinces.[8] They culminated in Weizmann's resignation from the Presidency of the World Zionist Organization and his address to a monster rally at the Pavilion Theatre, Whitechapel.[9]

These events dealt a fatal blow to Patriotic Zionism. In the process they helped give expression to that species of Anglo-Jewish ethnic separatism against which successive communal élites had battled for the best part of half a century. The extraordinary coincidence of a by-election in Whitechapel provided a perfect opportunity for a demonstration of the new reality.

The Whitechapel by-election of November–December 1930 was caused by the death of its Labour MP, Harry Gosling, who was both a Gentile and a pro-Zionist. In an electorate of some 37,000 voters, about 12,000 were Jewish, though whether *Poale Zion* 'had a strong hold over them', as Professor Gorny maintains, is open to doubt.[10] The Liberals played a shrewd game. They chose as their candidate an up-and-coming Jewish solicitor from South Wales, and a Zionist of rising fame, Barnett Janner (1892–1982), and they agreed that the official return of Janner's election expenses would incorporate the sums expended by an allegedly independent body, the Palestine Protest Committee (PPC), an *ad hoc* entity over which the East London Young Zionist League exercised great influence.[11] Officially the EZF maintained an air of studied neutrality. Its new General Secretary, Lavy Bakstansky (1904–71) declined to take part in the by-election campaign, but in fact the constituency was visited by almost every EZF leader of note.

[7] Cesarani, 'Zionism in England', 128–9.

[8] *JC* (25 July 1930), 27–8.

[9] Ibid. (24 Oct. 1930), 26–7; (31 Oct.), 24–5.

[10] G. Alderman, *The Jewish Community in British Politics* (Oxford, 1983), 112; Gorny, *British Labour Movement*, 91.

[11] *JC* (24 Oct. 1930), 27; (7 Nov.), 22; (14 Nov.), 22–3; (21 Nov.), 32; (28 Nov.), 16; see also Cesarani, 'Zionism in England', 136. The account given by Lady E. Janner in *Barnett Janner: A Personal Portrait* (London, 1984), 32–5, makes no mention of the activities of the Palestine Protest Committee.

Janner's election meetings were 'practically synonymous' with those of the PPC.[12]

The injection into Whitechapel of the politics of the Mandate placed *Poale Zion* in an embarrassing position. We know that Brodetsky was approached to stand as Labour candidate.[13] We know, too, that the courageous decision of *Poale Zion* to campaign for the man Labour eventually chose to defend the seat, the Irish Catholic James Hall, was greatly influenced by back-room discussions between Ernest Bevin, Secretary of the Transport & General Workers' Union, and Dov Hos, the emissary in Britain of the Palestine Labour Party.[14] *Poale Zion* condemned the White Paper, and Hall was prevailed upon to give an assurance that, if elected, he would vote against the Government should it attempt to put the White Paper into force.[15] When polling took place, on 3 December, the Labour majority was cut from 9,180 to just 1,099. Over the following two months MacDonald's Government came under great pressure to revoke the White Paper, not least from American Jewry but also from Professor Harold Laski (1892–1950), Nathan Laski's brilliant if rebellious son who had married out but whose Jewish sensitivities had been thoroughly aroused by what he perceived to be Passfield's anti-Jewish policies.[16] On 13 February 1931, in a letter addressed to Weizmann and printed in Hansard, Ramsay MacDonald indicated his Government's support for the principles enunciated by Winston Churchill in 1922; Lord Passfield's White Paper was, in effect, dead.[17]

What did the crisis of 1930 mean for Zionism in Britain? Leopold Greenberg had put the *Jewish Chronicle* at the service of the Zionist interest during the by-election, and the invocation of the Jewish vote, both by him and by the East London Zionist League, was certainly not a bluff.[18] Compared with the general election of 1929, and with turn-out practically unchanged, Labour suffered a negative swing of 18 per cent.[19] Labour Zionists were quick to use

[12] Cesarani, 'Zionism in England', 140–2.

[13] S. Brodetsky, *Memoirs* (London, 1960), 140.

[14] Gorny, *British Labour Movement*, 98–9.

[15] *JC* (28 Nov. 1930), 8, 16.

[16] Gorny, *British Labour Movement*, 98–9.

[17] *Commons' Debates*, 5th ser. 248. 751–7 (13 Feb. 1931).

[18] *JC* (7 Nov. 1930), 6.

[19] The term 'swing' is used here in the conventional sense, measuring one party's percentage gain in votes cast against another's percentage loss, and is based upon the total number of valid votes cast for all parties.

the explanation of there having been a Jewish anti-Labour vote as ammunition in their campaign against the White Paper.[20] And, even though we lack the evidence of opinion polls and of systematic surveys, it seems safe to conclude that many of these votes were lost due to Jewish anger at the policies of Lord Passfield.

It seems equally safe to conclude that many Jewish voters deserted Labour for quite different reasons. A feature of the by-election contest was the candidature of Harry Pollitt, Secretary of the Communist Party, who obtained over 2,000 votes, and over 2,500 in 1931, when the Conservatives dropped out of the contest and Janner won the seat. Many of these Communist votes were undoubtedly of Jewish origin, a sign of the growing Jewish infatuation with Communism that was to be a marked feature of Jewish life in Britain in the 1930s and 1940s. Janner naturally played the Zionist card, but more than this he played the Jewish card, which was a very different tactic. As Liberal MP for the premier 'Jewish' constituency in Britain, Janner threw himself into parliamentary work on behalf of Jewish interests. He angled for, and expected, the Jewish vote in return.[21] But by 1935 the Jewish vote in East London was overwhelmingly Labour. With no Communist intervention to take votes away from Labour, Janner lost the seat to Hall, and a year later himself joined the Labour Party, taking the route mapped out in 1934 by Major Harry Nathan (1889–1963; Lord Nathan of Churt), the Jewish Liberal MP for North-East Bethnal Green, who with his wife Eleanor (1892–1972; a Liberal member of the LCC) had defected to Labour in order to save their political careers.[22]

The message from Whitechapel was certainly that Zionism was a force to be reckoned with as a factor affecting Anglo-Jewish political behaviour, but the message was equally that it was much less potent than Labourism. The events of October–December 1930 put Zionism on the political map; the Board of Deputies was

[20] Gorny, *British Labour Movement*, 93.

[21] See Lady Janner, *Barnett Janner*, ch. 3; Alderman, *Jewish Community*, 114; Mocatta Library (University College London), Anglo-Jewish Archives, Neville Laski Papers, AJ33/90: typescript note by Laski, 14 Oct. 1936, 7 (now transferred to the Parkes Library, University of Southampton).

[22] *JC* (17 Feb. 1933), 27; (7 May 1937), 11; on Nathan see H. Montgomery Hyde, *Strong for Service: The Life of Lord Nathan of Churt* (London, 1968), and G. Alderman, *London Jewry and London Politics, 1889–1986* (London, 1989), 70–1.

cast into the shadows, a fact of some significance. A corner had been turned, but it did not lead at once to the position of communal dominance to which Zionists had been looking forward since 1917. Consider, for example, the explanation furnished to Lloyd George by his politial aide, Gareth Jones, concerning the political situation in Whitechapel: 'the Jews would like to hear something brief and personal about Palestine . . . they do *not* want the Government policy to be attacked at length . . . Many of them are not keen Zionists.'[23] Or the observation of a correspondent to the *Young Zionist* in December 1932 that among Jewish working-class young people Zionism 'has made no headway. The tendency in the best part of our Jewish working class . . . is to join the Communist Party'.[24] Or the view formed in June 1936 by Joe Jacobs, the Jewish secretary of the Stepney Communist Party, to the effect that 'The Jews in East London were not yet in favour of Zionism. That is not to say that many Jews were not Zionists. The majority did not see this as a solution to their problems. They saw themselves as British Jews.'[25]

Events in Germany certainly gave an edge to Zionist propaganda, and it was against that sombre background that the militant anti-Zionism that had characterized the lay leadership of British Jewry in the 1920s yielded ground to a pragmatic non-Zionism, in which those who thought of themselves as Jews of the British persuasion could play a full part in the development of Jewish Palestine as a haven for the persecuted, without, however, admitting that there might ever be such a thing as a Jewish nationality. In January 1933 the Presidency of the Board of Deputies fell into the hands of just such a person, Neville Laski (1890–1969), brother to Harold and son-in-law of *Haham* Gaster.[26] Neville Laski was a brilliant barrister and a communal servant of great stature and immense energy. He was not a 'Leaguer'; he did indeed accept an invitation to attend as a guest the 18th World Zionist Congress held in Prague in August 1933. But he was emphatically opposed to the idea that there might arise, in Palestine, a Jewish State which would give expression to and confer 'Jewish' nationality. In matters relating to

[23] Lloyd George Papers, House of Lords Record Office, G/26/1/34: typescript minute from Jones, 27 Nov. 1930.
[24] *Young Zionist* (Dec. 1932), 137.
[25] J. Jacobs, *Out of the Ghetto*, ed. J. J. Simon (London, 1978), 208.
[26] On Neville Laski see *JC* (28 Mar. 1969), 53.

the Jewish Agency (of whose Administrative Committee he became Chairman in 1934) he allied himself with leading American non-Zionists, such as Felix Warburg and Morris Waldman. To a British civil servant he calmly described Brodetsky as 'of non-British origin'.[27] So fearful was he of political Zionism that in August 1934 he made a secret offer to the Colonial Office to spy for them against the Agency, hoping thereby to influence the British Government against the political aims of the World Zionist movement.[28] By the late 1930s, and under the twin pressures created by the need to address the problem of Jewish refugees from Germany and Austria, and by the emergence of a new home-grown anti-Jewish movement, this preoccupation with the 'British' character of Anglo-Jewry was to become an obsession.

The installation of a Nazi government in Germany in January 1933, and the subsequent harassment of German Jews, culminating in the promulgation of the Nuremberg Laws in September 1935 (by which German Jews were stripped of German citizenship), raised for British Jewry a problem of much greater severity than that posed by the persecution of Russian Jewry a half-century earlier. Russian Jews could be sent on their way to America, or repatriated on the grounds that they were the victims of political rather than of religious or racial oppression, or that they were not refugees at all, but merely emigrants. These solutions could not be applied to German Jewry in its entirety, while the solution which Zionists offered—wholesale resettlement in the Holy Land—posed acute difficulties in terms of British policy in Palestine, where, in 1936, an Arab revolt was proclaimed.

The problem was further exacerbated by the social and economic composition of the German refugee body. Nazi policy was deliberately designed to squeeze Jews out of their positions as captains of industry, magnates of commerce and finance, and members of the professions and of the academic community. The prospect of such persons coming to live and work in Britain gave rise to an anti-refugee lobby among some of the most respected sectors of British middle-class society. In 1933 and 1934 the *British Medical Journal* began reporting hostility from the medical profession to refugee doctors, and in 1934 *The Times* carried a

[27] Shimoni, 'From Anti-Zionism to Non-Zionism', 35.
[28] G. Rey, 'Laski's Offer', *JC* (17 Aug. 1984), 18–19.

similar correspondence regarding university appointments.[29] An Academic Assistance Committee, established by non-Jews in May 1933, offered emergency help, but on a selective basis; its basic policy was one of re-emigration.[30] Of the many brilliant German and Austrian Jewish scientists and scholars who found (it is true) temporary refuge in Britain, few were offered permanent posts, and many were eventually persuaded or tempted to take up positions in the United States.[31] This policy of ultra-cautious selectivity was applied also to businessmen and industrialists. Where it could be demonstrated that their permanent resettlement in Britain would benefit the British economy, they were welcomed. It has been estimated that by 1938 Jewish refugees from Nazism had established some 250 businesses in Britain, providing perhaps as many as 25,000 jobs; their contribution to the revitalization of economically depressed areas (Tyneside, South Wales, West Cumberland, and Northern Ireland) is particularly noteworthy.[32]

The underlying principle which informed the attitude of Britain's National Government towards Jewish immigration in the 1930s was that Jews, by their presence and by their behaviour, created anti-Semitism. The least possible number would be allowed to enter Britain, and most of these (unless their potential contribution to British society could be clearly demonstrated) would acquire no right of permanent residence, but would enjoy the status of mere transmigrants; their well-being, moreover, would be the responsibility of British Jewry, not of the British taxpayer.[33] These norms were, by and large, accepted by the official Jewish leadership in Britain, and never challenged, for several reasons.

Firstly, in spite of, or perhaps because of, the confrontation with Downing Street over the 1930 White Paper, the conviction that the

[29] A. Sharf, *The British Press and Jews under Nazi Rule* (London, 1964), 161.

[30] See generally N. Bentwich, *The Rescue and Achievement of Refugee Scholars: The Story of Displaced Scholars and Scientists, 1933–1952* (The Hague, 1953).

[31] P. Hoch, 'No Utopia: Refugee Scholars in Britain', *History Today* (Nov. 1985), 53–6; 'Nobel Prize Winners Unwelcome', *Edinburgh Star* (Mar. 1990), 22–4; and see W. E. Mosse *et al.* (eds.), *Second Chance: Two Centuries of German-Speaking Jews in the United Kingdom* (Tübingen, 1991), 229–54.

[32] H. Pollins, *Economic History of the Jews in England* (London, 1982), 205–8; H. Loebl, 'Refugee Industries in the Special Areas of Britain', in G. Hirschfeld (ed.), *Exile in Britain* (London, 1984), 219–49.

[33] L. London, 'Jewish Refugees, Anglo-Jewry and British Government Policy, 1930–1940', in D. Cesarani (ed.), *The Making of Modern Anglo-Jewry* (Oxford, 1990), 164–5.

community must not be seen to be lobbying against the Government (putting sectional interests before the national interest) was never stronger than during the 1930s, when the British public's fear of Communism was—certainly down to 1938—much more widespread than fear of Nazism. In the aftermath of Hitler's victory in the German elections of March 1933, a movement sprang up both in East London and the provinces in favour of an economic boycott of Nazi Germany, and in November a Jewish Representative Council for the Boycott of German Goods and Services was established, with Morry Davis, the President of the Federation of Synagogues, as its Chairman.[34] Chief Rabbi Hertz supported the boycott, but only in private; he declined 'officially and openly' to have anything to do with it, citing the view of German orthodoxy that its implementation was likely to be counter-productive.[35] The Board of Deputies also cited the opposition of German Jewry, but pointed additionally to the fact of the *Ha'avarah*, the agreement between the World Zionist Organization and the German Government, by which German Jews resettling in Palestine could export some of their capital provided it was used to buy German goods.[36]

The opposition of German Jewry to the boycott, and the embarrassment of the *Ha'avarah*, were very real. But they came as convenient excuses for inaction which was dictated on another ground, namely that a boycott ran counter to the policy of 'economic appeasement' in which the British Government was engaged in the early years of the Nazi regime. It is worth remembering that in the United States the boycott was officially supported by the American Jewish Congress. The desire not to be seen in an anti-government pose surfaced again in 1938, when the Joint Foreign Committee expressed its opposition to public meetings of protest against the treatment of Jews in Austria.[37]

[34] Alderman, *Jewish Community*, 121; Federation of Synagogues Minute Book No. 3: Special Board Meeting, 9 July 1933.

[35] Hertz Papers, Office of the Chief Rabbi of the United Hebrew Congregations, General Correspondence, Misc. D. folder, files D–G: correspondence between Hertz and Davis, 23–5 Sept. 1935. See also V. D. Lipman, *A History of the Jews in Britain since 1858* (Leicester, 1990), 193.

[36] Cesarani, 'Zionism in England', 354; American Jewish Archives, Cincinnati, Felix Warburg Papers, 293/1: Minutes of meeting of the Joint Foreign Committee of the Board of Deputies and the Anglo-Jewish Association, 28 June 1933. See generally S. Gewirtz, 'Anglo-Jewish Responses to Nazi Germany 1933–39: The Anti-Nazi Boycott and the Board of Deputies of British Jews', *Journal of Contemporary History*, 26 (1991), 255–76.

[37] Lipman, *History*, 194.

During a debate on British refugee policy, initiated by the Labour MP Philip Noel Baker in the House of Commons on 21 November 1938 (twelve days after *Kristallnacht*), the Home Secretary, Sir Samuel Hoare, defended the Government's cautious approach by declaring that it was 'a fact that below the surface . . . there is the making of a definite anti-Jewish movement'; the mass immigration of Jews to Britain would, he warned, lead to further anti-Jewish manifestations.[38] By prior agreement, and so as not to give the impression of special pleading, no Jewish MP took part in this debate; the *Jewish Chronicle* acknowledged their restraint.[39] The first occasion upon which the Board of Deputies organized any form of official Anglo-Jewish protest against Nazism was on 1 December 1938, at the Royal Albert Hall, when the chair was taken by the former Lord Chancellor, Lord Sankey; Dr Hertz was the only Jewish speaker.[40]

The events of November 1938 and the dismemberment of Czechoslovakia led to a fundamental reassessment of communal policy towards refugees from Nazism. Until then, the community acted fully within the framework of policy as received from the British Government. In 1933 the major communal agency dealing with refugees was still the Jews' Temporary Shelter, to the Presidency of which Herman Landau had been succeeded by Otto M. Schiff (1875–1952), a banker of German origin who had received the OBE for his work on behalf of Belgian refugees during the First World War.[41] Schiff was also, at this time, one of the 'Overseers of the Poor' of the United Synagogue. To cope with the first wave of Jewish refugees from Nazism he founded the Jewish Refugees Committee, renamed the German Jewish Aid Committee in 1938; this tended to deal with adults and accompanied children.[42] Unaccompanied children under 16 were, from 1938, the responsibility of the Movement for the Care of Children from Germany.[43] Both bodies, and a host of others, were sustained by the Central British Fund for German Jewry (CBF), established in April 1933 under the aegis of the House of Rothschild, and so constituted as to maintain the most delicate of balances between

38 A.J. Sherman, *Island Refuge: Britain and Refugees from the Third Reich 1933–1939* (London, 1973), 180.

39 *JC* (25 Nov. 1938), 32.

40 Ibid. (9 Dec. 1938), 33–4.

41 On Schiff see ibid. (21 Nov. 1952), 9; (2 May 1975), 9.

42 N. Bentwich, *They Found Refuge* (London, 1956), 17, and ch. 4.

43 B. Wasserstein, *Britain and the Jews of Europe 1939–1945* (Oxford, 1979), 10.

Zionists and non-Zionists.[44] A similar balance was maintained in the disposition of the Council for German Jewry, a largely Anglo-American venture established in 1936, which raised funds for the resettlement of refugees, especially but not exclusively in Palestine; the Honorary Directors of the Council were Professor Norman Bentwich (1883–1971) and the Gentile Zionist Sir Wyndham Deedes; Schiff and Leonard Montefiore jointly chaired its 'London Refugee Committee'.[45]

The role of Otto Schiff was of pivotal importance to the pace and direction of Anglo-Jewish efforts to rescue and resettle German Jews. Armed with the provisions of the Aliens Act of 1919 and the Aliens Order of 1920, the British Government could refuse entry into Great Britain of any alien who could not demonstrate that he or she had a means of support (other than through obtaining employment, of course) while in Britain. There was no 'right' of asylum. That being so, such refugees as were permitted to enter Britain were admitted on a purely temporary basis, generally on the assumption that they would eventually re-emigrate, and certainly on the basis that they would under no circumstances become a charge on the state.[46] Jewish refugees, in particular, were to be admitted in very limited numbers, and on the basis of careful selection, particular attention being paid in this regard to the likelihood of their being easily assimilated into British society during their stay.[47]

In April 1933 the British Cabinet decided on a very limited relaxation of the rule that alien immigrants had to demonstrate financial independence. This concession was made on receipt of a remarkable pledge, personally signed by Neville Laski, Leonard Montefiore, Lionel Cohen (1888–1973; later Lord Cohen of Walmer and then Chairman of the Law, Parliamentary, & General

[44] Bentwich, *They Found Refuge*, ch. 2; and see J. Stiebel, 'The Central British Fund for World Relief', *TJHSE* 17 (1978–80), 51–69.

[45] Bentwich, *They Found Refuge*, ch. 3 and 208–9; on Norman Bentwich, the son of Herbert and the first Attorney-General of Mandated Palestine, who was dismissed from his post in 1931, see the entry in J. Comay, *Who's Who in Jewish History* (London, 1974), 91.

[46] *Commons' Debates*, 5th ser. 348. 189: statement by Osbert Peake, the Parliamentary Under-Secretary for Foreign Affairs. On the background to the 1919 Act, which was renewed annually and which formed (with associated Orders in Council, such as that of 1920) the basis of British immigration policy until 1971, see C. Holmes, *John Bull's Island* (London, 1988), 112–14.

[47] London, 'Jewish Refugees', 164–7.

Purposes Committee of the Board of Deputies), and Schiff; news of the existence of this undertaking inevitably leaked out, though its details were not made public at the time.[48] In this document the signatories asked the Government to admit refugees from Germany and to waive the rule that such persons should be able to demonstrate financial independence; their sojourn in Britain was to be temporary, while their 'ultimate transmigration . . . to countries other than England' was arranged; the signatories further undertook that 'all expense, whether in respect of temporary or permanent accommodation or maintenance, will be borne by the Jewish community without ultimate charge to the state'. This pledge was accepted by the Cabinet, and on the basis of its being honoured (in many cases by personal guarantees from British Jews) some 30,000 Jewish refugees from Nazism had, by the end of 1938, been permitted entry into Britain.[49]

There are two ways in which this guarantee might be viewed. The British Government need not have admitted a single Jewish refugee from Nazi persecution. That it did so was due to the pledge which Schiff and his colleagues had given, and which, down to December 1939, was honoured by British Jewry at a cost of some £3,000,000.[50] The guarantee was thus the means by which freedom was secured for some Jewish victims of Nazism—but only for some. Within the terms of the undertaking, the Government was entitled to permit entry only so long as, in its estimation, British Jewry could provide the necessary financial support. The guarantee only covered Jews of German nationality. It did not extend to Jews of Polish, Hungarian, or other nationality (or even to stateless Jews) who were living in Germany at the time of the Nazi take-over. Polish and Hungarian nationals had to obtain visas to enter Britain, and the view of the British Government, supported by Schiff and his colleagues, was that these unfortunates could return to their countries of origin.[51] Such repatriations were routinely enforced. In 1936 some 3,800 Jews in this category were returned, with the full approval of the

[48] Lipman, *History*, 195–6. The pledge was attached as an appendix to a Memorandum ('Proposals of the Jewish Community as Regards Jewish Refugees from Germany') by the Home Secretary, Sir John Gilmour, dated 6 Apr. 1933: PRO CAB 24/239, C.P. 96/33. It was not authorized by the Board of Deputies and there is no reference to it in the Board's Archives.

[49] Lipman, *History*, 196.

[50] Wasserstein, *Britain and the Jews of Europe*, 82.

[51] London, 'Jewish Refugees', 171.

Jewish authorities, to countries in eastern Europe. 'It is a tragic reflection', Bentwich later commented, 'that . . . the fatal insecurity of East European Jewry was not adequately recognized.'[52] Tragic, indeed.

The strict terms of the guarantee were used by those who articulated Anglo-Jewish refugee policy as a means of limiting not merely the numbers of Jewish victims of Nazism permitted to enter Britain, but also the type, or class. Schiff developed 'a close working relationship' with the Aliens Department of the Home Office, so that, in practical terms, German Jews were allowed into Britain on his authority.[53] In his apologia for Schiff's policies, Bentwich described how the Home Office 'had complete trust in Mr. Schiff and his assistants, and were prepared to accept their word that any particular refugee or group of refugees would be maintained'.[54] But the reverse was also true. At bottom, refugees were admitted, and were refused admission, on Schiff's say-so. The Home Office trusted Schiff and Bentwich because they knew that, in their approach to this task, they would bring to bear prejudices and preferences of which the Government approved. One of these was that persons over 45 years of age were unsuitable for eventual re-emigration, and so should not be admitted in the first place.[55] Another related to the occupational class of those applying for entry. Following the German occupation of Austria, at the beginning of March 1938, the Home Office reintroduced visas for German and Austrian immigrants.[56] They did so, in part at least, at the behest of Schiff, who wished to use the visa requirement as a means of exercising greater control over the quality as well as the quantity of Jewish refugees entering Britain.

As part of a delegation from the Board of Deputies to the Home Secretary on 1 April 1938, Schiff complained how very difficult it was 'to get rid of a refugee . . . once he had entered and spent a few months in this country. The imposition of the visa was especially necessary in the case of Austrians who were largely of the shopkeeper and small trader class and would therefore prove much more difficult to [re-]emigrate than the average German who had

52 Bentwich, *They Found Refuge*, 33.
53 London, 'Jewish Refugees', 174.
54 Bentwich, *They Found Refuge*, 52.
55 See N. Bentwich, *Wanderer between Two Worlds* (London, 1941), 29.
56 London, 'Jewish Refugees', 175.

come to the United Kingdom.' The Home Office note of Sir Samuel Hoare's reply is instructive:

> It would be necessary for the Home Office to discriminate very carefully as to the type of refugee who could be admitted to this country. If a flood of the wrong type of immigrants were allowed in there might be serious danger of anti-semitic feeling being aroused in this country. The last thing which we wanted here was the creation of a Jewish problem. The Deputation [from the Board of Deputies] said they entirely agreed with this point of view.[57]

This last point was perfectly valid, and was used by Hoare and by R. A. Butler (Under-Secretary at the Foreign Office) in answering parliamentary questions on refugee policy later that year.[58]

In 1938 the policy which had been underpinned by the 1933 guarantee collapsed under the weight of the multiple crises (the occupation of Austria, *Kristallnacht*, and the dismemberment of Czechoslovakia) of that year. Swayed by international pressure—focused upon the Evian conference which President Roosevelt had convened that summer—the Home Office put greater emphasis upon the humanitarian aspects of immigration policy.[59] Fortunately, the Jewish organizations could not cope with the vastly increased workload; at Bloomsbury House, home to a miscellany of Jewish and non-Jewish refugee bodies, chaos reigned. Earl Winterton actually warned the Jewish authorities that the Home Office reserved the right to admit as refugees persons whose applications they had not approved.[60] Schiff had already, in March, taken it upon himself to inform the Government that the Jewish relief organizations could not accept further financial responsibilities in respect of Jewish refugees who might be admitted in future; now he warned that the German Jewish Aid Committee could not be responsible for the upkeep of refugees from Czechoslovakia.[61]

[57] PRO HO 213/42: Minutes of meeting, 1 Apr. 1938, 3. See also the Memorandum submitted by the Board of Deputies to the Home Office on 24 Mar. 1938 ('Admission of Political, Racial or Religious Refugees from the former Austrian State') supporting the refusal to grant 'indiscriminate admission' to Jewish refugees from Austria: Mowshowitch Collection, YIVO Institute, New York, folder 153.

[58] *Commons' Debates*, 5th ser. 335. 843–4 (4 May 1938); 338. 2410–11 (21 July).

[59] London, 'Jewish Refugees', 178; Sherman, *Island Refuge*, 95–122.

[60] Sherman, *Island Refuge*, 155–6; the warning was given on 20 Oct. 1938.

[61] Bentwich, *They Found Refuge*, 45; Sherman, *Island Refuge*, 157–8.

But the flow of Jewish refugees to Britain did not stop. Indeed, it increased dramatically following the decision of the Chamberlain Government to respond positively to a deputation, led by Viscount Samuel (as Herbert Samuel had become) shortly after *Kristallnacht*. The deputation consisted, besides Samuel, of Viscount Bearsted (Marcus Samuel), Neville Laski, Lionel de Rothschild (President of the United Synagogue), and Chaim Weizmann. Schiff's absence was perhaps as important as Herbert Samuel's presence. Samuel had been a supporter of Chamberlain's foreign policy, and had even been prepared to believe that Hitler was 'a man with a conscience'.[62] Now, in his capacity as Joint Chairman of the Council for German Jewry, he asked for, and obtained, a considerable relaxation of entry rules, especially in relation to young persons under 17 years of age, who were to be admitted without visas and without their parents, and who were to be regarded as transmigrants undergoing training.[63] Between the end of 1938 and the outbreak of war with Germany in 1939 some 25,000 Jewish refugees from Nazism (including some 9,000 children) were allowed to enter Britain—almost as many as during the entire period since the beginning of 1933.[64] What is more, Chamberlain's Cabinet reversed the policy that such persons were not to become a charge upon the state. In July 1939 it agreed to afford a measure of financial assistance, though only to aid eventual emigration from Britain.[65]

To what extent the Cabinet really believed that resettlement was possible must remain an open question. On 17 May it had issued a White Paper designed to prevent any massive entry of Jewish refugees into Palestine. Other countries were adopting ever tighter immigration controls. During the Second World War many thousands of persecuted Jews admitted temporarily into Britain acquired, after very considerable privation, a degree of permanent residence about which the Home Office could do little; this resulted in the net addition of some 40,000 souls to the sum total of British Jewry by 1945.[66]

[62] J. Bowle, *Viscount Samuel* (London, 1957), 309.

[63] London, 'Jewish Refugees', 180–1.

[64] Sherman, *Island Refuge* 265, 271. On the Children's Transports see K. Gershon (ed.), *We Came As Children* (London, 1966), and B. Turner, . . . *And The Policeman Smiled* (London, 1990).

[65] Sherman, *Island Refuge*, 245–50; this agreement to give financial aid was contingent upon other governments making similar contributions.

[66] Bentwich, *They Found Refuge*, 115–16; Wasserstein, *Britain and the Jews of*

Could more have been done? Why did British Jewry wait until a situation of literally murderous proportions had developed in central Europe, before asking the British Government to adopt a generous policy of humanitarian assistance? And why was there not, at any time, a campaign, by the recognized official organs of British Jewry, with the aim of reorientating public and ultimately Government opinion into a more sympathetic frame of mind? At the time it was argued that a higher and more strident communal profile in the matter of refugee policy would have lent substance to the accusation that the loyalty of British Jews to their co-religionists in other lands was greater than their loyalty to their fellow citizens in Britain.[67] In other words, the old arguments between Zionists and anti-Zionists, about the fundamental nature of the Jewish presence in Britain, were resurrected, but in a more dangerous form: to what political entity did the Jews of or in Britain ultimately belong? Was their much-vaunted patriotism nothing more than a sham, or at least in need of heavy qualification?

The spectre of the cosmopolitan Jew, loyal to international Jewry but to nothing else, haunted Jewish communal leaders (and many of those whom they led) as much as it haunted British purveyors of anti-Jewish prejudice, of whom there was a growing number in the 1930s. It was precisely for this reason that Neville Laski turned his back upon the World Jewish Congress (WJC) formed in 1936 on the initiative of the American Zionist Rabbi Stephen Wise and the Lithuanian-German Zionist Nahum Goldmann. The WJC was designed as the Diaspora counterpart of the World Zionist Organization, and the complement to it.[68] Laski consistently and successfully argued against the affiliation to the WJC of the Board of Deputies and tried (in vain) to persuade the Foreign Office to have no dealings with it.[69] Jews in different countries, he told his colleagues in the Board, possessed 'differences of outlook, very largely the analogous differences of the general communities of which they form part'; 'the semblance of internationalism and unified action in the World Jewish Congress has therefore no basis

Europe, 82; London, 'Jewish Refugees', 190. During the war the *net* increase in the size of the Jewish refugee population of Britain was of the order of 10,000.

[67] Stein and Aronsfeld, *Leonard G. Montefiore*, 14.

[68] G. Shimoni, 'Selig Brodetsky and the Ascendancy of Zionism in Anglo-Jewry (1939–1945)', *JJS* 22 (1980), 128; J. Fraenkel, *The History of the British Section of the World Jewish Congress* (London, 1976), 4–5.

[69] London, 'Jewish Refugees', 187–8.

in fact', and could only provide ammunition for those who peddled 'the frequent and unfounded charge against Jews by the anti-Semites' that there existed an 'international Jewry'.[70] A British Section of the WJC was called into being, the creation of the Zionist Federation of Great Britain and Ireland (as the EZF had become), *Poale Zion*, British *Mizrachi*, and a collection of Jewish labour and trade-union groups, friendly societies, independent synagogues, and the Federation of Synagogues.[71] A delegation of twelve persons elected by this Section attended the founding conference of the WJC in Geneva, while Morry Davis received a separate invitation *ad personam*. In the context of the then continuing struggle between the Board and its detractors over the ultimate source and seat of communal authority within British Jewry, the composition of the original British Section of the WJC is highly significant, for it bore a striking resemblance to the panorama of groups which had established the Representative Council to further the Jewish economic boycott of Germany in 1933.[72]

At bottom, the approach of British Jewry to the refugee question, as to so many other items on the communal agenda in the era of Nazism, was very heavily influenced by the fear of anti-Semitism and by a diagnosis of its causes that gained wide communal currency. Some communal postures, particularly as they affected the treatment of Jewish refugees by British Jews, and the reaction of British Jewry to the British Government's treatment of Jewish aliens during the Second World War, will be considered in due course. But what took place in these spheres cannot be properly understood without a grasp of underlying motives and attitudes.

The activities of the British Union of Fascists (BUF) and its apparent success in gaining adherents, most noticeably in North and East London, sent shock waves throughout the Anglo-Jewish world. Sir Oswald Mosley, the estranged and embittered former

[70] BD C11/10/2: Memorandum by Laski on the WJC, 6 Jan. 1937. Compare Laski to Felix Warburg, 9 Apr. 1936, in Felix M. Warburg Papers, American Jewish Archives, Cincinnati, 328/11: 'The bogey of the international Jew which finds its crudest form in the Protocols, is if you will bear with me, definitely assisted both by Zionism and by its offshoot,—or, as I have termed it, facet,—the World Jewish Congress.'

[71] Fraenkel, *British Section*, 5.

[72] Alderman, *Jewish Community*, 121; it is equally significant that the Jewish Representative Councils of Leeds, Manchester, Glasgow, and elsewhere also affiliated to the WJC's British Section. The Board of Deputies did not affiliate until 1974, when it became the British Section: Fraenkel, *British Section*, 10.

member of the second Labour Government, was not at first regarded as unfriendly to Jewish interests. The 'New Party', which he formed in February 1931, may have attracted some Jewish support; the Jewish boxer Ted 'Kid' Lewis was certainly a member, and contested Whitechapel for the party at the general election of 1931.[73] Fascism itself was neither pro- nor anti-Jewish. Mussolini had enthusiastic support from the cream of Italian-Jewish society. When Mosley transformed the New Party into the BUF, in 1932, he effected to assure British Jewry that anti-Semitism formed 'no part' of its policy.[74] For a moment even the *Jewish Chronicle* accepted that this was so.[75] One of the members of Mosley's 'January Club', a half-way house for those who wished to support the Fascist cause without actually joining the BUF, was Sir Philip Magnus-Allcroft, the son of Laurie Magnus, the editor of the *Jewish Guardian*; in a letter written to Philip Guedalla, Chairman of the Press & Information Committee of the Board of Deputies on 25 October 1934, Magnus-Allcroft admitted that he was 'not quite the only one of my faith who was a member of the Club'.[76]

By 1934 Jews were being refused membership of the BUF, and the few Jews who had enrolled themselves into it, including 'Kid' Lewis, were 'frozen out'.[77] From then on (the autumn of 1934) anti-Jewish propaganda became a central feature and a formal element of BUF policy; by 1936 anti-Semitic policies dominated BUF strategy, culminating in an attempted provocative march through the East End which ended in the so-called 'battle' of Cable Street (4 October 1936) and the orgy of reprisals against Jewish property which was carried out at Mile End the following week.[78] At the LCC elections of March 1937, BUF candidates polled a respectable 14 per cent of the votes in Shoreditch, 19 per cent in Limehouse, and 23 per cent in Bethnal Green.[79]

In the East End of London, as in other areas of Jewish (especially Jewish immigrant) settlement, a certain level of 'street' anti-

73 Alderman, *Jewish Community*, 113.

74 Board of Deputies of British Jews, *Annual Report for 1932*, 43–4.

75 *JC* (13 Jan. 1933), 9.

76 CZA: Papers of Philip Guedalla, A159, file 3; in the *Jewish Community*, 195, I wrongly ascribe this letter to Magnus-Allcroft's grandfather, Sir Philip Magnus, who had died in 1933.

77 C. Cross, *The Fascists in Britain* (London, 1961), 102.

78 C. Holmes, *Anti-Semitism in British Society 1876–1939* (London, 1979), 193–4.

79 Alderman, *London Jewry*, 90.

Semitism was regarded as the norm, a residue left from the days of the British Brothers' League, but which could be exploited and expanded (as over conscription during the First World War) should circumstances permit. A degree of middle- and upper-class prejudice against Jews was also taken for granted; this might manifest itself at public schools or golf clubs, or even in the admissions policies of medical schools.[80] The Conservative Party proved a safe haven for out-and-out anti-Semites, such as Edward Doran (MP for Tottenham, 1931–5) and Archibald Henry Maule Ramsay (MP for Peebles & Southern, 1931–45, a fanatical anti-Bolshevik and a member of the Nordic League).[81] In June 1937 the anti-Zionist but none the less Jewish Mayor of Cheltenham, Daniel Lipson (1886–1963), won the Cheltenham by-election as the Independent Conservative candidate after the local Conservative Association has succumbed to an insidious anti-Jewish campaign and had refused to adopt him.[82]

The apparent success of the BUF in the mid-1930s seemed to suggest that the popular anti-Semitism of the streets had found an articulate and well-financed middle-class leadership, prepared to exploit social and economic grievances in order to whip up anti-Jewish feeling, which was itself then used as a major vehicle in its quest for political advancement. The Board of Deputies was not well equipped to counter-attack. A suggestion from Waley Cohen (now a Vice-President) that a Defence Committee be established, was vetoed by Laski on the grounds that such a move would create panic.[83] Instead, the Law & Parliamentary and Press & Information Committees were linked by a Co-ordinating Committee. This arrangement was intrinsically defective and could not last. In November 1938 the Co-ordinating Committee became the Defence Committee, with a full-time Secretary of its own, Sidney Salomon (d. 1965), a lawyer and son of a Manchester rabbi, who had worked on the *Jewish Chronicle* and later in the London office of

[80] T. Kushner, *The Persistence of Prejudice: Antisemitism in British Society during the Second World War* (Manchester, 1989), 96.

[81] Alderman, *Jewish Community*, 120, 197.

[82] *Gloucestershire Echo* (9 June 1937), 3; *JC* (25 June 1937), 12. Lipson was virtual head of the Jewish community in Cheltenham, which by then was reduced to a few families: B. Torode, *The Hebrew Community of Cheltenham, Gloucester and Stroud* (Cheltenham, 1989), 52; *The Times* (16 Apr. 1963), 14; *JC* (19 Apr. 1963), 31.

[83] Lipman, *History*, 187.

the *Yorkshire Post*.[84] At about the same time Laski became, in effect, the Board's first full-time President; money raised secretly by Waley Cohen enabled him to give up his own legal career in order to concentrate on Jewish defence.[85] By the outbreak of war, communal defence had assumed its place as the greatest of the Board's priorities; so it has remained.

But in fact there were (and have continued to be) two conflicting defence strategies. The first was aimed, naturally, at the detractors of British Jewry. This included intelligence gathering, media monitoring, and co-operation with the Special Branch. At times of municipal and national elections (the 1937 local elections, the North-East Leeds and Middleton & Prestwich by-elections of 1940), candidates in the major political parties were offered election literature, which they could then distribute as their own; in this way the Board hoped to encourage an anti-Fascist vote.[86] There was a continuous programme of publications and lectures on anti-Fascist themes, but emphasizing also the Jewish contribution to British life. In 1938 Salomon published *The Jews of Britain*, in which he played down Jewish involvement in finance and commerce, but stressed instead the Jewish contribution to the arts and medicine. An agreement was reached with the British Broadcasting Corporation, which undertook to submit to the Board the scripts of any programme 'of Jewish interest', and to abide by the Board's decision or to 'further discuss the matter' before the programme was broadcast.[87] In November 1940 the Chairman of the Defence Committee, M. Gordon Liverman, reached an agreement with Morris Myer, by which, in return for a loan from the Committee of £500, Myer gave 'an unqualified assurance' not to allow his newspaper, *Di Tsait*, 'to advocate a contradictory attitude to the official policy of the Board'.[88]

[84] On the foundation of the Co-ordinating Committee see Neville Laski to Nathan Laski, 22 July 1936, in Felix M. Warburg Papers, American Jewish Archives, Cincinnati, 328/11. On Salomon see *JC* (23 July 1965), 24.

[85] R. Henriques, *Sir Robert Waley Cohen* (London, 1966), 364.

[86] Mocatta Library (University College London), Anglo-Jewish Archives, Neville Laski Papers, AJ33/158: typescript memo. [undated but probably post-1945] by Salomon headed 'The Jewish Defence Committee', 8 (now transferred to the Parkes Library, University of Southampton).

[87] Ibid. 22–3.

[88] Neville Laski Papers, AJ33/155: typescript 'Note of an interview with Mr. Maurice [*sic*] Myer Regarding Proposed Loan', 22 Nov. 1940, signed by Myer and Liverman.

Much of the Board's defence literature, by reason of its timidity and condescension, arguably strengthened the anti-Semitic cause. Nor, in any case, did all this commendable effort represent the major thrust of the defence policy, which was aimed not so much at protecting Jews from their detractors, as at shielding the detractors from the Jews. In the aftermath of Cable Street Neville Laski arranged (through his brother Harold) a secret meeting with Harry Pollitt and Herbert Morrison (who had masterminded Labour's capture of the LCC in 1934, and was now Labour Leader at County Hall). Laski wished to discuss, with these two very experienced observers of and participants in the politics of working-class London, why there was such hostility to Jews. Morrison and Pollitt made some very unflattering remarks about Barnet Janner's invocation of the Jewish vote at Whitechapel: 'it was still remembered and talked about, and it was said that Jews were Jews first and Englishmen a long way after.' But the major burden of the analysis which Laski was offered was that, by their professional conduct, Jewish landlords, estate agents, and businessmen had contributed much to anti-Jewish feeling in East London.[89] Laski did not waste much time in accepting the truth of what he had been told. His view was shared by many other communal leaders.

During the early 1930s the Board of Deputies had had to deal with a number of issues of extreme sensitivity arising from the business practices of Jews, pre-eminently though not exclusively in London. The Board could have declined to address such matters, and could have argued that what was at issue was business conduct, not Jewish business conduct. This was precisely the attitude adopted by left-wing propagandists, many of whom were also Jews. But the members and leadership of the Board did not take this view, partly because they were heirs to a long-standing tradition of Jewish collective responsibility for the conduct of individual Jews, but partly also because the Fascist campaigns had come to concentrate forcefully on the activities of Jewish employers, Jewish shopkeepers, Jewish landlords, and even of Jewish members of the LCC.[90] These attacks seemed to demand a specifically Jewish

[89] Neville Laski Papers, AJ33/90: typescript note by Laski, 14 Oct. 1936; and see C. Holmes, 'East End Anti-Semitism, 1936', *Bulletin of the Society for the Study of Labour History*, 32 (Spring 1976), 26–7.

[90] Holmes, *Anti-Semitism*, 194; *JC* (12 Mar. 1937), 20.

response, for there could be no doubt that the BUF was managing to exploit grievances which, whether justified or not, were genuinely held against Jews and the Jewish community of London.

The hostility of some Jewish employers towards trade unionism in London was certainly a major cause of ill-feeling. Professor Skidelsky has noted that many of the BUF's most prominent activists came from the furniture trade, where intense competition led to anti-union practices.[91] Blackshirt propaganda drew attention to the paralysis affecting the unions in the furnishing trades, which was attributed to the fact that 'Jewish bosses employ outside labour whenever workers protest'.[92] The accusation was somewhat disingenuous, since Jewish workers were heavily involved in the National Amalgamated Furnishing Trades Association (NAFTA), the East London branch of which, 'Jewish in all but name', was 'especially noted for its militancy'.[93] None the less, what was alleged was basically true. In July 1936 the Board of Deputies itself felt constrained to complain to a Jewish proprietor about the physical harassment of NAFTA members at his factory in Tottenham. The following February Laski received a complaint from the President (a clergyman) of the Hackney Wick Workers' Club and Institute to the effect that the Jewish Board of Guardians had been supplying blackleg labour to a Jewish-owned firm intent on 'resisting Trade Union organization'. Later that year other communications were received, from equally reputable sources, alleging anti-union stratagems by other Jewish-owned furniture and upholstery firms operating in north London.[94]

In relation to such complaints, which could equally well have been made against non-Jewish firms, there was little that Board officials could do. We know that the Board used its influence with some of the large, Jewish-owned retail hire-purchase furniture stores to persuade them to compel factory owners to adopt a more generous wages policy and to recognize appropriate trade unions.[95] But the growth of anti-Semitism within the trade-union movement

[91] R. Skidelsky, *Oswald Mosley* (London, 1975), 394–6.

[92] *East London Pioneer* (5 Dec. 1936), in BD E3/245.

[93] E. R. Smith, 'Jews and Politics in the East End of London, 1918–1939', in Cesarani (ed.), *Making of Modern Anglo-Jewry*, 160; Pollins, *Economic History*, 190.

[94] These papers are in BD E3/245.

[95] J. A. Gillespie, 'Economic and Social Change in the East End of London during the 1920s', Ph.D. thesis (Cambridge, 1984), 270.

remained a major source of communal concern; in November 1939 the Board's Defence Committee authorized an investigation of this phenomenon.[96]

Complaints against Jewish shopkeepers were of several kinds. The greatest friction arose over the vexed question of Sunday trading, a matter that had arisen earlier in the century, but which reached crisis point in London following the passage of the Hairdressers' and Barbers' Shops (Sunday Closing) Act of 1930. The right to be able to trade on Sunday, provided the Jewish Sabbath (roughly sunset Friday to nightfall Saturday) was observed, was highly prized by orthodox immigrants. By the non- or not-so-orthodox, however, the opportunity to trade on Sundays as well as Saturdays had come to be exploited in a most cynical fashion. The 1930 Hairdressers' Act contained a clause, inserted at the behest of the Board of Deputies but in the face of overt opposition from non-Jews, which made special provision for Jewish barbers and hairdressers, who could operate on Sunday if they closed on Saturday; but the Act omitted to provide machinery for the policing of this concession.[97] Abuses of the concession were widespread, and in 1934 the Public Control Committee of the LCC expressed the view that it should be rescinded.[98]

On 6 December 1934 Laski, Janner, and Dr Bernard Homa (1900–91; a member of the Public Control Committee) summoned a meeting of Jewish hairdressers and barbers within the LCC area, in an attempt to put a stop to abuse of the 1930 concession.[99] That meeting was private, but Laski and his colleagues were soon compelled to abandon secrecy in appealing to the hairdressing fraternity to avoid action that Fascists were busy exploiting for their own ends.[100] These appeals appear to have had little effect. By 1935 the hairdressing problem had become subsumed within much wider issues of general Sunday trading, in which Jews were portrayed as a particular class of offender against the Christian

[96] BD E2/150.

[97] BD A/22: Minutes of Meeting, 17 Feb. 1929 (Report of the Law and Parliamentary Committee); and see PRO HO45/13812.

[98] BD E3/115(1): note of interview between B. A. Levinson (Chairman, Law and Parliamentary Committee) and B. H. Gibbens (Public Control Department, LCC), 24 Oct. 1934.

[99] BD E3/115(1).

[100] Ibid.: Secretary, Board of Deputies, to Editor, *East London Observer* (10 Nov. 1932); BD E3/115(2): typescript note of meeting between Laski and others and a deputation of hairdressers and shop assistants, 30 July 1935.

values of British society. The combined pressures generated by shopworkers, retail traders, and latter-day sabbatarians proved irresistible.

In 1936, under the auspices of the Early Closing Association, a Shops (Sunday Trading Restriction) Bill was introduced from the parliamentary back-benches and quickly passed into law; neither the Government nor the Board of Deputies dared to resist it.[101] Although some Jewish MPs (the Liberal Percy Harris and the Labourites George Strauss and Dan Frankel) tried to argue the case for sensible Sunday trading, they did so without much backing from within the Jewish community.[102] Strongly influenced by Bernard Homa, who had warned that action was needed to stem the tide of anti-Jewish feeling, the Board focused exclusively upon the need to protect the interests of those Jews who conscientiously objected on religious grounds to trading on the Jewish Sabbath.[103] For them, the right was maintained to trade on Sundays (but only up to 2 p.m.); doubtful cases could be referred by local authorities to a special 'Jewish Tribunal', serviced and funded by the Board of Deputies but technically appointed by the Home Secretary.[104]

But beyond the special case of Sunday trading, Jewish shopkeepers were subjected to increasing criticism on account of aggressive and innovative sales and marketing techniques for which the generality of non-Jewish retailers was ill-prepared, and which they did not like. The exploitation of 'loss-leaders' (the sale of items at below cost price in order to attract custom), the employment of eye-catching advertising gimmicks, and the abandonment of prices fixed by manufacturers (resale price maintenance) were projected in both the trade and the Fascist press as stereotypical aspects of an unacceptable face of capitalism which Jews were said (explicitly or implicitly) to embody. Laski was also of this view. Addressing a Cardiff audience in October 1933 he blamed Jews who 'by their own conduct fostered anti-Semitism'.[105] The diagnosis was one at

[101] There is a brief history of this measure in the *Report of the Committee of Inquiry into Proposals to Amend the Shops Act*, Cmnd 9376 (London, 1984), 2, 90.

[102] *Commons' Debates*, 5th ser. 308. 2178–93 (21 Feb. 1936); 311. 483–7, 2090–1 (24 Apr., 8 May); *East London Advertiser* (29 Feb. 1936), 3.

[103] BD E3/115(2): Homa to L. L. Cohen (Chairman, Law and Parliamentary Committee), 22 Apr. 1934.

[104] G. Alderman, 'Jews and Sunday Trading in Britain: The Private Control of Public Legislation', *Jewish Law Annual*, 8 (1989), 223–5.

[105] *JC* (20 Oct. 1933), 35.

which other communal leaders were also to arrive. In May 1937, for example, Louis Rabinowitz, Rabbi of the Cricklewood Synagogue, informed Laski that the 'disgraceful attitude' of Jewish traders towards the 1936 Sunday Trading legislation 'forms in my opinion an unanswerable argument in favour of Fascist allegations'.[106]

The theme was one to which Laski was to return again and again during his Presidency of the Board. That it amounted to an exhortation to his fellow Jews to accept—at least temporarily—a second-class status, was a price he was prepared to pay in order to dampen anti-Jewish prejudices. At the St John's Wood (United) Synagogue in May 1939 Laski condemned 'the price-cutting activities of some Jewish traders in the tobacco, grocery, cosmetic, and chemistry [i.e. pharmacy] businesses . . . It was no use replying to these charges by saying that there were non-Jewish price-cutters. He knew there were. But Jews must not trade in this way. Those who did were doing the greatest harm to their people.'[107]

This policy of low profile extended naturally into the housing question, to which there were two aspects. Firstly, the old allegation that Jewish households displaced Gentile families was resurrected as Jews moved into Bethnal Green, Stoke Newington, and Hackney.[108] More than that, it began to acquire the most uncomfortable religious overtones. In Hackney, the changing ratio of Jews to Christians resulted in falling church attendances and eroded church incomes. Jews not only profaned the Christian Sabbath (it was said), by trading on Sundays, but undermined the Christian basis of local society.[109] Secondly, the conduct of Jewish householders and landlords gave additional cause for concern. To the oft-heard charge that Jews were unscrupulous and rapacious landlords a new one was added. Jewish householders were accused, often rightly, of using their residential dwellings for non-residential purposes, as workshops or small factories. What had happened in Stepney and Shoreditch (it was argued) would happen in Stoke Newington, and Stamford Hill: 'our best residential roads are being

[106] BD E3/82(1): Rabinowitz to Laski, 19 May 1937.

[107] *JC* (19 May 1939), 18. For a discussion of the Board's approach to alleged problems in the grocery trade at this time, see M. Freedman, 'Jews in the Society of Britain', in M. Freedman (ed.), *A Minority in Britain* (London, 1955), 214–16.

[108] M. Rose, *The East End of London* (London, 1951), 266.

[109] *Hackney Gazette* (25 Apr. 1934), 5; (4 July), 4; (11 Feb. 1935), 4; BD C6/9/1/3: Memo. by Salomon, 19 Jan. 1937.

ruined by these pests', an 'Old Hackney Inhabitant' argued, because 'good private houses' were turned to industrial purposes.[110] The BUF exploited such hostility to the full during the 1937 LCC elections; BUF speakers were instructed to stress and support the feeling which was known to be widespread that when Jews moved into an area, respectable dwellings were transformed into 'poor unhygienic workshops'.[111]

As new LCC housing estates were brought into commission after the First World War, the severity of the anti-alien housing policy adopted in 1923 became all too real. Its impact was aggravated by the deliberately onerous conditions imposed by the Home Office on those desiring naturalization, more especially during the Home Secretaryship of Joynson-Hicks; although the minimum period of residence before naturalization was five years, in practice it was fifteen years in 1924 (in 1922 it had been twenty-two years), and the bias against 'Slavs, Jews and other races from Central and Eastern parts of Europe' was privately admitted.[112] The effect was 'to delay or deny naturalisation to a very large number of Jews of Russian or Polish origin'.[113] Neither Conservative nor Labour Governments could be persuaded to reduce the naturalization fee of £10.

In the Borough of Stepney by the early 1930s the alien (non-naturalized) population still amounted to 30,000 out of a total population of some 219,000,[114] Most of these foreigners were of course Jewish and, as a result, the Aliens Committee of the Board of Deputies, prompted by Nettie Adler, Morry Davis, and Barnet Janner, began to interest itself in the impact and legality of the LCC's housing policy.[115] Following the Labour take-over of the LCC in 1934, and the election as the new Chairman of its Housing

110 *Hackney Gazette* (14 May 1934), 4.

111 PRO HO144/21063/262–9: Brochure issued by BUF for speakers at LCC elections, Feb. 1937 (Special Branch report, 24 Feb.). I am grateful to my research student Thomas Linehan for drawing this document to my attention.

112 PRO HO45/24765/432156/17: Minute by Sir John Pedder, Permanent Under-Secretary at the Home Office, 28 May 1924. See generally D. Cesarani, 'Anti-Alienism in England after the First World War', *Immigrants & Minorities*, 6 (1987), 14–18.

113 J. M. Ross, 'Naturalization of Jews in England', *TJHSE* 24 (1970–3), 68.

114 *East London Observer* (2 Mar. 1935), 5.

115 BD A26: Minutes of Meeting, 15 Jan., 14 May, 23 July 1933 (Reports of Aliens Committee); see also *East London Observer* (20 Jan. 1933), 6; *JC* (24 Feb. 1933), 14.

and Public Health Committee of the Jew Lewis Silkin (1889–1972), hopes were entertained that the anti-alien housing policy of 1923 would be scrapped.[116] In fact the policy, like that relating to scholarships, remained intact, the London Labour Party being too fearful of a proletarian backlash to contemplate any amelioration.[117] At the Board of Deputies, too, the issue was quietly downgraded as a communal priority. In March 1935, after an unsatisfactory meeting between Silkin and the Stepney Housing Committee, it was left to another Jewish Stepney Councillor, Jacob Fine, to give expression to the immorality of a Labour-controlled LCC applying a Conservative policy on housing discrimination.[118] Fine's motion was carried unanimously. But at County Hall Silkin brushed the Stepney protest aside; Morry Davis kept his mouth firmly shut.[119]

Jewish agitation at the continued existence and application of the LCC's housing policy of 1923 was allowed to subside; after 1935 we hear no more of official or officially inspired efforts to have the policy rescinded.[120] In London's East End, Jewish activists, such as Michael Shapiro and 'Tubby' Rosen, were prominent in the Stepney Tenants' Defence League (formed 1937), whose policy of 'direct action'—especially rent strikes—acquired immense popularity locally, but not with the Board of Deputies.[121] The Board had already made clear its abhorrence of direct action in relation to the BUF. It argued that street confrontations with Fascists merely served to give them publicity, and resulted in situations in which the BUF could argue that Jews sought to protect themselves by denying freedom of speech to others.[122] Additionally, the Board (supported by Chief Rabbi Hertz) wished to avoid at all costs the charge that Jews were enemies of law and order.[123] The Board accordingly urged Jews to stay away from Mosley's planned march through the East End on 4 October 1936. This advice, too, was repudiated at

116 On Lewis Silkin, MP for Peckham 1936–50, and Minister of Town Planning 1945–50 (when he took a peerage) see *JC* (17 May 1972), 36.

117 *East London Observer* (21 July 1934), 5. For papers relating to the continued refusal of the LCC to admit alien Jewish children to its Central Schools, see BD B4/LO2 (Sept. 1938–Jan. 1939).

118 *East London Observer* (2 Mar. 1935), 5.

119 Ibid. (23 Mar. 1935), 5.

120 Ibid. (1 Jan. 1938), 2.

121 P. Piratin, *Our Flag Stays Red* (new edn., London, 1978), 32–49. Shapiro was one of the Communist councillors elected at Stepney in 1945.

122 G. C. Lebzelter, *Political Anti-Semitism in England 1918–1939* (London, 1978), 161–4.

123 *JC* (12 May 1933), 33.

the grass roots. In the summer of 1936 the Jewish Labour Council, which represented Jewish trade unions, socialist societies, and branches of the Bundist Workers' Circle Friendly Society, convened a conference with synagogal bodies, Zionist organs, and other Jewish friendly societies. Thus was formed the Jewish People's Council against Fascism and Anti-Semitism (JPC), the avowed objects of which were to defend 'the Jewish People' against Fascist attacks and, to this end, to co-operate with other anti-Fascist organizations; these included the Communist Party.[124] It was the JPC and its Communist ally which organized the physical blockade which prevented the BUF from marching from the Tower of London to Victoria Park (Hackney) on 4 October, and which were largely responsible for orchestrating the policy of physical confrontation with Fascists throughout 1937 and 1938.

Between those who controlled the Board and the miscellany of groups which had given life to the JPC there existed an inevitable and scarcely disguised antagonism. The policies of the JPC not only ran counter to those of Laski and his colleagues; in creating its own dialogue with local authorities and the Government, the JPC put itself forward as an alternative but authentic Anglo-Jewish voice, and thus threatened to undermine the Board's credibility.[125] The Board welcomed the hasty passage, at the end of 1936, of the Public Order Act, under the terms of which the Metropolitan Police Commissioner was able to ban provocative marches by Fascists until the BUF was itself proscribed in 1940.[126] But the major thrust of the Board's anti-Fascist activities lay in the quite different direction of dealing with what its Defence Committee termed 'the internal causes of antisemitism'.[127]

Laski had accepted the need for a Defence Committee, but in the context of a more systematic effort by the Board to police Anglo-Jewry. In May 1938 a subcommittee, set up at his suggestion on

[124] On the Jewish People's Council (of which A. R. Rollin was the Treasurer) see Lebzelter, *Political Anti-Semitism*, 140–2, 152–3; G. Shimoni, 'The Non-Zionists in Anglo-Jewry, 1937–1948', *JJS* 28 (1986), 93; and T. Kushner, 'Jewish Communists in Twentieth-Century Britain: The Zaidman Collection', *Labour History Review*, 55/2 (Autumn 1990), 67. See also the printed report of the Jewish Labour Council, 26 July 1936, and the pamphlet 'The Jewish People's Council against Fascism and anti-Semitism and the Board of Deputies' [1936] in the Mowshowitch Collection, YIVO Institute, New York, folders 154 and 153 respectively. I cannot endorse the view that the JPC was nothing more than a Communist 'front' organization.

[125] Lebzelter, *Political Anti-Semitism*, 141–2.

[126] Ibid. 130–5.

[127] BD C6/2/6: Defence Committee Memorandum, 1940.

10 December 1936 'to deal with such social conditions as sweatshops, bad employers, landlords and price-cutting in the East End', recommended the establishment of a special committee charged with the duty of enhancing communal awareness of the effect upon the communal image of 'individual malpractices'; in London and the provinces groups were to be established to investigate such cases, 'and to take such steps as may be fitting to check their continuance'.[128] As the Chairman of the Defence Committee, M. G. Liverman, wrote in November 1938:

> I submit that the time has passed for us to pretend that we are a perfect community and to ignore the fact that not a day goes by without anti-Semitism being created by Jews themselves . . . a new generation of unethical Jewish traders are by bankruptcy, due to complete irresponsibility and lack of principle, causing hardship over a wide field and manufacturing anti-Semitism at high pressure.[129]

In the short term, 'Vigilance Committees' were set up, covering both towns and trades, to investigate complaints relating to Jewish landlords, Jewish employers, Jewish refugee immigrants, and Jewish traders, and to try to bring pressure to bear where complaints appeared justified. These efforts were co-ordinated by an adjunct of the Defence Committee, an advisory body which was reconstituted in 1940 as an organization separate from but affiliated to the Board of Deputies, the Trades Advisory Council (TAC). The self-defined remit of the TAC was 'the elimination of friction between Jew and non-Jew in trade and industry'.[130] The deeper significance of its formal inauguration was not commented upon at the time, and has remained unrecognized. By the very fact of its conception, the Board signalled that British Jews were not, after all, just like other British citizens, but that British Jewry did possess—and was obliged to possess—at least some of the characteristics of a state within a state. To this extent the Emancipation was compromised, in the interests of communal safety.

Thus, in a manner which possessed much irony, the establishment of the TAC was a recognition of the enduring sense of Jewish

128 Lebzelter, *Political Anti-Semitism*, 147–8.
129 Ibid. 148.
130 Trades Advisory Council, *Forty Years of Service* (London, 1980).

separatism in Britain.[131] To this extent, the outlook of the established leadership came to have something in common with that of the Zionists: Jews in Britain could never exercise the same freedoms which the British State alleged was the birthright of all its citizens. We should not be surprised, therefore, that the first general secretary of the TAC was the *Poale Zion* activist Maurice Orbach (1902–79) a prominent member of the British section of the World Jewish Congress, as was his friend Noah Barou, the TAC's acting chairman.[132] Both used the TAC as a vehicle from which to launch bitter public attacks upon the wickedness of the Anglo-Jewish business community, so that by the summer of 1942, as the Board became preoccupied with Jewish involvement in the wartime black market, an open split developed between the TAC and the Defence Committee in which it had originated, the latter charging that the activities of the TAC verged upon the counter-productive.[133]

Armed with an appreciation of the internal strains and stresses to which Jews in Britain were subject during the 1930s, we are in a better position to understand two particular features of the Anglo-Jewish experience during that troubled period: the antipathy displayed towards Jewish refugees who managed to gain sanctuary in Britain, and the apparent attraction for many British Jews of Communist ideology.

As to the first, a myth has developed which has only recently begun to be systematically exposed. The treatment of Jewish refugees from Nazism by British Jews was neither uniformly uncritical nor uniformly benevolent. We have already traced the development and impact of a communal policy towards these refugees which resulted and was designed to result in the admission into Britain of a minimum number of Jews and Jewesses, from a

[131] Dr Lebzelter's view, that 'Anglo-Jewry's reaction against anti-Semitism in England [in the 1930s] above all illuminates the effect of successful integration, namely a marked loss in the minority's sense of identity' (Lebzelter, *Political Anti-Semitism*, 153) seems to me very wide of the mark, and to reflect a fundamental misunderstanding of the nature and purpose of communal defence policies at this time.

[132] On Orbach, later MP for East Willesden, see Alderman, *Jewish Community*, 129, 132, 139, 200, and *JC* (4 May 1979), 23; on Barou see Orbach's essay, 'Noah Barou and the Trades Advisory Council', in H. D. Infield (ed.), *Essays in Jewish Sociology, Labour and Co-operation in Memory of Dr Noah Barou 1889–1955* (London, 1962), 31–3.

[133] *JC* (31 July 1942), 8; for a discussion of Jewish involvement in the wartime black market see Kushner, *Persistence of Prejudice*, 119–22.

particular social and economic background, and of a particular age. But however small the number of refugees admitted, their presence and especially their concentration in certain areas, gave rise to a new anti-Semitic agitation. In London this agitation reached a climax at Hampstead, in 1945, where over 2,000 signatures were collected for a petition to Parliament asking that 'aliens . . . be repatriated and that, meanwhile, they . . . be housed in army or prisoner-of-war camps'.[134] The petition received national publicity. It was repudiated by Hampstead Borough Council, but had none the less carried the signature of the mayor.

The agitation in which the Hampstead petition had resulted had a long pre-history. It originated, in part, in a housing shortage which was of course made much worse by wartime conditions. In 1940 the *Hampstead and Highgate Express* had welcomed the policy of internment of aliens as 'a blessing in disguise'; in 1943 and 1944 both this newspaper (whose 'Heathman' column was singularly anti-Semitic) and the Jewish press agreed on the severity of prejudice against the refugees, which was definitely linked to a local housing crisis.[135] In nearby Kilburn in 1944 two local clergymen advocated that the Jewish (and not just the alien) population of the area be limited to 1 per cent of the total.[136] In 1939 only about 15,000 Jewish refugees lived in the boroughs of Hampstead and Hendon; by 1943 a local newspaper was claiming that refugees constituted a quarter of Hampstead's population of 80,000.[137] This claim was undoubtedly an exaggeration. But the very fact of overestimation reflected a local hostility that was as much anti-Jewish as xenophobic in origin, and which, indeed, could be seen at work at all levels of British society during the Second World War, as Jewish evacuees quickly discovered.

For many Jews evacuated from urban areas, as for their hosts in rural areas where few if any Jews had ever been seen before, the experience of evacuation itself constituted an educational exercise of deep and lasting significance. All too often, however, Jews (both adults and children) found themselves the targets of crude abuse and genteel antagonism, which could on occasion be reflected in the

[134] *Hampstead and Highgate Express* (12 Oct. 1945), 1; (2 Nov.), 5.
[135] Ibid. (7 July 1944), 6; *JC* (19 Feb. 1943), 5.
[136] *Kilburn Times* (9 June 1944), 3.
[137] *Hampstead and Highgate Express* (6 Oct. 1939), 1; (29 Oct. 1943), 2.

local press.[138] More generally, anti-Jewish stereotypes abounded—and were permitted to abound—in popular novels and in the press; the opinion was expressed in some 'respectable' quarters that a justification might be offered for at least some of Germany's anti-Jewish policies; the Jews themselves were blamed for the outbreak of war, and they were accused of shirking wartime service.[139] The official Jewish response to developments such as these was weak and defensive. A handbook, in English and German, issued jointly by the Board of Deputies and the German Jewish Aid Committee in January 1939, warned refugees not to make themselves conspicuous, not to talk 'in a loud voice', and not to take any part in political activities.[140] Gordon Liverman privately condemned 'the thoughtless behaviour' of many refugees; in June 1940 the Board's Aliens Committee, on the advice of its Public Relations Officer, went so far as to instruct refugees to spy on one another.[141] It is worth adding that Anglo-Jewish leaders found it all too easy to adopt themselves an anti-Semitic discourse when they blamed refugees for the rise in the incidence of anti-Jewish prejudice. In reporting to the Secretary of the Board of Deputies in 1943 on the situation of Jewish refugees in Cardiff, Otto Schiff enclosed the opinion of a Welsh-Jewish acquaintance lamenting that so many of them were of 'typical continental and Jewish outlook'; most Cardiff Jews, he added, were 'not a very likeable lot'.[142]

Afraid of appearing unpatriotic, most organizations (Jewish and

[138] See generally Kushner, *Persistence of Prejudice*, 65–77.

[139] These subjects are authoritatively and exhaustively treated in Kushner, *Persistence of Prejudice*, especially chs. 3 and 4. In fact, as Dr Kushner demonstrates (p. 123) the number of Jewish men and women in the armed forces during the Second World War amounted to 60,000, or 15% of British Jewry, whereas only 10% of the general population served in this way. Ironically, the most blatant case of anti-Jewish prejudice was the enforced resignation of the Minister of War, Leslie Hore-Belisha (1893–1957), in Jan. 1940: see Alderman, *Jewish Community*, 119, and A. R. Trythell, 'The Downfall of Leslie Hore-Belisha', *Journal of Contemporary History*, 16 (1981), 391–411. In 1951 Hore-Belisha became the first *Sephardi* peer.

[140] *JC* (20 Jan. 1939), 29; Sherman, *Island Refuge*, 219.

[141] BD C2/3/3/10/2: Liverman to Adolph Brotman (Secretary of the Board), 14 May 1940; C2/2/6.

[142] BD C2/2/5/1: Schiff to Brotman, 4 May 1943. See also the letter from Lieutenant E. A. Norman to Morris Waldman (Executive Vice-President of the American Jewish Committee) undated but early 1944, arguing from his own observations that anti-Jewish prejudice in Britain had been exacerbated during the war by the Anglo-Jewish capacity for 'shrewd, aggressive, ostentatious and devious' behaviour, and by 'the noisy showiness of some Jews in public': Morris Waldman Archives, YIVO Institute, New York, box 16.

non-Jewish) concerned with refugees supported the policy of wholesale internment ('Collar the Lot') instituted by Winston Churchill in the spring of 1940; indeed, there is evidence that internment was welcomed in certain prominent Jewish circles.[143] It was most definitely urged, and welcomed, by the *Jewish Chronicle*.[144] In principle, of course, and on grounds of wartime security, internment could not be criticized. But the task of protesting against some of its more absurd and grotesque aspects (such as the incarceration of elderly Jews who had fled from Tsarist Russia, and had never become naturalized) was left to the National Council for Civil Liberties and the Committee for the Protection of Refugee Aliens, from which bodies the Board of Deputies was careful to keep a safe distance.[145]

Two examples, drawn from two very different Jewish communities, reflect something of the common atmosphere of distrust and ill will that greeted Jewish refugees at this time. In May 1940 the Board of Management of the Hendon Synagogue refused to allow a special sermon to be preached to refugees because it did not want 'to encourage gatherings of German people'—even though they were Jews! At the 1940 Annual General Meeting of this synagogue the warden, S. Cohen, berated the community on account of its poor response to appeals for funds to aid the refugees: 'Committees had been set up for the relief of refugees, but the Hendon Synagogue was not represented, because of its fear at the attempt of collection [of money].' Mr Cohen went on to report that, notwithstanding such behaviour, attendances at the synagogue were excellent, but only on account of the presence of refugees.[146]

The Jewish aid organizations pursued a deliberate policy of dispersal of refugees from London.[147] Several thousand went to Scotland, primarily Glasgow, which in 1933 boasted the fourth largest Jewish community in Britain (after London, Manchester, and Leeds), with a resident Jewish population of about 15,000,

[143] Kushner, *Persistence of Prejudice*, 174. On internment see P. Gillman and L. Gillman, *'Collar the Lot'* (London, 1980), and R. Stent, *A Bespattered Page?* (London, 1980).

[144] *JC* (17 May 1940), 10.

[145] Kushner, *Persistence of Prejudice*, 175; some Jews who had been interned in the First World War were interned afresh in the Second.

[146] G. Alderman, *The History of the Hendon Synagogue 1928–1978* (London, 1978), 6–7.

[147] Wasserstein, *Britain and the Jews of Europe*, 92.

over half of whom lived in the notorious slum district known as the Gorbals.[148] There was much unemployment in Glasgow, but little overt Fascist activity. Yet the relationship between resident Jews and German and Austrian Jewish refugees was not good. A writer in the local *Jewish Echo* made unfavourable comparisons between Jews of Polish and Russian origin, who had been proud to maintain their Jewish cultural heritage, and the more recent arrivals from Germany, who, he alleged, despised their Jewish origins and were now spiritually bereft.[149] Some weeks later this theme was repeated in an article in which German and Austrian Jews were castigated for their aloofness.[150]

The reception and settlement of refugee children, who came unaccompanied on the Children's Transports, constituted a particularly painful episode. These children were initially traumatized, of course, by the experience of separation from parents whom (in very many cases) they were never to see again, and by the journeys they had been obliged to undertake to reach Britain. Had they all been found billets in Jewish homes, their sufferings might have been lessened. This could have been accomplished, but the will was lacking. In August 1939, for example, we find the editor of the *Birmingham Jewish Recorder* pleading with his readers to offer hospitality to refugee children, or at least to contribute to their care in a hostel.[151] At the end of December 1943 *Dayan* Dr Isidor Grunfeld (1900–75), of the United Synagogue's *Beth Din*, recalled how in 1938, when the Children's Transports began arriving, Jews who had been only too willing to donate money to refugee causes 'showed themselves very reluctant to take Jewish refugee children into their homes'.[152]

Many Jewish children thus found themselves, at the end of a process which was utterly haphazard, fostered with non-Jewish families, and there can be little doubt that (as Dr Grunfeld recorded) some were lured or lulled into Christianity, while others

[148] R. Kölmel, 'German-Jewish Refugees in Scotland', in K. E. Collins (ed.), *Aspects of Scottish Jewry* (Glasgow, 1987), 58–9; see also *Jewish Year Book*.

[149] *Jewish Echo* [Glasgow] (5 Jan. 1940), 3.

[150] Ibid. (1 Mar. 1940), 3; for similar prejudice in Birmingham see Z. Josephs, *Survivors: Jewish Refugees in Birmingham 1933–1945* (Warley, West Midlands, 1988), 174.

[151] Quoted ibid. 5.

[152] *JC* (31 Dec. 1943), 12. On Grunfeld see ibid. (12 Sept. 1975), 54–5.

were exploited as substitute domestic servants.[153] Some refugee children were fortunate in their billets and in their benefactors. 'Many of the girls and boys', Norman Bentwich later boasted, 'proceeded to the Universities and to other institutions of higher education.'[154] But it is clear that some, of above average intelligence, who could have profited from university education, were denied the opportunity so to do because of an unwillingness on the part of British Jewry to make the necessary funds available, due partly to fear of an anti-Jewish backlash.[155]

German and Austrian Jews with a vocation for the pulpit could find themselves treated by their British co-religionists with a prejudice that compared well with that evinced by British doctors and university teachers towards their German-Jewish refugee counterparts. Consider the letter written by an irate correspondent to the *Jewish Chronicle* in 1942, on learning that a young cleric originating from East Prussia had been appointed Minister at the Brondesbury (United) Synagogue:

> Your readers must have read—as I did—with incredulity and indignation of the appointment which those responsible . . . have thought fit to make at Brondesbury Synagogue. A youth, barely 20, of German nationality . . . is appointed to the ministry of a Synagogue . . . he was, until comparatively recently living in a country which will be, quite properly, abhorrent to all right-thinking people for generations to come.[156]

The target of this outburst was the 21-year-old Immanuel Jakobovits, subsequently Chief Rabbi of the United Hebrew Congregations.

[153] I base these assertions in part on testimony given to me by persons who came on the Children's Transports, including Mrs Clare Barrington and Mrs Paula Hill of London, and the late Mrs Marion Ferguson. The Union of Orthodox Hebrew Congregations later asserted that the placing of Jewish children in non-Jewish homes led to 'Child Estranging': *JC* (7 Jan. 1944), 6; (14 Jan.), 12. But the policy of placing orthodox child refugees only in orthodox homes was itself a subject of controversy within British Jewry, and was rejected by Waley Cohen: M. R. Ford, 'The Arrival of Jewish Refugee Children in England, 1938–1939', *Immigrants & Minorities*, 2 (1983), 147; J. T. Baumel, 'Twice a Refugee: The Jewish Refugee Children in Great Britain during Evacuation, 1939–1943', *JSS* 45 (1983), 177–8. See also M. Berghahn, *Continental Britons* (Oxford, 1988), 113–20.

[154] Bentwich, *They Found Refuge*, 72.

[155] The experience of John Grenville, later a professor at the University of Birmingham, is salutary: Josephs, *Survivors*, 68–9.

[156] *JC* (2 Jan. 1942), 18.

In the immediate post-war period, and aided particularly by the euphoria generated by the re-establishment of the Jewish State so soon after the catastrophe of the Holocaust, there developed within British Jewry a collective amnesia (the guilt of those who survived, perhaps) about the precise nature of its own reaction to news of the Final Solution and to the plight of its Jewish victims. Although the awful truth of the Final Solution was not officially confirmed by the British Government until 17 December 1942, the ultimate aim of Nazism in this regard was widely understood, and the complicity of the German people was a matter of common knowledge.[157] Yet Chief Rabbi Hertz himself, in a talk broadcast on the BBC in April 1942, said that he was prepared to excuse the fact that 'millions of German nationals have all along approved' of Nazi policies; 'punishment', he insisted, 'must be confined to the blood-stained leaders'.[158] Nazism was an unmitigated evil, but one—it was argued—which the Almighty had sent for a purpose as yet unrevealed. According to Rabbi Israel Mattuck of the Liberal Jewish Synagogue, 'Jewish martyrdom had a divine purpose for good'.[159] What this 'good' might be no one was prepared to say; but the tone adopted by some Anglo-Jewish publicists towards the Final Solution bordered (and still borders) upon the apologetic.[160] Thus we encounter the historian and journalist Cecil Roth (1899–1970) declaring to the Cambridge University Jewish Society in May 1942 that the sufferings of the Jews were a test: 'it was necessary for the instrument to be put through the fire before it could be tempered into the finest steel'.[161]

On the most delicate question of possible attempts by the allies to halt the planned destruction of European Jewry, British Jewry was decidedly ambivalent. By 1944 Auschwitz and other death camps

[157] A. Goldman, 'The Resurgence of Antisemitism in Britain during World War II', *JSS* 46 (1984), 43.

[158] J. H. Hertz, *Early and Late: Addresses, Messages and Papers* (Hindhead, 1943), 12.

[159] *JC* (1 Oct. 1943), 12.

[160] One interpretation of the Holocaust still favoured by some orthodox Jews in England is that the virtual destruction of European Jewry was a Divine and well-deserved punishment for defections from orthodoxy: see *Jewish Tribune* (7 Feb. 1991), 6: letter from A. Goldberg.

[161] *JC* (8 May 1942), 11. On Roth see L. P. Gartner, 'Cecil Roth: Historian of Anglo-Jewry', in D. Noy and I. Ben-Ami (eds.), *Studies in the Cultural Life of the Jews in England* (Jerusalem, 1975), 69–86. Roth was by this time already Reader in Post-Biblical Jewish Studies at Oxford.

were within easy range of allied bomber aircraft; on 30 June Weizmann led a delegation from the Jewish Agency to the British Foreign Office, to ask that the railway lines from Budapest to the extermination centre at Birkenau be bombed.[162] The matter was also raised with the Foreign Office by the Board of Deputies the following October.[163] As is well known, Churchill and Foreign Secretary Anthony Eden favoured the plan, but were out-manœuvred by Foreign Office officials on other grounds, stemming partly from the deterioration in relations with the Soviet Union and partly from an official irritation with the problems caused in Palestine and elsewhere by Jews and Jewish preoccupations. The excuses were offered that it was understood that deportations of Hungarian Jews to Auschwitz had come to a halt, and that any attempted bombing of death camps would divert the Allied war effort.[164]

What is important in the context of Anglo-Jewish reaction to the Holocaust is that no pressure of any significance was ever exerted upon the British Government on this question. There were of course numerous appeals to the Government to admit more refugees into Britain, and Palestine, and to grant a measure of British protection to Jewish refugees in neutral countries. There was an impressive gathering at the Albert Hall on 29 October 1942 to protest against Nazi persecution.[165] But in relation to the failure of the British Government to take active steps to rescue European Jewry there was never a mass lobby, or a public demonstration. It was never suggested—at least in any public forum—that the British Government might actually not care very much about the fate of European Jewry. What was suggested was that the patriotic duty of British Jews was to support the war effort, and the priorities associated therewith as laid down by the Government, and that to challenge these priorities was to endanger the good name of the community.[166]

[162] Wasserstein, *Britain and the Jews of Europe*, 309–13; C. Genese, *The Holocaust: Who Are The Guilty?* (Lewes, Sussex, 1988), 118. See generally M. Gilbert, *Auschwitz and the Allies* (London, 1981).

[163] BD C11/7/1/6: note by Brotman, 12 Oct. 1944; and see M. N. Penkower, *The Jews Were Expendable* (Chicago, 1983), 206.

[164] Wasserstein, *Britain and the Jews of Europe*, 308–9, 350–1.

[165] *JC* (6 Nov. 1942), 5.

[166] See letter from Captain Edmund de Rothschild in *JC* (17 Sept. 1943), 5. Anglo-Jewish reactions to the Holocaust are extensively examined in a forthcoming critical monograph by Dr Richard Bolchover.

In March 1944 the *Jewish Chronicle* (now edited by Leopold Greenberg's son, Ivan) carried a report of a remarkable speech made by Chief Rabbi Hertz at a prize-giving at the Finchley Synagogue. Stung by Anglo-Jewry's apparent unwillingness to agitate on behalf of oppressed co-religionists in Europe, Hertz did not mince his words:

> While they were sitting in that hall . . . hundreds of their brethren were being murdered. One feature of that unparallelled tragedy was the general indifference. 'Anglo-Jewry does not know what is going on, and the few who do, do not seem to care much!'[167]

To such behaviour two exceptions need to be recorded. The British Section of the World Jewish Congress did suggest, in a muted way, that the saving of Jewish lives might be elevated into an Allied war aim, and actually petitioned the British Government to authorize air attacks upon the death camps.[168] But the suggestion came in the context of the British Section's Zionist agenda, and was, in any case, bound to lack credibility given the hostility to the WJC by the Board of Deputies. Secondly, there were the efforts of Rabbi Dr Solomon Schonfeld (1912–84), who had succeeded his father as presiding Rabbi of the *Adath Yisroel* Synagogue in North London and of the Union of Orthodox Hebrew Congregations which had grown out of it.[169] Solomon Schonfeld became, in the post-war period, one of the most controversial leaders of rigid anti-Zionist orthodoxy, and a champion of independent orthodox primary and secondary education. He acquired a reputation for cutting corners in the pursuit of his entirely altruistic ends, and for an uncompromising disdain of established communal procedures. In the crisis of the Holocaust these characteristics were entirely consonant with the needs of the hour. He had already, on his own initiative, arranged for 300 Jewish children from Vienna to be brought to England and housed in the two schools of which he was

[167] *JC* (17 Mar. 1944), 11. On 13 Dec. 1942 Hertz had called for a 'Day of Mourning and Fasting'; the *JC* reported that in some districts Jewish shops remained open 'and the stall-holders in the East End made only a pitiful show of complying with official entreaty, compromising with plain duty by observing only a five minutes silence. After that, it was a case of on with the money game!': ibid. (18 Dec. 1942), 8.

[168] Fraenkel, *British Section*, 7.

[169] On Schonfeld see D. Kranzler and G. Hirschler (eds.), *Solomon Schonfeld: His Page in History* (New York, 1982), 19–32.

the Principal.[170] In 1939 he persuaded Chief Rabbi Hertz to establish a Religious Emergency Council, and to appoint him as its Executive Director; the following year he married Hertz's daughter, Judith. On the basis of his official position and his family connections, and by the use of bluffs and stratagems designed to deceive and outwit both the British and the Anglo-Jewish authorities, he succeeded between 1938 and 1948 in rescuing more than 3,700 children and adults, bringing many of them to England as permanent immigrants, contrary to the stated objectives of the older-established Jewish refugee organizations.[171]

In January 1943 Schonfeld found himself at the centre of a controversy surrounding his attempt to mobilize parliamentary support on the issue of rescue work. He had (and was to retain throughout his life) a flair for meeting and making friends with all manner of important and influential non-Jews, and for enlisting them in his many welfare and educational schemes. In December 1942, following confirmation of the Final Solution, he took the initiative in setting up a 'Council of Rescue from Nazi Massacres', and in obtaining the patronage of the Archbishop of Canterbury, Dr William Temple, and the distinguished Independent MP Eleanor Rathbone. No less than 277 Members of Parliament were persuaded to append their names to a Motion calling upon those in control of British Dominions and other possessions to permit the entry of Jewish refugees from Nazism. The impact of the Motion was designed to extend beyond its actual wording, however, since there was some justification for the view that satellites of Nazi Germany, such as Hungary and Romania, would have been encouraged to have afforded some protection from deportation, had they known that territories of the British Empire were willing to take in Jewish refugees.[172]

The Motion was never passed. The Board of Deputies launched against it a spiteful but well-directed campaign, as a result of which MPs were persuaded to sabotage its adoption.[173] The President of

[170] D. Kranzler, *Thy Brother's Blood* (New York, 1987), 13–16.

[171] Ibid. 176–84. The efforts of the British-born businessman and journalist Harry Goodman, Political Secretary of the orthodox and anti-Zionist World *Agudas Israel* Movement, in obtaining 900 visas for Jewish refugees from the Irish and Mexican Governments during the war, also deserve to be recorded: see ibid. 171–5, and Penkower, *Jews were Expendable*, 255.

[172] Kranzler, *Thy Brother's Blood*, 181.

[173] *JC* (29 Jan. 1943), 5: letter from Schonfeld.

the Board was candid enough to defend this action on the grounds that 'the intervention of an unauthorized individual, however well-intentioned, in a situation of this sort, naturally brings confusion and may have damaging effects'. Moreover, he later argued, any internal challenge from within British Jewry to the claim of the Board and its committees to have the exclusive right of audience with the British Government had to be resisted; otherwise there would result 'the diminution of the power of British Jewry to act on behalf of Jews . . . [which] . . . would be a crime against Jewish interests'.[174]

But there was another reason why the Motion was resisted. Schonfeld had omitted Palestine from the list of British-controlled territories named in it. The omission did not stem from Schonfeld's anti-Zionism, but from the need to obtain for the Motion as much parliamentary support as possible.[175] The failure to include the name of Palestine in the Motion incurred the uncompromising wrath of the Board's Zionist lobby, which was now growing considerably in size, and which was soon to effect that which it had not been able to achieve in 1917.

During the late 1930s the position of Zionism as a focus of loyalty within British Jewry had changed radically for the better. The process was gradual, and to pinpoint one moment in time as the watershed is to ignore the permeative quality of what took place. We might point to the 'rare appearance' of Simon Marks at the Board of Deputies in May 1933, to suggest that the temper of the times required the replacement of Neville Laski as President by Chaim Weizmann;[176] or to the election of Lavy Bakstansky as a member of the Board of Deputies in 1934; or to Otto Schiff's failure to be elected as Vice-President of the Board in 1938;[177] or even to the elevation of Selig Brodetsky to the Presidency, in succession to Laski, the following year. These are all important milestones, but there is a danger in focusing too much attention narrowly upon them.

It is beyond contention that the rise of Nazism, the refusal of the British Government to adopt a more generous policy on the

[174] Ibid. (5 Feb. 1943), 6: letter from Prof. Brodetsky; (9 Apr.) 11: speech of Brodetsky in Glasgow.

[175] M. Retter, 'The Setting', in Kranzler and Hirschler, *Schonfeld*, 44.

[176] D. Cesarani, 'The Transformation of Communal Authority in Anglo-Jewry, 1914–1940', in id. (ed.), *Making of Modern Anglo-Jewry*, 127–8.

[177] *JC* (13 Feb. 1938), 9; (20 Feb.), 24, 31.

admission of refugees into Britain, and the professed unwillingness of the communal leadership—certainly as exercised by Laski and Schiff—to mount a challenge to this policy played into Zionist hands. So too did the perceived failure of the Board of Deputies to adopt a more bellicose position *vis-à-vis* domestic Fascism. We have noticed the part played by trade unions, friendly societies, *B'nai B'rith*, and certain Zionist organs in the 1930 Whitechapel by-election, in the implementation of the German boycott in 1933, and in the establishment of the Jewish People's Council in 1936. These were straws in the wind. They were evidence of a growing antipathy towards the then existing communal leadership, a genuine (if limited) revolt at the grass roots against a leadership regarded as weak and passive, if not actually submissive. From this alienation there were two beneficiaries. Communism was one. Zionism was the other.

It was among young people, particularly, that Zionism, like Communism, held an attraction as a vehicle through which mounting anger at the many and varied varieties of appeasement practised by the communal leadership could be expressed, and acted out. During the inter-war period there was much wringing of hands in the community over what was seen as a drift (some said a stampede) of young Jews and Jewesses away from any identification with Jewish communal life. The rabbinical leadership had little doubt either as to the fact of this defection or that its origin lay in the lamentable manner in which religious education had been provided (or rather not provided) for both native and immigrant Jewish youngsters alike at the turn of the century. Rabbi Lerner had drawn the attention of the Federation of Synagogues to this lacuna—and to its long-term implications—as early as 1891,[178] and his concern was confirmed and shared by his successor, Rabbi Meir Tsevi Jung, who spent most of his period of office as Chief Minister of the Federation (1912–21) preoccupied with schemes designed to attract youths and adults alike back into the synagogal framework.[179]

On the eve of his departure to take up a post in Australia, in March 1923, the Reverend Israel Brodie (1895–1979; later Chief Rabbi of the United Hebrew Congregations), complained to the *Jewish Chronicle* that 'if one walked down Whitechapel Road and

[178] G. Alderman, *The Federation of Synagogues 1887–1987* (London, 1987), 31.
[179] Ibid. 47–9.

Commercial Road on a Friday evening and on the Sabbath, one would be surprised at the open breaking and profanation of the Sabbath . . . The great religious problem in the East End is to get hold of the younger generation and try to induce them to show more interest in, and more respect for Judaism.'[180] Brodie drew particular attention to the popularity of 'betting, boxing and gambling'; it was certainly the case that Jewish boys saw in sport, particularly boxing, an avenue to the social status, beyond the world of Jewry, which they felt could not be achieved in other ways.[181] The assessment which Brodie made was endorsed by numerous other contemporary observers of the communal scene: for example, by Anglo-Jewish writers of the period, such as Simon Blumenfeld (*Jew Boy*, 1935, and *Phineas Kahn*, 1937) and Willy Goldman (*East End My Cradle*, 1940); at a *B'nai B'rith* conference on intermarriage in 1931;[182] and by speakers (including Brodetsky) at a joint conference, on 'Problems of Youth', of the *B'nai B'rith* Women's Lodge and the Union of Jewish Women in 1933.[183]

What was true of London was also true in the provinces. Rabbi S. Y. Rabbinowitz of Liverpool observed in 1919 that 'Some . . . of our foreign ignorami [*sic*] think that in England one may do anything . . . that as soon as one crosses the Russian border . . . one is free and excused from everything' pertaining to religious obligation.[184] In Manchester immigrant mothers continued to wear *sheitels* (wigs), but their married daughters shunned what was admittedly religious custom rather than law, on the grounds that it was un-English and repulsive into the bargain.[185] Jewish sports clubs were happy to travel to and play matches with non-Jewish clubs on the Sabbath.[186] Partly—but only partly—as a result of

180 *JC* (16 Feb. 1923), 20, 23.

181 On Anglo-Jewish boxers, 1890–1945, see K. Blady, *The Jewish Boxers Hall of Fame* (New York, 1988), 263–82; see also *JC* Supplement (30 Aug. 1929), pp. v–vii: 'Is Anglo-Jewry Decadent?' by 'A Social Worker'.

182 *JC* (27 Feb. 1931), 14.

183 Ibid. (3 Mar. 1933), 13–14.

184 Quoted in L. P. Gartner, *The Jewish Immigrant in England, 1870–1914* (London, 1960), 195.

185 R. Livshin, 'The Acculturation of the Children of Immigrant Jews in Manchester, 1890–1930', in Cesarani (ed.), *Making of Modern Anglo-Jewry*, 92. For the abandonment of Sabbath observance in Manchester see R. Burman, 'Women in Jewish Religious Life 1880–1930', in J. Obelkevich, L. Roper, and R. Samuel (eds.), *Disciplines of Faith: Studies in Religion, Politics and Patriarchy* (London, 1987), 48–9.

186 Livshin, 'Acculturation', 90; *JC* (9 Jan. 1931), 14.

economic pressure, Sabbath desecration became commonplace. In Leeds there was a similar progression from religious observance to laxity.[187]

Some statistical support for this qualitative data is provided through evidence of declining attendances at part-time religion classes, contained in the reports prepared by the Council (later Central Committee) for Jewish Education.[188] The Council had been established on the proceeds of the Jewish War Memorial Fund (set up to commemorate the Jewish dead of the First World War), and was charged with the duty of co-ordinating and monitoring Jewish education.[189] According to the data which it collected, in 1920 (when it began publishing reports) about 12,000 children attended religion classes in London; by the late 1930s the number had fallen to less than 10,500. Attendances at the once-overfull *Talmud Torahs* of the East End, such as Brick Lane and Redmans Road, had shrunk by around 50 per cent. To some extent the depression was to be blamed for this state of affairs; parents could no longer afford the weekly attendance fees. It was equally true that some contraction in religious activity in the East End was to be expected, given the movement of Jews to the inner and outer suburbs; the *Talmud Torahs* of East and North London declined, but classes associated with suburban synagogues expanded by almost 40 per cent between 1919 and 1938.[190] Nevertheless, it was the view of Herbert Adler, the Council's Director of Jewish Education, that in 1939 only slightly over half of the Jewish children in London were being given some form of formal religious instruction, and just about half in the provincial Jewries.[191]

In 1945 the *Beth Din* of the United Synagogue issued a prohibition aimed at those men who had taken for themselves non-Jewish wives, or wives not converted to Judaism by orthodox rabbinical courts; such men were henceforth banned from membership of congregations acknowledging the authority of the *Beth Din* or, if they already enjoyed such membership, from holding congregational office. In fact, however, there is no evidence of substantial out-marriage during the inter-war period; on the

[187] T. M. Endelman, *Radical Assimilation in English Jewish History 1656–1945* (Bloomington, Ind., 1990), 176.

[188] D. Cesarani, 'The East End of Simon Blumenfeld's *Jew Boy*', *London Journal*, 13 (1987–8), 49.

[189] Lipman, *History*, 219.

[190] Ibid. 218.

[191] Report of the Central Committee for Jewish Education, 1938–9, 24.

contrary, the number of marriages celebrated annually in synagogues increased and the rate of synagogue marriages was remarkably similar to the marriage rate of the general population.[192] The communal Jeremiahs of the inter-war period made the mistake of confusing religious observance with ethnic identity. For many Jews attachment to Zionism provided that sense of Jewish commitment and participation which synagogue attendance and ritual observance no longer satisfied.[193]

British Zionism gained adherents in the 1930s, but at a price: its political and practical aims had to be incorporated within a wider social and cultural framework of activities.[194] To the purists, this accommodation came as a great disappointment, and was regarded as a sign of failure. A writer in the revived *Zionist Review* (which had ceased publication in 1926 but was resurrected in 1934) lamented the fact that many Jews in North London 'simply regard Zionist and other communal work as a relaxation'.[195] But the spread of cultural Zionism, and the opportunities Zionist work offered as an means of expressing Jewish ethnic separatism—and hence also of opposition to a timid and assimilationist leadership—had by the end of the decade made a definite impact upon the internal politics of the United Synagogue. Robert Waley Cohen and his fellow Honorary Officers were compelled to engage in ever more desperate procedural tactics to prevent the United Synagogue Council from affiliating to the Zionist Federation; a younger generation of synagogue Ministers, thoroughly Zionist in outlook, was repeatedly cautioned (though evidently to no effect) and reported to Chief Rabbi Hertz, who was, to Waley Cohen's intense annoyance, inclined to defend them.[196]

Zionism, in short, was becoming fashionable; more than that, it was displacing traditional religious values and Yiddish-based

[192] M. Davis, *Mixed Marriage in Western Jewry* (Jerusalem, 1969), 215. Professor S. Prais and Mrs M. Schmool have calculated that the synagogue marriage rate (9.9%) was higher than that of the general population (7.8%) in the decade 1901–10, almost the same in the following decade (8.2% compared with 8.3%), and slightly higher (8.0% as against 7.8%) in the decade 1921–30; in the following decade the Jewish rate fell to 8.4%, that of the general population rose to 8.8%: S. J. Prais and M. Schmool, 'Statistics of Jewish Marriages in Great Britain: 1901–1965', *JJS* 9 (1967), 151.

[193] D. Cesarani, 'Introduction' to D. Spector, *Volla Volla Jew Boy* (London, 1988), p. viii.

[194] Cesarani, 'Zionism in England', 163–6.

[195] *Zionist Review* (Feb. 1935), 185.

[196] Cesarani, 'Zionism in England', 181.

cultural norms as a major weapon of communal self-identification and self-preservation.[197] Its popularity was most marked among Jewish youth. *Habonim* (The Builders), an anti-assimilationist scout movement founded in 1929, became militantly Zionist; by 1939 it boasted 4,000 members.[198] A merger of the Association of Young Zionist Societies with the University Zionist Council resulted, in 1935, in the establishment of the Federation of Zionist Youth, which exploited sporting links to entice into affiliation a number of nominally non-Zionist groups, and could claim to represent the interests of perhaps 2,500 members.[199] The arrival of young people from Germany and Austria (who, after all, had been admitted to Britain only on condition that they were trained and prepared for re-emigration) stimulated the establishment of agricultural training settlements, to which some English-born Jewish youngsters were also attracted; in 1936 the first ten English 'pioneers', trained in this manner, embarked for Palestine.[200]

The limited but real expansion in the scope and breadth of Zionist activities at local level in the 1930s provided the essential prerequisite for a strategy of permeation at the communal centre of British Jewry, in which Zionists were able to exploit growing dissatisfaction with the leadership in order to overturn it. As Vice-President of the United Synagogue Waley Cohen was in a position to browbeat Zionist leaders of constituent congregations; at the Board of Deputies these local leaders were free to act as they pleased. Morry Davis could deliver the votes of Deputies (of whom there were no less than seventy in 1937) representing Federation Synagogues, the lay heads of which either agreed with his Zionist viewpoint or were obliged to follow his directions as a result of the stranglehold he had by then acquired upon Federation affairs.[201] Under Bakstansky's direction, the Zionist Federation began exert-

[197] Zionism was, indeed, paraded as the answer to assimilation: J. H. Hertz, *Sermons Addresses and Studies*, i (London, 1938), 332–3; I. Cohen, *Jewish Life in Modern Times* (2nd edn., London, 1929), 317–18.

[198] *JC* (6 Jan. 1933), 21; Cesarani, 'Zionism in England', 380; Lipman, *History*, 180.

[199] Cesarani, 'Zionism in England', 395; Lipman, *History*, 180.

[200] *JC* (28 Aug. 1936), 20.

[201] Referring to the support for the WJC which the Federation gave at the Board of Deputies, Neville Laski explained to Felix Warburg that Federation Deputies 'have to vote as their master, the President, dictates for a variety of reasons': Felix Warburg Papers, American Jewish Archives, Cincinnati, 328/11: Laski to Warburg, 26 May 1936.

ing influence in respect both of the election of persons as Deputies and of the election of Deputies to committees of the Board, notably the Palestine Committee.[202] The Zionist Federation itself formed a Board of Deputies Committee in 1936. As a result of the election of Deputies the following year, it could count on the support of around 125 Deputies in the new three-year session. This was only a third of the total number of Deputies (377), but it must be remembered that there was a great deal of absenteeism at Board meetings. There was now a Zionist majority on the Palestine Committee; on the Board itself Zionists and non-Zionists were more evenly matched than ever before.

In that year—1937—relations between the Zionist and non- and anti-Zionist wings of the Board of Deputies reached a crisis point. Following the outbreak of the Arab Revolt in Palestine, the British Government had established a Royal Commission to inquire into the unrest; its recommendation in favour of partition (the creation of a Jewish State and an Arab one, with a corridor from Jerusalem to Jaffa remaining under British rule) was accepted by the British Government, and endorsed by the House of Commons (21 July 1937).[203] The prospect of a partitioned Palestine aroused acute anxieties among Zionists and non-Zionists, but for very different reasons. Weizmann was prepared to accept partition, even though this would have resulted in the creation of a miniscule Jewish state, minus Jerusalem, because the situation in Central and Eastern Europe demanded some form of sovereign territory under Jewish control. The 'Revisionist' Zionists, led by Vladimir Jabotinsky (and which included Ivan Greenberg) rejected what was offered as inadequate.

All but the most left-wing Zionists (who clung still to the idea of a binational Arab-Jewish State) welcomed the notion of Jewish statehood, however. This was precisely why non- and anti-Zionists opposed partition in principle. During the summer of 1937 these groups (represented by Osmond d'Avigdor-Goldsmid, Neville Laski, Lionel Cohen, Robert Waley Cohen, and Lord Reading (Rufus Isaacs)) plotted together, and on 23 November they presented to the Colonial Office a 'Non-Zionist Memorandum'—in effect a definitive repudiation of the idea of Jewish nationality.[204]

[202] Cesarani, 'Zionism in England', 236.
[203] Laqueur, *History of Zionism*, 514–18.
[204] Cesarani, 'Zionism in England', 221–2.

Zionists manœuvred to have the matter brought before the Board's Palestine Committee, where in January 1938 a resolution was carried calling for the establishment in Palestine of a Jewish State as a British Dominion; the full Board endorsed this resolution by 200 votes to 10.[205] Lionel Cohen resigned his position as a Vice-President of the Board; in the ensuing contest for his replacement, Otto Schiff was defeated by the Zionist candidate, the physician Dr Israel Feldman (1888–1981).[206]

On the Board of Deputies the position of the non- and anti-Zionists became increasingly untenable, and was further undermined by the intensification of the Nazi persecutions, the final rejection of the partition of Palestine by Neville Chamberlain's Government in November 1938, and the White Paper of 17 May 1939, in which the Balfour Declaration was abandoned in favour of a policy designed to bring about the creation of an independent Palestine in which Jews would be in a permanent minority. The 1939 White Paper aroused almost universal hostility in Anglo-Jewry; even Robert Waley Cohen was moved to condemn it.[207] Neville Laski had already made his position clear in his book *Jewish Rights and Jewish Wrongs*, published in April 1939, in which he condemned Jewish statehood.[208] Later that year he and his immediate allies on the Board launched a clumsy attempt to suspend its activities for the duration of the war, and run Anglo-Jewry through a small executive committee.[209] The move was bound to fail, not least because it would have placed enormous power in the hands of the Joint Foreign Committee, which was still in existence and on which the Board was compelled to share power with the Anglo-Jewish Association. At the Board meeting held on 19 November 1939 Laski unexpectedly announced his resignation; one month later (17 December) Selig Brodetsky, the child immigrant from the Pale of Settlement, was elected, unopposed, as the Board's first Zionist President. He had attended his first Board meeting, as the representative of the United Synagogue of Leeds, as recently as 15 October.

[205] *JC* (3 Dec. 1937), 36; (10 Dec.), 36–7; (21 Jan. 1938), 8.

[206] Ibid. (25 Feb. 1938), 24; Feldman obtained 127 votes, Schiff 121—a true measure of Zionist strength on the Board at this time.

[207] Henriques, *Waley Cohen*, 369–70.

[208] N. Laski, *Jewish Rights and Jewish Wrongs* (London, 1939), 149–55.

[209] *JC* (17 Nov. 1939), 16; Cesarani, 'Communal Authority', 136.

The victory was as much Bakstansky's as Brodetsky's, and was itself symbolic in two respects. In practical terms it merely confirmed a transfer of power that had already taken place. More importantly, as Dr Shimoni has observed, it 'was not necessarily an accurate gauge of Zionist strength' on the Board.[210] Bakstansky had managed to create a coalition of malcontents, united mainly in their opposition to communal government 'by a clique . . . who have little contact with the masses of Jewry'.[211] During the early years of the war arch-assimilationists such as Anthony de Rothschild and the Conservative MP Louis Gluckstein threatened still to present the Government with a view of Palestine and its future which ran counter to Zionist philosophy. In preparation for the Board's triennial elections in June 1943, Bakstansky and his allies carried to perfection a well-laid plan to 'pack' the Board with their own nominees, often using for this purpose synagogues which had never bothered to apply for Board membership, or whose Board representation did not reflect their full entitlement. On 4 July 1943, at the largest-ever meeting of the Board (339 Deputies attending out of 420 elected), a tightly disciplined Zionist caucus, 'whipped' by Bakstansky, succeeded in dissolving the Joint Foreign Committee—but only by six votes (154 to 148 with 37 abstentions).[212]

Opponents of Zionism retreated to the protective cover of the Anglo-Jewish Association, with which the Board of Deputies conducted a war of words (in private and occasionally in public) until, in April 1947, the Association withdrew its representation on the Board.[213] The social worker Basil Henriques (1890–1961) joined Louis Gluckstein, Sir Jack Brunel Cohen, Rabbi Israel Mattuck, and others in forming the short-lived Jewish Fellowship (7 November 1944–7 November 1948) to uphold 'the principle that the Jews are a religious community' and that there were no grounds 'for forming a Jewish state'.[214] The Fellowship attracted some nominally orthodox Jews, such as Robert Waley Cohen and

[210] Shimoni, 'Selig Brodetsky', 131.

[211] Confidential circular letter, 8 Dec. 1939, quoted ibid. 131.

[212] Ibid.; see also *JC* (9 July 1943), 1, 6. For a hostile but accurate description of Bakstansky's modus operandi see Morris Waldman Archives, YIVO Institute, New York, box 16: Lieutenant E. R. Norman (England) to Waldman, 21 Jan. 1944.

[213] Shimoni, 'Selig Brodetsky', 149.

[214] Ibid. 150; Alderman, *Jewish Community*, 125–6. There is a short appreciation of the Jewish Fellowship in G. Shimoni, 'The Non-Zionists in Anglo-Jewry, 1937–1948', *JJS* 28 (1986), 102–6.

Ewen S. Montagu (then a Vice-President, and from 1954 to 1962 the President of the United Synagogue), and at least one practising orthodox member, Émile Marmorstein. But its guiding lights—principally Henriques and Gluckstein—were leading members of the Liberal Jewish Synagogue. In opposing the re-establishment of the Jewish State they thus made common cause (though on very different grounds, of course) with the ultra-orthodox Jews who also baulked at Israel's Declaration of Independence.

It has been truly said that the proclamation of the State of Israel consoled the Jewish people for the tragedy of the Holocaust. In Britain Zionism itself became, in this immediate post-war period, a central component of the social theology of British Jewry, something to which, on the level of pure emotion, the majority could subscribe without wishing themselves to go on *aliyah*. But we should make careful note of the fact that some of the victories of the Zionist lobby at the Board of Deputies were achieved by the narrowest of margins. And we would be much mistaken in supposing that its triumph at the Board of Deputies reflected its triumph as a mass movement in the purely political sense.

Anti-Zionists like Basil Henriques were genuinely shocked at the spread of Zionism among Jewish youth.[215] Zionist youth groups had been equally shocked at the strength of Communist politics among those whom they hoped to recruit. Between 1930 and 1950 or thereabouts, the hope that *Poale Zion* would act as an effective bridge, over which committed socialists would find their way to Zionism, was fulfilled, but only in a most qualified sense. Even as late as 1946 *Poale Zion* in Britain could boast a membership of only 2,000; in 1943 its membership had stood at just 1,300.[216] These adherents were drawn largely from the lower middle class; the leadership comprised some first generation British-born sons of immigrants, such as Maurice Rosette (subsequently the first Speaker of the Israeli Parliament, or *Knesset*) and the Labour MP Sydney Silverman, and a group of foreign-born socialists, foremost among whom were Schneier Levenberg, who came to England from Russia in 1936, and Berl Locker, who came to London two years later as head of the Political Bureau of the Jewish Agency.[217]

[215] C. Bermant, *The Cousinhood* (London, 1971), 381–2; S. Bunt, *Jewish Youth Work in Britain* (London, 1975), 102–10.

[216] G. Shimoni, 'Poale Zion: A Zionist Transplant in Britain (1905–1945)', in P. Y. Medding (ed.), *Studies in Contemporary Jewry*, ii (Bloomington, Ind., 1986), 254.

[217] Ibid. 251.

Poale Zion acted as a small but powerful pressure group within the British Labour and trade-union movements, and could claim much credit for the fact that opposition to the 1939 White Paper became official Labour Party policy.[218] The Labour Party conference of 1944 took the momentous step of including, in its post-war programme, a policy based on the idea that the Arabs should be 'encouraged to move out [of Palestine] as the Jews move in'.[219] It was at a *Poale Zion* conference in May 1945 that Hugh Dalton announced, on behalf of Labour's National Executive Committee, the party's support for a 'free and prosperous Jewish State in Palestine'.[220] These pronouncements were considered of prime importance at the time, and were cited as bench-marks against which the Labour Government's treachery (announced by Foreign Secretary Ernest Bevin on 13 November 1945), in adhering to the terms of the 1939 White Paper, was measured and wept over by the Anglo-Jewish Left.[221] But *Poale Zion* itself 'was never more than a small component of the Zionist movement', and that movement, even at the end of 1945, had managed to attract the support of—at most—31,000 British Jews: perhaps 7 per cent of the total Jewish population of Britain at that time.[222] To the extent that the bulk of British Jewry voted Labour at the 1945 general election, this was a result of socio-economic considerations: it had very little to do with *Poale Zion*, and probably little to do with Labour's apparent endorsement of Jewish statehood.[223] In particular, the attempts of *Poale Zion* to achieve a mass following in London's East End were uniformly unsuccessful.

This lack of success was attributed to the strength of Communist sympathies.[224] Other Zionist groups also noted the tendency of Jewish working-class people to support Communist politics, and even to join the Communist Party (CP). 'Against a creed which promises economic salvation on an international scale', a writer in the *Young Zionist* observed in 1934, 'the Zionist offer of national

[218] Ibid. 255–6; *JC* (26 May 1939), 28; (8 Mar. 1940), 1, 6.

[219] Ibid. (15 Dec. 1944), 1, 5.

[220] Ibid. (25 May 1945), 1; Shimoni. 'Poale Zion', 257; and see J. Gorny, *The British Labour Movement and Zionism 1917–1948* (London, 1983), 182–4.

[221] Alderman, *Jewish Community*, 128–9; Gorny, *British Labour Movement*, 202–11.

[222] Shimoni, 'Poale Zion', 158–9.

[223] Alderman, *Jewish Community*, 126–7.

[224] See *Zionist Review* (21 Oct. 1938), 17: report of a meeting (chaired by Dr Levenberg) of *Poale Zion* with secretaries of Jewish trade unions.

freedom appears a nebulous and insubstantial thing.'[225] What Barnet Litvinoff has aptly characterized as the 'Jewish infatuation' with Communism in Britain was of strictly limited duration (roughly 1935–55) and sprang from two distinct causes.[226] We can distinguish firstly a number of Jews from middle-class and/or intellectual backgrounds who joined the CP from motives of conviction and idealism: Ivor Montagu, for example, grandson of Samuel Montagu, and Jack Gaster, son of the *Haham*.[227] Secondly, there was a small group of Bundists, congregated together in the Workers' Circle Friendly Society, the membership of which had grown to around 2,500 by 1945; associated with the Workers' Circle was a generation of Jewish Communist trade-union leaders, notably Sam Elsbury (the Russian-born founder of the United Clothing Workers' Union), P. Marks of Leeds (a member of the Cabinet Makers' Alliance and a founder-member of the CP), and Mick Mindel (elected in 1939 as Chairman of the United Ladies' Tailors' Trade Union).[228]

In the mid-1930s this core of CP members was able to achieve a mass Jewish following because the CP alone had taken the BUF seriously from the start, and was prepared to offer a defence (both verbal and physical) of Jewish interests against Fascist attacks which did not rely on a policy of low profile. Communists were seen as people who evinced a genuine and at the same time unpatronizing concern for Jewish needs in London's East End, and who matched words with deeds.[229] In 1937 the political fruits of this concern began to show; Phil Piratin was elected as the lone

[225] *Young Zionist* (Sept. 1934), 3.

[226] B. Litvinoff, *A Peculiar People* (London, 1969), 158.

[227] I. Montagu, *Youngest Son* (London, 1970), 115–18, 338; C. C. Aronsfeld, 'Communists in British Jewry: A Zionist Socialist Analysis', *Jewish Monthly*, 1 (1947), 33. For the attraction of Communism for Jewish 'proletarian' writers in East London at this time, such as Blumenfeld, see K. Worple, *Dockers and Detectives* (London, 1983), 94–118.

[228] H. Srebrnik, 'Communism and Pro-Soviet Feeling among the Jews of East London, 1935–45', *Immigrants & Minorities*, 5 (1986), 287; E. R. Smith, 'East End Tailors, 1918–1939: An Aspect of the Jewish Workers' Struggle', *Jewish Quarterly*, 34/2 (1987), 26–9; E. R. Smith, 'Jews and Politics in the East End of London, 1918–1939', in Cesarani (ed.), *Making of Modern Anglo-Jewry*, 160–2; H. Pelling, *The British Communist Party* (London, 1975), 56–7, 85; Alderman, *Jewish Community*, 116. The activities of the Workers' Circle (formed 1909) are discussed in Kushner, 'Jewish Communists in Twentieth-Century Britain', 68–9.

[229] The prominence of the CP and its ally, the Workers' Circle, in combating the BUF in Manchester is also noteworthy: see B. Williams, *Manchester Jewry: A Pictorial History 1788–1988* (Manchester, 1988), 97.

Communist member of Stepney Borough Council, representing the largely Jewish Spitalfields East ward. In 1945 Piratin was returned to Parliament for Mile End: the distinction of being the last Communist MP thus went to the son of a religious Jewish immigrant.

Britain's wartime alliance with the Soviet Union provided a special opportunity for the spread of Communist propaganda among British Jews; in 1943 the CP established a 'National Jewish Committee', which campaigned vigorously against wartime anti-Semitism in Britain and against Mosley's release from detention.[230] Nationally it seems likely that Jews constituted about a tenth of CP membership—roughly 5,000 out of 50,000.[231] I have estimated elsewhere that about half Piratin's 1945 vote (roughly 2,500, that is) came from Jews, and that in Stepney in 1945 it is possible that as much as a third of the Communist membership was Jewish. In East London Communist fortunes also benefited from the increasingly corrupt and dictatorial rule of Morry Davis, both as President of the Federation of Synagogues and as Labour Leader of Stepney Borough Council.[232] Davis's removal through imprisonment at the end of 1944 dealt a blow to the image of Labour which was temporary, but severe while it lasted. Local Communists reaped a predictable harvest, capturing ten seats on the Borough Council in 1946; seven of these were won by Jewish candidates, and all ten victories were registered in Jewish wards.[233] That same year Jack Gaster was elected as one of the two Communist Councillors on the LCC for the Mile End division.[234]

Writing in 1937 William Zuckerman declared that 'It is not the Jews who make the East End "Red", but the East End, which during the last generation . . . made the Jew "Red"'.[235] Communist

[230] Aronsfeld, 'Communists in British Jewry', 31; H. Srebrnik, 'The British Communist Party's National Jewish Committee and the Fight Against Anti-Semitism During the Second World War', *Immigrants & Minorities*, 8 (1989), 82–96. The high point in Anglo-Jewish adulation of Stalin's Russia came with the visit to Britain, in the autumn of 1943, of the Soviet Yiddishists Itzhak Feffer and Shloime Mikhoels.

[231] Alderman, *Jewish Community*, 118.

[232] Alderman, *London Jewry*, 97–8.

[233] H. Hopkins, 'Painting the East End Red', *John Bull*, 11 (Jan. 1947), 14–16; there were 2 further Jewish Communist victories in by-elections for the Stepney Council in 1947 and 1948: *East London Advertiser* (12 Dec. 1947), 1; (27 Feb. 1948), 1.

[234] Ibid. (18 Jan. 1946), 1.

[235] W. Zuckerman, *The Jew in Revolt* (London, 1937), 74.

sympathy among Jews of that generation had about it some of the qualities of a group identification, a means, perhaps, of ethnic self-assertion.[236] It certainly showed remarkable staying power; as late as 1957 every Communist (four in all) elected to Stepney Borough Council was Jewish.[237] But East London Jewish Communism was rarely able to break out of its Stepney heartland, and when the Jews moved away they frequently lost sight of their Communist youth; Sir Alfred Sherman, who fought for the Communists in the Spanish Civil War, became a journalist on the *Daily Telegraph* and the first Director of the Thatcherite Centre for Policy Studies.[238] In 1950, fighting in a new, amalgamated Stepney division, Piratin lost his seat in Parliament, coming bottom of the poll.[239] Communist representation on the LCC also disappeared. Whatever sentimental attachment Jews might have harboured towards Communism was eroded by news of Soviet anti-Semitism under Stalin and by disenchantment with the realities of East European totalitarianism. Jews were prominent in the mass defections from the CP at the time of the Soviet invasion of Hungary (1956), and there were further rifts following the decision of the USSR and its allies to break off diplomatic relations with Israel in 1967. Leading Jewish intellectuals either left the party or, like Professor Hyman Levy, were expelled.[240]

Surveyed from the perspective of the late 1940s, British Jewry was united neither communally, nor politically, nor socially, nor (as we shall see) religiously. The final bloody years of the Palestine Mandate, from the assassination of Lord Moyne in Cairo (6 November 1944) through the blowing-up of the King David Hotel in Jerusalem (22 July 1946) to the proclamation of the Jewish State (14 May 1948) constituted a period of great anguish for communal leaders, and played a major part in the revival of

[236] H. F. Srebrnik, 'The Jewish Communist Movement in Stepney: Ideological Mobilisation and Political Victories in an East London Borough, 1935–1945', Ph.D. thesis (Birmingham, 1983), 15–18, 230–4.

[237] *JC* (11 Jan. 1957), 9.

[238] *Sunday Times* (4 June 1978), 6.

[239] *East London Advertiser* (3 Mar. 1950), 1.

[240] Alderman, *Jewish Community*, 162. In 1958 Levy (d. 1975; Professor of Mathematics at Imperial College, University of London), produced a short book, *Jews and the National Question*, in which he defended the right of the Jews to remain a distinctive people, and which was adjudged to be anti-Marxist; he was expelled on 30 Mar. See H. Srebrnik, 'British Communism and Left-Wing Jews: The Hyman Levy Affair and the Parting of the Ways', *Eye* (Aug. 1983), 3, 15–16.

Fascism at this time and in a resurgence of anti-Jewish violence.[241] British Jews proclaimed their loyalty to their country of residence but in general supported the efforts of the *Yishuv* to rid itself of British rule. In 1947, in response to Revisionist-inspired military operations against the British Army in Palestine (and specifically the execution by hanging of two British Army sergeants) there were serious outbreaks of anti-Jewish rioting in Liverpool, Glasgow, Manchester, London, and elsewhere.[242] The Labour Party declined to endorse a proposal that anti-Semitism be outlawed, and the House of Commons refused to entertain a Bill to this effect.[243] At the Board of Deputies Neville Laski made an equally fruitless attempt to have Brodetsky removed as President.[244]

The re-establishment of the Jewish State, and its recognition *de jure* by the British Government in April 1950, mark a convenient watershed also in the history of modern British Jewry. A particular feature of the affairs of Anglo-Jewry during the 1940s—certainly as they were perceived both by those who were and by those who were not located at the epicentre of events—was the underlying feeling that the community was badly organized, and even that it was descending into chaos.[245] To some extent this view was an outcome of the multiple frustrations engendered by the Holocaust and British policy in Palestine.[246] But inasmuch as there had grown up a multiplicity of overlapping agencies and committees to deal with refugees and rescue work, a multiplicity of bodies claiming to represent the views of British Jews on matters of communal as well

241 On Mosley's post-war Union Movement, and its impact in East London, see C. T. Husbands, 'East End Racism 1900–1980', *London Journal*, 8 (1982), 14–15, and Skidelsky, *Oswald Mosley*, 490–2, 505–20.

242 *JC* (8 Aug. 1947), 1; S. Temkin, 'Three Centuries of Jewish Life in England, 1656–1956', *American Jewish Yearbook*, 58 (1957), 53; D. Nathan, '1947 The Agony of Anglo-Jewry', *JC* (26 Aug. 1977), 17; Kushner, *Persistence of Prejudice*, 199.

243 Sharf, *British Press*, 203; for evidence of anti-Jewish feeling at this time on the Hackney and Stepney Borough Councils see Alderman, *London Jewry*, 98.

244 *JC* (12 Mar. 1948), 12; Laski had argued that a situation whereby the President of the Board of Deputies was also a member of the Executive of the Jewish Agency—as Brodetsky was—was 'fraught with danger to the Anglo-Jewish Community'.

245 *JC* (4 Feb. 1944), 1, 10: speech of D. I. Sandelson, President of the United Hebrew Congregation of Leeds; for criticism of the training and funding of 'the Jewish civil service' see ibid. (26 Mar. 1943), 5: speech of Neville Laski; and ibid. (7 Jan. 1944), 5.

246 Ibid. (30 July 1943), 9: letter from Israel Feldman.

as Zionist politics, and a multiplicity of fund-raising entities, all competing for a limited amount of potential revenue, there was substance in the allegation that 'faction and discord' were the overriding communal characteristics at this time.[247] Bakstansky's institution of the caucus system at the Board of Deputies was not universally welcomed even by Zionists. Brodetsky warned him in September 1943 that it was bound to compromise the Board's 'representative character', a view endorsed by Ivan Greenberg in the *Jewish Chronicle* the following January.[248]

By the end of the decade there was in fact a multiplicity of Zionist 'groups' on the Board itself, 'a phenomenon as near to a party system as the procedure, functions and history of a purely voluntary body such as the Board allowed'.[249] Zionism, in fact, had not been and was not a unifying force among British Jews; but now that Jewish statehood was a reality, the precise role of Zionism in communal affairs had to be redefined. British Jewry itself was in a state of socio-economic transformation and associated demographic change. Religious pluralism was a fact of life. Lip-service was conventionally paid to the need for communal unity. But there was no agreement even that this ought to be regarded as a priority; an increasing proportion of British Jewry came to regard the promotion and protection of diversity as of higher importance. This conflict, between those who pursued unity and those who championed diversity, was to be the major theme of the history of the Jews in Britain over the next forty years.

[247] *JC* (18 Feb. 1944), 14: letter from Mrs J. Jacobs.

[248] Brodetsky to Bakstansky, 23 Sept. 1943, quoted in Shimoni, 'Selig Brodetsky', 142; *JC* (21 Jan. 1944), 10. See also the discussion in S. A. Cohen, 'Selig Brodetsky and the Ascendancy of Zionism in Anglo-Jewry: Another View of his Role and Achievements', *JJS* 24 (1982), 26–9.

[249] Israel Finestein, 'The Group System at the Board', *Concord* (published by the Jewish Defence Committee) (June 1949), 1–2; see also the critique of the group system by M. G. Liverman in *JC* (26 Dec. 1947), 11.

7
A House Divided

IT is just possible that in the mid-1950s there were as many as 450,000 Jews in Britain. In 1950 the *Jewish Year Book* offered this figure as its estimate of the Jewish population of Great Britain, claiming that Jews then constituted about 0.8 per cent of the total population—the highest proportion in the history of British Jewry. The *Jewish Year Book* computation was derived from estimates calculated by Dr Hannah Neustatter.[1] These estimates were the best then available; the story of their downward revision is itself an object-lesson in the dynamics of communal image defence in the recent past. For many years the overall figure of 450,000 was accepted by communal spokesmen, some of whom were known to further inflate it and to talk about 'half a million' (or more) British Jews.[2] Informed opinion knew very well that there was a need to take account of multiple synagogue membership and—more seriously—that it was most unwise to accept at face value the returns provided by synagogues, which were (and still are) known to use artificially inflated returns for ulterior purposes, such as representation at the Board of Deputies.[3]

In 1968 Professor S. J. Prais and Mrs M. Schmool (respectively the Honorary Consultant to and the Research Officer of a Statistical and Demographic Research Unit which the Board of Deputies had established three years earlier) published revised estimates, based upon adjusted returns of burials and cremations carried out under Jewish auspices. While agreeing with Dr Neustatter that London Jewry was about 280,000 strong, Prais and Schmool put the provincial figure at 130,000 (compared with that of 170,000 given in the *Jewish Year Book*), and so arrived at an

[1] H. Neustatter, 'Demographic and other Statistical Aspects of Anglo-Jewry', in M. Freedman (ed.), *A Minority in Britain* (London, 1955), 74–6.

[2] G. Alderman, 'Tadmit u-metsiyyut be-yahadut britanyah ka-yom' (Hebrew; 'Image and Reality in Contemporary British Jewry'), *Gesher* (Summer 1987), 24.

[3] Such had been one legacy of Bakstansky's policy of 'packing' the Board in 1943.

overall Jewish population of Great Britain of some 410,000.[4] In the early 1980s Dr Barry Kosmin, appointed as the first Executive Director of the Board's Research Unit, completed a fundamental reassessment of the size of British Jewry, using the traditional bench-mark of mortality rates but refining them to take a more systematic account of rates of synagogue affiliation, as well as of age and sex. The revisions of Prais and Schmool had suggested that the size of British Jewry was contracting at a rate of 1.5 per cent per annum. Kosmin and his collaborators put the rate at less than 1 per cent per annum; none the less, they argued that the overall size of British Jewry in the early 1980s was of the order of 354,000, and perhaps as low as 330,000.[5]

Within the Executive Committee of the Board there was an intense debate focused upon the wisdom of releasing this new estimate.[6] The argument was put that the influence of the Board depended upon the perceived size of the community it was supposed to represent. But the academic rigour of Kosmin's computations was strong enough to withstand this onslaught. With a bad grace, the Board's leadership accepted the findings and published them.[7] Undervalued and generally unloved by the community it served, the Research Unit was therefore consistently underfunded. Kosmin sought preferment in the United States, where he became Director of the North American Jewish Data Bank at City University, New York.[8] But his considered judgement, that British Jewry in 1985 comprised no more than about 330,000 persons, was generally accepted.[9]

[4] S. J. Prais and M. Schmool, 'The Size and Structure of the Anglo-Jewish Population, 1960–65', *JJS* 10 (1968), 7–8.

[5] S. Haberman, B. A. Kosmin, and C. Levy, 'The Size and Structure of British Jewry in 1977' (Board of Deputies mimeo., 1983), 4. A more detailed explanation of these findings, by the same authors, was published as 'Mortality Patterns of British Jews 1975–79: Insights and Applications for the Size and Structure of British Jewry', in *Journal of the Royal Statistical Society*, ser. A, 146 (1983), 294–310.

[6] Alderman, 'Tadmit u-metsiyyut', 23–4.

[7] But note the thinly veiled attack on them voiced by the then President of the Board, Labour MP Greville Janner, quoted ibid. 24. See also G. Alderman, 'Anglo-Jewry: The Politics of an Image', *Parliamentary Affairs*, 37 (1984), 161–2.

[8] See my review of S. Waterman and B. Kosmin, *British Jewry in the Eighties* (London, 1986), in the *London Journal*, 14 (1989), 94–5.

[9] Waterman and Kosmin, *British Jewry*, 7; the figure of 330,000 appeared routinely thereafter in the *Jewish Year Book*. The *JC* (6 Sept. 1991), 1, reported that new estimates then being considered by the Board of Deputies' Community Research Unit suggested an Anglo-Jewish population, in 1988, of just 300,000 plus or minus 10,000.

TABLE 7.1. *The Size and Location of British Jewry, 1955–1985*

Area	1955	1985
London	289,000	201,000
Contiguous Home Counties	—	18,000
Manchester	36,000	30,000
Leeds	29,000	14,000
Glasgow	15,000	11,000
Liverpool	9,000	5,000
Birmingham	8,000	6,000
Brighton and Hove	4,500	10,000
Southend	3,500	4,500
Nottingham	2,500	1,000
Newcastle upon Tyne	2,300	1,500
Cardiff	2,300	1,250
Hull	2,000	1,500
Sheffield	1,850	1,000
Belfast	1,800	270
Edinburgh	1,500	1,000
Bournemouth	1,500	3,000
Sunderland	1,500	275
Rest of UK	38,750	19,705
TOTAL	450,000	330,000

Sources: Neustatter in Freeman (ed.), *A Minority in Britain*, 77, 249; Waterman and Kosmin, *British Jewry*, 21, supplemented by *Jewish Year Book*.

Some fundamental features of the demography of British Jewry since the Second World War have attracted a consensus, which is reflected in the material reproduced in Table 7.1. No one seriously doubts that there has been a substantial contraction in the size of British Jewry. Very little of this contraction can be ascribed to emigration. In particular, emigration to Israel has remained small (though high by western European standards); at the end of the 1950s there were less than 3,000 Jews in Israel of British birth, though by 1972, under the impetus of the spur to *aliyah* generated by the Six Day War (1967), the number had more than doubled, and by the end of the following decade (1983) it exceeded 13,000; on the other hand, the 1981 British census revealed the presence in

Britain of just over 7,000 persons of Israeli birth.[10] There has also been a small post-1945 emigration of Jews from Britain to the United States, Australia, South Africa, and particularly Canada (to which over 5,500 British Jews emigrated in the period 1961–81); but it is most unlikely that the total number involved can have exceeded 10,000.[11]

The Anglo-Jewish death rate has remained high as the population has contracted. During the period 1965–9 it averaged 4,751 annually; between 1975 and 1979 the average rose to 4,874; between 1980 and 1983 it fell, slightly, to 4,761.[12] Overall, Anglo-Jewry has failed to reproduce itself in sufficient numbers to make good this shortfall, let alone provide for a net increase in population. During the 1960s an average of 5,100 Jewish children were born in Britain each year. In the 1970s the average was only 4,500, and in the early 1980s less than 3,500.[13] Put another way, the excess of deaths over births was of the order of 400 or so in the later 1970s, and 1,200 in the early 1980s; in 1988 the gap was calculated at 954.[14]

Two explanations can be offered to account for this shortfall. There might have been a collapse of the birth rate. At first sight this seems unlikely. During the period 1965–9 there was an average of 2.4 births per synagogue marriage; this average rose to 2.9 in 1980–2, and in 1989 alone the average was 3.5.[15] This statistic is, however, a crude measurement, since it does not relate each birth to the marriage which produced it. A better measurement is to calculate changes in the fertility ratio, and we are able to do this for three Jewries (Redbridge, Hackney, and Sheffield) from survey data collected by the Board's Research Unit.[16] In the City of Sheffield, in 1971, the ratio was 429 for the entire population, and 439 for the Jews; but by 1975 the Jewish ratio had fallen to 242.[17] In Hackney in 1971 the ratio was 404, whereas in the borough as a whole it was

[10] Waterman and Kosmin, *British Jewry*, 17, 19.

[11] Ibid. 18–19.

[12] B. A. Kosmin and C. Levy, 'Jewish Circumcisions and the Demography of British Jewry 1965–82', *JJS* 27 (1985), 9.

[13] Haberman, Kosmin, and Levy, 'Size and Structure', 5; Waterman and Kosmin, *British Jewry*, 9.

[14] Report of the Community Research Unit of the Board of Deputies, 1989–90, 1.

[15] Ibid.; Kosmin and Levy, 'Jewish Circumcisions', 9.

[16] The fertility ratio is calculated by dividing the total number of children aged 0–4 in a given population by the total number of women aged 15–44.

[17] B. A. Kosmin, M. Bauer, and N. Grizzard, *Steel City Jews* (London, 1976), 15.

437, and even within Hackney's white population it stood at 409.[18] In 1977, in the London Borough of Redbridge, the birth rate was 11.4 per thousand; in England and Wales as a whole it was 12.5; amongst Redbridge Jews it was only 10.1. Between 1967 and 1977 the fertility ratio in England and Wales fell by 29 per cent; in Redbridge the fall was of the order of 17 per cent; amongst Redbridge Jewry the fall was in excess of 31 per cent.[19]

The factors which have led to low fertility rates among British Jews are not to be found in any inability to produce offspring; on the contrary, the Redbridge statistics reflect a very high level of fecundity among Jewish married women compared with national averages for specific marriage cohorts.[20] Limitations in family size appear to have been deliberate, and to have been grounded partly in economic considerations. Even among Hackney's extreme orthodox Jewish populations there is evidence of a trend to later marriages for females—again grounded in economic as well as educational considerations.[21] But the Hackney survey also revealed anecdotal evidence of a greater recourse to contraception among 'ultra-orthodox' women; if this has happened in respect of a Jewish community which is alleged to abide by rabbinical opposition to birth control, how much more likely it is that family planning has been systematically adopted by the mass of British Jews who are not susceptible to fundamentalist influences.[22]

One inevitable consequence of the failure of British Jewry to reproduce itself has been the development of a serious imbalance between the young and the elderly. In the period 1975–9, the proportion of the population of England and Wales aged over 64 was 14.5 per cent, while the economically active population (aged 20 to 64) by whom they were supported comprised 55.7 per cent. Within British Jewry, however, the economically active proportion amounted to 54.7 per cent, but the over-64s accounted for 18.1 per cent.[23] In 1985 the Board of Deputies' Research Unit projected that over the following two decades the elderly population would expand by some 6.4 per cent of the 1985 figure, while the

[18] B. A. Kosmin and N. Grizzard, *Jews in an Inner London Borough (Hackney)* (London, 1975), 16.

[19] Calculated from the figures in B. A. Kosmin, C. Levy, and P. Wigodsky, *The Social Demography of Redbridge Jewry* (London, 1979), 17.

[20] Ibid. 18–19.

[21] Kosmin and Grizzard, *Hackney*, 16–17.

[22] Ibid. 18 n. 2.

[23] Haberman, Kosmin, and Levy, 'Size and Structure', 4.

economically active population would decline from 56 to 49 per cent.[24]

Of far deeper significance in explaining the failure of British Jewry to replace itself since the Second World War has been the decline in the number of synagogue marriages. These reached a peak in the 1940s, when they averaged 2,876, but in the 1950s the average dropped to 2,088; although there was a modest increase in the late 1960s and early 1970s, the number of synagogue marriages fell drastically thereafter, to 1,250 in 1978, 1,075 in 1982, and 1,057 in 1989.[25] This decline is much greater than we should expect even given the contraction of the community as a whole. On the basis of recorded births in the 1950s and 1960s, the number of synagogue marriages contracted by these offspring ought to have been almost twice the actual figures.[26] 'Relevant factors', Drs Kosmin and Waterman argue, 'include civil marriage between Jews, out-marriage with Gentiles, net emigration of young persons, apostasy, and non-marriage or "alternative life-styles". In the two latter cases, the increasing tendency of provincial Jews to settle in London, the most secularized city in the country, may well be an additional factor.'[27]

The strain which an ageing population has placed upon communal welfare agencies is axiomatic. One inevitable result has been to encourage (if not actually force) amalgamation and rationalization.[28] A start was made in 1972, when the Central Council for Jewish Social Service was established to co-ordinate the activities of the Jewish Welfare Board (the renamed Jewish Board of Guardians in London), Norwood Child Care (which had developed on the foundations of the Norwood Jewish Orphanage, founded in 1795), the Jewish Blind Society (established 1819), and the Home and Hospital for Jewish Incurables (founded 1889). The Central Council proved to be a false start, dogged by resistance to

[24] Waterman and Kosmin, *British Jewry*, 15.

[25] S. J. Prais and M. Schmool, 'Statistics of Jewish Marriages in Great Britain: 1901–1965', *JJS* 9 (1967), 154; B. A. Kosmin and S. Waterman, 'Recent Trends in Anglo-Jewish Marriages', *JJS* 28 (1986), 51; Report of the Community Research Unit of the Board of Deputies, 1989–90.

[26] S. J. Prais and M. Schmool, 'Synagogue Marriages in Great Britain: 1966–8', *JJS* 12 (1970), 25; Kosmin and Waterman, 'Recent Trends', 51.

[27] Ibid. 56.

[28] See generally J. Wolkind, *London and Its Jewish Community* (London, 1985), 18–25.

centralization and fear of bureaucratization.[29] But in the 1980s the Ravenswood Foundation, which has an international reputation for the care and treatment of the mentally handicapped, absorbed the Jewish Society for the Mentally Handicapped, while the Jewish Society for Deaf Children was taken over by Norwood Child Care. On 1 January 1990 the Jewish Blind Society formally merged with the Jewish Welfare Board to form Jewish Care, which now constitutes the largest Jewish welfare agency in Britain, providing residential and domiciliary facilities at no less than thirty-three centres in London and the provinces.[30]

It remains to be seen whether Jewish Care is a success, and, if so, whether other, smaller welfare agencies (of which there were still almost one hundred in existence at the end of the 1980s) will be encouraged to forgo the luxury of independence in the interests of economies of scale and elimination of unnecessary duplication. However, the fact that a shrinking community can still sustain so many agencies is not simply a reflection of the longevity of bureaucracies—a hallmark of modern Anglo-Jewry—and of the importance attached to the social status which association with them still brings.[31] It is equally a proof of the fact that British Jewry, taken as a whole, is exceedingly well off. The welfare agencies have adopted an entirely pragmatic approach to the capacity of the State to provide funds for social provision; the philosophy of total self-help has been discarded. Central government now provides around 60 per cent of the operating costs incurred by the Jewish welfare agencies, amounting to about 30 per cent of total income (£6.7 million out of £22.7 million in 1983).[32] The remaining moneys are derived from investments, legacies, the sale of services to those who (or whose relatives) can afford to pay, and fund-raising.

It is true that a handful of individuals feature disproportionately in these fund-raising efforts: the great 'Jewish' charitable foundations, such as Wolfson, Ronson, and Clore, are major contributors to welfare projects, and to educational schemes. In 1983, when Jews accounted for perhaps 0.6 per cent of the total population of

29 S. Brook, *The Club: The Jews of Modern Britain* (London, 1989), 244–5.

30 There is a full list in the 1990 *Jewish Year Book*, 112.

31 J. Moonman, *Anglo-Jewry—An Analysis* (London, 1980), 56–7.

32 Brook, *The Club*, 246; A. A. Kessler, 'Fund-Raising and Finance in the British Jewish Community, 1983', in U. O. Schmelz and S. DellaPergola (eds.), *Papers in Jewish Demography 1985* (Jerusalem, 1989), 397.

the United Kingdom, no less than 15 per cent of the top 200 grant-giving charities were established and operated by Jews, though not all of these necessarily identified with the Jewish community.[33] None the less, in that year the average contribution made annually by individual Jews to communal organizations worked out at £144, compared with only £28 as the average contribution within the general population of the United Kingdom.[34] For most Jews, this contribution, or the major part of it, will have been made in the form of synagogue dues; studies have consistently shown a high rate of post-war synagogue affiliation, which in 1977 stood at 85 per cent of all identifying Jewish households, and at 88 per cent in 1983.[35] Avraham Kessler, of the Economic Research Corporation in Jerusalem, has calculated that in 1983 total Jewish household income in Britain amounted to £1,800 million; on that basis, the income was approximately £5,450 per capita, as against a per capita household income of about £4,200 for the entire population of the United Kingdom.[36] Put another way, British Jewry is roughly 30 per cent wealthier than the general population amongst which it dwells.

This situation is far removed from that which obtained in the inter-war period, and is, of course, directly related to upward social mobility. Jews give disproportionately to communal charities because they are disproportionately represented in the higher social classes, and—consequently—enjoy a higher disposable income. The social pyramid which we observed as the socio-economic model of British Jewry in the mid-nineteenth century has now been turned—roughly speaking—upside down.

The exigencies of wartime evacuation and conscription resulted in the mushrooming of Jewish communities over a wide geographical area. The United Synagogue established 'membership groups' in places such as Amersham, Beaconsfield, Guildford, High Wycombe, Peterborough, St Albans, Staines, Windsor, and Worcester.[37] Other already established provincial communities experienced a temporary

[33] Brook, *The Club*, 246; A. A. Kessler, 'Fund-Raising and Finance in the British Jewish Community, 1983', in U. O. Schmelz and S. DellaPergola (eds.), *Papers in Jewish Demography 1985* (Jerusalem, 1989), 398–9.

[34] Ibid. 399.

[35] Ibid.; Haberman, Kosmin, and Levy, 'Size and Structure', 5.

[36] Kessler, 'Fund-Raising', 401; my Jewish per capita average differs slightly from Kessler's because I use a total Jewish population of 330,000 as the basis of the calculation.

[37] *Jewish Year Book* (1945–6); A. Newman, *The United Synagogue 1870–1970* (London, 1977), 161.

surge in membership, and some rural areas which had never known an organized Jewry found themselves so blessed: Buxton, for example, Hitchin, Ilkley, Letchworth, Newbury, and Penrith. Jewries which had been located in declining industrial and coalfield areas, and which would themselves probably have disappeared in the depression of the 1930s, were temporarily reprieved. In 1934 the office of the Registrar-General listed 310 buildings as registered for Jewish worship; by 1952 this number had increased by over 38 per cent, to a record 428.[38]

By 1970 the number of synagogues in Britain had reduced to 375, and in 1983 to 295 synagogue buildings and 328 congregations.[39] A few of the wartime communities survived and grew—Staines is one such example—but most have disappeared. In addition, there has been a growth in the size of Jewries in certain coastal resorts (in part a function of the ageing population), as Table 7.1 indicates. For the most part, however, the provincial communities have contracted without respite, and as they have done so migration from them to larger surviving centres has tempted those Jewish families who have sought a reasonably vibrant Jewish environment within the same region. There is much truth in the adage that British Jewry is becoming 'a tale of two cities'—London and Manchester. But within these centres, and pre-eminently within the Greater London area, Jews have moved away from the original areas of settlement into the suburbs; wartime bombing helped here, by greatly accelerating a process which, as we have seen, was already well under way in the inter-war period.

Thus by the mid-1980s London's East End (the City of London plus the boroughs of Tower Hamlets and Hackney) which at one time accounted for two-thirds of London Jewry, contained just over one-eighth, while the outer London area accounted for almost 64 per cent. More specifically, five outer London boroughs (Barnet, Brent, and Harrow in the north-west and Enfield and Redbridge in

[38] S. J. Prais, 'Statistical Research: Needs and Prospects', in J. Gould and S. Esh (eds.), *Jewish Life in Modern Britain* (London, 1964), 124.

[39] S. J. Prais, 'Synagogue Statistics and the Jewish Population of Great Britain, 1900–70', *JJS* 14 (1972), 216; Waterman and Kosmin, *British Jewry*, 28. The discrepancy between the number of congregations and the number of buildings is explained by the fact that some congregations can make do without permanent accommodation. By 1990 the number of congregations had increased to 357, partly the result (according to the Community Research Unit of the Board of Deputies) of the proliferation of small orthodox congregations in Manchester and north London.

TABLE 7.2. *The Pattern of Jewish Settlement in London, 1985*

Anglo-Jewry	330,000
London Jewry (GLC area)	201,000
Outer London	127,650
Barnet	48,200
Brent	14,400
Enfield	5,300
Harrow	10,300
Redbridge	19,400
Inner London (LCC area)	73,350
Hackney	19,700
Camden	11,200
Westminster	9,600
Tower Hamlets and City	8,300
London North of the Thames	180,000
London South of the Thames	21,000

Source: Adapted from Waterman and Kosmin, *British Jewry*, 23.

the north-east) came to contain almost half the Jewish population of the capital (see Table 7.2). The pattern has been repeated, albeit on a lesser scale, in other cities. In Leeds, Jews have moved out of The Leylands and Chapeltown into suburban districts such as Moortown and Alwoodley, while in London they have moved beyond the county boundary into areas of south Hertfordshire and south-west Essex.[40] In Greater Manchester and its surrounding districts the bulk of the community is now to be found in the northern and north-western suburbs, such as Prestwich and Whitefield in the Metropolitan Borough of Bury, with lesser concentrations in Salford to the west and in south Manchester, spilling over into parts of neighbouring Cheshire, such as Sale and Gatley.[41] In Glasgow the once great Jewish concentration in the

[40] On Leeds see E. Krausz, *Leeds Jewry* (Cambridge 1964), 24–5, and R. O'Brien, 'The Establishment of the Jewish Minority in Leeds', Ph.D. thesis (Bristol, 1975), 330.

[41] B. Williams, *Manchester Jewry: A Pictorial History 1788–1988* (Manchester, 1988), 115–16; Waterman and Kosmin, *British Jewry*, 27.

Gorbals has disappeared; affluence accelerated the movement of Jews deep into the 'South Side', to Pollockshields, Newlands, Giffnock, and Newton Mearns.[42]

Moving out is a function of moving up, from the ranks of the working classes and the petty bourgeoisie into a more comfortable middle-class existence, but also into a middle-class framework of social reference. Self-perception is as important in this regard as any objective measurement of social-class composition. Even amongst Jews whom sociologists would have no difficulty in classifying as 'working class'—skilled, and not-so-skilled wage-earning manual workers—social habits, and most importantly a desire for home ownership, reflect a yearning for middle-class values which is certainly in part an outcome of a fervent desire for social integration and acceptance; this, in turn, is a function of a deep-seated insecurity which few British Jews would admit to in public. As a result, however, the 'Jewishness' of the Anglo-Jewish working classes 'operates as an element which results in the acquisition of middle class norms by objectively situated working-class Jews'.[43]

A genuine Anglo-Jewish working class has survived into the post-1945 era, but it is exceedingly small by comparison with the situation that obtained even at the outbreak of the Second World War. An examination of the occupations (as given on the death certificates) of a sample of Jews who died in 1961 revealed that Jews who were not members of synagogues, but who had nevertheless been buried under Jewish auspices, were 'found somewhat more frequently in lower social classes'; specifically, only 14 per cent of synagogue members had been engaged in 'partly skilled' occupations, but for non-members the proportion was 22 per cent.[44] The same authors had already reported that a third of non-members lived in East London and 'generally followed working-class occupations', and they concluded that their findings indicated the existence of 'a broad class which may be precluded by financial reasons from joining a synagogue, and which must be expected to have a style of life rather different from the middle-class Jewish stereotype'.[45]

42 Brook, *The Club*, 279–80.

43 J. W. Carrier, 'A Jewish Proletariat', in M. Mindlin and C. Bermant (eds.), *Explorations* (London, 1967), 134.

44 S. J. Prais and M. Schmool, 'The Social Class Structure of Anglo-Jewry, 1961', *JJS* 17 (1975), 9.

45 Prais and Schmool, 'Size and Structure of the Anglo-Jewish Population', 11: a

It is also worth noting that as recently as 1978 the *Jewish Chronicle* reported that the Jews' Free School (relocated at Camden Town, north London) was sometimes called upon 'to buy shoes for children from poverty-stricken families';[46] that the various Jewish welfare agencies routinely provide financial support for an Anglo-Jewish poor; and that Jews in contemporary Britain have been found working in manual occupations as varied as a security guard, a railway guard, a postman, a bus-driver and conductress, and as automobile production workers.[47] Dr Carrier's study of the survival of a Jewish proletariat in East London during the 1960s found that it was (so to speak) alive and well, located in blocks of council flats.[48] This picture was supported by the Board of Deputies' Hackney survey a decade or so later, which showed that about 40 per cent of Hackney Jewry lived in less than desirable council estates and industrial dwellings, and that Jewish women in that locality formed a significant segment of the semi-skilled workforce.[49]

Working-class Jews are certainly not confined to the older districts of settlement, and Jews with non-manual and professional occupations are to be found in what used to be thought of as declining inner-city areas.[50] But working-class Jews exhibit characteristics very different from those of working-class non-Jews; 'the intimacy of the card table is preferred to the bingo hall, the living room to the pub.'[51] In his study of the Jews of Edgware (now part of the London Borough of Barnet), Professor Ernest Krausz

substantial proportion of these non-members comprised pensioners, the chronically ill, and persons in receipt of national assistance. The estimate made by these authors, that non-members represented 39% of the Jewish population, must be regarded as excessive in view of more recent research (see n. 23 above).

[46] *JC* (31 Mar. 1978), 22.

[47] H. Pollins, *Economic History of the Jews in England* (London, 1982), 214–15. As a member of the North London Defence Sub-Committee of the Board of Deputies in the early 1970s I had to deal with employment problems encountered by an orthodox Jewish bus-driver; a first cousin of my mother was a bus-conductress; my sister's father-in-law is a security guard.

[48] Carrier, 'A Jewish Proletariat', 120–40.

[49] Kosmin and Grizzard, *Hackney*, 29–30.

[50] For evidence of Jewish professionals and managers still living in Chapeltown, Leeds, in 1979, see N. Grizzard and P. Raisman, 'Inner City Jews in Leeds', *JJS* 22 (1980), 26.

[51] B. A. Kosmin and D. J. de Lange, 'Conflicting Urban Ideologies: London's New Towns and the Metropolitan Preference of London's Jews', *London Journal*, 6 (1980), 169.

showed that although Edgware Jewry in the early 1960s was thoroughly working class in origin (53 per cent of his sample having been born in London's East End), over 80 per cent regarded themselves as belonging to the middle class, while only just over 8 per cent said they belonged to the working class.[52]

From the point of view of occupation, however, Jewish men in Edgware were to be found predominantly in the professional, managerial, skilled, and self-employed groups—the exact opposite of the picture for the general population of the district.[53] The trend illuminated by Professor Krausz has been confirmed by both aggregate analysis and other surveys carried out since his work was completed. Estimates prepared by Professor Prais and Mrs Schmool of the social-class structure of Anglo-Jewry in 1961 emphasized the tendency for British Jews to be found among the higher social classes (see Table 7.3). Their work suggested that in the early 1960s over 40 per cent of Anglo-Jewry was located in the upper two social classes, whereas these categories accounted for less than 20 per cent of the general population.

The survey of Sheffield Jewry carried out by the Board of Deputies' Research Unit in 1974 demonstrated that over half the male sample fell within the categories of employers, managers, professional, and middle-ranking non-manual workers, compared with less than one-fifth in the City of Sheffield as a whole.[54] The Research Unit's Hackney survey (1974–5) put about a third of the economically active Jewish sample in these categories; in the general working population of the borough as a whole only 12 per cent were within these groups.[55] The analysis of Redbridge Jewry, carried out in the winter of 1977–8, showed that no less than 70 per cent of the Jews there belonged to the professional, managerial, and skilled non-manual occupational classes; for all economically active males in the borough the proportion was about 50 per cent.[56]

52 E. Krausz, 'A Sociological Field Study of Jewish Suburban Life in Edgware 1962–63 with special reference to Minority Identification', Ph.D. thesis (London, 1965), 93, 103. A few years later a similar pattern of response was found among Jews in Hackney: J. W. Carrier, 'Working Class Jews in Present-Day London: A Sociological Study', M.Phil. thesis (London, 1969), 346.

53 Krausz, 'A Sociological Field Study', 67.

54 Kosmin, Bauer, and Grizzard, *Steel City Jews*, 22.

55 Kosmin and Grizzard, *Hackney*, 27.

56 Waterman and Kosmin, *British Jewry*, 44.

TABLE 7.3. *Estimated Social-Class Distribution of the Live Jewish Population, 1961*

Social class	Population distribution	
	Jews %	General %
I Professional	10	4
II Intermediate	34	15
III Skilled	36	49
IV Partly Skilled	10	19
V Unskilled	—	8
Other	8	5

Source: S. J. Prais and M. Schmool, 'The Social-Class Structure of Anglo-Jewry, 1961', *JJS* 17 (1975), 11.

Throughout Greater London it seems that Jews in the 1970s were roughly twice as numerous as non-Jews in these socio-economic groups. It is also worth noting the heavy representation of Jews in self-employed occupation: 55 per cent of Edgware Jewish males were found to be self-employed, 44 per cent in Sheffield, 34 per cent in Redbridge, and 21 per cent in Hackney; in Great Britain as a whole the 1971 census placed less than 8 per cent of the economically active population in this category.[57] A survey of Glasgow Jewry carried out in the mid-1970s found that 81 per cent of Jewish males living in Newton Mearns were self-employed; this contrasted with just 28 per cent of non-Jewish men.[58]

Within the category of self-employment, Jews in post-war Britain are biased heavily towards the running of small firms, the management of shops, and of modest manufacturing enterprises: in short, the securing and maintenance of 'an economic independence that has the appearance of control of destiny . . . [and which] represents the security of personal decision-making'.[59] 'The "typical" Jewish business', Dr Pollins reminds us, is now the small firm, manufacturing or distributing products such as foodstuffs, timber, plastics, jewellery, leather goods, footwear, and clothing.[60] The

57 Waterman and Kosmin, *British Jewry*, 44.
58 Brook, *The Club*, 286, referring to the research of Tova Benski.
59 Kosmin and de Lange, 'Conflicting Urban Ideologies', 169–70.
60 Pollins, *Economic History*, 219–20.

large, nationally known Jewish-owned distribution chains, such as the Dixons Group (the electrical retailers of which Stanley Kalms, the former Chairman of Jews' College, is the head) and Lex Service (the garage chain and transport conglomerate directed by Trevor Chinn, a Governor of the Jewish Agency), and the Jewish-controlled property empires, such as the Freshwater Group and the pyramid of companies run by the Berger family, are, despite their size, very much the exceptions to the rule.[61]

Jews are also attracted by occupations such as market trading and taxi-driving; it has been estimated that perhaps as many as one third of taxi-drivers in London are Jewish.[62] Contemporary British Jewry is also over-represented in some professions, notably law, medicine, dentistry, pharmacy, estate agency, accountancy, and higher education.[63] This reflects the importance placed by Jewish parents in the immediate post-war years on encouraging their able children to take full advantage of educational opportunities made available under the 1944 Education Act. Professor Krausz found that a quarter of Jewish children in Edgware aged 15 and over were attending universities or colleges, that another 13 per cent were preparing to do so, and that the common parental expectation was that their children would progress through the educational system until at least the age of 21.[64]

The demonstrable upward social mobility of British Jewry has played a central role in its movement away from Labour and towards Conservative politics. At the moment of Labour's victory in the 1945 general election this development scarcely seemed credible. In 1945 Labour was the party towards which Jews with political ambitions naturally gravitated. Of the twenty-eight Jews—a record—elected to Parliament in 1945, no less than twenty-six took the Labour whip; of the remaining two one was the Communist Piratin, the other the rebel Conservative Lipson. We have already seen how the love affair between Jews and Communism turned sour. Daniel Lipson's presence in the House of Commons from 1937 to 1950 was a potent reminder of the strength of anti-Jewish prejudice then to be found in the Conservative Party.

[61] On Jews in the property business see ibid. 227–30.
[62] Ibid. 216; Waterman and Kosmin, *British Jewry*, 44.
[63] Pollins, *Economic History*, 234–5.
[64] E. Krausz, 'The Edgware Survey: Occupation and Social Class', *JJS* 11 (1969), 75.

Official Conservative MPs who were Jewish did not reappear at Westminster until 1955, when Sir Henry d'Avigdor Goldsmid (1909–76) was returned for Walsall South; the following year he was joined by Sir Keith (now Lord) Joseph (b. 1918), elected for Leeds North-East. Sir Henry and Sir Keith had both been educated at Harrow and Oxford; neither was remotely typical of British Jewry.[65]

In due course Sir Keith was to play a central role in alerting his party colleagues to the advantages to be gained from harnessing the power of the Jewish vote for the Conservative cause. But in the 1950s the hostility with which sections of the party regarded Jews was still strong, and had indeed been reinforced by the popular anti-Semitism that had accompanied the collapse of the Palestine Mandate. The only Member of Parliament to have been interned during the Second World War was the Conservative anti-Semite A. H. M. Ramsay, and in 1950 (no doubt with Ramsay as well as the embarrassment of Lipson very much in mind) the party's Standing Advisory Committee on Candidates took the extreme step of vetoing the local choice of Andrew Fountaine as the candidate at Chorley, Lancashire, on the grounds of Fountaine's attitude to Jews.[66] It is also worth recalling that those who led the Conservative Party at the time of the Suez crisis (1956) were not friends of Israel, and that the mood of the party as a whole, if it was anti-Egyptian, was certainly not pro-Israeli.[67]

It must also be emphasized that although anti-Jewish prejudice was rampant in some Conservative associations in rural areas, it was by no means confined to the countryside.[68] In post-war Britain the most blatant example has come from Finchley (now part of the London Borough of Barnet). At the local borough council elections of 1957 Liberals alleged that the Finchley Golf Club, 'officered by prominent Conservatives', was implementing a policy of excluding

[65] G. Alderman, 'Converts to the Vision in True Blue', *Times Higher Education Supplement* (10 July 1987), 15.

[66] On Ramsay see G. Alderman, *The Jewish Community in British Politics* (Oxford, 1983), 120; on Fountaine see A. Ranney, *Pathways to Parliament* (London, 1965), 42–8.

[67] L. D. Epstein, *British Politics in the Suez Crisis* (London, 1964), 176–8.

[68] G. Alderman, 'Changing Political Allegiances', in J. M. Merrick (ed.), *The Lit. At Home: A Celebration of the Centenary of the Edinburgh Jewish Literary Society 1888–1988* (Edinburgh, 1988), 34.

Jews from membership.[69] The allegations turned out to be true and they were followed, three years later, by revelations of Jewish quotas operated by other golf clubs, in such prominently Jewish areas as Hendon and Stanmore.[70] These events were subsequently held to have been responsible for a swing of Jewish voters away from the Conservative Party and towards the Liberals. There is some statistical support for this view, and it is also the case that Liberals did well in Jewish wards. In 1957 there had not been one Liberal member of Finchley Council. By the time of the 1959 general election there were seven (all elected at the expense of the Conservatives), and at the 1963 local polls the Liberals advanced still further, winning nineteen of the twenty-four council seats; six of the nineteen, including the new Mayor and Deputy Mayor, were Jews.[71] These Liberal victories were essentially the result of protest votes, and they owed something to the national Liberal revival at this time. None the less, their relationship to Jewish sensitivities could not be ignored. When the young Mrs Thatcher was first elected as MP for Finchley, in 1959, she quickly embarked on a pro-Jewish policy from which—in broad terms—she rarely deviated.

At the general election of 1945 only eight of the thirty-four Jewish Labour candidates failed to secure election, whereas all five official Jewish Conservatives and all sixteen Jewish Liberals had been defeated; indeed, the 1945 contest was the first since the Emancipation at which no Jewish Liberals were returned. The evidence of the fate of parliamentary candidates, therefore, points to a very strong attachment on the part of British Jewry to the Labour Party. But the situation in reality was not nearly as straightforward as this parliamentary analysis might suggest. The vast majority of constituencies where Jews were to be found in large numbers had indeed all returned Labour MPs.[72] This did not mean that all or nearly all Jews had voted Labour.

[69] B. Donoghue, 'Finchley', in D. E. Butler and A. King, *The British General Election of 1964* (London, 1965), 241–53; *JC* (3 May 1957), 10. See also BD C6/1/2/5: Minutes of the Metropolitan Area Committee of the Defence Committee, 10 July 1957.

[70] *Hendon Times* (1 Apr. 1960), 6.

[71] Donoghue, 'Finchley', 250–2; R. W. Johnson, 'Is This Successful Management?', *London Review of Books* (20 Apr. 1989), 3.

[72] The 2 seats at Bethnal Green, the 3 at Hackney, 2 of the 3 at Stepney, the Stoke Newington seat, the 2 seats at Ilford, Central and North-East Leeds, North Salford, South Tottenham, the 2 Walthamstow seats, the 2 at Wembley, the 2 at Willesden, and Glasgow Gorbals.

Evidence relating to the make-up of Anglo-Jewish political preferences at this time is largely qualitative. In 1947 the research unit of the Jewish Fellowship conducted a wide-ranging survey of 40,000 Jews; 22.5 per cent of the respondents identified themselves as Conservative supporters, 33.1 per cent as Liberals, 32.9 per cent as Labour supporters or 'socialists', and 2.3 per cent as Communists.[73] These percentages, as indications of any overall pattern, must be treated with a great deal of scepticism, because the number of respondents who answered the question dealing with party preferences amounted to less than 8 per cent of those to whom the questionnaire was sent. What is important, however, is that even in 1947 Jews were fully prepared to identify themselves as Conservative supporters. In 1964 a much more reliable survey was carried out by Dr Bernard (now Lord) Donoghue in the Finchley constituency. In a random sample of 130 electors, two-fifths voted Conservative and only one-fifth Labour; in 1959 the ratio had been three Conservative votes for every one cast for each of the Liberal and Labour Parties.[74]

The survival and careful nurturing of a tradition of Jewish support for the Conservative Party was to pay handsome dividends in the outer-suburban areas of the large conurbations. In London this tradition had remained intact during the inter-war period; to the Toryism of the established Jewish gentry was added the Toryism of the Jewish *nouveaux riches*.[75] Even in an area as strongly working class as Hackney had become by the 1950s, Jews could be found standing as Conservatives: five Jews stood in the Conservative interest in the Hackney Borough Council elections of 1953.[76] In the following year a Jew secured election as a Conservative in the Cricklewood ward of Willesden, then an area of expanding Jewish settlement in north-west London. A Jew was elected as Mayor of Richmond-upon-Thames in 1930 and 1946, another became Mayor of Hendon in 1950, and yet another served

[73] *JC* (2 Sept. 1949), 9.

[74] Donoghue, 'Finchley', 251.

[75] G. Alderman, *London Jewry and London Politics, 1889–1986* (London, 1989), 107–8. For some discussion of Jewish Conservatism in inter-war Stepney, see E. R. Smith, 'Jews and Politics in the East End of London, 1918–1939', in D. Cesarani (ed.), *The Making of Modern Anglo-Jewry* (Oxford, 1990), 145–6.

[76] *JC* (1 May 1953), 25; (25 May), 11: out of a total of 51 Jews elected to London borough councils in 1953, no less than 12 were Conservatives.

as Mayor of Finchley in 1952–3; all were Conservatives.[77] It is also worth observing that at the 1945 general election there were a few constituencies, already heavily populated with Jews, which were held by the Conservatives: Hendon South, Finchley, Leeds North, and Middleton & Prestwich (north Manchester). Significantly, these were all marginal seats situated in outer suburbs.

During the 1950s and 1960s two quite separate but complementary processes eroded the foundations of the inter-war alliance between Anglo-Jewry and Labour. One, to which we have already referred, was sociological and demographic. The other was political, grounded in developing Labour attitudes towards Zionism and the State of Israel. The decision (announced in November 1945) of the Labour Foreign Secretary, Ernest Bevin, to uphold the terms of the 1939 White Paper was greeted with profound dismay in Anglo-Jewish circles; the sense of shock was compounded by the evident helplessness of the Jewish Labour MPs, few of whom proved willing to step out of line and publicly oppose government policy. In April 1946 only six Jewish Labour MPs, 'after desperate "lobbying" by the Poale Zion', could be persuaded to venture even the slightest parliamentary opposition to Ernest Bevin's Palestine policy.[78] Some Jewish Labour supporters hoped that, with Bevin's death (1951) and the State of Israel a fact of life, relations between the Labour Party and British Jews could be restored to something like their former level. But the Suez affair thwarted efforts at reconciliation, the more so because Labour was then out of office, and so could not plead the burdens of government in defence of its attitude towards Israel.

Within Anglo-Jewry (and judging by the many communal gatherings held in October and November 1956) there was general unanimity that Israel had been justified in attacking Egypt in order to bring to an end years of terrorist incursions across the Gaza Strip; the Israeli conquest of Sinai was a further source of pride.[79] The seventeen Jewish Labour MPs returned in the 1955 election were therefore expected to support Israel's position. This expectation was natural but most naïve. All seventeen obeyed the three-line whip and voted against Anthony Eden's Conservative Government

[77] *JC* (15 Nov. 1946), 15; (24 Mar. 1950), 6; (21 Mar. 1952), 7; *Richmond Herald* (14 Nov. 1931), 10; (3 Nov. 1934), 6; (16 Nov. 1946), 4.

[78] *JC* (26 Apr. 1946), 5.

[79] See Alderman, *Jewish Community*, 131–2.

on 1 November 1956, and all but one (Emanuel Shinwell, then in Australia) behaved similarly a week later.[80] On 30 October, in an unexpected division that had not carried a three-line whip, seven Jewish Labour MPs had abstained; of these only Shinwell and Harold Lever (who sat for Manchester Cheetham) made it clear that their abstentions had been deliberate.[81]

The standard response of Jewish Labour MPs to criticism from the community was to state that in Parliament they represented their constituents, not their fellow Jews.[82] This was constitutionally correct, but was widely regarded within the community as little more than an excuse. The failure of Maurice Orbach, elected MP for East Willesden in 1945, to even accidentally abstain caused deep resentment, and was certainly a factor in his defeat there at the 1959 general election.[83] The failure of Barnett Janner to abstain became a communal scandal.[84] Janner had been elected Labour MP for North-West Leicester in 1945; in 1955 he had become President of the Board of Deputies, and by 1956 he was also President of the Zionist Federation. He supported the official Labour Party position, but at the same time refused to resign his communal offices. On 18 November 1956 he won, by a large majority, a vote of confidence at the Board of Deputies: an indication of the extent to which the caucus machinery so delicately cultivated by Bakstansky had fallen into disrepair once the Jewish State had been re-established. In any case, any sanction against Janner would probably have been a breach of parliamentary privilege.[85] But the affair, particularly in view of his past wooing of Jewish voters, did him little credit, and the fact that he had put party considerations before Jewish commitment did his reputation irreparable harm.

But of more fundamental significance for the future relationship between Jews and the Labour Party was the attitude of Clement Attlee's successor as Labour Leader, Hugh Gaitskell. Gaitskell's previous record had been that of a friend to Israel. At the time of Suez, however, he likened the British Prime Minister, Anthony Eden, to a policeman who had determined 'to go in and help the

[80] *JC* (9 Nov. 1956), 8; Epstein, *Suez Crisis*, 188–9.
[81] Alderman, *Jewish Community*, 132.
[82] This had been Ian Mikardo's defence of his obedience to the Labour whip: *JC* (16 Nov. 1956), 1.
[83] Alderman, *Jewish Community*, 133, 139–41.
[84] Ibid. 132; E. Janner, *Barnett Janner* (London, 1984), 135–7.
[85] Epstein, *Suez Crisis*, 195; *JC* (16 Nov. 1956), 1; (23 Nov.), 1.

burglar [i.e. Israel] shoot the householder [Egypt]'.[86] This comparison was neither easily nor quickly forgiven, and it had certainly not been forgotten by the time of the Six Day War (1967), when the Labour Government of Harold Wilson (again regarded as a good friend of Israel hitherto) went to great lengths to distance itself from Israeli policy.

It is generally recognized that the Six Day War marked an ominous turning-point in the history of left-wing anti-Semitism in Britain.[87] Israel's Arab neighbours had never accepted the re-creation of a Jewish State in part of the realm of Islam, and had thus never accepted the partition of mandated Palestine in 1948. Gaza had been occupied since then by Egypt, while East Jerusalem, and the provinces of Judea and Samaria, on the West Bank of the River Jordan, had been annexed by the Hashemite Kingdom of Transjordan; in this way the Arabs had themselves deliberately prevented the creation of a Palestinian Arab state in just these territories, hoping that in time the Jewish State might be destroyed. With the capture of Gaza and East Jerusalem, Judea and Samaria, Israel—till then the underdog of the Middle East—could henceforth be regarded as an imperialist, colonial power, ruling by force of arms over a downtrodden Palestinian-Arab population.

This aspect of Israeli policy can of course be criticized without questioning the legitimacy of the Jewish State or the justice of its re-establishment; many Jewish citizens of Israel have done so over the past two decades. However, elements of the left in Britain (as elsewhere in western Europe) used the events of 1967 as an excuse to attack the very fact of Israel's existence and, by scarcely concealed implication, the entire basis of the movement for Jewish self-determination. The force of this attack was made all the greater by the resolution of the General Assembly of the United Nations (10 November 1975) equating Zionism with racism. Those who supported the Zionist cause could henceforth be branded as racists, and racism could be portrayed as part of a new 'world Jewish conspiracy' that was already alleged to embrace capitalism and imperialism.[88]

[86] This remark, made in the House of Commons on 3 Nov. 1956, is quoted in Epstein, *Suez Crisis*, 192.

[87] On the origins and development of modern left-wing anti-Semitism in Britain see S. Cohen, *That's Funny You Don't Look Anti-Semitic* (Leeds, 1984).

[88] Ibid. 38–49.

By the time of the Yom Kippur War (October 1973) Zionism had ceased to be a matter of contention within Anglo-Jewry. Actual emigration to Israel ran at between 500 and 1,000 persons a year, mainly of young people or those in early middle age; most British Jews have been deterred from undertaking *aliyah* through material and practical considerations.[89] None the less, a survey of Jewish adults conducted by National Opinion Polls in 1970 showed that 80 per cent supported the idea of a Jewish state.[90] In Newton Mearns, a survey conducted in 1973–4 found that Zionism 'seems to be the new focal point of Jewish identity'.[91] The 1978 Redbridge survey concluded that 'support for Israel is a given fact'.[92] Attacks upon the legitimacy of the Jewish State are now routinely regarded as anti-Semitic. In consequence, however vigorously left-wing anti-Zionists deny that their motives are in any way anti-Jewish, the reaction of Anglo-Jewry has been and is one of scepticism and disbelief.

Following Labour's defeat at the general election of 1979, the 'hard'—or 'outside'—left began to make very significant inroads into the machinery of Labour policy-making at all levels. The Israeli invasion of the Lebanon in 1982 whipped the anti-Zionism of the left to fever pitch. In May 1982 the Labour Party's National Executive Committee, which had already endorsed Palestinian-Arab self-determination and urged participation of the PLO in peace talks, passed a motion criticizing Israeli policies on the West Bank and the bombing of the Lebanon. Anti-Zionist motions had, by then, become standard items on the agenda papers of many constituency Labour parties.[93] The manifesto prepared by the Labour Party for the 1983 General Election proclaimed the right of Israel to live within 'secure internationally recognised borders', but at the same time urged the establishment of a Palestinian state.[94] Labour lost that election in disastrous fashion. But in London the

[89] V. D. Lipman, *A History of the Jews in Britain since 1858* (Leicester, 1990), 232; B. A. Kosmin and C. Levy, *Jewish Identity in an Anglo-Jewish Community* (London, 1983), 29.

[90] Kosmin and Levy, *Jewish Identity*, 25.

[91] T. Benski, 'Identification, Group Survival and Inter-Group Relations: The Case of a Middle-Class Jewish Community in Scotland', *Ethnic & Racial Studies*, 4 (1981), 313.

[92] Kosmin and Levy, *Jewish Identity*, 32. See also S. Harris, 'The Identity of Jews in an English City', *JJS* 14 (1972), 80–1.

[93] *JC* (7 May 1982), 10; (28 Aug.), 6.

[94] *The New Hope for Britain* (London, 1983), 38.

party, dominated by the hard left, had won control of the Greater London Council in 1981 and, under the leadership of Ken Livingstone, embarked upon a five-year period of intense anti-Zionist activity that brought it and the Jewish community of London to a state of conflict unprecedented in British or Anglo-Jewish history.[95]

These developments—by themselves—would have had a profoundly adverse effect on the former close relationship between Jewry and Labour in Britain. But—by themselves—they would not necessarily have caused an irreparable rupture, and they would not—by themselves—have driven Jews into the arms of any other party. In the years immediately following the 1967 war it was the Young Liberals who carried the banner of anti-Zionism with most enthusiasm.[96] Both anti-Zionism and unadulterated anti-Semitism were to be observed at work in the Conservative Party at this time. Left-wing politics certainly pushed Jews into seeking political camps other than those of Labour in which to dwell. What pulled them towards the Conservatives was socio-economic advancement, of precisely the sort that had propelled them from run-down city centres into a thoroughly suburban existence.

The class structure of Anglo-Jewry, as it has developed over the past forty years, marked out British Jews as a group that would be particularly receptive to Conservative ideologies as they were redeveloped first under Edward Heath (1965–75) and then under Mrs Thatcher who succeeded him as Tory Leader (1975–90). We must bear in mind in this connection that in 1970 about 64 per cent of the A, B, and C1 occupational groups (as conventionally used by psephologists, and embracing professional, administrative, managerial, and non-manual occupations) over the country as a whole voted Conservative, and that although this proportion fell somewhat over the five subsequent general elections, it has not since then dropped below 50 per cent; whereas the percentage of the combined A, B, and C1 categories supporting Labour has contracted fairly steadily from 25 per cent in 1970 to just 18 per cent in 1987.[97]

One particular aspect of British electoral sociology in the 1980s was the relationship between voting behaviour and housing tenure.

[95] I deal with this unhappy history in *London Jewry*, ch. 5.

[96] Ibid. 117.

[97] G. Alderman, *Britain: A One-Party State?* (London, 1989), 8.

At the general elections of 1983 and 1987 about half of all owner-occupiers (that is, people who had bought or were buying their own homes, as opposed to those who lived in rented accommodation) voted Conservative; only about a quarter of owner-occupiers voted Labour, and about the same proportion supported the Social-Democratic/Liberal 'Alliance'. We know that in Redbridge at the end of the 1970s over 90 per cent of Jews were owner-occupiers, and that in those parts of Barnet, Brent, and Harrow where Jews reside in large numbers the proportion of owner-occupiers is not less than a half and often much higher.[98]

General societal factors as well as particular Jewish sensitivities have thus combined to reorientate British Jewry in a Conservative direction. That this is so can be demonstrated by reference to both quantitative and qualitative data. Table 7.4 gives the results of surveys of Jewish voters which I have carried out at general elections since 1974 in three heavily Jewish constituencies in London: Hendon North and Finchley (both in Barnet) and Ilford North (Redbridge).[99] For comparative purposes the table also shows, in square brackets, the proportions of the combined A, B, and C1 categories found, by national opinion surveys, to have supported the political parties at each election.[100] It will be readily apparent that the broad trend of Jewish electoral behaviour in these constituencies has been very much in line with that of the top social classes; indeed, usually the Jews have proved somewhat more Conservatively inclined.[101] Table 7.4 also shows the findings of a similar survey I conducted in Hackney North in 1983, and here the percentages in square brackets refer to the national pattern of the C2, D, and E categories—that is, skilled and unskilled manual workers, casual workers, and state pensioners. Again, the remarkable

[98] Kosmin, Levy, and Wigodsky, *Social Demography*, 25; R. Waller, *The Almanac of British Politics* (3rd edn., Beckenham, 1987), 40–2, 46, 70. The very close correlation between Jewish areas of settlement and areas of high owner-occupancy is demonstrated in S. Waterman, *Jews in an Outer London Borough, Barnet* (London, 1989), 44–6; more than 90% of all households in 'Jewish' Edgware in 1981 were owner-occupied.

[99] The methodology of the Hackney, Hendon, and Ilford surveys, as recorded in Table 7.4, is explained in Alderman, *Jewish Community*, 202–5; the methodology of the Finchley surveys follows that employed at Ilford.

[100] The full data may be found in Alderman, *One-Party State?* and D. Butler and D. Kavanagh, *The British General Election of 1979* (London, 1980), 343.

[101] For a fuller discussion see G. Alderman, 'London Jews and the 1987 General Election', *Jewish Quarterly*, 34/127 (1987), 14.

TABLE 7.4. *Jewish Political Preferences in London, 1974–1987*

Constituency	Conservative [ABC1] %	Labour [ABC1] %	Liberal/Alliance [ABC1] %
Hendon North (Feb. 1974)	59	16	25
(N=150)	[53]	[22]	[23]
Hendon North (Oct. 1974)	68	22	10
(N=178)	[51]	[25]	[21]
Ilford North (1979)	61	35	4
(N=143)	[60]	[23]	[16]
Finchley (1983)	52	24	24
(N=120)	[55]	[17]	[28]
Finchley (1987)	60	22	18
(N=205)	[54]	[18]	[26]
	[C2DE]	[C2DE]	[C2DE]
Hackney North (1979)	36	49	13
(N=130)	[35]	[50]	[14]

Note: Hendon North, Ilford North, and Finchley percentages are based on those who stated an intention to vote; Hackney North percentages are based on those who actually voted.

similarity between the Jewish pattern and that of these lower social classes needs no further emphasis, and reflects the social-class composition of Hackney Jewry—an ageing community drawing its political inspiration from memories of the vibrant left-wing Jewish tradition with which the area was once saturated.

One aspect of Jewish political sociology not touched upon in these surveys is the relationship (if any) of partisanship to degree of religiosity. It is tempting to suppose that the more traditional and fundamentalist a British Jew is in religious terms, the more likely he or she is to be a Conservative supporter. The Conservative Party has a long history of support for denominational schools, and its emphasis on the centrality of religious commitment (Christian or otherwise) in the moral and ethical underpinning of the State is, it is argued, likely to enhance its attraction for what are often but unfortunately termed the 'right-wing' orthodox.

The growth of the practising orthodox (in both absolute and relative terms) is a phenomenon of the greatest significance in the religious—and hence communal—development of British Jewry in recent times. Its extent, and consequences, will be considered in due course. Here it is necessary to state that such evidence as we possess by no means leads conclusively to the view that identification with Conservative politics is an inevitable concomitant of 'right-wing' or 'ultra-'orthodoxy. In May 1978 Josef Lobenstein won, in a heavily ultra-orthodox ward, the only Conservative seat on an otherwise entirely Labour-controlled Hackney Borough Council; Councillor Lobenstein, a leading member of British *Agudas Israel* and of the Union of Orthodox Hebrew Congregations, subsequently became President of the North London *Adass Yisroel* Synagogue (the founding synagogue of the Union) and Conservative Leader on the Hackney Council.[102] Hackney is one centre of ultra-orthodoxy in post-war London; Hendon and adjacent Golders Green (Barnet) is the other. In a survey of a small number of members of the Hendon *Adass Yisroel* Synagogue (also a constituent of the Union), carried out in 1976, Dr Sabine Roitman found that 70 per cent of her respondents identified themselves as Conservative supporters.[103]

But what we do not know is whether these pieces of evidence reflect a true correlation between religious and political commitment, or whether they are simply reflections of other criteria, such as socio-economic group or even housing tenure. It is worth remembering that some aspects of orthodoxy—especially its teachings concerning the duties owed by those who happen to possess wealth—incline more to a socialist than to a neo-liberal political philosophy.[104] In May 1982, on what is believed to have been the first occasion on which a rabbi has gained election to a local authority in Britain, Rabbi Avroham Pinter topped the poll—for Labour—in Hackney's Northfield ward. Members of Hackney Jewry's fundamentalist (and anti-Zionist) Satmar community also identify themselves with Labour politics.[105] It is also possible, of course, that such well-known local Jewish celebrities as Lobenstein

[102] Alderman, *Jewish Community*, 159–60.

[103] S. Roitman, 'Les Juifs anglais de 1966 à 1976—pratiques, mentalités, compartements', Ph.D. thesis (Université des Sciences Humaines, Strasburg, 1978), 220.

[104] See G. Alderman, 'Continuity and Change in Jewish Political Attitudes and Voting Patterns in England since 1945' (Paper presented at the Institute of Contemporary Jewry, Hebrew University of Jerusalem, 1989), 22–3.

[105] *Jewish Tribune* (9 May 1991), 1.

and Pinter polled a personal vote, or that they polled a specifically Jewish (and perhaps Yiddish-speaking) vote.[106]

Mrs Thatcher won the Conservative leadership contest in 1975, and entered upon her eleven-year tenure of the premiership in 1979. The genuineness of her own admiration for Jewish people is not in doubt. 'Mrs Thatcher comes from the sort of provincial suburban background in which a mild anti-semitism has traditionally been quite pervasive, but one of the most attractive things about her is the entirely open-hearted way she has related to the Jewish community.'[107] At the same time this respect—even admiration—dovetailed most conveniently with other of her preoccupations, more particularly her overriding concern to promote entrepreneurship, self-help, and a spirit of independence among the entire citizenry of the United Kingdom. During her tenure of the Conservative leadership, Mrs Thatcher was fond of holding up British Jewry as a prime example of these characteristics at work. Finchley is the only constituency Mrs Thatcher ever represented in the House of Commons and, as we have seen, she entered upon this inheritance at a time of acute local tensions between the Jews and sections of the Finchley Conservative hierarchy. Fence-mending became a top priority. A new Tory agent was hired in 1962, and by 1964 the proportion of Jews persuaded to vote Conservative had increased by 50 per cent.[108]

Moreover, in refashioning both the Conservative Party and Conservatism, Mrs Thatcher appears to have turned to Jews as counterweights to the influence of public school 'one-nation' Toryism, embracing the welfare state and the regulated economy, that ruled triumphant in the days of Harold Macmillan and Edward Heath. The influence of Sir Keith Joseph upon her economic thinking has been enormous; her appointment of so many Jews to ministerial and Cabinet positions was and is without precedent.[109] Only once, indeed, since 1979, has the Conservative Party been in serious danger of losing Jewish support. In the early 1980s, when Lord Carrington was in charge of the Foreign Office,

106 Alderman, *Jewish Community*, 206; G. Alderman, 'What is the Strength of the Jewish Vote?', *JC* (4 May 1990), 29.

107 Johnson, 'Is this Successful Management?', 3.

108 Donoghue, 'Finchley', 251.

109 Alderman, *One-Party State?*, 118, 135; at one time Mrs Thatcher had no less than 5 Jews in her Cabinet simultaneously: Keith Joseph, Nigel Lawson, David Young, Malcolm Rifkind, and Leon Brittan.

the relationship of the Conservative Government with British Jewry underwent a period of strain, following Carrington's statement (17 March 1980) that the PLO was not a 'terrorist' organization.[110] There was a number of well-attended protest meetings in synagogues in north-west London; in letters to the local press and to the rabbi of the Finchley United Synagogue the Prime Minister carefully distanced herself from the policy of her Foreign Secretary.[111]

With unemployment rising and inflation over 20 per cent, Finchley was not then considered a very safe Conservative seat. Soundings were taken with a view to moving the Prime Minister to safer territory.[112] These events took place before the Falklands conflict (1982), which helped change the fortunes of the Conservative administration and which (fortuitously from the point of view of relations with Anglo-Jewry) resulted in Lord Carrington's resignation. From 1983 Mrs Thatcher arguably pursued policies more pro-Jewish than that of any Prime Minister since Lloyd George. It is true that her Government concluded an arms deal with Saudi Arabia, and more recently (1989) called upon Israel to negotiate with the PLO. But the Prime Minister and the party she led went out of their way to support Soviet Jewry. The Foreign Office ended complicity in the Arab boycott of Israel (through the certification of signatures on boycott documents), and Prime Minister Thatcher visited Israel and was careful to distance herself from some of the more extreme pro-PLO utterances of her ministers.[113] She also demonstrated extreme sensitivity to other Jewish concerns, such as *shechita* and the prosecution of alleged Nazi war criminals living in Britain.[114]

The peerage which she bestowed at the beginning of 1988 upon Immanuel Jakobovits had a significance the importance of which can hardly be overestimated. Lord Jakobovits's admiration for Mrs Thatcher, and for the encouragement of wealth creation and

[110] *The Times* (18 Mar. 1980), 5.

[111] Alderman, *Jewish Community*, 170–1.

[112] I. Bradley, 'A Finchley Problem for Mrs. Thatcher', *The Times* (29 Oct. 1981), 14. A proposal was mooted to move the Prime Minister to the adjacent Hendon South constituency.

[113] *Jewish Herald* (20 Jan. 1989), 1; *JC* (20 Jan. 1989), 10.

[114] G. Alderman, *Anglo-Jewry: A Suitable Case For Treatment* (Egham, 1990) (Inaugural Lecture), 22–4; G. Alderman, 'Risking the Jewish Vote too?', *The Times* (23 Apr. 1990), 14; *JC* (15 June 1990), 44; (29 June), 1. In 1991 the Conservative Government of John Major used the Parliament Acts to enact a Nazi War Crimes Bill which had been defeated in the House of Lords.

acquisition, became hallmarks of his tenure of the office of Chief Rabbi of the United Hebrew Congregations, to which he was elected in 1966.[115] As early as 1977 he had condemned the welfare state for undermining individual responsibility and for encouraging a 'get something for nothing' attitude.[116] In particular, he faithfully reflected a feeling of antipathy towards the aspirations of Britain's Black communities that is undoubtedly widespread within British Jewry.

Most British Jews resent the 'race-relations industry', and many object to being termed an 'ethnic minority'.[117] They realize that the 1976 Race Relations Act can protect them (and are occasionally grateful for it), but nevertheless they feel uncomfortable in its presence. During the 1970s many Jews blamed the Blacks for the resurgence of racist politics and for the rise of the National Front. Sir Keith Joseph's plea to the Jews of Ilford North, during the 1978 by-election there, to support Mrs Thatcher's policy of tight immigration control, was condemned by the *Jewish Chronicle*, but caught the communal mood exactly. The Conservatives won back Ilford North on a swing of 6.9 per cent, but among Jewish voters the swing to the Conservatives was no less than 11.2 per cent.[118]

Sir Keith's intervention was itself a landmark: for the first time in over half a century, a leading Conservative politician had appealed to Jewish voters to support the party on a major issue, and had met with resounding success. Since then the growing anxieties of British Jews surrounding the quality of urban life served only to strengthen their support for Thatcherite values. During the 1980s Mrs Thatcher found herself under increasing attack from within the Established Church of England on fundamental questions of social policy, especially in relation to inner-city areas. Her most consistent theological support came from within the circle of orthodox Jewry.

In a pamphlet published by the right-wing Social Affairs Unit in 1985 Rabbi Dr Jonathan Sacks (the then Principal of Jews' College who in 1990 was elected Chief Rabbi of the United Hebrew Congregations in succession to Lord Jakobovits) contrived to offer thinly veiled support from the Hebrew Bible for major elements of

[115] See e.g. his interview with Walter Schwarz in the *Guardian* (29 Dec. 1988), 20.

[116] *Jewish Tribune* (17 June 1977), 4.

[117] G. Alderman, 'Census Sensibility', *JC* (9 Mar. 1990), 28.

[118] Alderman, *Jewish Community*, 148–9.

Conservative domestic legislation; Rabbi Sacks's selected texts, the political commentator Hugo Young argued, served to confer 'ethical legitimacy on a series of economic measures that Christian churchmen have denounced'.[119] Nowhere were such denunciations more eloquently expressed than in the pages of the report, *Faith in the City*, of the Commission on Urban Priority Areas set up by Archbishop of Canterbury Robert Runcie. It was Immanuel Jakobovits who came to Mrs Thatcher's rescue, by issuing in 1986 a sharp riposte, exhorting the disadvantaged not to insist upon public help ('self-reliant efforts and perseverance eventually pay off'), and criticizing the Blacks for wishing to change the character of British society into 'a multi-ethnic form'.[120] 'This being Thatcher's Britain, these sentiments . . . earned him a place on the Honours List.'[121]

These views were themselves controversial, and certainly did not represent the opinions of all orthodox Jews in Britain, or even of all orthodox clergy. But they did accurately mirror a feeling widespread within an Anglo-Jewish community that was rapidly turning its back on the welfare state and its face against collectivism. Some features of the general election of June 1987 reflected these developments. Cecil Parkinson, one of Mrs Thatcher's closest political colleagues, received the endorsement of Alan Plancey, Rabbi of the Elstree and Borehamwood (United) Synagogue (and subsequently elected Chairman of the Rabbinical Council of the United Synagogue), in spite of the fact that Mr Parkinson is a self-confessed adulterer.[122] Martin Savitt, a former Vice-President of the Board of Deputies and at that time a Vice-Chairman of the Zionist Federation, assisted the campaign of the Conservative Harriet Crawley against Ken Livingstone, the Labour candidate at Brent East.[123] The Livingstone candidature was always controversial, and his election to Parliament, on a much-reduced Labour

[119] J. Sacks, *Wealth and Poverty* (London, 1985); *Guardian* (27 May 1986), 23.

[120] Sir I. Jakobovits, 'From Doom to Hope', *JC* (24 Jan. 1986), 26–8.

[121] Johnson, 'Is this Successful Management?', 3.

[122] Alderman, 'Changing Political Allegiances', 35–6.

[123] Alderman, 'London Jewry and the 1987 General Election', 15. Livingstone had won the Labour nomination at Brent East after a prolonged campaign, by an unholy alliance of anti-Zionists, anti-Thatcherites, anti-racists, and supporters of the Irish Republican Army, to force out the sitting Labour MP, Reg Freeson, a Jew and co-chairman of *Poale Zion*: Alderman, *London Jewry*, 126, 136.

vote, was entirely predictable. Mr Savitt is, however, entitled to claim a little credit for the narrowness of his victory.

Sixty-three Jewish candidates stood at the 1987 election: twenty-five for the Conservatives, fifteen for Labour, twenty-one for the Alliance, and two independents. Of these there were returned sixteen Conservative and seven Labour MPs. The number of Jewish Labour MPs reached its peak (38) in 1966; following the 1987 election the Jewish Labour contingent at Westminster was smaller than at any time since 1935. The Jewish Conservative total returned in 1987 was smaller by one than in 1983, but was still the second largest ever, and the pattern established in 1983, of the political balance among Jewish MPs lying with the Conservative Party, was thus maintained and indeed strengthened.

We must be wary of drawing too many conclusions from the success or failure of Jewish parliamentary candidates. None the less, the fact that a third of all Jewish candidates in 1987 stood for the Alliance, that over a third were Conservatives, and that, while the number of Jewish Labour candidates declined (there had been twenty in 1983), the number of Jewish Conservative candidates (eighteen in 1983) increased, does tell us something about the changing political balance within British Jewry as a whole. The strength of the picture increases, and its definition is sharpened, when considered in conjunction with the Jewish voting pattern in Finchley. Compared with 1983, Mrs Thatcher increased her share of the total poll by just 2.8 per cent; but her share of the Jewish poll (see Table 7.4) increased by nearly three times that amount. At Finchley there was in fact a swing *from* the Conservatives *to* Labour of 1 per cent. The Prime Minister clearly owed some of the increase in her own share of the vote to her Jewish supporters: the Jewish vote there swung heavily (5.0 per cent) against the trend. Of course—as the Finchley statistics themselves indicate—there are still Jews who vote Labour, and the centre parties can expect some Jewish support. Equally clearly, however, 'Thatcherism has seen the Jewish identification with Labour stood on its head'.[124]

On 10 January 1988 the editor of the *Sunday Telegraph*, Peregrine Worsthorne, described Judaism as 'the new creed of Thatcherite Britain'.[125] There was no communal protest at this turn of phrase. When the bulk of Anglo-Jewry lived in areas of

124 Johnson, 'Is this Successful Management?', 3.

125 *Sunday Telegraph* (10 Jan. 1988), 20.

deprivation in the inner cities, its relationship to the Labour Party and to the Labour ethos was bound to be strong, and it was made stronger still by the anti-Jewish prejudice then to be found in large measure within the Conservative Party. It matters little that this prejudice has not entirely disappeared.[126] The Labour Party is—for the time being at any rate—not perceived as a party serving Jewish interests. Many Jews will define these interests in empirical terms, and they will point (for example, and depending on their own referential framework) to the anti-Israeli foreign policy of the Greater London Council under Labour control from 1981 to its abolition in 1986, or to the enthusiasm expressed in certain quarters for the Black American demagogue Louis Farrakhan, or even to the opposition of the Labour-controlled Inner London Education Authority (abolished by the Conservative Government in 1990) to the granting of financial support to Jewish schools.[127] Underlying and informing all these matters of complaint is the basic fact that, from a purely socio-economic point of view, the Labour Party and the British-Jewish community now inhabit very different worlds.

Rabbi Lord Jakobovits presided over and personified this sea change. Paradoxically, he was unable to exploit it in order to maintain over British Jewry the primacy of the Chief Rabbinate as it existed in the days of Joseph Hertz, and he has bequeathed to his successor an office less recognized throughout Jewish Britain than at any time since the Emancipation. Conventional wisdom ascribes this failure to the undeniable religious polarization that has affected British Jewry since 1945. But the roots of the problem may certainly be traced back beyond 1939, and indeed, in some respects, they may be linked directly with the unresolved conflict between Hermann Adler and the immigrant religious die-hards whom he was never able totally to subdue.

We noted in Chapter 3 how in 1905 the *Machzike Hadath* had been prevailed upon to recognize the authority of the Chief Rabbi in relation to *shechita*, and also in matters relating to the solemnization of marriages. But a section of its adherents, who constituted the North London *Beth Hamedrash*, refused to be so bound. In 1909 this community acquired its first rabbinical leader,

[126] G. Alderman, 'Antisemitism', *Jewish Quarterly* (Spring 1991), 42–3.

[127] These themes are explored in Alderman, *London Jewry*, 117–38. On Farrakhan, see *JC* (10 Aug. 1990), 19.

the Hungarian Rabbi Dr Victor Schonfeld (1880–1930), and some years later a new synagogue, the *Adass Yisroel*, near Highbury, north London. Other small but like-minded London communities attached themselves to the *Adass*, initially for burial purposes. Such were the origins of what became, on 27 March 1926, the Union of Orthodox Jewish [later Hebrew] Congregations (UOHC). In 1913 the *Adass* synagogue applied to the Board of Deputies for certification to enable a marriage secretary to be appointed. The application was referred to Chief Rabbi Hertz, who declined to approve it because the synagogue would not recognize his authority and, more especially, because its rabbi insisted on his right to sanction divorces and arrange *chalitza* ceremonies without reference to any higher authority. In 1919, and under threat of legal proceedings, Hertz repented as part of an historic agreement by which the *Adass* agreed to provide his office with details of every marriage, divorce, and *chalitza* authorized by it, but only after the ceremony had been conducted.[128]

Hertz's extreme sensitivity in this matter reflected a growing preoccupation with the developing religious pluralism amongst British Jews, which he realized must affect adversely his claim to be and to be recognized as the religious head over all of them. The Liberal Jewish movement, while still small, did not remain a socially exclusive clique, as the Reform movement had done in the nineteenth century. Under the guidance of Claude Montefiore and Lily Montagu it grew, acquired other patrons of status such as Louis Gluckstein and Basil Henriques, and became, as we have seen, a religious refuge for anti-Zionists in the inter-war period. More than that, it was during these years that Liberal Judaism 'captured the imagination and support of those within Anglo-Jewry who were searching for something "modern" in terms of religious observance'.[129] Three new synagogues were opened in the 1920s, in north London, south London, and Liverpool. In 1926 Montefiore, Montagu, and Israel Mattuck took the first step in establishing

[128] B. Homa, *Orthodoxy in Anglo-Jewry 1880–1940* (London, 1969), 24–8; Union of Orthodox Hebrew Congregations, *Silver Jubilee Brochure* (London, 1951), 6–9: 'The Story of the Union'; *Souvenir Book published on the occasion of the consecration of the new Adath Yisroel Synagogue* (London, 1957); Adath Yisroel Synagogue, *Golden Jubilee* brochure (London, 1961).

[129] A. J. Kershen, '1840–1990: One Hundred and Fifty Years of Progressive Judaism', in A. J. Kershen (ed.), *150 Years of Progressive Judaism in Britain* (London, 1990), 14.

what became (in 1928) the World Union for Progressive Judaism. Other Liberal congregations were founded in the 1930s in Birmingham and Brighton.

In London, by 1939, the Liberal Jewish Synagogue could boast a membership (1,622) greater than that of the West London Reform Synagogue (1,386).[130] But for Reform Judaism the 1930s were also years of growth, fuelled by the influx of German refugees, among whom were a clutch of talented Reform rabbis, such as Werner Van der Zyl and Ignaz Maybaum, who were able to underpin British Reform Judaism with a more robust, distinctive, and radical German Reform ideology.[131] Presiding over them was Rabbi Harold Reinhart, a graduate of the American Reform centre at Hebrew Union College, Cincinnati, who had in 1929 become the Senior Minister at West London; under Reinhart's direction a new prayer book was completed (1931) and new headquarters opened (1934).[132]

Of major significance, too, was the establishment of Reform congregations in the expanding suburbs of Golders Green and Edgware, as well as in Glasgow. In 1942 these communities joined those of West London, Bradford, and Manchester in forming the Associated British Synagogues—later, in 1958, the Reform Synagogues of Great Britain (RSGB); in 1948 a Reform *Beth Din* was inaugurated: this was, in effect, a declaration of total religious separatism.[133] For the Liberal movement the war years were also a period of consolidation. In 1944 the movement became the Union of Liberal and Progressive Synagogues (ULPS) of which there were then eight constituents. Both Liberal and Reform communities benefited from the presence in London, after the war, of Rabbi Dr Leo Baeck (1873–1956), the charismatic leader of non-orthodoxy in Nazi Germany, a survivor of the Holocaust—and a pro-Zionist—who became President of the World Union for Progressive

[130] S. Sharot, 'Reform and Liberal Judaism in London: 1840–1940', *JSS* 41 (1979), 222.

[131] J. Romain, 'The Changing Face of British Reform', in Kershen, *150 Years of Progressive Judaism*, 44.

[132] M. Leigh, 'Reform Judaism in Britain (1840–1970)', in D. Marmur (ed.), *Reform Judaism* (London, 1973), 41–2.

[133] Kershen in id., *150 Years of Progressive Judaism*, 14–15; M. Curtis, 'The *Beth Din* of the Reform Synagogues of Great Britain', in Marmur, *Reform Judaism*, 137–9.

Judaism.[134] The Reform and Liberal movements in Britain have never merged, partly because of a recurrent and obstinate strand of traditionalism in British Reform.[135] But their dogmas, while distinctive, were none the less sufficiently similar for the ULPS to agree, in 1964, to become a partner in the Leo Baeck College, the theological seminary which the RSGB had established in 1956.[136]

In the 1930s Chief Rabbi Hertz still believed that he could somehow contain the progressive movements within his orthodox umbrella. This belief led him, in 1934, to attend the opening of the West London Reform Synagogue's extension, the Stern Hall, and to declare that the Liberal Jewish Synagogue was a body of persons professing the Jewish religion, so that it might be certified by the President of the Board of Deputies for marriage purposes.[137] During the Second World War (and perhaps influenced by the presence in Britain of many non-orthodox American Jewish servicemen) he extended further courtesies to the progressives, for example by including Louis Gluckstein in his 'Jewish War Services Committee' and by acquiescing in the appointment of non-orthodox clerics, such as the Revd Leslie Edgar (Associate Minister of the Liberal Jewish Synagogue) as an armed forces chaplain.[138]

But these concessions to the progressives, made (so it was proclaimed) in order to preserve communal unity during a period of great crisis for British and for world Jewry, caused outrage among the practising orthodox, towards whom Hertz applied a policy of counter-productive confrontation. As orthodoxy was swept by the tide of non-observance and secularism that characterized inter-war Jewry, its remaining adherents became bolder and more outspoken

[134] On Leo Baeck see *JC* (9 Nov. 1956), 30; *The Times* (3 Nov. 1956), 11; and A. H. Friedlander, *Leo Baeck* (London, 1968). The change of attitude on the part of progressive Judaism towards Zionism following the re-establishment of the Jewish State is examined in J. D. Rayner, *Progressive Judaism, Zionism and the State of Israel* (London, 1983), 12–13.

[135] Romain in Kershen, *150 Years of Progressive Judaism*, 43–9.

[136] J. Magonet, 'A Rabbinic Seminary for Europe', in Kershen, *150 Years of Progressive Judaism*, 37–41.

[137] Homa, *Orthodoxy*, 33–5; A. Newman, *Chief Rabbi Dr Joseph H. Hertz* (London, 1973), 16–17. In 1939 Hertz gave similar recognition to the Liberal community in Liverpool. See *JC* (25 Jan. 1935), 17; BD C13/1/12: Minutes of the Law and Parliamentary Committee, 1934–41; and Archives of the Office of the Chief Rabbi, Greater London Record Office, Acc. 2805/72: Liberal Judaism and Intermarriage, 1935–43.

[138] B. Homa, *Footprints on the Sands of Time* (Gateshead, 1990), 197–9.

against Hertz's 'progressive conservatism'. *Yeshivot—Talmudical* colleges on the lines of those to be found in eastern Europe, and which offered an intensive training leading to the conferment of *semicha*—had been established in London in 1903 and in Manchester in 1911.[139] Hertz was prepared to tolerate and even welcome them, as bastions of *Torah*-true orthodoxy, because they did not effect to become independent communities. But when, in 1926, a small and separatist group at Gateshead announced its intention to found there a *yeshivah* the effective patron of which was the saintly Rabbi Yisroel Meir Kagan of Radin (Poland), Hertz made a clumsy and ill-considered attempt to quash the initiative by prevailing upon the Home Secretary, Joynson-Hicks, to refuse entry to the Rabbi, Abraham Sacharov, whom the Gateshead rebels had invited to head the new institution.[140] Eventually, in 1929, the Gateshead *Yeshivah* was inaugurated, and the following year it appointed as its head, and on Kagan's recommendation, Rabbi Nachman Landynski. Supported by refugee businessmen who were permitted to operate in the depressed north-east, and with its associated schools, teacher-training, and postgraduate facilities, it became the largest orthodox *yeshivah* complex in post-war Europe.[141]

Hertz accepted the reality of Gateshead, but was never reconciled to it. He refused for a considerable time to grant it the necessary certification for marriage purposes, but he could hardly deny that its synagogue was composed (and composed exclusively) of professing Jews. Meanwhile, rather than subjugate themselves to his authority, the Gateshead community suffered the inconvenience of having to invite to its wedding ceremonies the local non-Jewish registrar, so that religious and civil ceremonies could be combined.[142] In 1935 Hertz relented, and conveyed the necessary declaration to the President of the Board of Deputies, in an attempt to stifle orthodox criticism of his simultaneous certification of the Liberal Jewish Synagogue.[143] Later that year he overcame the objections of the United Synagogue in insisting on the appointment to his *Beth*

[139] Lipman, *History*, 219.

[140] *JC* (12 Feb. 1926), 10; (19 Feb.), 7, 15.

[141] The best (if incomplete) account of Gateshead is in L. Olsover, *The Jewish Communities of North-East England 1775–1980*, 221–50. See also A. Levy, *The Story of Gateshead Yeshivah* (Taunton, 1952), and M. Donbrow, *They Docked at Newcastle and Wound Up in Gateshead* (Jerusalem, 1972).

[142] Homa, *Orthodoxy*, 33.

[143] Ibid. 35.

Din of Rabbi Yechezkel Abramsky (1886–1976), a *Talmudic* genius and a victim of Stalinist persecution, who had been permitted to leave the Soviet Union in 1932 after an international campaign, and had served from 1932 to 1935 as Rabbi of the *Machzike Hadath* in London.[144]

Abramsky served as a *Dayan* on the United Synagogue's *Beth Din* until his retirement in 1951. His influence on its outlook was profound, more especially in matters relating to conversions and *shechita*; it was primarily through him that the porging and sale of cattle hindquarters was subjected to increasing control and eventually (1941) forbidden altogether.[145] Adherents of 'progressive conservatism' complained bitterly that 'a handful of orthodox extremists' were now 'in the saddle'.[146] This was an exaggerated view, but the developments which prompted it were very real. We have already noted how *shechita* supervision had been customarily regarded as a litmus-test of orthodoxy—the bench-mark by which Hermann Adler's claim to be the religious head of British Jewry had been declared deficient, and against which, in 1911–12, the very idea that there was a need for one 'Chief Rabbi' had been seriously questioned. Under Hertz matters in this regard reached a crisis point.

In 1928 Parliament had legislated for the slaughter of animals in Scotland; 'the Chief Rabbi' was made the sole licensing authority for *shochetim* in that kingdom.[147] The Federation of Synagogues, the UOHC, and the Spanish & Portuguese congregation had no interest in the Scottish situation *per se*, but they were extremely angered that a precedent had been set by which (in the words of Rabbi Victor Schonfeld) 'no Rabbi in Scotland should have the right to grant Kaboloh [i.e. a religious licence] to Shochetim except through the Chief Rabbinate of the United Synagogue'.[148] Thus,

[144] *JC* (28 June 1935), 9; (24 Sept. 1976), 12.

[145] Ibid. (12 July 1935), 17; (2 Aug.), 9; (21 Mar. 1941), 6; (28 Mar.), 16. London Board for Shechita, Minute Book 1934–53: entries for 18 Oct. 1935 and 27 Mar. 1941. Orthodox precept requires that the sciatic nerve be removed from cattle hindquarters; Abramsky took the view that sufficiently skilled labour to perform this task did not exist; the ban on the sale of hindquarters was enforced as a wartime measure, but has never been rescinded.

[146] *JC* (2 Aug. 1935), 9.

[147] Slaughter of Animals (Scotland) Act, 1928, section 8. This section incorporated the definite article ('the Chief Rabbi') which had been rejected as part of the United Synagogue Act of 1870.

[148] University College London, Gaster Papers, Union of Orthodox Jewish Congregations file: typescript memo. by Dr V. Schonfeld, Dec. 1929.

when Parliament turned its attention to England and Wales, a fierce and very public campaign was launched against the extension of Hertz's authority.[149] *Haham* Gaster argued that 'an audacious attempt' was being made 'by taking advantage of the ignorance of Parliament of the true situation of the Jewish communities—to induce them to establish what would be tantamount [to] a Jewish state church by the sanction of a single Chief Rabbi under the authority of Parliament'.[150]

This fear, that a state of affairs which the United Synagogue had failed to bring about in 1870 would now indeed come to pass, was shared by many rabbis throughout the United Kingdom. On 12 January 1930 a conference of rabbis convened by the Federation and the Union declared the proposal to endow the Chief Rabbi of the United Hebrew Congregations with the statutory power to act as the sole licensing authority for *shochetim* in England and Wales to be 'inimical to Judaism and contrary to Jewish law'. This resolution was supported by rabbinical leaders in every major provincial centre where Jews dwelt in large numbers, including Glasgow, Leeds, Sheffield, Hull, Manchester, Liverpool, Newcastle, and Sunderland, and by Rabbi Dr Herzog of Dublin, as well as by eminent Continental rabbis.[151] Hertz launched a vicious counter-attack, aimed especially at 'the so-called Union of Orthodox Jewish Congregations'.[152] But his claim to be the sole licensing authority for *shochetim* in England and Wales was not accepted by Parliament. Under what became the Slaughter of Animals Act of 1933 *shochetim* in England and Wales were (and still are) licensed by a Rabbinical Commission, of which the Chief Rabbi is the ex-officio chairman, the designated rabbi of the Spanish & Portuguese Jews the ex-officio deputy chairman, and which comprises also three rabbis appointed by the United Synagogue, two by the Federation of Synagogues, one by the Union, and two by the President of the Board of Deputies to represent provincial communities.[153]

[149] Homa, *Orthodoxy*, 28–9; Alderman, *Federation*, 50.

[150] University College London, Gaster Papers, Union of Orthodox Jewish Congregations file: typescript memo. by Gaster, undated but probably Dec. 1929.

[151] G. Alderman, 'The British Chief Rabbinate: A Most Peculiar Practice', *European Judaism*, 45 (Autumn 1990), 52.

[152] Ibid.

[153] The Scottish anomaly has never been rectified. I have been informed by the Secretary to the Rabbinical Commission, Mr M. Carr (interview, 17 Feb. 1989), that in practice the Commission deals with Scottish applications too.

It was not only the progressive wing that gained adherents as a result of the immigration to Britain of Jews from central Europe during the 1930s and 1940s. In 1934 Rabbi Dr E. Munk (1900–78), who had come to London from Berlin in 1930 and who had acted as temporary Rabbi of the UOHC following Victor Schonfeld's death the following year, established in Golders Green a community of strictly orthodox German-Jewish refugees.[154] The philosopher Rabbi Dr Alexander Altmann (1906–87) came from Berlin in 1938 to the post of Communal Rabbi and 'father' of the *Beth Din* in Manchester.[155] A crop of other orthodox refugee rabbis, such as Isidor Grunfeld and Julius Jakobovits (both subsequently *Dayanim* in London) found employment as ministers of congregations in London, and elsewhere. The cumulative impact was to strengthen very considerably the hitherto limited opposition to 'progressive conservatism'. This opposition had been previously orchestrated by *Haham* Gaster. But with his death in 1939 the leadership passed to Solomon Schonfeld, under whom the UOHC emerged as the bastion of an uncompromising orthodoxy—a far cry from Hertz's orthodox vision—that was determined to prevent any further undermining of the major communal institutions by infiltration of non-orthodox personnel.

Hertz's ability to hold British Jewry together came under increasing strain during what turned out to be the last five years of his life; perhaps it was only the extreme emergency of the war and the fact of the Holocaust that induced others not to challenge his authority more openly. He encountered continual friction with Robert Waley Cohen over his support for Zionism.[156] He seems, as a widower, to have come increasingly under the influence of Solomon Schonfeld, his son-in-law, who in 1944 felt strong enough to make public his desire that the UOHC, though affiliated to the Board of Deputies, should act independently of it.[157] A formal orthodox caucus within the Board had been established as early as 1934.[158] It was unable to prevent Waley Cohen from insisting (in 1947, during the interregnum that followed Hertz's death) that the

[154] C. Bermant, *Troubled Eden* (London, 1969), 226–7; on Munk see *JC* (17 Mar. 1978), 26.

[155] See ibid. (12 June 1987), 30.

[156] C. Bermant, *The Cousinhood* (London, 1971), 373–4.

[157] Jabotinsky Institute, Tel Aviv, Papers of Abraham Abrahams, 2F, file 5/5: Jewish Telegraphic Agency report of annual general meeting of the UOHC, Feb. 1944.

[158] *JC* (9 Nov. 1934), 23.

post-war 'Jewish Committee for His Majesty's Forces' contain official representatives of the Reform and Liberal movements.[159] But on 24 April 1949 it succeeded (by seventy-eight votes to sixty) in defeating at the Board a motion put forward by the progressives that would have obliged the President of the Board to certify henceforth for marriage purposes synagogues indicated by the President of the Liberal Jewish Synagogue.[160]

Behind this apparently narrow issue there lurked much greater ones: were Liberal and Progressive Jews, whose religious precepts (by then) incorporated a substantial rejection of orthodox criteria for Jewish identity, Jewish marriage and divorce, and conversion to Judaism, still 'persons professing the Jewish religion'?[161] If the Liberal and Progressive movements were allowed representation on the Board, and were therefore taxed for the privilege, why should their ecclesiastical authorities not have some status in its deliberations, parallel with that enjoyed by the Chief Rabbi of the United Hebrew Congregations and the spiritual head of the Spanish & Portuguese Jews? As Deputy Chief Rabbi, *Dayan* H. M. Lazarus (1879–1962) had set his face absolutely against appeasement. In May 1948 a new Chief Rabbi was appointed, Israel Brodie (1895–1979). He proved to be just as obstinate. After their defeat the following April, the progressives walked out of the Board, and refused to elect deputies for the 1949–52 triennial session; they were joined in this boycott by the West London Reform Synagogue.[162]

Israel Brodie was not the first Chief Rabbi to have been born in Britain (that honour belonged to Solomon Hirschell), but he was the first to have been both born and educated in England, at Jews' College, University College London, and Oxford. He was by all

[159] Homa, *Footprints*, 210–11; both the UOHC and the Federation of Synagogues agreed to be represented on the new body.

[160] *JC* (29 Apr. 1949), 1, 19. The negotiations which preceded and followed this defeat may be followed in BD E1/32: correspondence between the Office of the Chief Rabbi and the Board of Deputies.

[161] Ibid. 19: speech by Lady Hartog at the Board of Deputies.

[162] *JC* (13 May 1949), 6; the Spanish & Portuguese Synagogue also refused (until May 1951) to elect Deputies, apparently as a protest against 'the decline of the Board from its former representative and independent status': *JC* (6 May 1949), 10; (25 May 1951), 1, 8. But the Manchester Congregation of British (i.e. Reform) Jews and the Withington (Manchester) Congregation of Spanish & Portuguese Jews continued to be represented throughout this crisis, a remarkable demonstration of provincial autonomy.

accounts a gentleman, but he was neither a scholar nor an original thinker; the bibliography of his writings is embarrassingly thin. In choosing him the selection committee passed over many eminent rabbis, resident in Britain, with skills as orators, researchers, writers, and galvanizers. Brodie was none of these things. He had a good pastoral record, both in London's East End and as Senior Jewish Chaplain to the Forces. His major qualifications for the Chief Rabbinate in 1948 seem to have been his English birth and upbringing and his reputation as a conciliator. So far as his ecclesiastical policy was concerned, he was completely overawed by his erudite orthodox colleagues, more particularly *Dayanim* Abramsky and Dr Grunfeld and the much-published Rabbi Dr Isidore Epstein, appointed in 1939, in succession to Dr Adolph Büchler, as Principal of Jews' College.[163]

The Liberals did not obtain an amendment of the constitution of the Board of Deputies requiring the President of the Board to certify them as persons professing the Jewish religion, for the purposes of obtaining marriage secretaries. They had to content themselves with a Bill (introduced by Sir Keith Joseph in 1958 and which became law the following year) giving Liberal-Jewish synagogues the same rights as the Reformers had obtained—also by special legislation—in 1856.[164] Meanwhile, Brodie had found himself confronted with a very different issue, which at first sight had little to do with his opposition to the enhancement of the status of progressive Jews, but which in fact dovetailed with it in one crucial respect: namely, the suspicions it aroused among the more Anglicized, latitudinarian, members of the United Synagogue, devotees of Hertz's 'progressive conservatism', that the Chief Rabbinate was becoming the prisoner of a resurgent, triumphalist, and fundamentalist orthodoxy, by no means located exclusively within the expanding UOHC.

What became known as the 'Jacobs Affair' turned the internal

[163] On Brodie see *JC* (16 Feb. 1979), 23, and J. M. Shaftesley, 'A Bibliographical Sketch', in H. J. Zimmels, J. Rabbinowitz and I. Finestein (eds.), *Essays Presented to Chief Rabbi Sir Israel Brodie* (London, 1967), pp. xi–xxxix.

[164] Marriages (Secretaries of Synagogues) Act, 1959. See *JC* (5 Dec. 1958), 13; (19 Dec.), 11; (20 Feb.), 5. The progressives had attempted unsuccessfully to amend what became the 1949 Marriage Act: see *PP [House of Lords]* 1948–49, v (29-v. 168): Report of the Joint Committee on the Marriage Bill and Minutes of Evidence, 7–16: evidence of Louis Gluckstein; and see Archives of the Office of the Chief Rabbi, Greater London Record Office, Acc. 2805/72: sub-files for 1946–7, 1949, 1951.

politics of British Jewry into an object of intense media attention.[165] The Manchester-born Rabbi Dr Louis Jacobs, a graduate both of University College London, and of Gateshead, at one time an assistant minister at Dr Munk's synagogue in Golders Green, had in 1954 been appointed Rabbi at the New West End Synagogue. Dr Jacobs (then 34 years of age) had already earned for himself a reputation as a *Talmudic* scholar of great promise. But he had one flaw. He did not accept that every word of the Pentateuch had been dictated to Moses by the Almighty, and he had had the courage to say so in a book, *We Have Reason To Believe*, published in 1957. There is an interesting hiatus between the publication of the book and the commencement of the 'Affair'. Privately, Israel Brodie was disposed not to take too much notice of the book; its appearance did not lead to any Chief Rabbinical condemnation, neither did it prevent the Chief Rabbi from approving Dr Jacobs's appointment to the staff of Jews' College (as Moral Tutor and Lecturer in Pastoral Theology) in 1959, nor from encouraging Dr Jacobs in the belief that he would succeed Dr Epstein as College Principal.

But when this opportunity arose, in 1961, Dr Jacobs was not offered the post. Dr Brodie seems to have been swayed by the opinions of his *Beth Din*, and by an embittered Dr Epstein, who—rightly—regarded his own enforced retirement in July 1961 as a waste of talent. Louis Jacobs was neither promoted nor dismissed. He resigned, along with Sir Alan Mocatta (1907–90), the Chairman of the Council of Jews' College, and its other Honorary Officers, and his many supporters founded for him a Society for the Study of Jewish Theology (September 1962), of which he became the Director, occupying himself with addressing public meetings and university campuses, and thus making himself arguably at least as well known outside the confines of Anglo-Jewry as was the Chief Rabbi himself.

In 1963 the pulpit of the New West End Synagogue again fell vacant. In January 1964 Louis Jacobs was invited to reoccupy it. This appointment also required the Chief Rabbi's approval, and Dr Brodie was prepared to give it, on condition that Dr Jacobs furnish a written declaration of repentance for his former published

[165] The controversy is summarized in Bermant, *Troubled Eden*, ch. 19; there is a blow-by-blow account in Louis Jacobs's autobiography, *Helping with Inquiries* (London, 1989). Some additional materials are in Archives of the Office of the Chief Rabbi, Greater London Record Office, Acc. 2805/109–110.

views on the nature of Divine revelation. Rabbi Jacobs refused to do any such thing. On 1 March 1964 an extraordinary general meeting of members of the New West End Synagogue resolved to appoint Louis Jacobs as their Rabbi notwithstanding the Chief Rabbi's fiat. The Affair thus became, for the United Synagogue, a matter of constitutional propriety. But the United Synagogue itself had begun to feel and respond to the winds of change generated by resurgent orthodoxy. Since 1962 its Presidency had been held, not by a member of one of the upper-crust families that had dominated its governance hitherto, but by Sir Isaac Wolfson (1897–1991), the son of immigrant parents, born in the Gorbals, who had become the head of Great Universal Stores and 'the first President of the United Synagogue to be a practising Orthodox Jew'.[166] On 23 April 1964 Sir Isaac summoned a special meeting of the United Synagogue's Council, at which a motion to dismiss the Honorary Officers and the Board of Management of the New West End Synagogue was carried by acclamation.[167]

The Jacobs Affair did not lead to a split in the United Synagogue, most of whose members had never cared deeply enough about theology to bother reading the offending book, and most of whom had—in any case—an instinctive loyalty to the Chief Rabbinate as an institution that must be supported at whatever cost. This cost, however, was not negligible. Dr Jacobs's views had attracted support from a small but influential group of mainly professional Jews and Jewesses, who had come to the conclusion that a stand had to be made against the religious fundamentalism of which the Chief Rabbi appeared to be a prisoner. In May 1964 over 300 of them resolved to form an independent congregation, under Louis Jacobs's spiritual leadership, and so 'to work for the return of the United Synagogue to its own traditions of tolerance and the "Progressive Conservatism" referred to in the preamble to its Bye-laws'.[168] For a time the communal hall of the Spanish & Portuguese Synagogue in Maida Vale was made available to this flock for their services. Eventually the premises of the former St John's Wood (United) Synagogue were purchased as the permanent home of what became the 'New London Synagogue'.

166 Bermant, *Troubled Eden*, 143; *The Times* (21 June 1991), 16.
167 Newman, *United Synagogue*, 184–6.
168 Jacobs, *Helping with Inquiries*, 179–80.

At the time of its conception, there was a tendency to dismiss the New London Synagogue as a creature of its time. 'Its general influence in the community as a whole is not striking', Chaim Bermant wrote in 1969, 'and those who had hoped that the breakaway would herald a new movement within Anglo-Jewry were disappointed.'[169] His description of its 800 or so members as including 'a rich sprinkling of barristers, bankers, stockbrokers, estate agents and businessmen from the plushier enclaves of Kensington, and some very elegant wives' was certainly correct.[170] They were mainly 'from older families, and deeply resented being pushed around by the new boys from the United Synagogue'.[171] But the belief that the New London would wither away has not come to pass. As a synagogue its form of worship (separation of the sexes, a mixed choir, traditional *Torah* readings) is indistinguishable from that to be found in many United Synagogues of pre-war days. Its offering of traditionalism without fundamentalism provided a haven—and a model—for those disturbed at the seemingly relentless move to the religious right within the United Synagogue. It now has about 1,000 members, and has sprouted branches in Finchley, Edgware, South Woodford, and Wimbledon. Together these are constituents of the *Masorti* Assembly of Synagogues, formed in 1985 and modelling itself upon the American Conservative Jewish movement.

The UOHC and kindred ultra-orthodox communities have also grown in size. The most visible manifestation of this expansion has been the post-war immigration, particularly from Communist eastern Europe, of adherents of various pietistic (and, some would say, excessively narrow-minded and anti-intellectual) *chassidic* sects, each following a particular rabbinical dynasty, all recognizable by a very distinctive style of dress (typically, beards, stockings, long frock coats, and fur-brimmed hats for the men, long-sleeved dresses and wigs or large scarves for the women), and each family doing its very best to bring into the world as many children as possible. *Chassidim* were not unknown in pre-war Anglo-Jewry. Some of the *chevrot* of the early Federation of Synagogues were *chassidic*; Rabbi Avigdor Chaikin was an adherent of the Lubavitch move-

[169] Bermant, *Troubled Eden*, 251. [170] Ibid. 252.
[171] Brook, *The Club*, 150.

ment.[172] In Manchester in the 1930s a group of *chassidic* refugees established their own *Machzike Hadath* community, with its own separate *shechita* arrangement, under the spiritual leadership of Rabbi Dovid Feldman.[173] Within the post-war influx, concentrated in Stoke Newington and Stamford Hill in north London, Hendon and Golders Green in the north-west, and in Manchester, two groups stand out: the pro-Zionist Lubavitch and the anti-Zionist Satmar (both exceedingly wealthy and both with world headquarters in New York). Many of the *chassidic* sects naturally attached themselves to the UOHC, which could provide *shechita* and burial facilities of the required standard. Coincidentally, perhaps, while Solomon Schonfeld lived, the older groups of German origin, combining strict orthodoxy with a respect for western culture, continued to control the UOHC's destinies. But within a few years of his death, in 1984, we can detect a profound change in the balance of power within the UOHC and its associated 'Joint Kashrus Committee' (*Kedassia*), which deals with the manufacture and supervision of food products. In 1990 adherents of Satmar made substantial inroads into the power-structures of these two bodies. Satmar is inward-looking. Adherents of Lubavitch are missionaries within Jewry, seeking out the irreligious and converting them to strict orthodoxy.[174]

In 1953 Dr Redcliffe Salaman felt confident enough to assert that 'the *Chassidim* . . . play little part in Anglo-Jewry, nor would they seem likely to do so'.[175] When Chaim Bermant published *Troubled Eden* in 1969, he paid no attention to Lubavitch; indeed, ultra-orthodoxy in general merited only one chapter, in which the world of *chassidism* was located as an exotic if eccentric one, living on the margin of Anglo-Jewish existence. Stephen Brook's update, *The Club*, which appeared in April 1989, devoted three chapters to

[172] H. M. Rabinowicz, *Hasidism: The Movement and its Masters* (Northvale, NJ, 1988), 379–81.

[173] Homa, *Orthodoxy*, 36.

[174] On the Lubavitch movement see Brook, *The Club*, ch. 5, and G. Alderman, 'Militants with £1 Million to Spend', *Manna*, 25 (Autumn 1989), 8, 10. Since 1962 the 'ultra-orthodox' communities in London and the provinces have been served by an English–Yiddish newspaper (now weekly, originally fortnightly) the *Jewish Tribune*, an organ of British *Agudas Israel*; the paper is rarely informative about the internal workings of the communities for which it caters, concentrating instead on *Torah*-learning and smug attacks on the non- and not-so-orthodox.

[175] R. N. Salaman, *Whither Lucien Wolf's Anglo-Jewish Community?* (London, 1954), 9–10.

'ultra-orthodoxy', one of them exclusively to Lubavitch. The opinions of Lubavitch rabbis are to be found scattered throughout the book, holding forth on such subjects as the role of women and the interface between Jewry and politics. Lubavitch-trained rabbis, such as Zvi Telsner at Finchley (Federation) Synagogue and Shlomo Levin at South Hampstead (United), appear only too happy to work within what now passes as mainstream orthodoxy. Who, at the time of Sir Israel Brodie's retirement (1965), would have predicted that Lubavitch *chassidim* would have found employment within the United Synagogue, or that 'Lubes' would have featured, as they now clearly must, among the opinion-formers of British Jewry?

In 1970, in London, the Reform and Progressive elements accounted for 20.6 per cent of male synagogue members; by 1990 the proportion had increased to 29.3 per cent. The so-called 'right-wing orthodox' increased as a proportion of London Jewry from 2.6 per cent to 8.8 per cent over the same period. The 'central orthodox'—mainly the United Synagogue and the Federation—declined from 72.3 to 58.2 per cent, and the *Sephardim* from 4.5 per cent to 3.7.[176] Although these figures refer to the position in London, they are within a few percentage points of the situation within British Jewry as a whole in 1990: Reformers and Progressives around 22 per cent, 'right-wing orthodox' about 6.2 per cent, *Sephardim* just under 3 per cent, and 'central orthodox' 68.5 per cent.[177]

The pattern and the trend is one of increasing polarization, with the centre being squeezed by the extremes as the whole of British Jewry itself contracts. But the bare statistics themselves convey little of the qualitative changes at work. Within the so-called 'central orthodox' are now to be found many younger families who have rebelled against the religious laxity and cloying materialism of their parents, whose ostentatious and irreligious life-styles were a favourite subject of the 'Golders Green novelists' of the post-war era—most controversially so in Brian Glanville's *The Bankrupts*

[176] Prais and Schmool, 'Synagogue Statistics', 219; Waterman and Kosmin, *British Jewry*, 31; information supplied by the Board of Deputies of British Jews.

[177] Information supplied by the Board of Deputies of British Jews. Statistics of Jewish marriages in 1990 break down as follows: Progressives 20.5%; central orthodox 65.8%; *Sephardim* 4.3%; right-wing orthodox 9.4%: see B. A. Kosmin, 'Localism and Pluralism in British Jewry 1900–80', *TJHSE* 28 (1981–2), 114, where the long-term trend since 1920 is discussed.

(1958).[178] The parents belonged to synagogues, but they rarely bothered to visit them; their children, in many cases, have adopted life-styles really very little different from that of many adherents of the so-called right-wing orthodox: the dietary and Sabbath laws are rigidly adhered to, as are those relating to sexual intercourse in marriage; men wear beards, women wear *sheitels* (now very fashionable), and the sexes are separated for the purposes of dancing at weddings and *barmitzvah* parties. A number of the constituents of the United Synagogue (for example, Hendon and Kingsbury) now run voluntary *chevra kadisha* societies, to prepare the dead for burial; this would have been unthinkable in 1965, although in declining provincial communities voluntary, unpaid burial societies had always to be sustained.

There are probably more Jews—and Jewesses—undertaking advanced studies in Judaism in Britain today than there have ever been, in a variety of part-time modes, through learning projects such as 'Seed' (one-to-one study of the *Talmud*), the Yakar centre in Hendon, the Spiro Institute (which operates in London and the provinces), Jews' College, the (non-orthodox) Sternberg Centre, and within Jewish studies programmes in universities and polytechnics. The demand for full-time Jewish schooling, at both primary and secondary levels, cannot be satisfied. But this burgeoning of demand is a comparatively recent development.

During the Second World War Jewish education for children, both part-time (after school and at weekends) and full-time (at Jewish day schools) suffered severe disruption; so did facilities for the training of teachers.[179] For the time being a Joint Emergency Committee for Jewish Education did its best to maintain standards amidst the difficulties posed by evacuation. But its efforts to create a unified Jewish response were hampered by lack of funds and, much more seriously, by deep religious divisions. Chief Rabbi Hertz vetoed formal co-operation with the progressives, while the Jewish Secondary Schools Movement (JSSM), headed by Solomon Schonfeld, struck out on a path of its own, and refused to become

[178] E. Sicher, *Beyond Marginality: Anglo-Jewish Literature After the Holocaust* (Albany, NY, 1985), ch. 6. See also H. Pollins, 'Sociological Aspects of Anglo-Jewish Literature', *JJS* 2 (1960), 35–8.

[179] B. Steinberg, 'Jewish Education in Great Britain during World War II', *JSS* 29 (1967), 36.

part of the London Board of Jewish Religious Education (LBJRE), established in 1946 with Dr Homa as its first chairman.[180]

In 1945 only two of the seven state-aided Jewish day schools which had existed in London in 1939 were still functioning; the Jews' Free School had been bombed; day schools in Birmingham, Liverpool, and Manchester were still in being, but were suffering from falling enrolments.[181] The formation of the LBJRE was the most significant outcome of a fundamental reappraisal of Jewish education in Britain which it was generally recognized needed to be undertaken at the end of the war, in the light especially of the necessity of raising large sums of money to erect new buildings.[182] Dr Hertz had pinned his hopes on the opportunities provided for denominational schooling by the 1944 Education Act, which envisaged a generous financial partnership between the State and the religious bodies in the maintenance (and in some cases the relocation and rebuilding) of denominational schools. British Jewry failed magnificently to take early advantage of these opportunities: 'apart from lack of motivation, there was also communal disunity'.[183] The Zionist Federation, searching for a new role now that the State of Israel had been re-established, determined to embark upon an ambitious school-building programme that competed for resources with that of the LBJRE.[184] Dr Schonfeld would have no truck with the Zionists, and was prepared to co-operate with the LBJRE only to a limited extent, and on condition that some of the moneys derived from the trusts of defunct Jewish day schools be put at the disposal of the JSSM.[185]

These very public disagreements were not resolved until 1954, and meanwhile prevented the Ministry of Education from allocating funds for Jewish voluntary schools. An agreement made at the Rothschild headquarters, New Court, led Dr Schonfeld to withdraw his objection to the rebuilding of the Jews' Free School as a large comprehensive school, catering for 1,500 pupils, at Camden Town

[180] *JC* (9 May 1941), 5; Alderman, *London Jewry*, 105–6; Archives of the Office of the Chief Rabbi, Greater London Record Office, Acc. 2805/65: correspondence relating to Jewish education, 1941–5.

[181] B. Steinberg, 'Anglo-Jewry and the 1944 Education Act', *JJS* 31 (1989), 83.

[182] S. S. Levin, 'The Changing Pattern of Jewish Education', in id. (ed.), *A Century of Anglo-Jewish Life 1870–1970* (London, 1970), 68.

[183] Steinberg, 'Anglo-Jewry', 89; and see Alderman, *London Jewry*, 104.

[184] Moonman, *Anglo-Jewry*, 25, 40.

[185] Steinberg, 'Anglo-Jewry', 101.

in 1957.[186] The unified system of Jewish day schools in London envisaged in a memorandum prepared for Chief Rabbi Brodie in 1952 has never emerged.[187] However, in an admittedly haphazard and certainly unco-ordinated way, there has been a distinct improvement in the provision of Jewish education in Britain over the past thirty years. In part this has been due to the efforts of independent orthodox bodies, pre-eminently in London but also in Manchester and Gateshead, in raising the funds to build private schools (in which, in some instances, Yiddish is the medium of instruction). The Zionist Federation and the LBJRE (now part of the United Synagogue) maintain a network of primary and secondary schools, some, though state aided, still relying on 'voluntary' parental contributions for Hebrew and religious instruction. For those parents who can afford it, a Jewish boarding school, Carmel College, founded in 1948 by Rabbi Kopul Rosen (1913–62) flourishes in the Berkshire countryside. The net result of all these efforts has been that whereas in 1967 only a quarter of Jewish children in Britain were educated in day schools, by 1982 the proportion had increased to almost a half.[188]

The precise impact of all this education is a matter of some dispute. Dr Stephen Miller, of London's City University, has recently suggested that while Jewish primary schools, and part-time education, have positive effects, mainstream Jewish secondary schools reinforce the ritual dimensions of Judaism but appear to have a negative effect upon perceptions of faith and spirituality.[189] If this is so in respect of children attending Jewish schools full-time, the risk of alienation run by children attending non-Jewish schools, and whose parents make little or no special provision for Jewish studies, must be at least as great.[190]

[186] *JC* (8 Feb. 1957), 23; (7 Mar.), 6; Moonman, *Anglo-Jewry*, 40.

[187] S. S. Levin and V. D. Lipman, *Towards an Integrated System of Jewish Schools* (London, 1952).

[188] Waterman and Kosmin, *British Jewry*, 39; see the useful discussion by the late Dr J. Braude, 'Jewish Education in Britain Today', in S. L. Lipman and V. D. Lipman (eds.), *Jewish Life in Britain 1962–1977* (New York, 1981), 119–29.

[189] S. Miller, 'The Impact of Jewish Education on the Religious Behaviour and Attitudes of British Secondary School Pupils', in J. Aviad (ed.), *Studies in Jewish Education*, iii (Jerusalem, 1988), 150–65; as Dr Miller notes, his findings do not apply to schools of the ultra-orthodox, which declined to take part in his survey.

[190] The relationship between spirituality and Jewish identity in modern Britain is examined in H. Cooper and P. Morrison, *A Sense of Belonging* (London, 1991); and see G. Alderman, 'Fears and Hopes for British Jewry', *JC* (17 May 1991), 21.

The funding of Jewish education in Britain has been substantially assisted by the Jewish Educational Development Trust, founded on the initiative of Rabbi Dr Jakobovits in 1971. The Trust, which has recently (1990) announced the funding of a Jewish secondary school in Hertfordshire (Immanuel College) gives assistance on a non-discriminatory basis; it has supported the Akiva School, set up by the Reform and Liberal movements in London in 1981, and the fact that it has done so was a reflection of Rabbi Jakobovits's early efforts to restore communal unity after the furore over the Jacobs Affair. Not long after Rabbi Jakobovits had been installed as Chief Rabbi of the United Hebrew Congregations in succession to Dr Brodie, it became known that he had given the necessary certificate to the Board of Deputies to enable the New London Synagogue to have a marriage secretary.[191] As we shall see, Dr Jakobovits was to make other overtures to the non-orthodox in later years, as he searched desperately for ways of underpinning and bolstering his presumed authority to speak for the whole of an increasingly fragmented British Jewry.

Dr Brodie retired, at the age of 70, in 1965. The Federation of Synagogues had taken no part in his election (1947–8), partly on the grounds of its objection to the continued subordinate status of the United Synagogue's *Beth Din*, and partly because of its demand for proportional representation on the electing body.[192] In truth, however, the Federation was but a shadow of its former self. The Presidency of Morry Davis had rapidly descended into a dictatorship, in which elections were dispensed with and control was maintained with the assistance of willing sycophants. A consequence of this, and of the resulting acute controversies, was that the Federation lost the opportunity to fulfil the role which the UOHC came to play, as the natural home for practising orthodox refugee Jews from central and eastern Europe.[193] Much more serious, however, were the consequences of wartime destruction of East

[191] Information supplied by the late Dr B. Homa and the late Mr H. Diamond (then Chairman of the Law, Parliamentary, & General Purposes Committee of the Board of Deputies). In 1983, when the *Beth Din* of the United Synagogue cast doubts on the validity in orthodox eyes of marriages and conversions carried out under Dr Jacobs's auspices, Rabbi Dr Jakobovits maintained a strange silence: see Dr Judith Freedman's review of *Helping with Inquiries* in *JJS* 32 (1990), 55–6.

[192] Alderman, *Federation*, 71.

[193] G. Alderman, 'M. H. Davis: The Rise and fall of a Communal Upstart', *TJHSE* 31 (1988–90), 249–68.

End synagogues and communities, and the rapid disappearance into the suburbs of the Jewish families who had sustained the Federation hitherto. In 1937 the Federation had comprised—on paper—some sixty-eight congregations serving the needs of perhaps 52,000 souls. By 1964 the total membership of Federation synagogues (males plus females who were members in their own right) was returned to the Board of Deputies as approximately 16,000, whereas that of the United Synagogue was then about 36,000.[194] By 1974 Federation membership had further contracted, to 10,000 or so.[195]

The Federation had not neglected the suburbs. But precisely because it was a federation of legally independent entities, it could not use moneys from redundant East London synagogues to build in the suburbs without the consent of those who were the trustees of the East London properties. The very independence which affiliation to the Federation had made so attractive in its early years now became a grave handicap. 'Constituent' synagogues—built and ultimately controlled by the Federation—did not appear until 1946, when such a synagogue was established at West Hampstead as a base for Kopul Rosen, appointed Principal Rabbi of the Federation the year before.[196] Rabbi Rosen's great talents lay in the fields of oratory, organization, and education. He looked to a major constitutional revision (effected in 1947) as the means by which the Federation would become the spiritual training-centre for a new religiously inclined élite, needed to spearhead the religious renaissance of post-war British Jewry.[197]

Rabbi Rosen's call for the putting aside of 'local patriotism and parochial interests' was not heeded.[198] Other constituent synagogues were established in due course—at Willesden in 1946, at Edgware (opened 1950) and at Ilford (originally opened 1927)—but the major theme of Federation history well into the 1950s was the virtual civil war between those who saw only too clearly the need to amalgamate and close East End synagogues which were no longer needed, so that resources could be released for the use of suburban communities, and those who remained in the East End, in control of these synagogues, and who challenged Federation

194 Alderman, *Federation*, 58, 104.
195 Ibid. 117.
196 Ibid. 72, 76.
197 K. Rosen, *The Future of the Federation of Synagogues* (London, 1946).
198 Alderman, *Federation*, 74.

members in the suburbs to build synagogues with money of their own. In February 1949 a disenchanted Rabbi Rosen resigned his post. While the dwindling membership of the Federation continued to fight over its future, Federation members in the suburbs joined the ready-made United Synagogues they found there. The Zionist activist Aaron Wright (elected President of the Federation in 1945) and Bernard Homa (for whom the post of Chairman of the Federation was created in 1946) resigned in 1947; Jack Goldberg, a well-known communal worker, was elected President in 1948 but resigned through ill-health in 1950.[199]

In 1951 the Federation elected as its sixth President Morris Lederman, a *shochet* of Polish birth (1908) who had come to England with his family in 1920; he was to remain President (with a short break in 1952–3) until his retirement in the spring of 1989. Mr Lederman was a Federation man, and he and his colleagues did their best to encourage the contraction of its East End so that new communities might grow. In time this end was achieved, but the process was painfully slow. By the early 1960s the expanded size and geographical coverage within Greater London of the United Synagogue was such that the leadership of the Federation was seriously attracted by the prospect of a working arrangement (agreed on 26 February 1965) by which the United Synagogue's *Beth Din* would be reorganized to include members of the Federation's rabbinate.[200] This was clearly envisaged as a prelude to an amalgamation of the two synagogal bodies.

The contraction of the Federation had been paralleled by the stagnation of the Spanish & Portuguese community. By the onset of the Second World War Bevis Marks had become little more than a historical monument. The spiritual centre of the London *Sephardim* was in Maida Vale, where a new synagogue had been opened in Lauderdale Road in 1896.[201] Although *Haham* Gaster formally retired in 1918, he continued, as we have seen, to play a full part in Anglo-Jewish affairs. It was not until a decade after his death that the *Sephardim* elected for themselves (1949) a new *Haham*, Rabbi Dr Solomon Gaon (b. 1912), a native of Yugoslavia but a graduate of Jews' College. The immigration to London and Manchester in the 1950s and 1960s of *Sephardi* families of considerable wealth from the Middle East, whose members in due course came to

[199] Alderman, *Federation*, 69–70, 83–6. [200] Ibid. 105–6.
[201] A. Levy, *The Synagogue at Lauderdale Road* (London [n.d.]).

eclipse the Spanish & Portuguese families of ancient lineage, resulted in tensions which have never been satisfactorily resolved. When in 1977 Dr Gaon resigned his post to become spiritual leader of the World *Sephardi* Federation in New York, there was no agreement on a successor (1984), and ecclesiastical power was formally split between the Moroccan-born Rabbi Pinchas Toledano and the Gibraltar-born and Carmel College-educated Rabbi Dr Abraham Levy.[202]

Under Dr Gaon's leadership the British *Sephardim* had maintained a spiritual as well as an organizational independence, but they had never allowed this to compromise the public status of Chief Rabbi Brodie. It appears that Dr Gaon's views on the possible appointment of Dr Louis Jacobs as Principal of Jews' College (of which the *Haham* was Vice-President) did not coincide with those of the *Ashkenazi* Chief Rabbi.[203] There was no public rift. When Dr Brodie intervened, those in charge of the Maida Vale Synagogue dutifully told Dr Jacobs and his disciples that they could no longer meet in the Montefiore Hall there.[204] In short, the British *Sephardim*, though they had played no part in his election, in practice acknowledged the suzerainty of Chief Rabbi Brodie, and hence of the United Synagogue which in large measure funded his office. The prospect that the Federation of Synagogues would do likewise opened up the possibility that the religious fragmentation that had increasingly characterized British Jewry since the 1930s might be contained, if not reversed.

This was not to be. The agreement which the Federation and the United Synagogue concluded in 1965 was never ratified by the United Synagogue.[205] The Federation did not, therefore, participate in the election of Rabbi Dr Jakobovits in 1966—or indeed of Rabbi

[202] Alderman, *Anglo-Jewry*, 13. There is no satisfactory treatment of the British *Sephardim* in the post-Gaster era; but see Bermant, *Troubled Eden*, 211–12; Brook, *The Club*, 142–6; and the series of articles by J. F. Silverman in the *JC*'s 'London Extra', 8, 15, 22, and 29 June 1990. The activities of the various *Sephardi* communities in Britain are co-ordinated by a Sephardi Federation of Great Britain and the Commonwealth.

[203] See Dr J. Freedman in *JJS* 32 (1990), 54.

[204] Bermant, *Troubled Eden*, 212.

[205] Alderman, *Federation*, 106–7. From the point of view of the United Synagogue the attraction of the agreement lay in the subvention (amounting to £2,750 p.a.) which the Federation would have made to the Chief Rabbinate; but at the end of the day the view seems to have prevailed that the Federation could best be killed off by attrition, not by kindness.

Dr Sacks as his successor in 1990.[206] In April 1966 the Federation announced the formation of its own *Beth Din*, which began authorizing marriages and divorces, and dealing with conversions and other matters which are within the normal purview of an orthodox Ecclesiastical Court.[207] This schism also had its effect upon *shechita* arrangements in London. For a time (1984–8) the Federation ran its own *shechita* operation; in 1989 the United Synagogue withdrew from the London Board for Shechita (which was left in the effective control of the Federation and the *Sephardim*) and established a rival body using former London Board staff.

At bottom this *shechita* 'war' was not so much about money as about power and status, not merely within London Jewry but in relation to British Jewry as a whole. As British Jewry has become more pluralistic in a religious sense, its members have become less willing to acquiesce in a situation in which the representative communal bodies fail to embody and reflect this diversity to the full. In 1957 the then President of the United Synagogue, Ewen Montagu, told the Federation that 'as long as he was President of the United Synagogue, there would only be one Religious Authority of the *Ashkenazim* in this country, and that would be the Chief Rabbi and nobody else'.[208] The result of such intransigence was to bring an additional *Beth Din* into being. Perhaps with this lesson in mind, Rabbi Dr Jakobovits did not, in his early years of office, pursue a policy of confrontation with those who did not, in practice, recognize his authority.

We have already noted some steps taken by him shortly after assuming office in the direction of conciliating the non-orthodox. Although the Liberals and Progressives had returned to the Board of Deputies after obtaining separate legislation for marriage-authorization purposes, they did not abandon their ambition that the constitution of the Board be altered to afford some status for their ecclesiastical authorities. The essential justice of this demand was recognized in October 1971, when, in an atmosphere of crisis and following a further withdrawal of progressive Deputies, the

[206] On 18 May 1989 the Executive Committee of the Federation decided that though it had no objection to being consulted about the choice of a new Chief Rabbi of the United Hebrew Congregations, it would recognize neither his status nor his authority: Alderman, *Anglo-Jewry*, 15–16.

[207] Alderman, *Federation*, 107.

[208] Quoted in Alderman, *Federation*, 96.

Board agreed to amend Clause 43 of its constitution so as to give rights of consultation to the ecclesiastical authorities of groups of congregations not under the jurisdiction of either the Chief Rabbi of the United Hebrew Congregations or the spiritual head of the Spanish & Portuguese Jews.[209]

This amendment had the approval of Rabbi Dr Jakobovits, who refused to accede to demands from the religious right that the Board be 'secularized', and a separate orthodox agency be set up to carry out the Board's religious functions.[210] In fact, the constitutional revision merely regularized a situation which had existed *de facto* ever since the commencement (in 1967) of the six-year Presidency of Mr Michael Fidler (1916–89; Conservative MP for Bury and Radcliffe 1970–4).[211] During the 1970s Dr Jakobovits and Mr Fidler gave further signs of encouragement to the progressives. In January 1972 the Board informed a Law Commission inquiry that there were two variants of Jewish marriage practice—the orthodox and the non-orthodox: the figment of one Jewry was thus abandoned.[212] In 1971 Dr Jakobovits only withdrew from an agreement to give the Lily Montagu Memorial Lecture after protests; but three years later (according to Dr Homa) he delivered an address at the Leo Baeck College.[213]

But if the Chief Rabbi of the United Hebrew Congregations had managed for the moment to preserve his status in the eyes of the left, he had begun to lose it in the eyes of the right. Immediately following the passage of the constitutional amendment in 1971, the UOHC walked out of the Board—and has never returned or shown the slightest enthusiasm for so doing. In the United Synagogue steps were taken to strengthen its orthodox posture. In 1984, under the Presidency of Sidney Frosh, the United Synagogue took the initiative in imposing upon the Board of Deputies a 'Code of Practice' that was designed, to some extent, to recoup the ground lost in 1971.[214] That same year the appointment was announced of Rabbi Chenoch Ehrentreu as Head of the United Synagogue's *Beth*

209 A. Bornstein and B. Homa, *Tell It In Gath* (London, 1972), sect. II.

210 Homa, *Footprints*, 224–6.

211 Alderman, *Anglo-Jewry*, 5.

212 Ibid. 7.

213 Homa, *Footprints*, 248; *Jewish Tribune* (10 Dec. 1971), 7; C. Bermant, *Lord Jakobovits* (London, 1990), 93.

214 The incidents which resulted in the promulgation of this Code (which is not an amendment of the Board's constitution) are outlined in Alderman, *Anglo-Jewry*, 6–7, and S. Frosh, 'Clause 74 And All That', *Hamesilah* (Pesach 5745/1985), 24–5.

Din; Rabbi Ehrentreu (b. 1932; a refugee from Frankfurt-on-Main) had, while the 'Father' of the Manchester *Beth Din* in 1982, refused to meet the Pope because, in meeting and shaking hands with the Pope (to which apparently he had no objection) he would have been part of a delegation that included a Reform Jew.[215]

We might note that it was also in 1984 that Dr Jakobovits issued a private memorandum to his clergy warning them against modes of conduct 'which could be construed as according legitimacy to non-traditional Judaism'. But we must also note that he apparently continued to meet, in his home and in his official capacity, leaders of the non-orthodox congregations.[216] This behaviour both bemused and outraged some sections of orthodox opinion. In 1987, following his public acceptance of modifications to *shechita* demanded by the Government as concessions to placate the animal welfare lobby, a coalition of orthodox interests (including the UOHC, the Federation, the *Sephardim*, the communal rabbis of Manchester and Gateshead, and a miscellany of independent orthodox rabbis acting on the initiative of the Campaign for the Protection of Shechita) in effect repudiated his assumed mandate to speak on behalf of orthodoxy in Britain, and addressed the Government directly.[217]

The modifications which this loose alliance obtained (embodied in Regulations approved by Parliament in July 1990), and the fact that the Ministry of Agriculture had agreed to receive deputations of British Jews neither sanctioned nor approved by the Chief Rabbi of the United Hebrew Congregations or the Board of Deputies of British Jews, have a symbolism and a significance that extends well beyond the specific matters then under discussion. The *shechita* controversy of the 1980s did nothing to enhance the reputation of the Board of Deputies. The insistence of the Board's leadership in recent years on the need for 'communal discipline', epitomized in the view of Dr Lionel Kopelowitz (President 1985–91) that 'there's got to be a Jewish view at the end of the day; there can't be two Jewish views or three Jewish views', is simply no longer grounded

215 *JC* (4 June 1982), 1.

216 Alderman, 'British Chief Rabbinate', 54–5; 'Not Definitive', *Hamaor*, 26/1 (Pesach 1991), 24–5.

217 Alderman, *Anglo-Jewry*, 8–24; *The Times* (23 Apr. 1990), 14; Rabbi H. B. Padwa (Principal Rabbinical Authority of the UOHC) and others to the Ministry of Agriculture, 27 July 1989 (copy in the possession of the author).

in reality—if indeed it ever was.[218] Attempts to stifle dissent are not merely inappropriate and capricious. In a free society they must inevitably backfire.[219]

British Jewry is polarized. It is also pluralized. The Board of Deputies does not reflect this diversity. Several attempts to reform the Board's constitution (most recently in 1988) have focused primarily upon streamlining its procedure and restricting its overall size. It continues, however, to represent (primarily synagogal) interests—and a narrow range of interests at that—rather than Jewish individuals, many of whom have become alienated from it.[220] In recent years its affairs have been clouded by serious financial problems, largely attributable to the unwillingness and refusal of member congregations to pay for its upkeep—in itself (of course) a vote of no confidence in what it does and what it stands for. The Kopelowitz presidency was ill-fated in other respects. 'Most men and women of any distinction', Stephen Brook wrote, 'have better things to do with their time than spend a dozen Sundays watching Dr Kopelowitz mismanage a meeting.'[221]

This statement was cruel. But it was also true. All too often the Board provides a platform for those who think they have a right to be heard; but these well-intentioned individuals, as a collectivity, are not representative. The view of Sir Sidney Hamburger, the elder statesman of Manchester Jewry, also quoted by Mr Brook, is worth reproducing here: 'If the Board didn't exist, it would make very little difference to the life of the Manchester community.'[222] The UOHC has already left the Board. Arnold Cohen, the newly elected President of the Federation of Synagogues, warned in 1990 that the Federation would drift away from the Board; the subsequent establishment, through the good offices of the Federation, of a National Association of Jewish Orthodox Lawyers, will certainly assist in this process.[223]

The Board's contemporary claim, to represent British Jewry as

[218] Interview with Dr Kopelowitz, 2 Mar. 1988.

[219] I deal with these themes in *Anglo-Jewry*, 25–6, 32–41.

[220] This point was made in the useful short critique made by Dr H. Kimmel, *The Structure and Regime of the Board of Deputies of British Jews* (London [1967?]). See also 'The Board of Deputies of British Jews: Report of Working Party' (The Wolkind Report) (mimeo., Feb. 1975), section D.

[221] Brook, *The Club*, 224; Mr Brook's treatment of the Board of Deputies (ch. 16) is admirably focused.

[222] Ibid. 270.

[223] *JC* (28 Sept. 1990), 1; the National Association of Jewish Orthodox Lawyers was established at a meeting held at the rebuilt *Machzike Hadath* synagogue,

completely now as it did a half-century ago, is grounded in myth. To an extent, the Government and its agencies have also come round to this view. To the example of its *shechita* negotiations we can add another of a very different kind, namely the decision of the Independent Broadcasting Authority in 1989 to award the London community radio franchise not to the consortium backed by the Board of Deputies, but to Spectrum Radio, whose Jewish component—the United Kingdom Jewish Community Radio Foundation—is fortunately totally free of Board control.[224]

We talk instinctively of 'the Anglo-Jewish community'. There is today no such thing, but rather a series of communities some of which overlap to a greater or lesser extent.[225] These range from the anti-Zionist ultra-orthodox through a panorama of religious, socio-economic, and even local identifications to the totally irreligious secular Jews who might none the less admit to an ethnic Jewishness if pressed, or when confronted with the reality of recurrent anti-Jewish prejudice which manifests itself on university campuses (inspired by Arab propaganda), in attacks on Jewish cemeteries and even on live Jews in broad daylight (inspired by neo-Nazi groups), and in the anti-Semitism that has always been a part of genteel society in Britain.

British Jewry is contracting but it is also, simultaneously, outgrowing the norms that it has inherited from a more élitist and centripetal age. There are many challenges facing the Jews of Britain as the twenty-first century approaches. None is more pressing than the need to construct a new institutional framework that will reflect diversity, and allow for its expression and articulation in an atmosphere that is at once as free from internal oppression as it ought to be from external threat.

Golders Green, on 26 May 1991. On 16 June 1991 the Board elected a new President, Israel Finestein, QC (b. 1921), a former Crown Court judge, under whose leadership it is felt the status and reputation of the Board will be enhanced. The following month, the Board elected a Reform Deputy, Aubrey Rose, as its Senior Vice-President, and a woman, Rosalind Preston, as Junior Vice-President. These elections, landmarks in themselves, will of course do nothing to attract back into the Board the ultra-orthodox elements which have turned away from it.

224 B. Bond and I. Sweiger, 'Radio for the 5750s', *Hamaor* (Pesach 1990), 13–14.

225 This reality formed the theme of Kosmin, 'Localism and Pluralism', *passim*; Dr Kosmin pointed out (p. 115) that the communities and congregations which acknowledged the authority of Rabbi Dr Jakobovits in 1982 amounted to only 62% of synagogue members in the United Kingdom as a whole, and to only 53% in London. I make the same point in relation to the election of Rabbi Dr Sacks as Chief Rabbi of the United Hebrew Congregations in 1990: Alderman, *Anglo-Jewry*, 15–16, and 'British Chief Rabbinate', 55.

Glossary

(The following terms, unless otherwise indicated, are transliterations from Hebrew)

aliyah: the act of migration to and settlement in Palestine/Israel.

Ashkenazi (plural *Ashkenazim*): Jews of central and eastern European origin, following the Polish or German rite.

Barmitzvah: the attainment of his religious majority by a Jewish boy on his thirteenth birthday, when he is able to participate in a *minyan*; usually accompanied by a ceremony and celebration.

Beth Din: House of Judgement; a Jewish ecclesiastical court.

Beth Hamedrash: House of Study, typically used also for prayer.

Bimah: the reading-desk in the synagogue; according to orthodox precept, it should be placed centrally, and not attached to the Ark at one end of the synagogue building, a practice adopted by the Reform movement.

chalitza: the ceremony, invariably conducted under the auspices of a *Beth Din*, by which a childless widow releases her unmarried brother-in-law from his obligation to marry her following the death of her husband, his brother; without this ceremony, the widow will not be free to marry any other man in an orthodox synagogue.

chassidim (adjective *chassidic*): members of pietistic sects, originating in eastern Europe in the second half of the 18th century, following charismatic rabbinical leaders who are generally chosen on the basis of hereditary dynastic attachment.

chazan (plural *chazanim*): the cantor or reader who leads the synagogue service from the *Bimah*.

chedorim (rooms): makeshift religious-instruction classes, usually held in a room or rooms in the teacher's house.

chevra (plural *chevrot*): a society or fraternity, usually formed for religious purposes; hence, a small synagogue (sometimes spelt *hebra*, *hebrot*).

chevra kadisha (holy society): a society whose members undertake to prepare the bodies of the Jewish dead for burial; traditionally this work is voluntary and unpaid, but very often communities will engage the services of paid professionals to perform these duties.

Dayan: a judge, a member of a *Beth Din*.

get: a bill of divorcement, given by the husband to the wife, normally under rabbinical authority.

Haftorah: the portion of the Prophets read after the portion of the *Torah* in the synagogue on Sabbaths and festivals.

Haham (Wise Man): the supreme rabbinical authority of the *Sephardim* in Britain.

halacha: Jewish law, as opposed to custom, or *minhag*.

herem: a ban, accompanied by a variety of pains and penalties (not excommunication, the concept of which does not exist in orthodox Judaism as in, say, Catholicism).

kashrut: the system of providing and maintaining supplies of *kosher* food; the observance of the dietary laws.

kehilla (plural *kehillot*): a self-governing community of Jews, typically with its own *shechita* and *Beth Din*.

Keren Hayesod: Palestine Foundation Fund, established at the end of 1920 to bear the running costs of the World Zionist Movement.

Keren Kayemet: Jewish National Fund, established in 1901 to purchase and reclaim land in Palestine.

kosher: fit for consumption and use according to orthodox Jewish law; see also *kashrut*.

landsmannschaft (plural *landsmannschaften*) (Yiddish): a fraternity or community of persons originating from the same town or district.

maggid: preacher.

melammed (plural *melammdim*): teacher.

mikvah (plural *mikvaot*): a ritual bath used by a married woman at a specific time after menstruation, prior to sexual intercourse, and by a convert on his or her acceptance into Judaism.

minhag: religious rite or custom.

minyan: a quorum of ten adult males meeting for prayer; a prayer-group.

Oral Law: see *Talmud*.

piyuttim: liturgical poems or hymns, typically of medieval origin.

semicha (plural *semichot*): the rabbinical diploma.

Sephardi (plural *Sephardim*): Jews originating from Spain and Portugal, and from south-eastern Europe, north Africa, and the Middle East, following a common and distinctive rite.

sha'alot: questions and problems put to a rabbi or *Beth Din* concerning the interpretation and application of Jewish law.

Shulchan Aruch: the standard code of orthodox Jewish law.

shechita: the slaughter of *kosher* animals for food according to orthodox Jewish law (see also *shochet*).

sheitel: a wig worn by a married Jewess, to prevent her natural hair being admired by the male public; the custom of wearing a *sheitel* is of *Ashkenazi* origin.

shiva: the period of confined mourning following the death of a near relative, usually of seven days' duration.

shochet (plural *shochetim*): a slaughterer of animals for consumption according to orthodox Jewish law (see also *shechita*).

succah (booth): a temporary structure, the roof of which is made of leaves, in which the Jew should 'dwell' during the festival of *Succot* (Tabernacles).

tallesim (popular plural form; singular *tallis*): prayer-shawls, traditionally of wool.

Talmud: the sixty-three volumes of rabbinical discussion and prescription, comprising the Oral Law (see also *Torah*).

Talmud Torah: a religion school.

trefah: food the consumption of which is forbidden by Jewish law; the opposite of *kosher*.

Torah: the Five Books of Moses, the Written Law (see also *Talmud*).

Yom Kippur: the Day of Atonement, accompanied by twenty-five-hour fast; the Sabbath of Sabbaths.

yeshivah (plural *yeshivot*): a religious seminary, the course of studies in which can lead to the conferment of the rabbinical diploma (see also *semicha*).

Yishuv: the Jewish community in Palestine before the re-establishment of the Jewish State in 1948.

Index